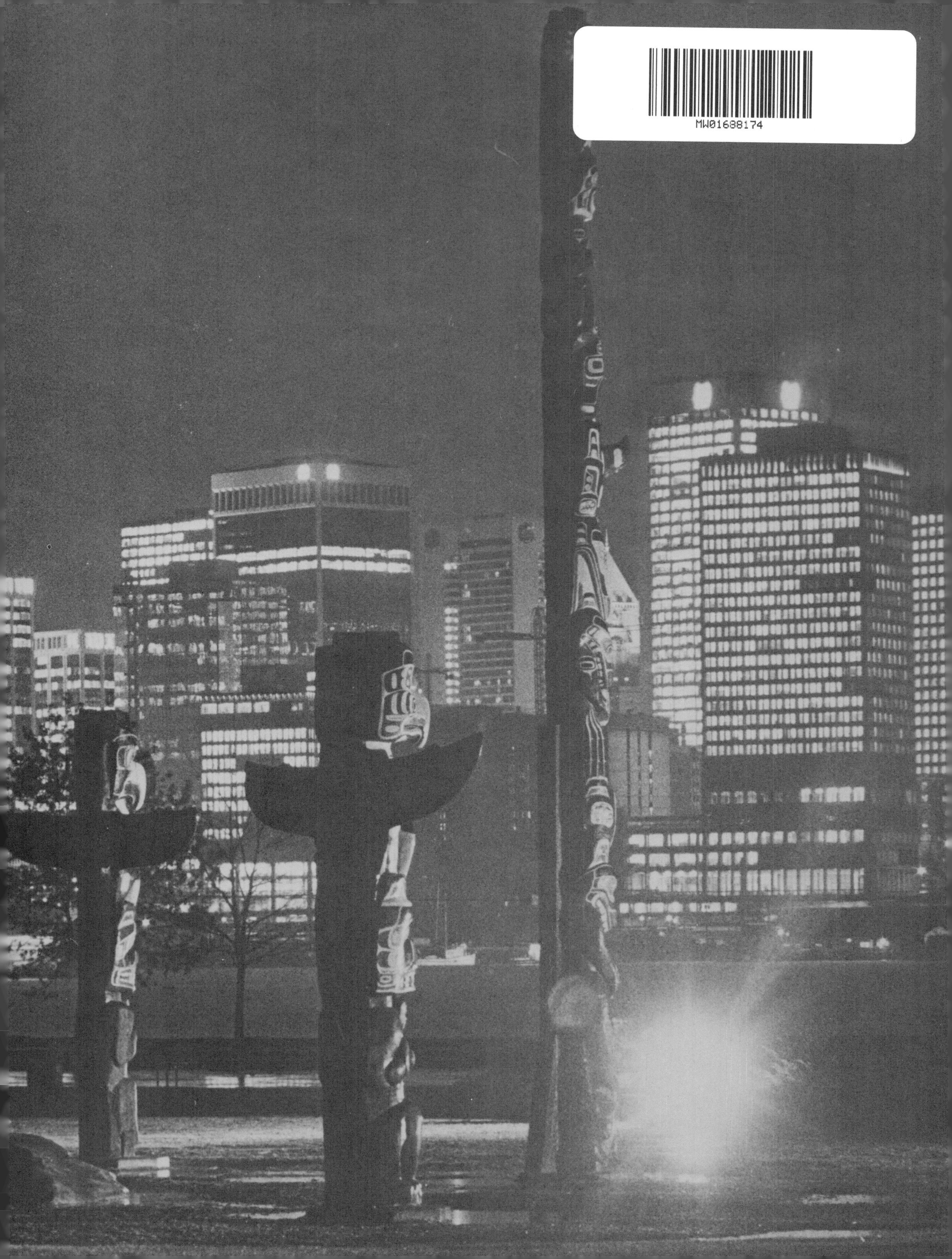

The Totem Carvers

Charlie James, Ellen Neel, and Mungo Martin

Phil Nuytten

For Vicki . . .
With my best
Regards
[signature]
T'LAXWSAM

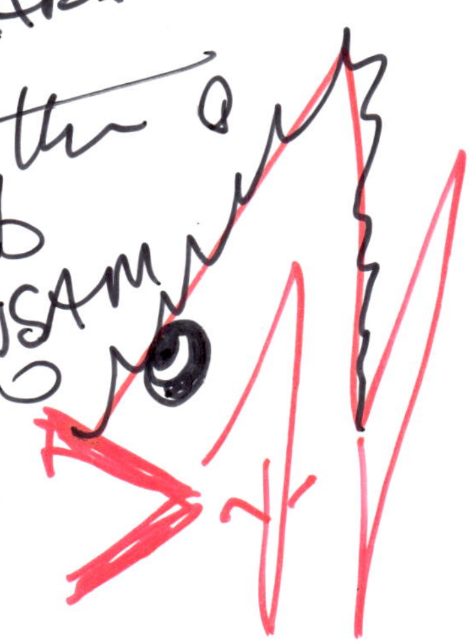

The Totem Carvers

Charlie James, Ellen Neel, and Mungo Martin

Phil Nuytten

Panorama Publications Ltd.
Vancouver Canada

DEDICATION:

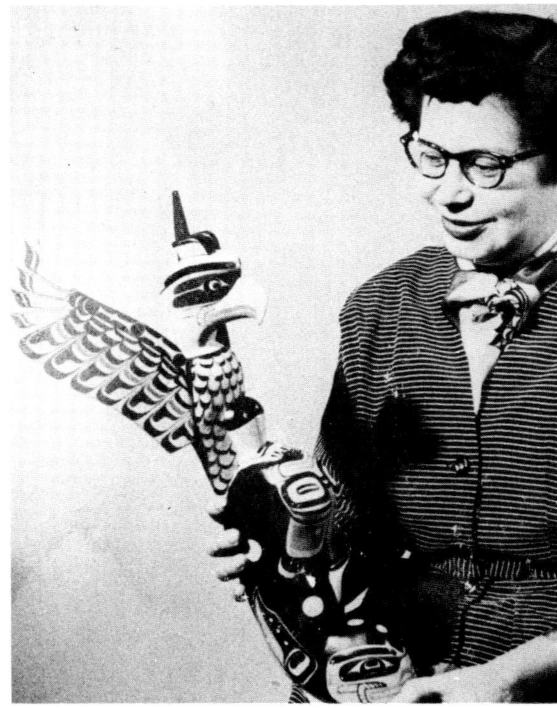

to Ellen...

Printed in Canada by Hazeldine Press Ltd, Vancouver, BC.
Typeset 9 point Souvenir. Panorama Publications Ltd, 3732 West Broadway, Vancouver, BC V6R 2C1.
Layout, design, and production: Panorama Publications Ltd.

Canadian Cataloguing in Publication Data
Nuytten, Phil.
The Totem Carvers.

ISBN 0-919317-02-2

1. Kwakiutl Indians—Wood-carving. 2. Indians of North America—British Columbia—Wood-carving. 3. James, Charlie. 4. Martin, Mungo. 5. Neel, Ellen. 6. Totem poles—British Columbia.
I. Title.
E99.K9N89 730'.8997 C82-091364-2

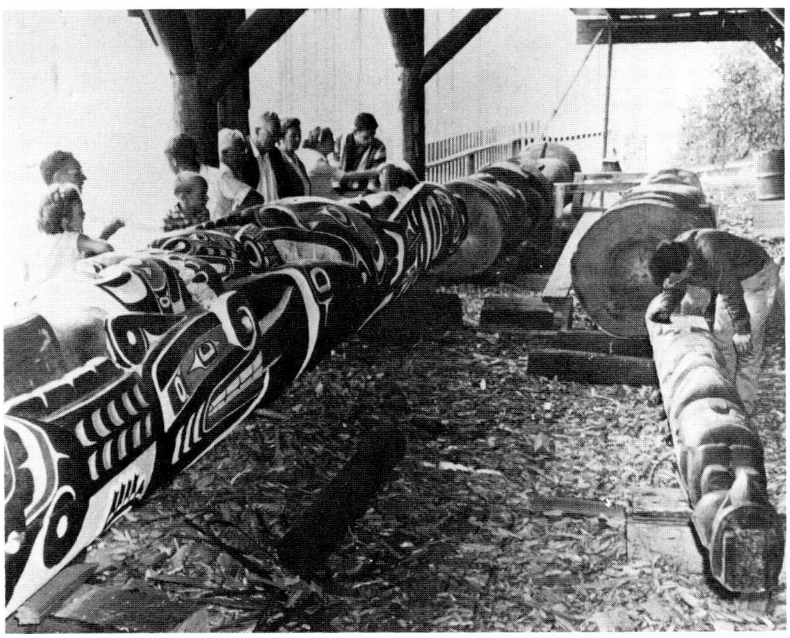

ACKNOWLEDGEMENTS

My thanks to these people for their assistance. Together their help ranged from the provision of extensive source data to brief conversations which caused isolated fragments to fall into place:

Arthur Alfred, Agnes Alfred, Jumbo Bell, Chick Chamberlain, Kathy 'Honey' Cook, Louise Dallaire, Amos Dawson, Arthur Dick, David Denbigh, Leslie Drew, Harry Duker, Hattie Ferguson*, David Hancock, Audrey Hawthorn, Tony Hunt, Michael Kew, Harold Lando, Renee Landry, John Livingston, Dr. Joe MacInnis, Peter L. Macnair, Mardonna AustinMcKillop, Lynne Meranda, Gus Matilpi, Bud Mintz, Richard Oman, Bill Reid, Alice Rosso, Larry Rosso, Jim Ryan, Dan Savard, Audrey Shane, Sharon Simpson, Daisy Sewid-Smith, Mabel Stanley*, Hilary Stewart, Emma Tamilin, Lloyd Wadhams, Gloria Cranmer-Webster, Tom 'McKenzie' Willie, Bob Wilson*, Rupert Wilson, David Young.*

The Neel family; Cora Beddows, Theo McBurnie, Bob Neel, Teresa 'Bitty' Neel and Pamela Wurmuth—for their long friendship and patient co-operation.

Shirley Ayling, Saretta Rogers and Carol Scott, for their typing skills.

Jessie Wharf for editing.

Special thanks to Bill Holm, for always finding time in his busy schedule.

My wife Mary—and daughter Virginia—for their patience.

Phil Nuytten—T'łax̱wsa̱m
North Vancouver, B.C.
1982

*deceased.

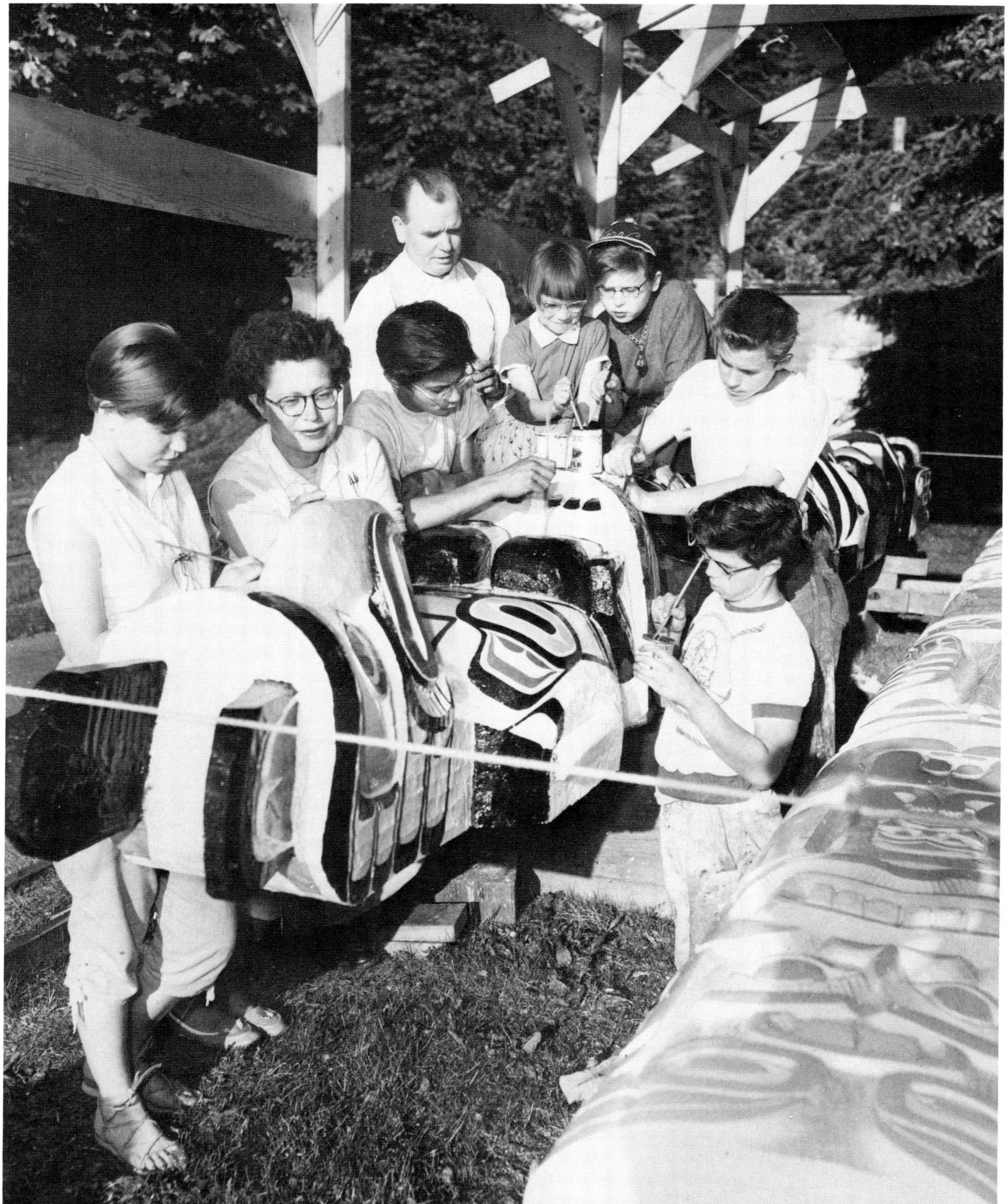

Contents

Author's Foreword

They called the exhibition, 'Arts of the Raven—Masterworks of the Northwest Coast Indian'. It was held at the Vancouver Art Gallery during the summer and early fall of 1967. The purpose of the showing was clearly stated in the foreword of the exhibition catalogue:

'This is art, high art, not ethnology. It proposes to bring together many of the master works of this art to show the wide range and excellence of its forms, and to explicate and establish its claim to greatness.'

The exhibition was excellent. 'Arts of the Raven' was one of the first major treatments of Northwest Coast Art—as art, rather than as a collection of curiosities. It was well-received in the Canadian province of British Columbia and served to introduce many to the art and culture of the Haida, Nootka, Tsimpshian, Salish, Tlingit and Kwakiutl people of Canada's western sea coast.

A number of consultants worked closely with the art gallery personnel to assemble the exhibits; notably, Bill Reid, Bill Holm and Wilson Duff. Wilson Duff was with the Department of Anthropology of the University of British Columbia and he was a craftsman; both in the acuity of his perception of the native people and in his writings of their culture. Duff was the logical person to write the introductory notes to the various sections of the exhibit and he did so; describing eloquently, the history of Northwest Coast Indian Art.

He pointed out that several of the distinctly different styles of these art forms had been almost completely lost, for a number of reasons, and had to be re-discovered by labourious study and painstaking reconstruction of the principles involved. One style that refused to succumb, however, was that of the Kwakiutl. Duff described it in a section entitled 'Gallery 8—The Art Today.'

'Art styles, it would seem, have greater viability than the cultures that produce them. The old Indian cultures of the coast are dead, but the art styles continue on in new and modern contexts. The Kwakiutl style never did suffer a full eclipse, but was kept well alive by such artists as Charlie James, Mungo Martin and Ellen Neel.'

Charlie James, Mungo Martin and Ellen Neel. Three people who spanned a century, living and working in an art form that, today rides a wave of renaissance. Barely two decades ago, Northwest Coast Indian art was viewed by most people as a quaint, folksy craft, something like Ukrainian Easter egg painting. Only a few saw it in the context of a powerful, indigenous art form, with traditions and disciplines as rigid as any school of European art. This was true of the artists as well as the collectors and patrons. Only a very few; and these three stand out among them. Surely, they should have some small measure of credit and recognition for their contribution. The objects that they made speak well of the art, but say little of their creators.

James, Mungo and Ellen. The story of who they were, how they were, and what they did, even now grows dim and distant. All three are gone today, and Wilson Duff is with them. Duff managed to sum up their contribution, accurately, in one sentence. This book is simply an expansion of that sentence.

These pages were originally to be a book solely about Ellen Neel. I knew her, learned much from her, and felt that I could repay a sort of debt by putting some of her contributions clearly on record.

It soon became obvious that a story about Ellen Neel could not be complete unless it gave at least some background on her grandfather and mentor, Charlie James—and his stepson and protege—Mungo Martin.

The work of these three people and the impact that their efforts had on the survival and continuity of Kwakiutl art is tightly interwoven—so interwoven that it seemed, at first, a relatively easy task to present a cohesive piece with each participant in their proper place, and few, if any, loose ends to tidy up.

Since their respective stories actually happened, it seemed that it would be a further simple task to assemble a chronological sequence of events that would join together to present a complete picture. At least, that was the theory.

This complete picture has proven, in practice, to be incredibly illusive!

Ellen and her grandfather were, by definition, generations apart. Mungo Martin did most of the work that made him famous late in his life, many years after he had last worked with his stepfather. Of Charlie James, so little is recorded that even a brief sketch required countless hours of sifting, cross-checking, interviewing elderly informants and reliance on maddeningly incomplete field notes taken many years before.

I have described the purpose of these pages as an attempt to assemble a record that will help to explain how a specific art survived to the present in an unbroken manner. Charlie James, Mungo Martin and Ellen Neel are important links in this continuous chain.

They were not, however, the only links. Kwakiutl artists such as Willie Seaweed, Charlie George Sr., Dick Price, Arthur Shaughnessey and Henry Speck, come to mind immediately and there were others. As a group, all of these people played an important role in ensuring that Kwakiutl art did not die out, but it is probable that none of them could claim the combined impact and continuity of James, Martin and Neel.

The efforts of these three people were significant and unique in that each was responsible for a different facet of an overall contribution.

Charlie James was best known as an innovator and the creator of a specific, well-defined style of Kwakiutl art. Mungo Martin, through circumstance rather than design, had one foot firmly planted in the time of Charlie James and the other in the second half of the twentieth century.

Mungo acted as a cultural bridge, producing not just objects, but recording something of their purpose and context. Ellen Neel was largely responsible for bringing this style of art to the general public in a popular form.

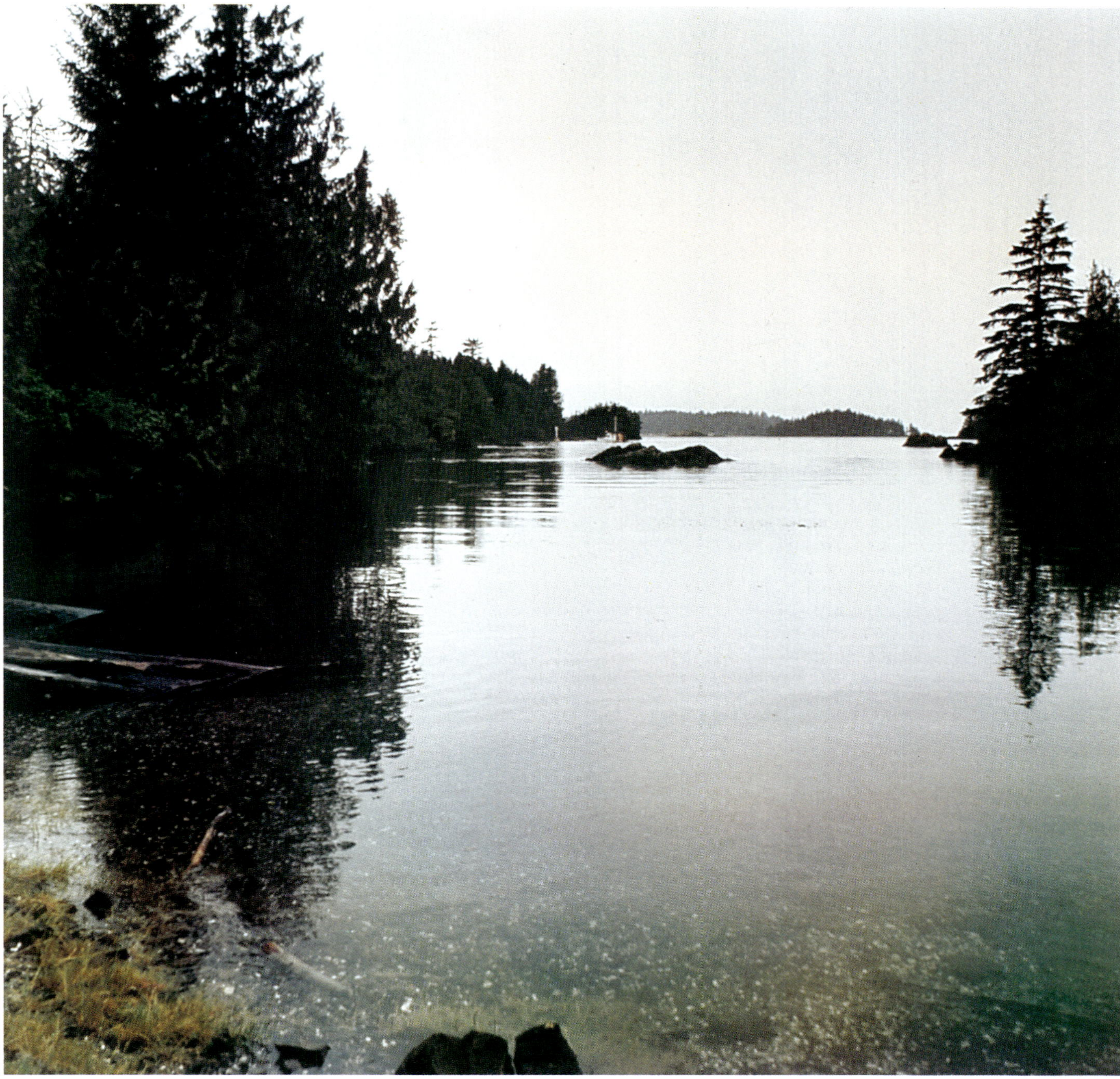

Through lectures, demonstrations, exhibitions and the production of thousands and thousands of commercial carvings, she reached a huge audience.

I hope that this book will have some ongoing value to students and researchers, of course, but primarily I want to tell a little of the personal stories of these three people; to show that they lived and laughed, and unlike many of the objects that they've left behind, they were not dusty museum pieces. To tell of these three people is to tell of Kwakiutl art—and to tell of Kwakiutl art is to tell of the Kwakiutl people. I will be satisfied if this book tells a little of all these things.

My personal intrusion on these pages is deliberate. I can't tell you how Charlie James, Mungo or Ellen really felt or what they thought. I can tell you how I felt, and though some may think it high-handed, I have done so.

As mentioned earlier, I tried hard to develop a format that would show Charlie James, Mungo Martin and Ellen Neel in one unified setting. I tried to accomplish this initially and once again, after the draft manuscript was completed, all without success. The gaps in information are too great and too much time has passed to allow a simple dovetailing of events. That is a bridge that you will simply have to build in your mind.

What follows then, is three incomplete stories about three individuals. Together they make up a small part of one story. That story started long before the first European set foot on these shores and it goes on, still.

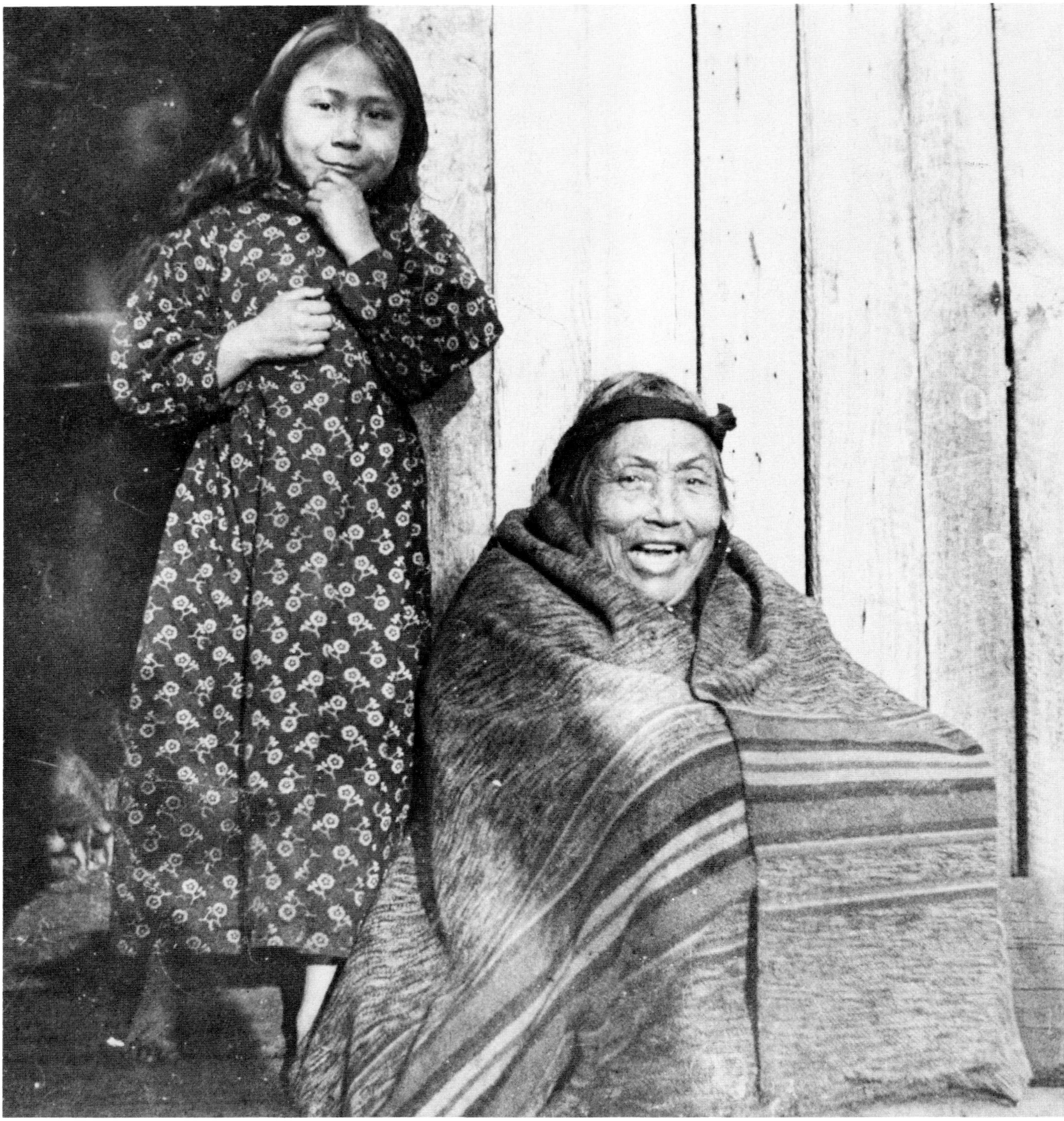

'My people start to laugh when they're really small . . . an' I guess they never really learn how to quit!' Old Fort Rupert Chief (Bob Wilson). (Photo: Courtesy BCPM PN-10-171.)

Note on Indian Words in This Text

Most of the Kwakiutl words and names appearing in this text have been rendered in a standardized orthography developed by the U'mista Cultural Center of Alert Bay, B.C. The U'mista orthography was selected over a number of different spelling conventions that have been used in the past, because it is the most common form being taught to young Kwak̓wala speakers today.

There are three exceptions to the use of the U'mista orthography in this text:

Where the Kwakiutl word was not recognizable—usually potlatch names that have become abbreviated over the years and are not currently in common use; and where the Kwakiutl words are rendered as part of a direct quotation from a written source. In both cases, the words are spelled as in the orginal source.

The third exception is the use of the term Kwakiutl. It should be written 'Kwagu'ł', but I have retained the commonly-used version for ease of recognition. Some examples of the source spelling and the given orthography are:

Charlie James' name 'Yaḵugłas' (always giving things away) is rendered here as YAḴUDŁAS—even though Charlie James used the written form 'Yakuglas' as taught to him in the orthography developed by Rev. Alfred Hall.

Mungo Martin used the spelling 'Nakapenkim' (ten times over) for his name—it is given here as NA̱KA̱'PA̱NKA̱M.

Ellen Neel's name 'Kakasolas' (people come from afar for advice) becomes ḴAḴA̱SO'LAS in the U'mista orthography.

In the Kwak̓wala alphabet used here, there are five vowels—they have these sounds:

a—the 'a' in a sneeze, 'ah-choo'.
a̲ (underlined)—the 'a' sound in 'what'.
e—the 'e' sound in 'bet'.
u—the 'u' sound in 'rude'.
o—the 'o' sound in 'sorry', or the 'oa' sound in 'oar'.
i—the 'i' sound in 'pizza'.

There are 37 consonants, many of which sound quite different from English consonants. For example, there is a series of explosive sounds marked with a raised comma (p̓, t̓, k̓, t̓s, etc.): these are pronounced with a slight 'click'.

There is a series of sounds which are pronounced at the back of the mouth (ḵ, g̱, x̱, w̱x, ḵ̓, etc.).

Some sounds are pronounced with a rounding of the lips that makes them sound as if they are followed by a 'w' (kw, qw, xw, etc.).

There is also a whispered 'L' that is written ł and a catch in the breath called a glottal stop that is written as an apostrophe (').

The following diagram, courtesy of the U'mista Cultural Society, shows the entire Kwak̓wala alphabet and illustrates some common words using the form. The diagram is copyrighted by the Society. The illustrations were drawn by Nola Johnston, specially to appeal to young Kwak̓wala learners.

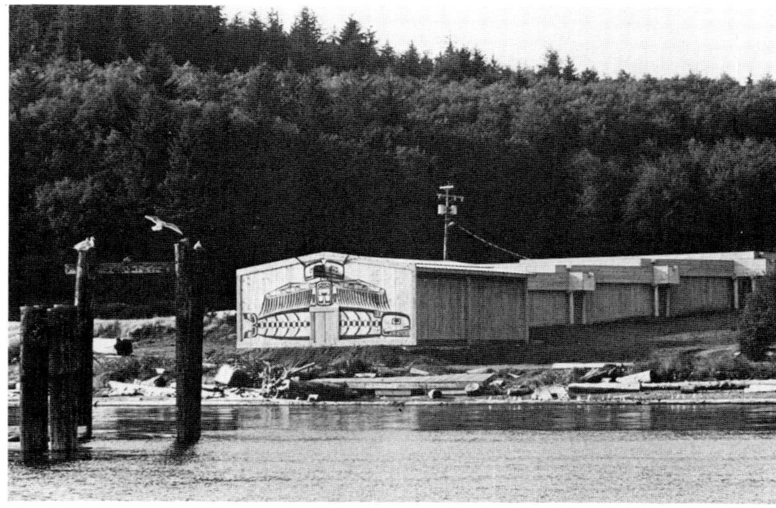

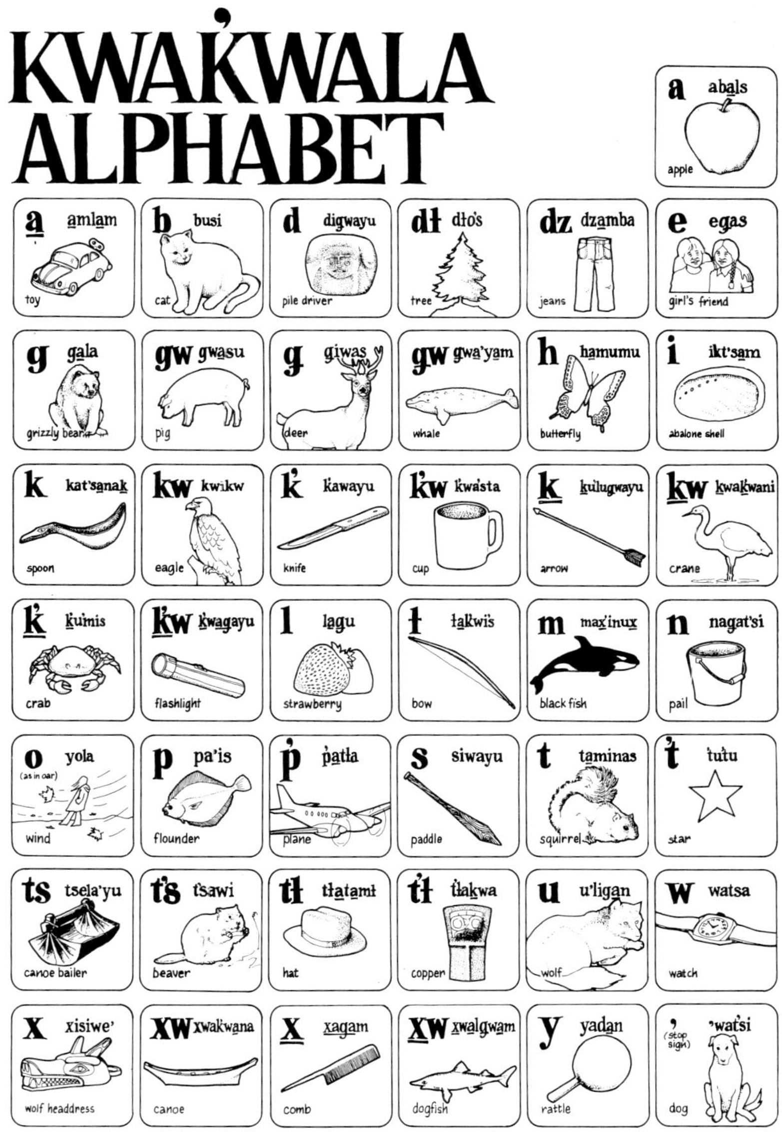

© U'mista Cultural Society, 1979

illustrations by Nola Johnston

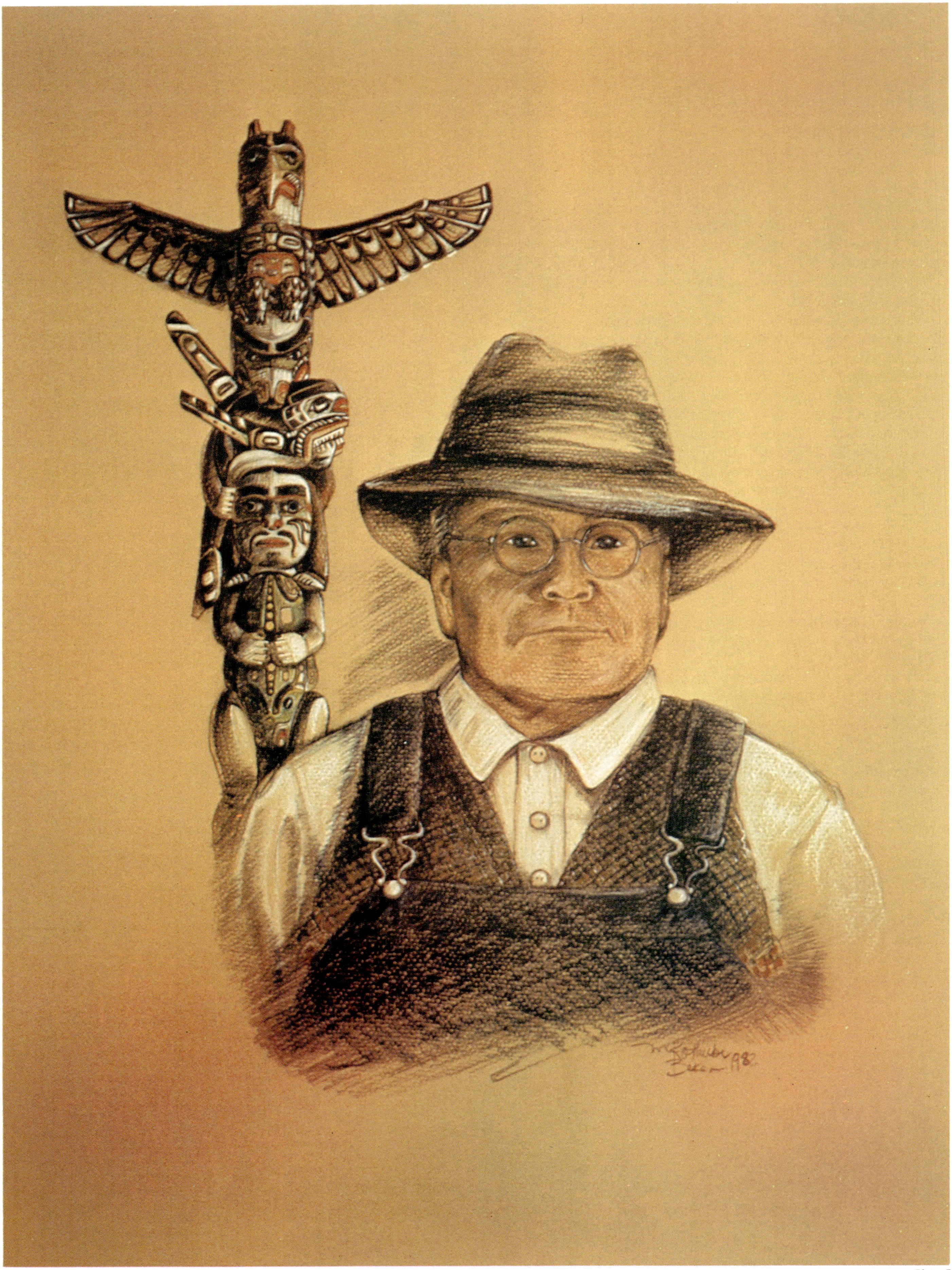

Plate: 7

Charlie James
Part 1

Charlie James was born in Port Townsend, Washington, around 1867. He died in Alert Bay, British Columbia, in 1938. In his seventy-odd years of life, James accomplished a great deal. He was Mungo Martin's stepfather and Ellen Neel's grandfather. He taught them to be as he was; a powerful artist in the Kwakiutl style.

James was called 'an innovator', a 'trend-setter', and even 'without a doubt the best carver in this whole area.' His work is known from those pieces which are displayed in the major public and private collections of the world. To most collectors, however, little is known of the man himself.

There is brief written mention of James in the works of Barbeau, Hawthorn, Malin, Macnair, Rasmussen, and many others. Often, even these small pieces of information are contradictory. His origins, his life, and his contributions are controversial.

Some museums have pieces that they attribute to James, but they were collected shortly after he was born. Other museum exhibits, obviously from his hands, are simply titled 'N.W. Coast, North America.' Copies of James' work are legion and his style is apparent in the work of many of his contemporaries, as well as those who came after. He is sometimes said to be the single major influence in Kwakiutl art from the turn of the century to current times.

His works are famous, however their creator is obscure. But some things *are* known. His masks and paintings, model poles and elaborate potlatch paraphernalia—the things that he made—are quite different. They provide stark contrast to other more restrained pieces that slumber quietly in glass coffins beside them. James' work seems somehow alive and barely contained in the quiet halls of solemn institutes.

These pieces are strongly expressive and powerful, yet strangely lost. They now dwell so far from the smell of the sea, so distant, in years, from the acrid smell of power and prestige. But so eloquent are these works, that surely they must sometimes stir! All over the world, in Germany and in England, in the United States and even on the cliffs of Point Grey, they must sometimes stir. When the fires are lit at Kingcome and Blunden, and during the June nights at 'Yalis, when the old people beat time in the remembered cadence and the clack, clack of the Huxwhukw beak is heard again, they must stir.

Who can say that the pull-strings don't tauten, and the cedarbark fringes don't tremble in some den, or glass case, or forgotten corner of an attic.

Surely, when the potlatch dances are underway, these 'carvings', these 'specimens' must know some small feeling, must be somehow aware that those ceremonies which give them meaning and reason for existence—are going on without them.

These objects that Charlie James made, even now, whisper in this strange manner to some people. Some appreciate the scarcely contained power and call it 'primitive art in the highest sense'. Others feel vaguely ill at ease and call the pieces 'barbaric' and 'grotesque.' Few are unaffected.

Charlie James was born Charles Jameson in Port Townsend, Washington, U.S.A., around 1867. His father was a white sawmill owner named Thomas Jameson and his mother was a Kwakiutl Indian woman named 'Kugwisi'la̱'og̱wa' from Fort Rupert, British Columbia.

Before James was ten years old, his mother died, leaving him and his two sisters in the care of his grandmother—'Kugwisi'la̱'og̱wa's' mother. The grandmother wanted to bring all of her daughter's children back to Canada, but Tom Jameson decided to keep his two daughters and raise them as white children. Jameson agreed at least partially to his mother-in-law's wishes, and allowed her to take his son to Victoria, B.C.

It is said Charlie James spoke english well, for a small boy, and Kwak̓wala only a few words. Why his father let him go is not known; his appearance could bring no stigma, for he was blue-eyed and fair-skinned—hardly a typical 'native.' Charlie James spent his early years with his grandmother in Victoria, before moving back to her people's village at Fort Rupert—near present-day Port Hardy, B.C. He later changed his name from Jameson to James, because as Mabel Stanley explained, 'He said Jameson was too long!'

When he was quite young, he was badly injured by

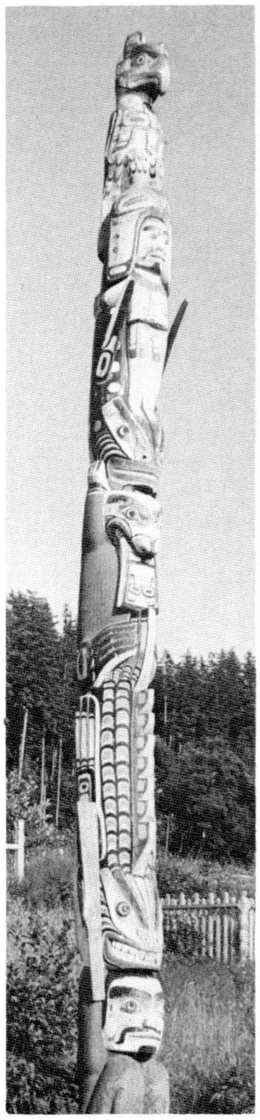

***Plate 8:* A Charlie James pole in the graveyard at Alert Bay. Note the killer-whale crest on the chest of the Thunderbird. (Alert Bay 1953. Photo: Wilson Duff Courtesy: B.C.P.M. PN-2093)**

the accidental discharge of a shotgun. This misfortune left him with only the thumb and the major part of the forefinger on his left hand. Although still functional, his left hand was ugly in appearance and James hid it from view. His sensitivity and self-consciousness over his crippled hand did not diminish as he got older. If anything, these feelings grew stronger. Those people who knew him well, say that his hand was always hidden in a pocket of his coveralls or smock when he worked, and in his pants or jacket pocket on other occasions.

He wore a light mitten over his damaged hand in addition to keeping it in his pocket, and only a very few people ever saw it. In the presence of strangers, he acted like a person with only one arm, doing everything one-handed. When alone or with his family, he used his damaged hand to hold objects through the cloth of his outer garments, while he carved or painted with his right hand.

It is likely that Charlie James began his career of carving because his crippled hand would not allow him to participate in the activities available to other young men in Fort Rupert. He learned the basics from his relatives and applied them, initially, to the carving of canoes. His son-in-law, Charlie Newman, said, 'he carved canoes up to 30′ and 40′ long—also many small ones, about 18′ or smaller. The small ones were used for transportation between the islands, for hunting and fishing and clamming.'

The cedar trees for the large canoes came from Vancouver Island or the mainland of British Columbia. James chose his trees while they were standing. The heart of the tree was plumbed first with an axe, to be sure that it was sound. Many large cedars are hollow or 'conked' and those were left standing. When a suitable tree had been selected, it was toppled and cut to the correct length. The excess outer wood was trimmed away and the portion of the wood with the fewest knots was selected and freed from the balance. The rough log was partially hollowed at the forest site and was then dragged to the beach using rollers, ropes and a number of helpers. The log was towed to the bay in front of the village and with many helping hands was hauled up onto the beach to be finished.

Charlie Newman continued his description by saying, 'Some people helped him in chopping out the canoes—some for a few days, some for shorter times—and an awful lot of people watched! Those who helped were paid off by a bit of potlatch.'

James did all the finishing work on these canoes with a 'D' adze, imparting the precise fluted texture that was to become characteristic of his later large poles. The paddles were made from the heavy, dense wood of the yew tree. This material was difficult to work but unbelievably strong.

Around 1895, Charlie James married a woman named Sara Nina, in the Indian fashion, at Fort Rupert, B.C. Sara Nina was also called Sara Finlay, and she was the daughter of a Kwakiutl woman named Ḵasa̱'las, and a Scottish employee of the Hudson's Bay Company named George Finlay. Sara Nina's name in Kwak̓wala was 'Na̱gedzi,' which means 'mountain of wealth,' although she was often called 'Ḵu̱migа̱.'

Before her marriage to Charlie James, Sara Nina had been married, at a young age, to a man named 'Yax̱'nukwa̱las,' meaning, 'no one leaves his home without gifts.' The white people, however, simply called him 'Martin.' During her marriage to Martin, Sara Nina had four sons, one of whom died in infancy. The eldest son was called Spruce Martin, and the youngest, Herbert Martin. The second born son was destined to become a famous man. He was named Mungo.

After Martin/Yax̱'nukwa̱las died, Sara Nina remarried to Charlie James, and James took her three sons as his stepsons. Charlie James and Sara Nina later had two daughters. One was called Emma and the other Lucy.

It is interesting to note that the marriage of Charlie James and Sara Nina was sanctified by clergy many years after the fact. Charlie James and Sara Nina, their

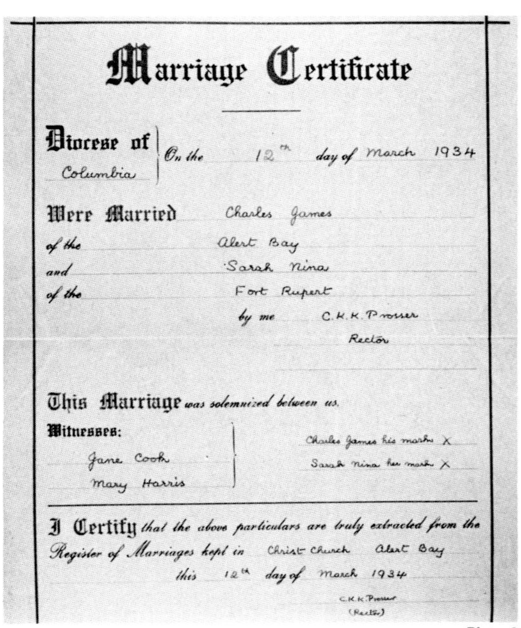

Marriage Certificate

Diocese of Columbia | On the 12th day of March 1934

Were Married Charles James
of the Alert Bay
and Sarah Nina
of the Fort Rupert
by me C.K.K. Prosser
Rector

This Marriage was solemnized between us.
Witnesses:
Jane Cook
Mary Harris

Charles James his mark X
Sarah Nina her mark X

I Certify that the above particulars are truly extracted from the Register of Marriages kept in Christ Church Alert Bay this 12th day of March 1934
C.K.K. Prosser
(Rector)

Plate: 9

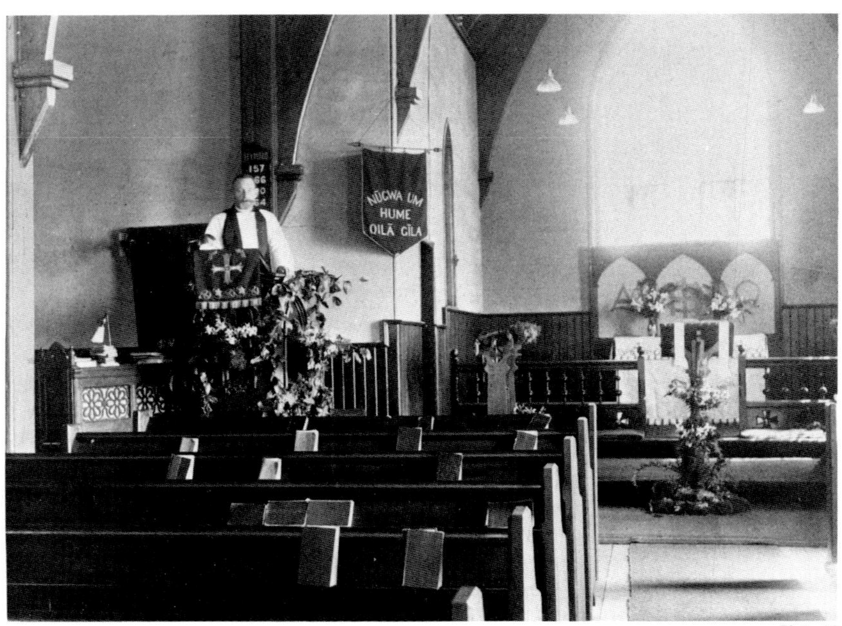

Plate: 10

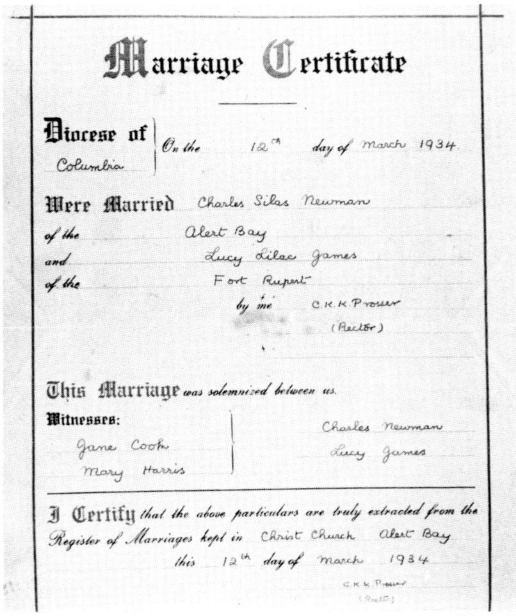

Marriage Certificate

Diocese of Columbia | On the 12th day of March 1934

Were Married Charles Silas Newman
of the Alert Bay
and Lucy Lilac James
of the Fort Rupert
by me C.K.K. Prosser
(Rector)

This Marriage was solemnized between us.

Witnesses:
Jane Cook
Mary Harris

Charles Newman
Lucy James

I Certify that the above particulars are truly extracted from the Register of Marriages kept in Christ Church Alert Bay this 12th day of March 1934

C.K.K. Prosser
(Rector)

Plate: 11

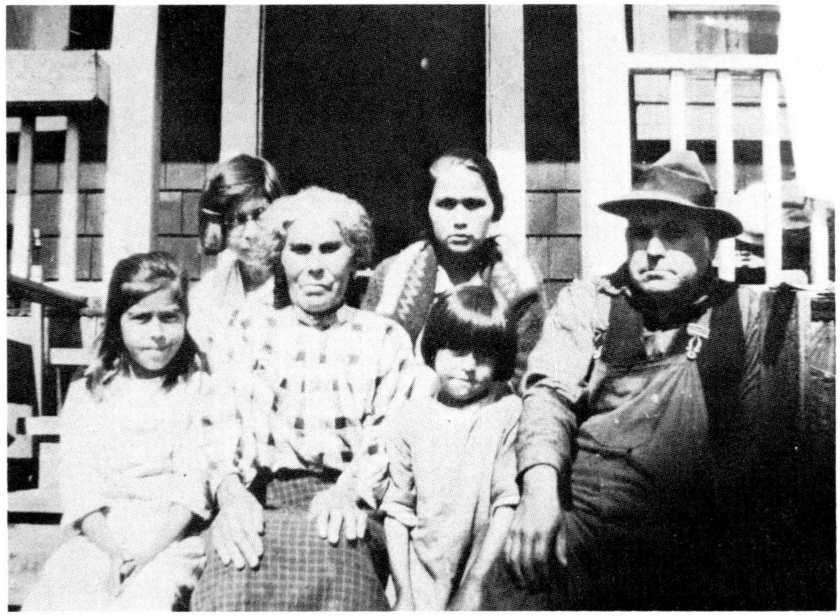

Plate: 12

Plate 11: **Marriage certificate of Lucy James and Charlie Newman. (Alert Bay, 1934. Photo: Courtesy Neel Family.)**

Plate 12: **Charlie James and Sara Nina pose with some of their nieces and grand-children. Ellen Newman is in the back left—with glasses. As always, James has his damaged left hand in his pocket. (Alert Bay, c. 1926. Photo: Courtesy Neel Family.)**

Plate 9: **Marriage certificate of Charlie James and Sara Nina (Sara Finlay) . . . Reverend Prosser presiding. (Alert Bay, 1934. Photo: Courtesy Neel Family.)**

Plate 10: **Christ Church at Alert Bay. This anglican church was the scene of most of the marriages in the area including some large-scale mass marriages. Reverend A.W. Corker in the pulpit—the legend on the banner reads, in Kwakwala, 'I am here to pray.' (Alert Bay, c. 1923/24. Photo B.C.P.M. PN-2305.)**

daughter Lucy and her husband Charlie Newman, were all married on the same day! The old people laugh when this period is recalled and say that the minister, in a fit of zeal, simply lined up everyone he could find and performed marriage ceremonies in wholesale quantities .

Since James' damaged hand prevented him from the usual occupations, such as salmon fishing, he was one of the few who carved full time. He carved for the tourist trade, but also produced ceremonial and functional articles commissioned by others of the tribe.

With his stepson Mungo, Charlie James travelled a good deal. 'Wandering,' Ellen Neel called it. She said, 'He made totem poles everywhere. He lived and carved in Victoria, then he went back north. Then he and Mungo lived in Vancouver, and then went back to Fort Rupert. He and Mungo always wandered back and forth, although most of the time they lived in Fort Rupert. After my mother married (about 1915) my grandfather and Mungo came to live in Alert Bay and then spent most of their time there.'

Alert Bay became Charlie James' home and there he did most of the work that made him well known. He worked from a shed on the beach—a small shed measuring perhaps 6 feet by 8 feet. When working on large poles, he would erect a shelter, next to the shed, to protect the poles from the rain. I asked the late Mabel Stanley where Charlie James carved. She remembered the shed on the beach, but said, 'It (where he carved) wasn't always on the beach—before that, it was right next to the house where Charlie Newman and Lucy and the kids lived. 'Dak̓uma' and his wife stayed there too, and Dak̓uma had a little shack, alongside the main house.' His son-in-law—Charlie Newman said, 'He carved in a shed on the beach, right in front of old man Drabble's house,' or, 'He carved on the beach by Gideon Whannock's house.'

Recently, I stood on the beach, about where Charlie James' shed used to be, and I thought of the various people's descriptions of this spot, 'in front of my smoke house'—'in front of old man Drabble's house,' and who knows how many in between—and now it's in front of Fred Cook's house. These things change, but the beach stays the same. I shielded my eyes from the June sun and looked across to Vancouver Island. In my mind I could see the old man laying down his adze, standing up from the small stool he used and brushing the sweet-smelling cedar chips from his lap. How many times did he stand, straighten up to stretch and relieve the pressure on his back, and then shield his eyes and squint across the bright water to the dark green forests beyond? Who knows. Amos Dawson was with me and seeming to catch some semblance of my thoughts, he said quietly, 'I remember an old shack here, from when I was a kid. I used to play in it.' 'Was it the same one that Charlie James used to carve in?' I asked. He shrugged, 'Who knows.'

James was a methodical man in his carving. To start the small tourist poles he cut pieces of yellow cedar to the correct length with a saw. He rounded them on three sides, leaving the backs flat, and then put them into a wood stave barrel full of rain water. The blank poles were left soaking for several days to render the wood soft and easily carved.

In his small shed he kept an old metal vise. Here the blank was placed and deep saw cuts made—to block out the thunderbird's beak and shoulders—the bear's chin and paws—or whatever was required according to the figures to be used. Then he did something unusual (according to current carving practice). He used an elbow adze to rough out the figures. His use of an adze on poles measuring only 16″-20″ high speaks well of his deftness with a traditional tool meant for much larger pieces. When much of the carving was finished with an adze, he would complete the fine work with a knife. He made all his own knives from old files.

Years ago, Dave Neel gave me one of Charlie James' knives. I never mentioned it to Ellen because I strongly suspected that he wasn't allowed to give away things that were not his, and that knife belonged, most certainly, to Ellen. The blade is thin, beveled on both sides and shaped like a bulbous triangle. The underside of the blade is flat and resembles a chisel in cross section. The blade is set into a yew wood handle, on one side, and bound there with thin, strong cod-line. The binding is covered with several layers of old-fashioned, cloth-based electrical tape. I thought it an awkward knife when I first tried it. Ellen and the boys had taught me to use a conventional knife of European style—but I later learned such a knife was well-designed. You could cut away as well as toward yourself without reversing the work piece, and you could cut alongside a projection without having the hilt of the handle force the blade into an awkward position. James knew his stuff.

Charlie James seldom used chisels except for a narrow one to cut the deep mortise for insetting the separate wings of the thunderbird. The wings of his tourist poles were all closely fitted into the deep mortises in the shoulders of the thunderbird without benefit of nails or glue. This treatment is a good identifying characteristic of a James pole. When all of this was complete, he sometimes sanded them and sometimes not, as sandpaper was costly.

James is often said to be the last carver in this century to use native paints. This is not strictly true. He had a mortar and pestle in his beach shack and would grind charcoal and add the powder to dried salmon eggs to make a good, permanent black. The mixture was soaked and the colour pressed out. Most of the other colours he used were European watercolours, and, in later years, poster paints filched from the residential school.

Characteristically, the backs of the wings were painted black midway and the backs of the figures were fully painted except for a square left blank and then painted with his name, CHARLIE JAMES. Sometimes his signature was accompanied by his Kwakiutl name 'YAKUGLAS' (Yakudłas) meaning 'always giving things away.' Curiously, the articles made for people in the tribe, or the poles made while teaching others, were not signed, nor was his very early work. James never varnished his poles although many of the subsequent owners did later, to protect the fragile water colours. These tourist poles were produced by the hundreds and are now truly scattered around the world. Occasionally among them is found a finely-wrought, beautifully detailed piece—a model or 'study' for a larger work.

Almost all of the totem poles carved by Charlie James, both miniature and fully-sized pieces, have a painted device or crest on the chest of the thunderbird. On tourist poles, this was most often a simple humanoid face, similar to the centre face of a 'sisiyutł' or double-headed snake, in a number of variations. On many full-sized poles, and some carefully done minatures, this device takes the form of James' personal crest, the killer whale.

The killer whale crest is rendered in a very abstract form, and was often used by Ellen Neel on the thunderbird figures surmounting her more elaborate pieces. Whether Ellen regarded the use of this crest as an inherited privilege from her grandfather or simply an elaborate decoration learned from him, is not known. When I first worked with Ellen, I had no idea what this design meant, though I dutifully copied it onto my rough versions of her work. Ellen explained that it was a killer whale and she pointed out that the central ovoids and their trailing 'U' forms represented, simultaneously, both the eyes of the killer whale and its

Plate 13: **The beach at Alert Bay. Charlie James used to carve the larger poles here. (Alert Bay, 1979. Photo: Author.)**

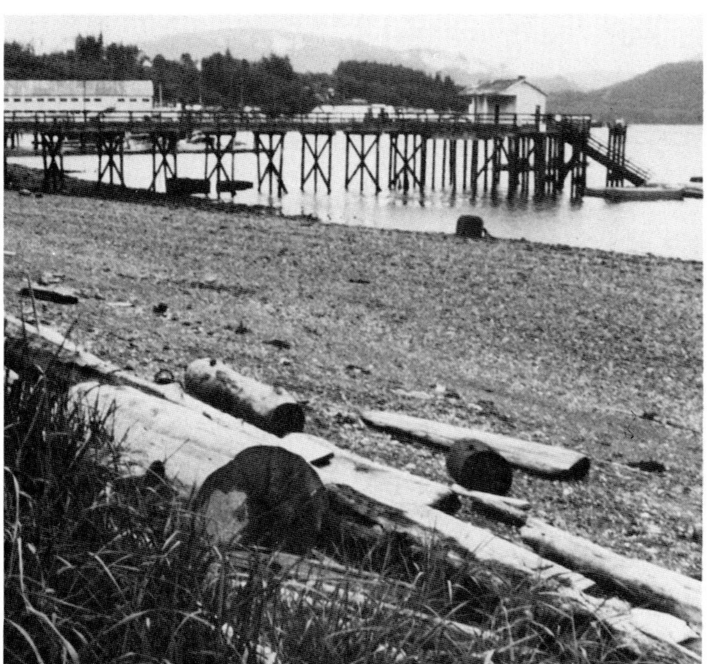

Plate: 13

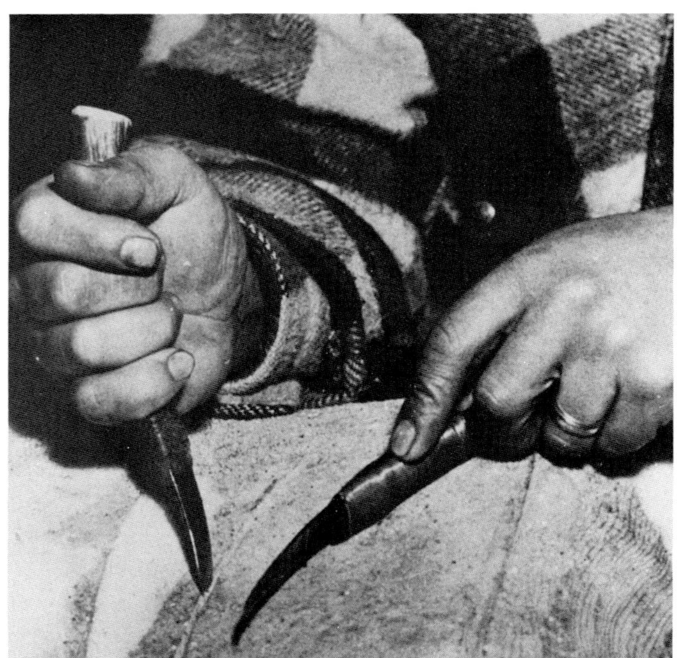

Plate: 14

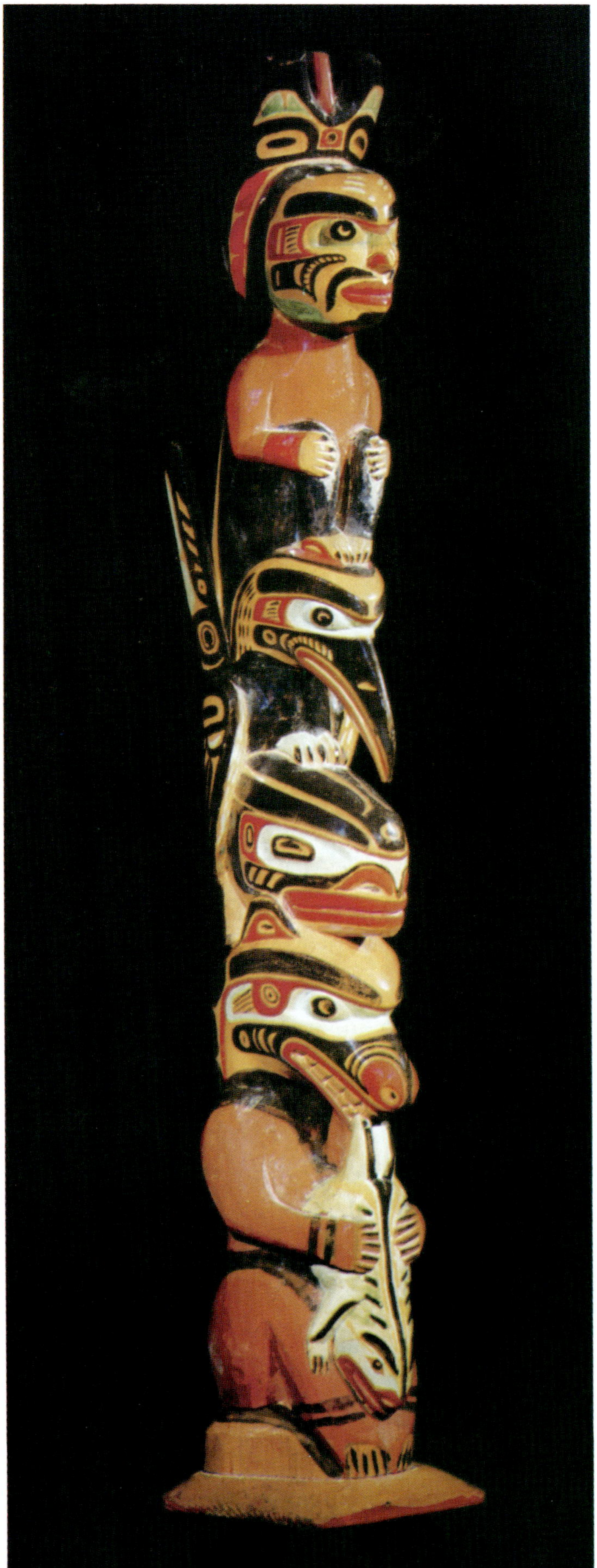

Plate: 15

Plate 15: A Charlie James carving in the collection of the B.C. Provincial Museum, Victoria, B.C. This model pole is 66 cm high and represents a good example of the 'midway' style of James—if such a thing exists. Peter Macnair, of the B.C.P.M., suggests that it might simply be a case of taking more time to 'Carve out the orbits and define the orbs,' as James did in this example. The date of this carving is unknown. (Victoria, date unknown. Photo: B.C.P.M. PN-6786.)

Plate 16: A model pole by Charlie James. This design of the Thunderbird surmounting a grizzly bear clutching a potlatch 'copper' with a human face above . . . is one of James' most often used designs . . . it appears with only minute variation, in dozens of James' model poles in various collections. This particular one is unusual in that it has the killer whale crest on the chest of the Thunderbird instead of a stylized human face similar to that shown on the copper. (See *Plate 19*.) This style of model pole is from the 1920/30 era. (Vancouver, c. 1950. Photo: Courtesy U.B.C. A-5329.)

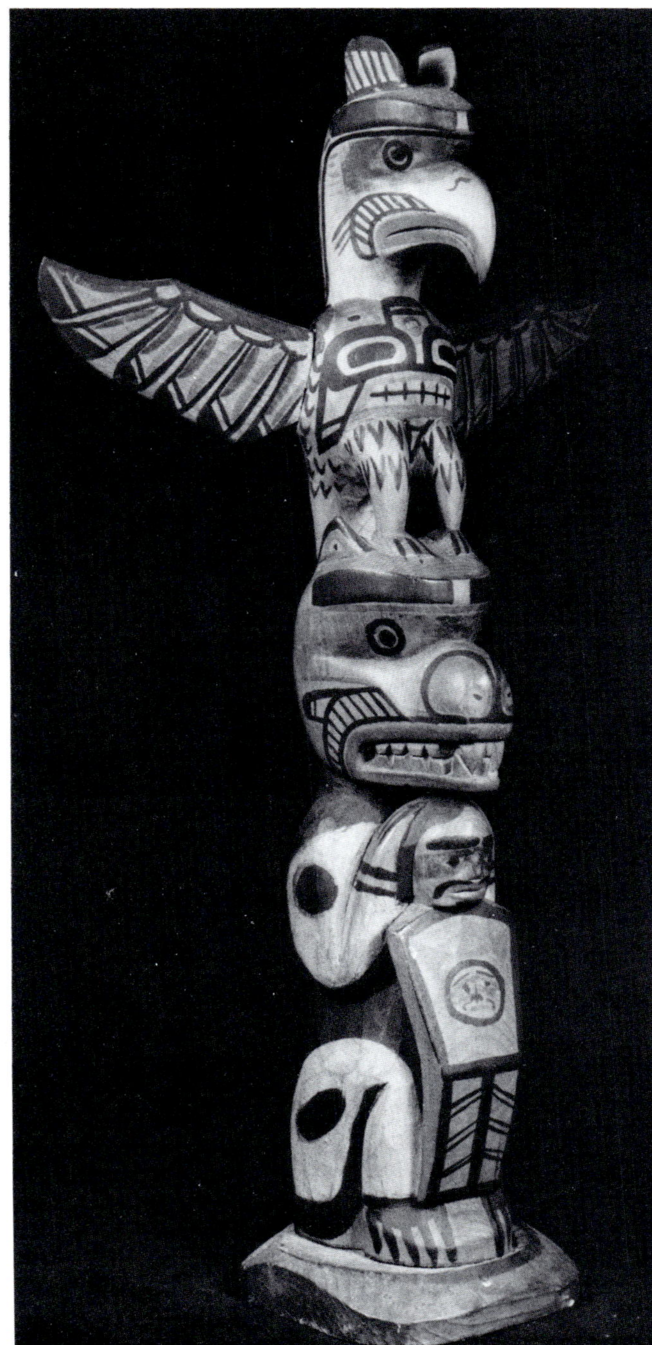

Plate: 16

Plate 17: The lower figures from a Charlie James pole. Kwakiutl carvers today, marvel at the power with which James could endow his figures . . . 'Sea bear' and seal. From the period 1920-30. (Photo: Author, 1981.)

Plate 18: Charlie James model pole. A kneeling human figure above a giant bear with a killer whale in its mouth. The whale has the dorsal and pectoral fins added as separate pieces. (Vancouver, c. 1950. Photo: Courtesy U.B.C. A-5334.)

Plate 19: Charlie James model pole. The 'K̲ulus'—(no horns) shown above a human figure holding a seal. (Vancouver, c. 1950. Photo: Courtesy U.B.C. A-5335.)

Plate 20: A Charlie James pole in the graveyard at Alert Bay. The design is similar to the 'grizzly bear houseposts.' Killer whale crest on the chest of the top figure. (Alert Bay, c. 1940. Photo: Parney Williams. Courtesy: B.C.P.M. PN-1936-A.)

Plate 21: A Charlie James carving in the Alert Bay cemetery. The killer whale crest is the simplified version more often found on much smaller model poles by James. (Alert Bay, no date given. Photo W.H. Gould. Courtesy: B.C.P.M. PN-2287.)

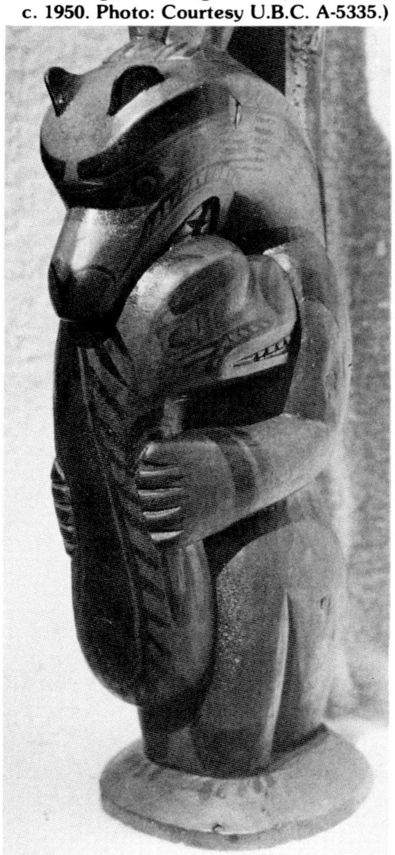

Plate: 17

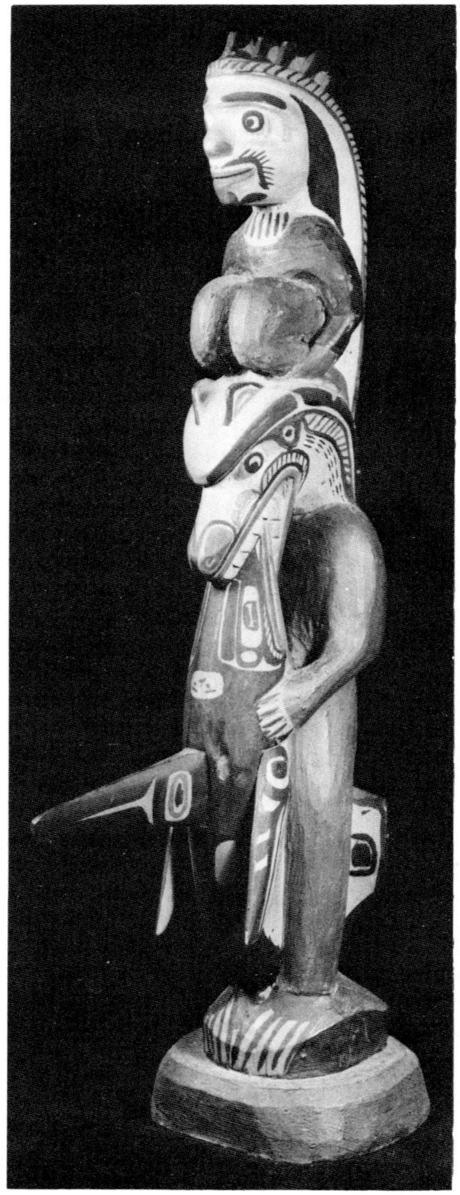

Plate: 18

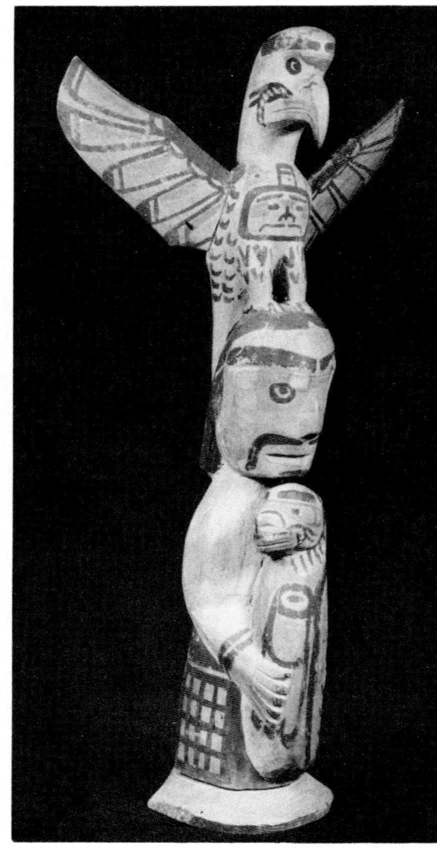

Plate: 19

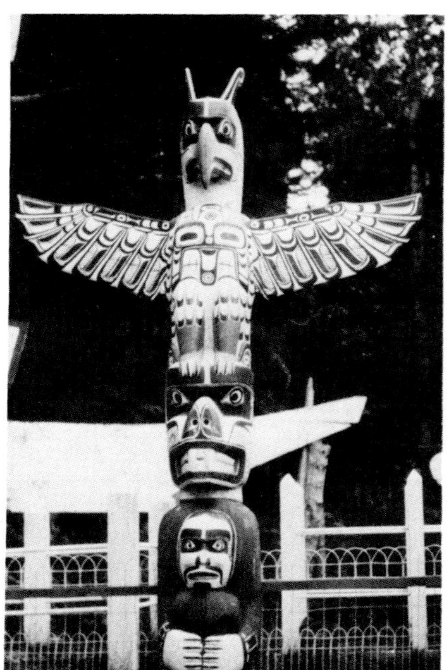

Plate: 20

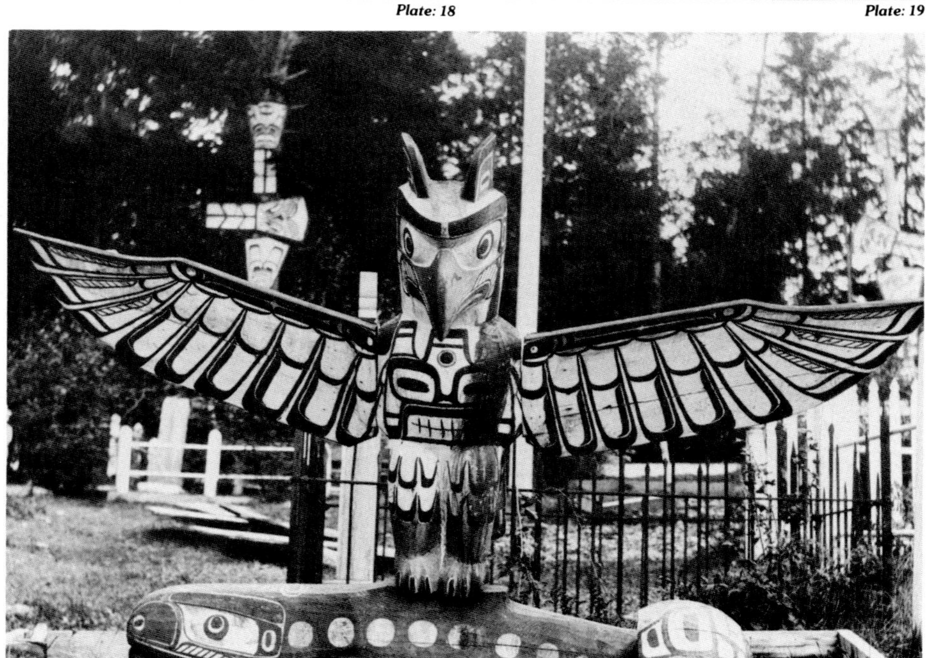

Plate: 21

tail flukes. (Though the terminology of 'ovoids' and 'U' forms came much later, courtesy Bill Holm.) When Ellen used it in simplified form on very small poles, it was hard to recognize, since a number of elements were omitted. James used the crest in a simple, but complete version on many small poles and elaborated it on large poles. The use of this crest, in its varying forms, is another important identifying characteristic of a Charlie James pole.

The cedar trees used for large, traditional totem poles were initially selected in the same manner as the trees for canoes from those standing in the forests on Vancouver Island. Several places, in the area of Alert Bay, held good cedar—Hardy Bay, for example. Later, as logging operations became more commonplace there, James would ask his son-in-law or other relatives to watch the beaches for drift logs that had broken loose from log booms during transport. These were pulled from the beach at high tide and towed behind a fishboat to the beach at Alert Bay.

The cedar log was dragged ashore using short sections of smaller diameter logs as rollers. Once it was in position beside his shed, James pried the log up to waist level and used wedges in conjunction with the short roller sections to secure it there. The bark and outer sap wood were removed first, using a double-bitted broad axe with a short handle. This same axe and a crosscut saw were used to block out the main figures. Handling these heavy tools must have been quite a feat since James was a small man and, of course, worked with only one hand.

The top and bottom figures were blocked out before the centre figures. The central space was measured and divided into the lengths needed for the middle figures. As with the small tourist poles, saw cuts were made and the pungent cedar chopped away to leave a bulky form. Most of the large poles produced by Charlie James were full-figured—that is, the figures were fully-carved at the back of the pole as well as the front. This was the main reason for the use of large wedges to hold the log in position. It was a relatively simple matter to drive out the wedges on one side, allow the log to roll 180 degrees and re-wedge it so that the back area could be carved.

When the figures were completely blocked out, front and back, the log/pole was rolled to its original position and work started with the elbow adze. James used five different-sized adzes—a very large one to start, changing to progressively smaller ones as the final form took shape. James' poles followed the traditionally flamboyant style of the Kwakiutl. The large figures were not tightly compressed to follow the round shape of the log, as was common in the more northern style, but were deeply cut and almost released from the log. The three dimensional aspect was further accentuated by the use of separate projecting pieces—the beak of a raven, for example, or the pectoral and dorsal fins of a killer whale. These separate pieces were driven into deeply-cut mortises and finally shaped once in place. It is said that James never used a single nail, but relied on his skill in fitting to achieve a degree of permanence that took many years to succumb to decay, weather and the innocent vandalism of small, agile children.

After the figures were fully carved, they were gone over with a 'D' adze to impart the parallel fluted lines that were the hallmark of the finished surface. During the finishing stages, particularly while cutting incised lines, the surface of the wood was kept wet to allow clean cuts to be made across the grain, without fear of the edges of the cuts tearing.

His early poles, particularly the model ones, show

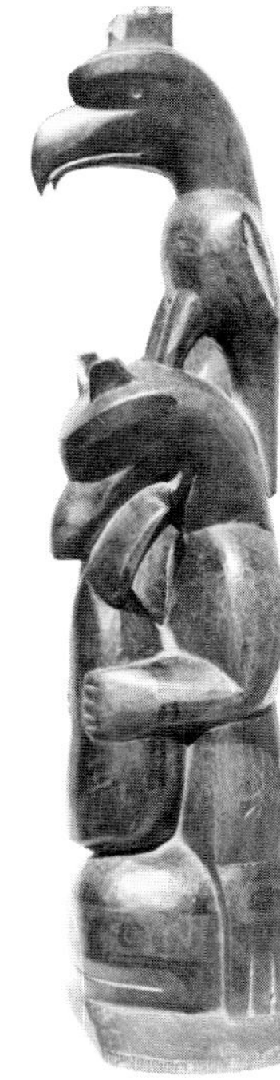

Plate 22: A Charlie James pole in the author's collection. This particular pole is made of a heavy, dense wood, probably western yew, rather than the red or yellow cedar usually used. The pole has almost no paint left and has a deep, polished patina from much handling. Purchased in London, England in 1979. (c. 1920-30. Photo: Author, 1981.)

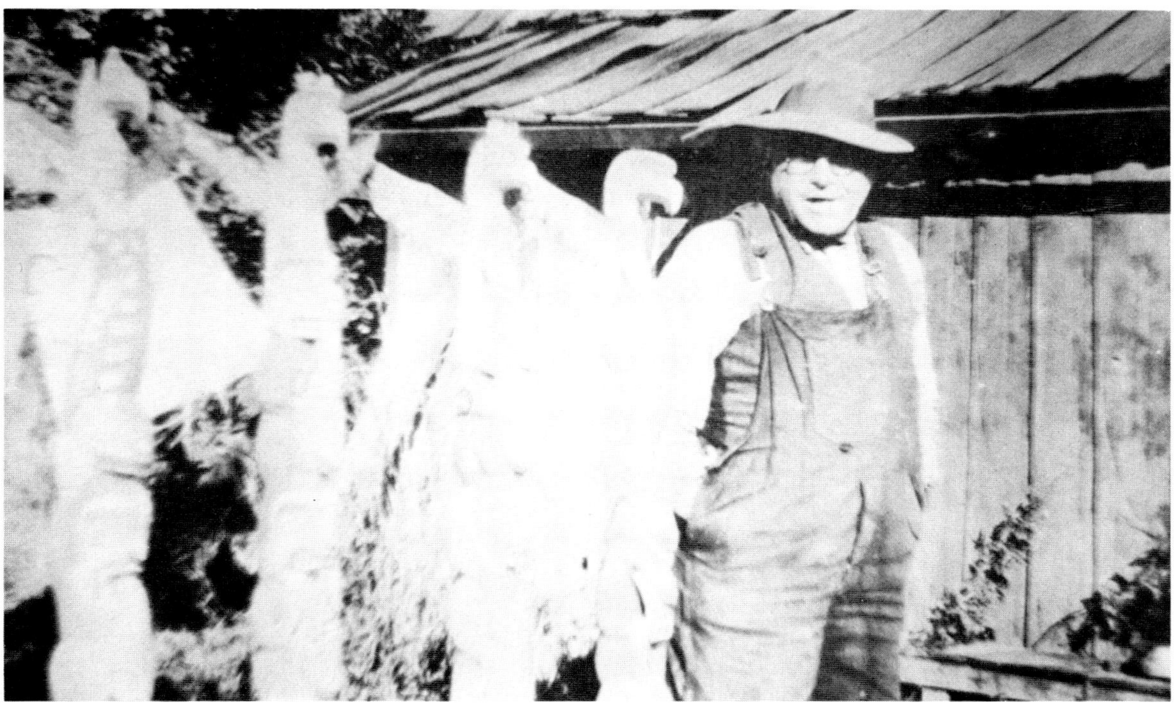

Plate: 23

Plate 23: Charlie James—'Dak̓uma'—outside his carving shed at Alert Bay. The 'tourist' poles are of a quality seldom seen today. (Alert Bay, 1930. Photo: Courtesy Neel Family.)

Plate 24: A 'study' or model of the Victoria pole shown in *Plates 26* and *27* (Vancouver, 1982. Photo: Author's collection.)

Plate 25: One of a number of model poles carved by Charlie James that are now in the Centennial Museum, Vancouver, BC. This model is similar to the 'Victoria' pole—except for the bottom figure. Note the killer whale on the chest of the Thunderbird. (Vancouver. Photo: V.M.P.A.)

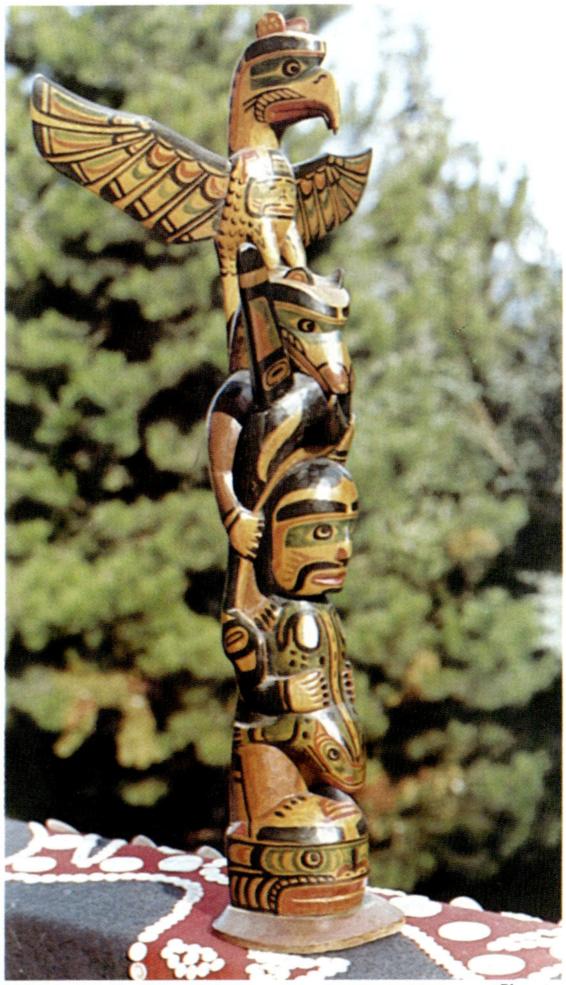

Plate: 24

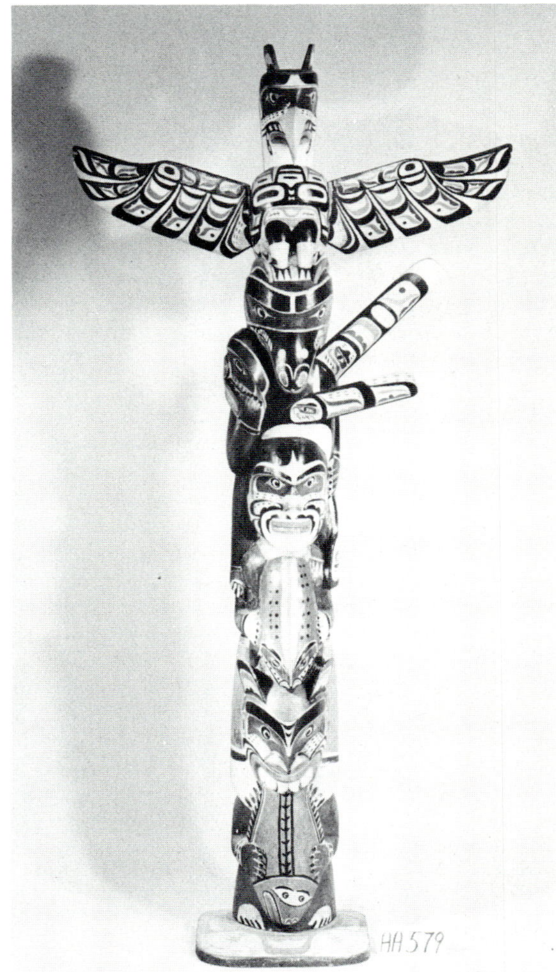

Plate: 25

little paint, and then only to accentuate carving. In later years James used commercially available exterior paint, in bright colours, almost completely covering the large poles. This 'polished' paint style was in demand from his clients and he worked according to their wishes. His own preference is not known, but it can be noticed that many of the pieces that he did as gifts revert to the earlier style with the wood itself prominent and the painting more subdued.

Each of the real full size totem poles has its own distinct history. Not just the legend or the interpretation of the figures so dear to tourists' hearts, but the actual story surrounding the pole itself. Who commissioned the pole and why? Who carved it and how? Where did it stand and for how long? Where is it now? And, most important, what of the people involved with it?

When a carver such as Charlie James was chosen to do an important piece of work, the enterprise was treated seriously from start to finish. Important pieces were such things as potlatch paraphernalia, event markers, memorial poles and the like. Each called for lengthy discussion. The figures that the prospective owner wanted to use, how to best portray them in a manner that was traditional and, at the same time, different. A small model or study was often produced to show the prospective client what he could expect in the finished article. In some cases, a number of models were made, all with the same figures, but each given a slightly different treatment in the carving or the painting.

Usually the artist himself would decide on what would be most effective, having heard the owner's crest stories related or having listened attentively to the details of the events to be recorded.

Many of the full size totem poles that Charlie James carved still exist today. They are changed, though, through time and rain coast weather, and only his deeply contoured carving remains, often hidden under many coats of paint, later applied by hands lacking his skill and imagination.

One notable exception to this aging process is a totem pole that remained indoors and under cover from the time it was carved and painted until now. It is in Victoria, British Columbia, standing in the Memorial Hall of Christ Church Cathedral. It is particularly interesting since a photograph exists of Charlie James doing the final painting in a shack on the beach. James' son-in-law, Charlie Newman, described it during an interview with Marius Barbeau. The pole still stands—unchanged—in perfect condition, with the original paint intact.

Charlie Newman supplied the details of how and why it was carved:

'I told the old man—Charlie James—let's do something for the girls, the girls in Victoria (The Women's Auxiliary to the church—Church of England—P.N.) They were always sending gifts to my children.' James replied, 'That's a good idea. Look for a cedar log for me and I'll make a totem pole for them.' I went hunting for cedar logs and I found a good one on

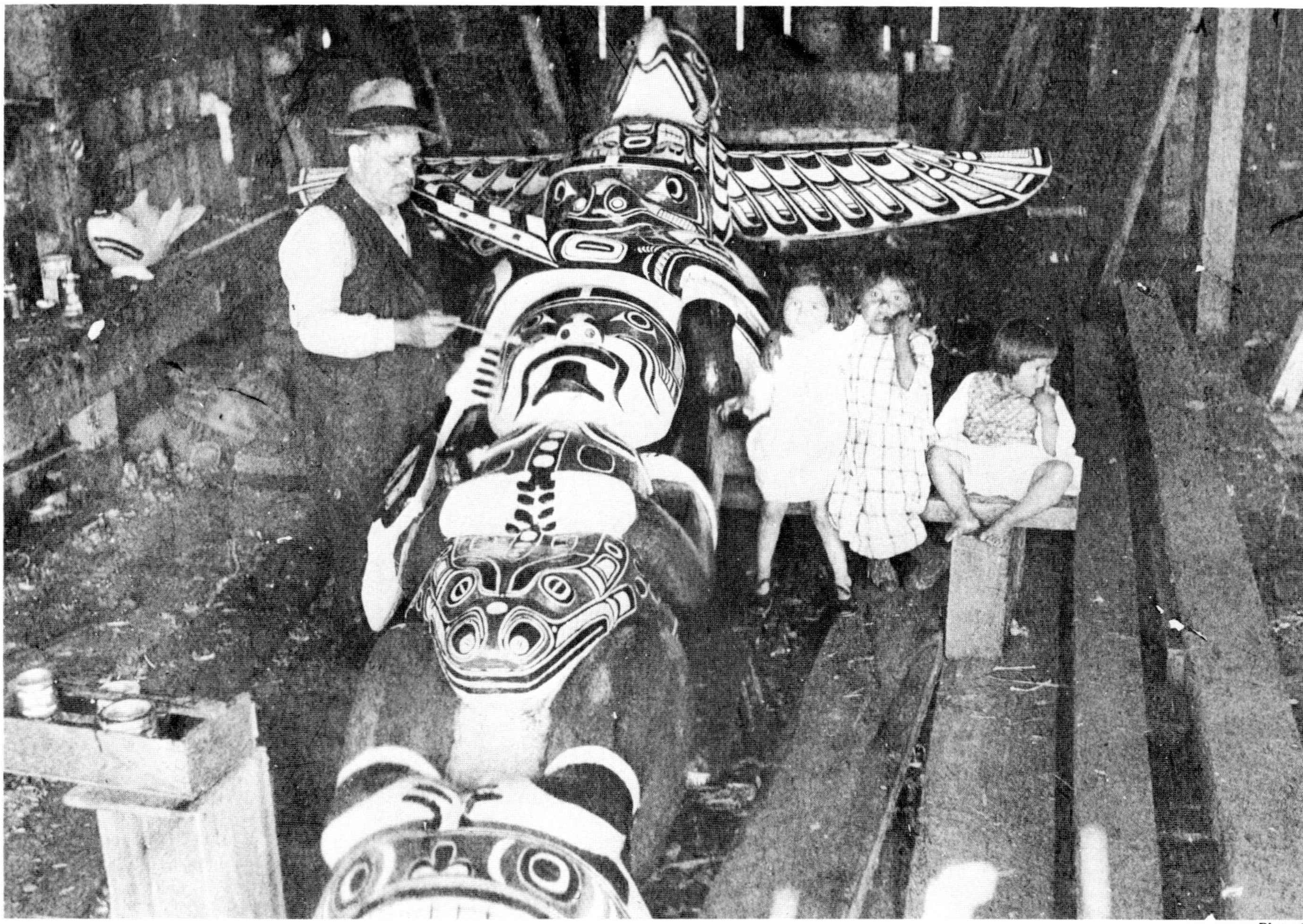

Plate: 26

this island (Alert Bay—Cormorant Island). It was about 18 feet long and about 30 inches in diameter. He (James) carved the thunderbird at the top, the bear with a whale, a Tsonoqua (the wild person of the woods) and a frog. When it was finished, he sent it down to Victoria. It stood in the Memorial Hall and I guess it is still there. It was really well painted. All this happened more than 20 years ago (about 1925). All the people here were glad and proud of it and they danced around it when it was finished. We gave it as a gift from our whole family to the girls in Victoria. Doctor Maudy took a lot of pictures of this pole while it was being carved. Doctor Maudy used to live here in Alert Bay. He was the first one to run the picture show here. Anyhow, he took lots of pictures while it was in the shed on the beach. It was in a shed because of the rain—along the beach in front of my smokehouse. Charlie James carved many big poles and he carved the posts for the big houses here. He got all those to do. Charlie James was the best carver on the coast!'

Whether or not James was 'the best carver on the coast' is a matter of opinion, but the fact remains that he was skilled and his work was as actively sought by his own people as it was by collectors and tourists.

It is said that each totem pole has its own story—a beginning and an end. The story of the Victoria pole is brief and simple but many of the stories are more complex. The degree of detail that can be located is limited only by the years that have passed.

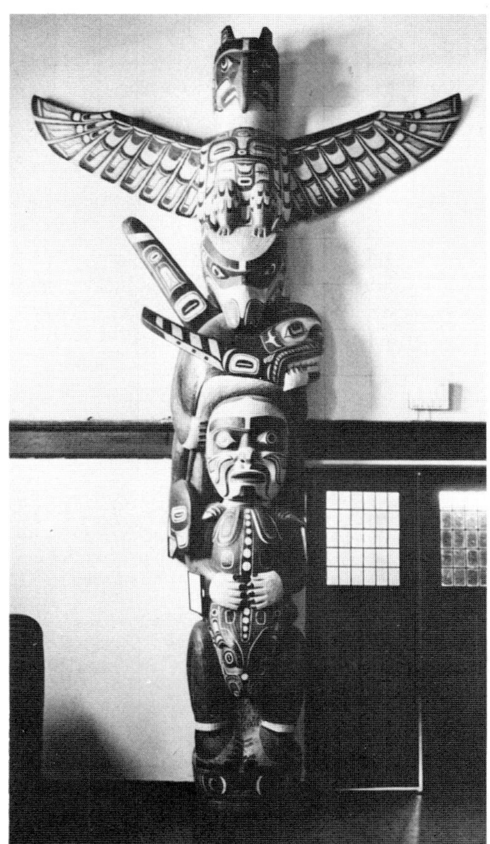

Plate: 27

Plate 26: **Charlie James applies the finishing paint to the totem pole destined to go to Victoria. (Alert Bay, c. 1925. Photo by Rev. Corker or Doctor Maudy. Courtesy: B.C.P.M. PN-2315.)**

Plate 27: **Totem pole shown in *Plate 26* as it stands today in Memorial Hall, Christ Church Cathedral, Victoria, BC. Note that the original paint is completely intact in this photo taken in 1979. (Victoria. Photo: Alex Barta.)**

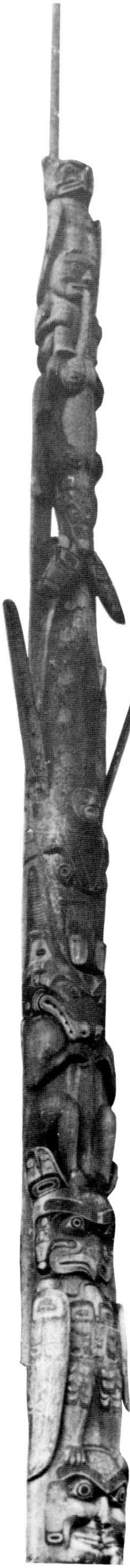

Plate: 28

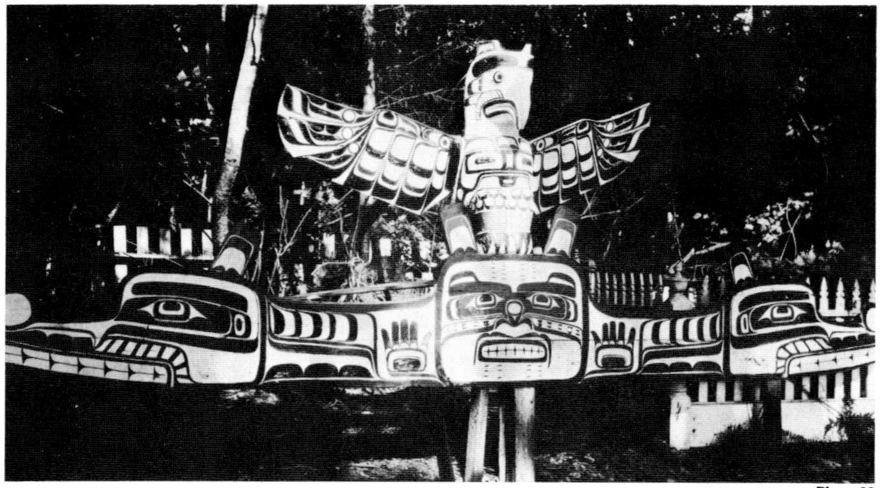

Plate: 29

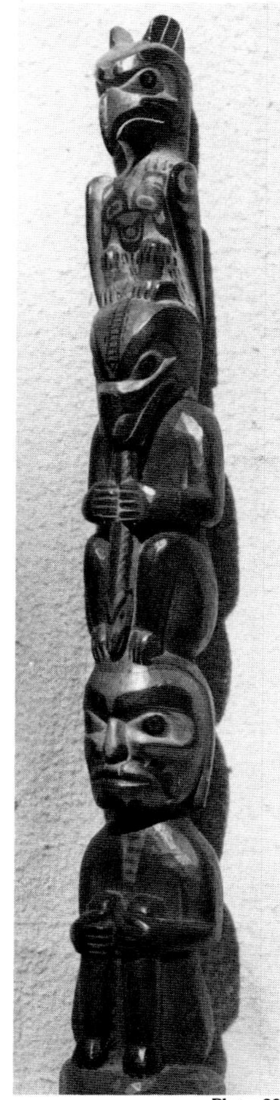

Plate: 30

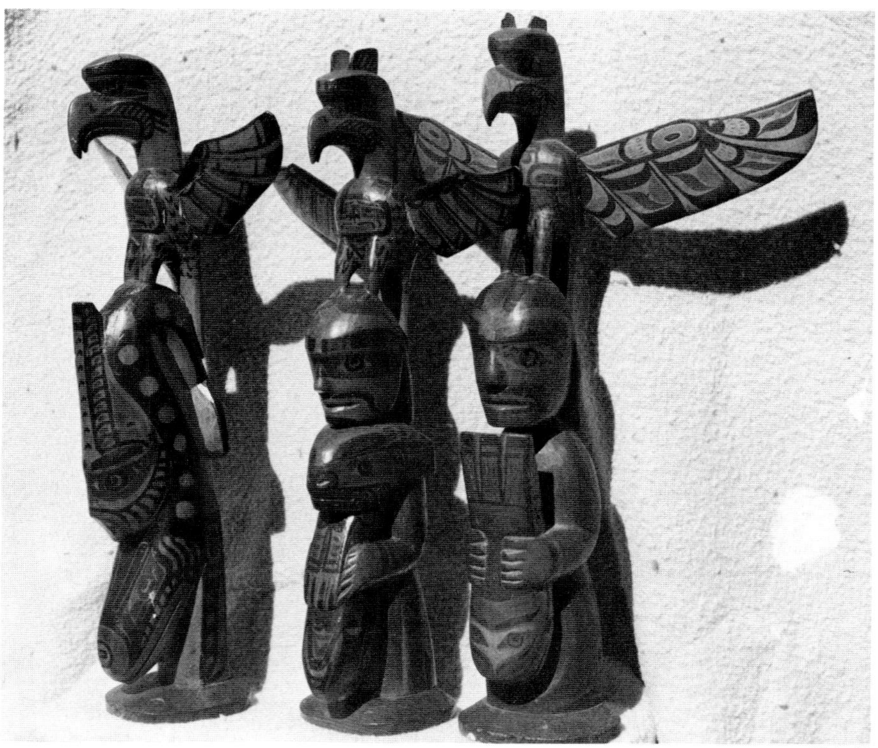

Plate: 31

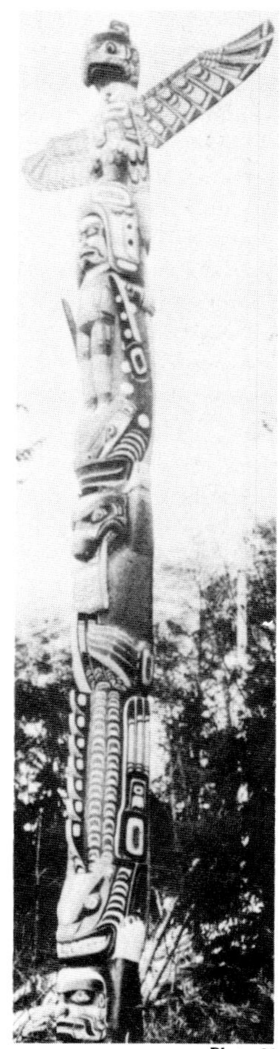

Plate: 32

Plate 28: A full-size totem pole carved by Charlie James sometime before 1910, which stood in front of Peter Smith's house at the village of Ḵalugwis, on Turnour Island. It shows an early James style quite different than that of his prolifically-produced tourist poles of later years. (c. 1933 or 1934. Photo: F.J. Barrows. Courtesy: B.C.P.M. PN-1960.)

Plate 29: A grave totem by Charlie James. Figures shown are the Thunderbird and the 'Sisiyutł' (double-headed snake or serpent.) This photo and was taken in the cemetery at Alert Bay, sometime between 1912 and 1915. (Alert Bay, c. 1915. Photo Courtesty: City Archives, Vancouver.)

Plate 30: A Charlie James model pole. Note the short beak on the thunderbird and the manner in which all the figures are contained within the round shape of the 'log.' Also note the killer whale crest . . . one of James' trademarks, on the crest of the thunderbird. (c. 1900. Photo: Author, 1981.)

Plate 31: Charlie James totems. The pole on the left has a young thunderbird 'Ḵulus' and killer whale . . . note the personification of the whale's blow-hole and dorsal fin into a seperate figure. The pole on the right has Charlie James' killer whale crest on the chest of the thunderbird . . . the wings on this pole were later replaced by Ellen Neel. (c. 1920-1930. Photo: Author, 1981.)

Plate 32: A Charlie James totem shown in its original location in the cemetery at Alert Bay, BC. Photo from the album of A.M. Wastell, a longtime resident of the Alert Bay area. (Alert Bay, c. 1910. Photo Courtesy: City Archives, Vancouver IN.N.52P.104.)

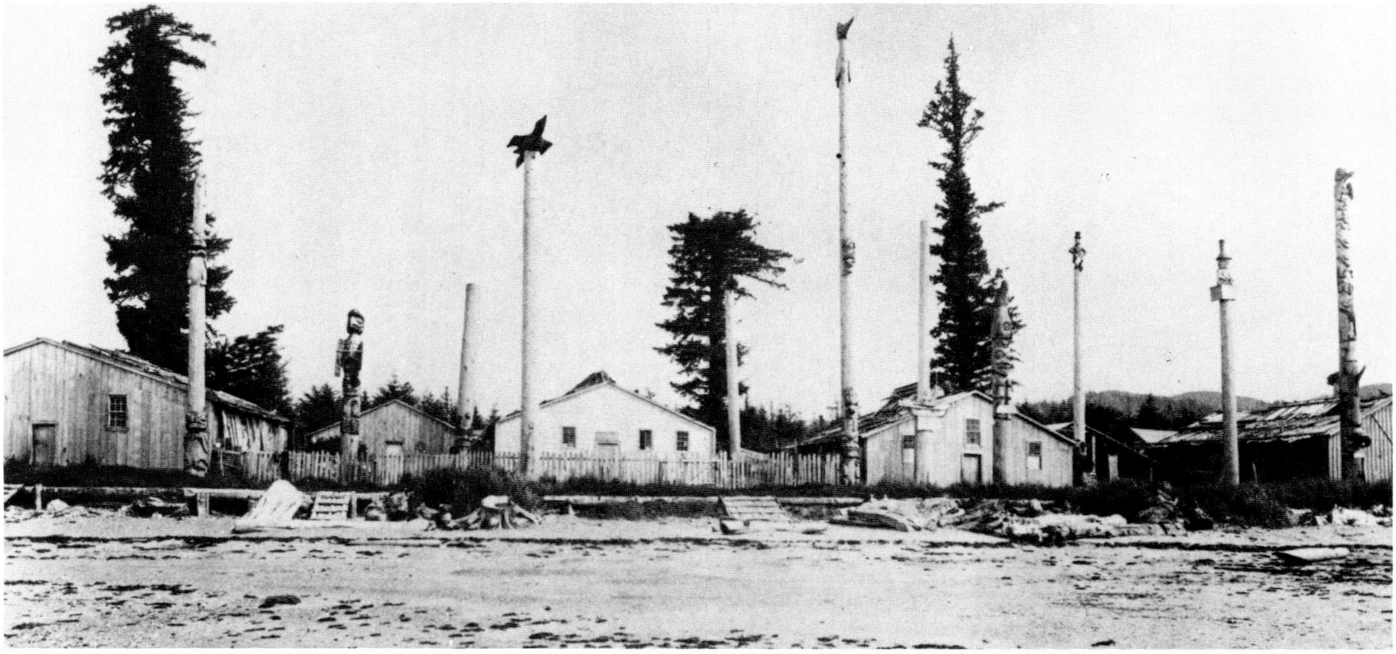

Plate: 33

Plate 33: **The village of Tongass, Alaska, near the turn of the century (1899). The original 'Hunt' pole is at the far right. This pole was removed by a group of Seattle business-men in that same year and placed in Seattle's Pioneer Square on October 18, 1899. (Tongass, Alaska, c. 1899. Photo Courtesy: University of Washington Press.)**

To begin to undestand a particular totem pole, one must know something of the reason for its existence and something of the people that commissioned it. Often, this can be a difficult task because of the tendency to stray from the point. A simple question leads to an elaborate explanation. Further questions are required to understand the original answer and on it goes. All of these byways have relevance, but call for patience and perseverance when the links become tenuous.

An example is the story of the Hunt 'Raven' pole commissioned by David Hunt of Fort Rupert, B.C., to honour his great-grandmother. This sixty-foot pole was carved by Charlie James, around the turn of the century to duplicate the crest figures of a pole that once stood at the grave of a Tlingit woman in Tongass, Southern Alaska. The dead woman was the daughter of a famous Tlingit chief named 'Shaiks'. Her daughter—'Shaiks' granddaughter—was called 'Anen' or Mary Ebbets.

Mary Ebbets was born in Alaska in 1823 and died at Fort Rupertt in 1919. She was married to a white man, Robert Hunt, who was involved in the fur trade for the Hudson's Bay Company. Hunt came to British Columbia from Dorsetshire, England, in the spring of 1850 aboard the sailing vessel 'Norman Morison', and spent some time on Vancouver Island before being posted to a trading area at the Nass River. Mary Ebbets and Robert Hunt first met at Fort Rupert, where she and her parents stopped during a voyage to Victoria, B.C.

They met again in the north and were married in Indian fashion at the Nass River. During this period in history, it was the policy of the Hudson's Bay Company to have their factors marry the daughters of native chiefs and thereby establish peace between the natives and the company. Robert and Mary Hunt lived for some years in the North, and then moved south to Fort Rupert, where they lived for the rest of their lives.

By the time that they moved to Fort Rupert, the Hunts had already started a family. One of their daughters, Elizabeth Hunt (later Elizabeth Wilson) said that she was 'just a baby; crawling' when they moved to Fort Rupert.

Robert and Mary Hunt went on to have eleven children, seven daughters and four sons. One of the sons was George Hunt, well known to ethnographers as the primary informant, interpreter and collaborator to Dr. Franz Boaz during his Kwakiutl research work.

Mary Hunt was known, in Fort Rupert, for her skill at weaving Chilkat blankets—the shawl-like garment worn by important people on public occasions. Chilkat blankets were known to the Kwakiutl through trade with the more northern people. The Chilkat blankets were expensive, scarce and much sought after. When Mary Hunt accompanied her husband to Fort Rupert, she brought her pattern boards with her and wove many Chilkat blankets during her long years there.

One such blanket was shown in 1977 as part of a huge travelling museum exhibition of Indian Art, called 'Sacred Circles.' The exhibitions had showings in Europe and North America and was sponsored by the Arts Council of Great Britain, with the support of British/American Associates. The patrons for this important artistic display were: HRH, the Duke of Edinburgh and Nelson A. Rockefeller, the Vice-President of the United States of America.

The display data for this particular exhibit read:

'Exhibit #356—Chilkat Blanket c. 1900 AD— Northwest Coast—Tlingit/Kwakiutl—wool, cedar bark warp—1.24 metres high—1.47 metres wide. Lent by Mr. & Mrs. Sosland. This hybrid is pure Chilkat style, but the colours are in Kwakiutl taste. It was woven by Mary Hunt, a Tongass Tlingit, who took her pattern boards to the south when she married into the Kwakiutl Hunt (!) family. Some eight or nine blankets of this type were made and are still mostly owned by the Kwakiutl.

Collected by Norm Feder from Mary Waddams (Wadhams?—P.N.) at Alert Bay—but formerly owned by Ed Whannock.'

Mary Hunt's daughter, Elizabeth Wilson, said of her mother, 'She wove blankets here (Fort Rupert) after we were born. She learned how from her people at Tongass. She wove until she was very old, but her back was straight as an arrow! She would stop working

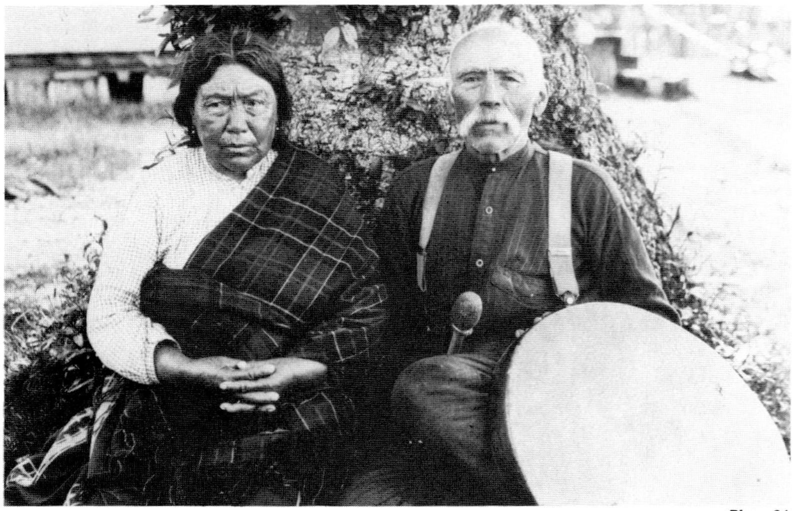

Plate: 34

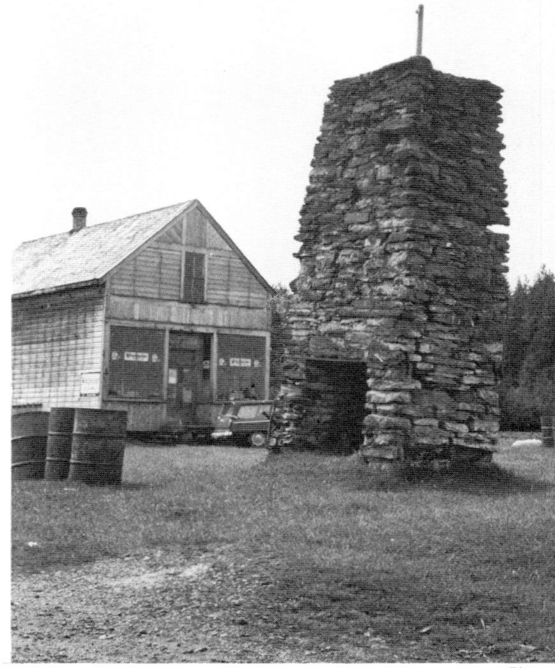

Plate: 35

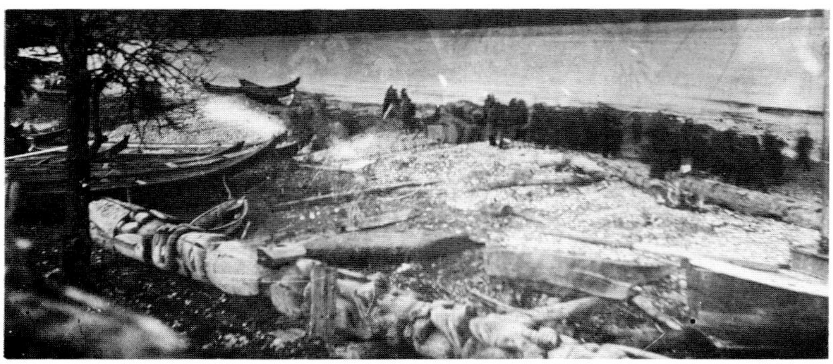

Plate: 36

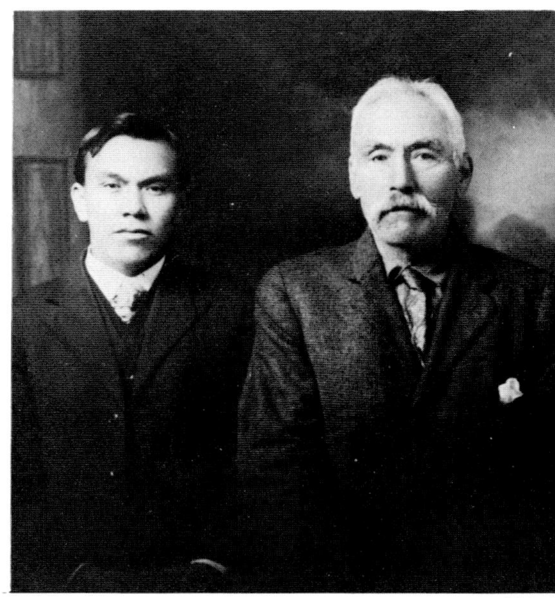

Plate: 37

Plate 34: **George Hunt and his wife at Fort Rupert, BC.This one man is responsible for the bulk of the published material on the Kwakiutl people. His accomplishments as a linguist and an author are well-known, but he was also a skilled artist, as are many members of the Hunt family today. (Fort Rupert, c. 1930. Photo: J.B. Scott. Courtesy: B.C.P.M. PN-9533.)**

Plate 35: **Fort Rupert, BC in 1966. The stone chimney is all that remains of the Hudson's Bay Company trading post established in 1849. Robert Hunt was one of the first factors of this post and his family line subsequently became prominent among the Kwakiutl people. General store in the background of the photo was owned by Bill Cadwallader. (Fort Rupert 1966. Photo: J. Smyly. Courtesy: B.C.P.M. PN-7346.)**

Plate 36: **The 'Raven pole' of the Hunt family. This old photo shows the Charlie James carving in an unfinished state, lying on the beach at Fort Rupert, B.C. (c. 1900. Photo: George Hunt. Courtesy: American Museum of Natural History PN-104467.)**

Plate 37: **George Hunt on the right, Jonathan Hunt, his son (and Tony Hunt's grandfather) on the left. Photo reportedly taken in a box car studio in Vancouver, B.C. (Vancouver, exact date unkown. Photo: Courtesy American Philosophical Society.)**

whenever the people from Fort Rupert walked in to try and learn how it was done. She would not teach them because it belonged to her people.'

Perhaps because of this, some of the people at Fort Rupert found the Hunt family 'haughty' and 'snobbish' and ridiculed them, saying they were not descended from an important northern family at all, but were commoners.

The pole that Charlie James was commissioned to carve was a replica of one that a Seattle group sponsored by the Board of Trade and the Seattle Times had appropriated in Alaska and moved to Seattle. (The sarcastic term 'appropriated' is used by the informants —although payment was later made to the owners of the pole.) The idea behind the commissioning of this replica was to prove that the Hunt family had come from a powerful northern family and thereby deserved respect from the Fort Rupert people.

The Hunt 'Raven' pole was erected in front of David Hunt's house, at Fort Rupert, as the climax to a huge and lavish potlatch. The potlatch had many purposes combined in one gala holiday; the distribution of possessions in the form of gifts to indicate the giver's wealth, a payment to the people present for acting as witnesses to specific claims on such things as names, positions, and privileges—but, most of all, a public challenge to those who might refute those claims to do so, or forever remain silent.

Before the Hunt pole was raised, a copper shield, symbolic of wealth and power, was broken and placed into the hole that would receive the base of the totem pole. This 'copper' was to 'guard' the pole and acted as a substitute for a slave that would have been sacrificed in earlier times.

The elaborate potlatch and the pole raising took place around 1905, when Charlie James was still a relatively young man.

The pole stood for nearly half a century, to remind people of the Hunt potlatch, and finally fell between 1952 and 1955. Bill Holm told me: 'I first saw the Hunt

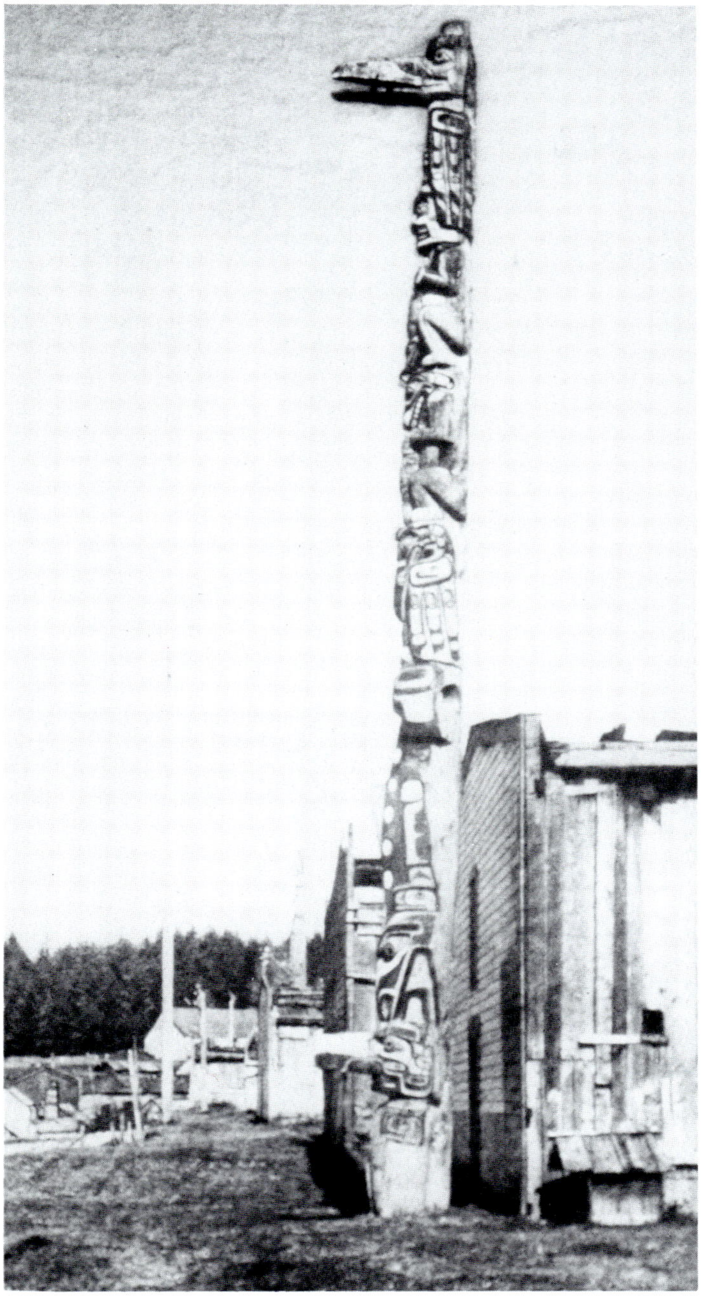

Plate: 38

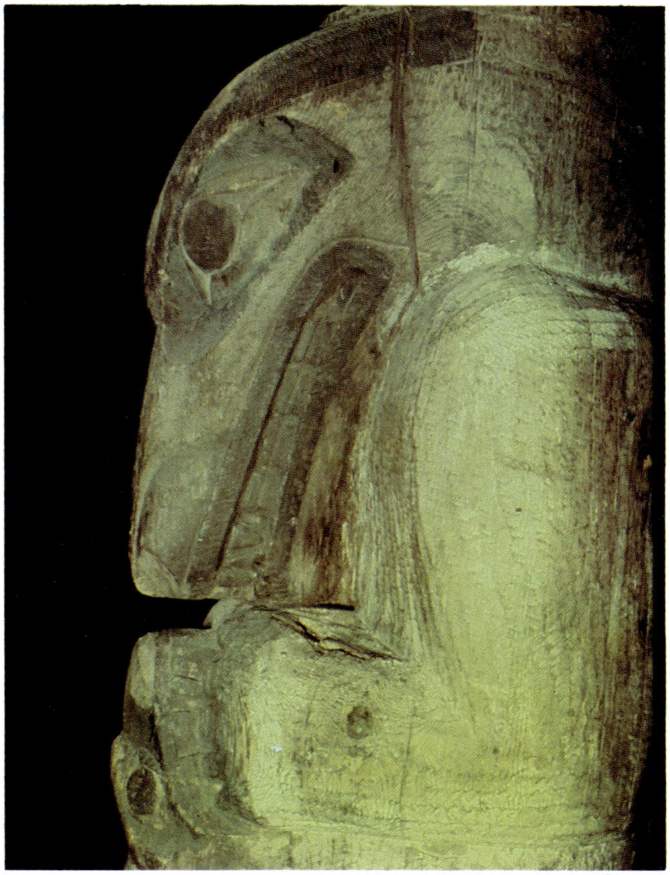

Plate: 39

Plate 38: **The 'Hunt pole' erected at Fort Rupert. This photo is one of a number of 'large plates supplementing *Volume Ten* of *The North American Indian*, and the caption reads, in part: '*QAGYUHL Village at Fort Rupert.*The heraldic column in the foreground commemorates the legendary history of a Tsimshian family. It's presence in this Kwakiutl settlement is due to the following circumstances: a party of Seattle men, innocently removed a totem pole from what they supposed was an abandoned village. A prominent member of the wronged family, had a local carver (Charlie James—P.N.) produce a totem pole according to her description of the lost one, and had it erected at the house of her eldest son's eldest son.' (Fort Rupert, c. 1915. Photo: E.S. Curtis. Courtesy: Larkspur Landing Fine Arts.)**

Plate 39: **A fragment of the Hunt 'Raven pole', now located in the Glenbow Museum, grizzly of the sea holding a seal to its chest. (Calgary, Alberta, 1979. Photo: Author.)**

pole in 1959. It had been cut up and stored under a house—I think it was Bill Hunt's house—at Fort Rupert.'

The dismembered pole subsequently found its way into at least one museum. It was there that I tracked down a couple of pieces that had the dubious distinction of having been separated by means of a chain saw:

Calgary, Alberta, in midwinter, is not a place for the fainthearted! The freezing wind tried to follow me into the Glenbow Museum, but the doors closed behind me and choked off its howling. I shook the snow off my parka and stamped the snow from my boots and proceeded into the elevator and up to the Indian exhibit. The entrance to the exhibit had two carved figures mounted against support pillars and they looked for all the world like brooding sentinels, on guard against who knows what. One figure represented a raven with its wings folded and its beak resting on its breast, the other figure was a fierce-looking bear grasping a seal. These figures were some of the final remains of the Hunt 'Raven' pole carved by Charlie James. The 60-foot totem pole that they had been a part of had been commissioned in pride and defiance, raised amid a huge celebration and stood for nearly a lifetime at Fort Rupert, British Columbia. Now these pieces dwelt here, with the Rocky Mountains between them and the rain forests of their origin. I sat on a dias beside a large oolichan oil dish and gazed at the bear figure probably meant to depict 'Na'nis' the bear of the sea, I thought, even though Barbeau described it as a grizzly bear.

The carving was strong, full-figured and carried one of the Charlie James signatures in the eye masks round at the front and sharp at the back, instead of the reverse which is usually seen on other Kwakiutl carvings. Only slight traces of the paint remained but the parallel fluting imparted by the 'D' adze was still strong and crisp.

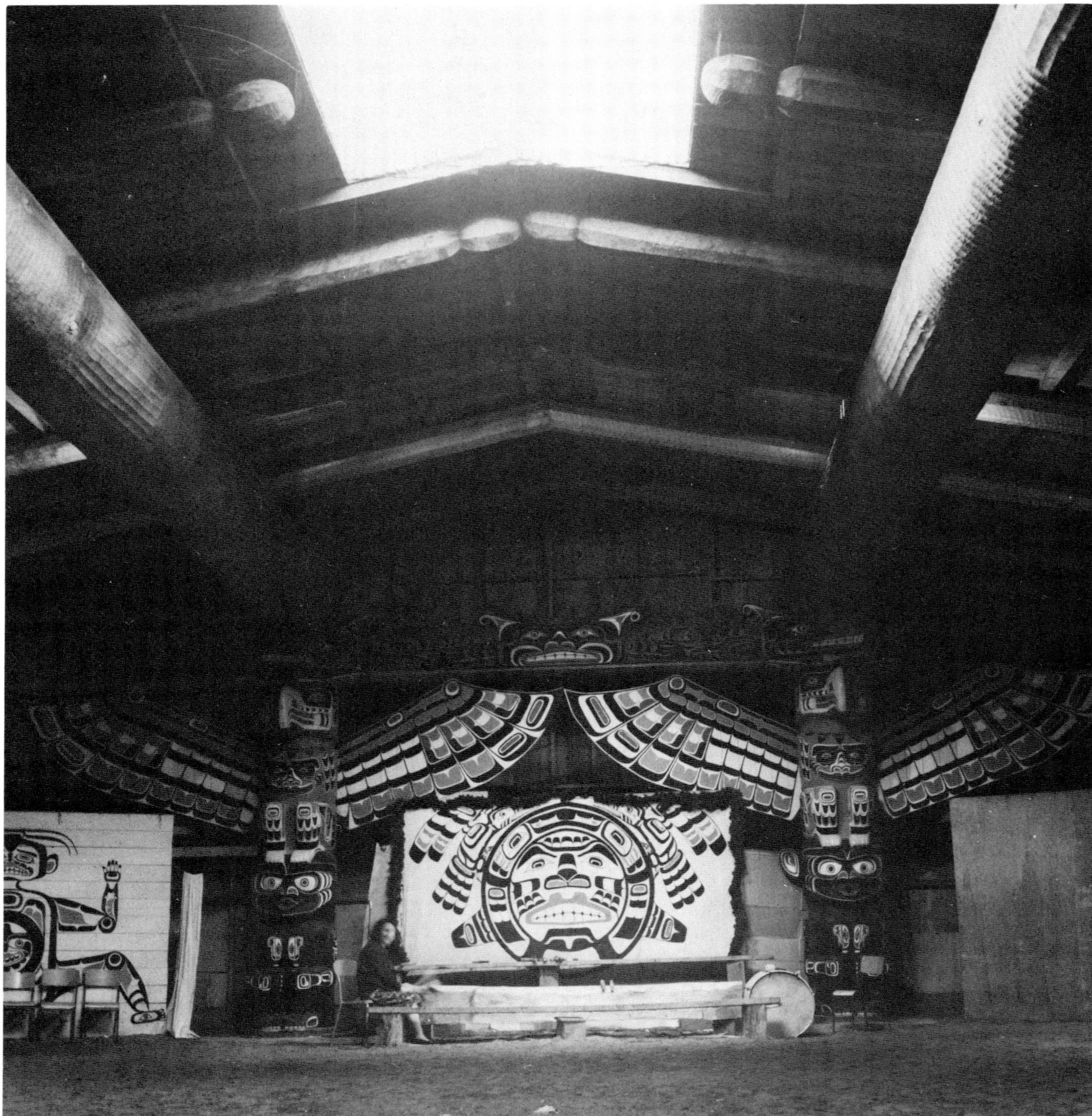

Plate: 40

Plate 40: The communal longhouse at Alert Bay. This illustration gives a clear indication of how the carved houseposts were used to support the massive main house beams. (Alert Bay, 1972. Photo: Jean Andre. Courtesy: B.C.P.M. PN-12922.)

My feelings were a mixture of indignation that these figures had been sawn apart and pleasure that they still existed at all. Many of my native friends believe that these old poles should be allowed to quietly decay back into the earth once their purpose is done. Others feel that they should be preserved to show coming generations something of what was gone before. I don't pretend to know the answer, only that there are many truths in the same situation. It's true that this pole is an example of the carving of Charlie James. It's true that it was meant to show the greatness of the Hunt family and it's also true, as the museum attendant told me, that—my indignation notwithstanding—a 60-foot pole would not fit into the museum.

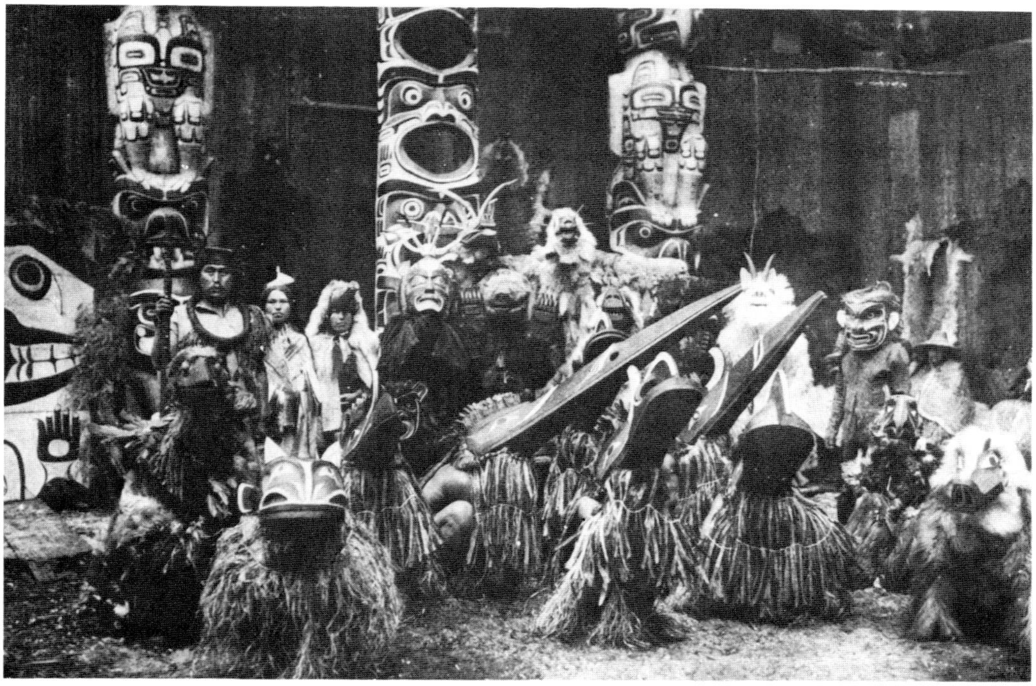

Plate: 41

Plate 41: A scene from the Curtis film 'In the Land of the Headhunters'—the Thunderbird houseposts can be seen in the background on either side of the central 'Hemspek' pole. (Blunden Harbour, 1914. Photo: V.M.P.A.)

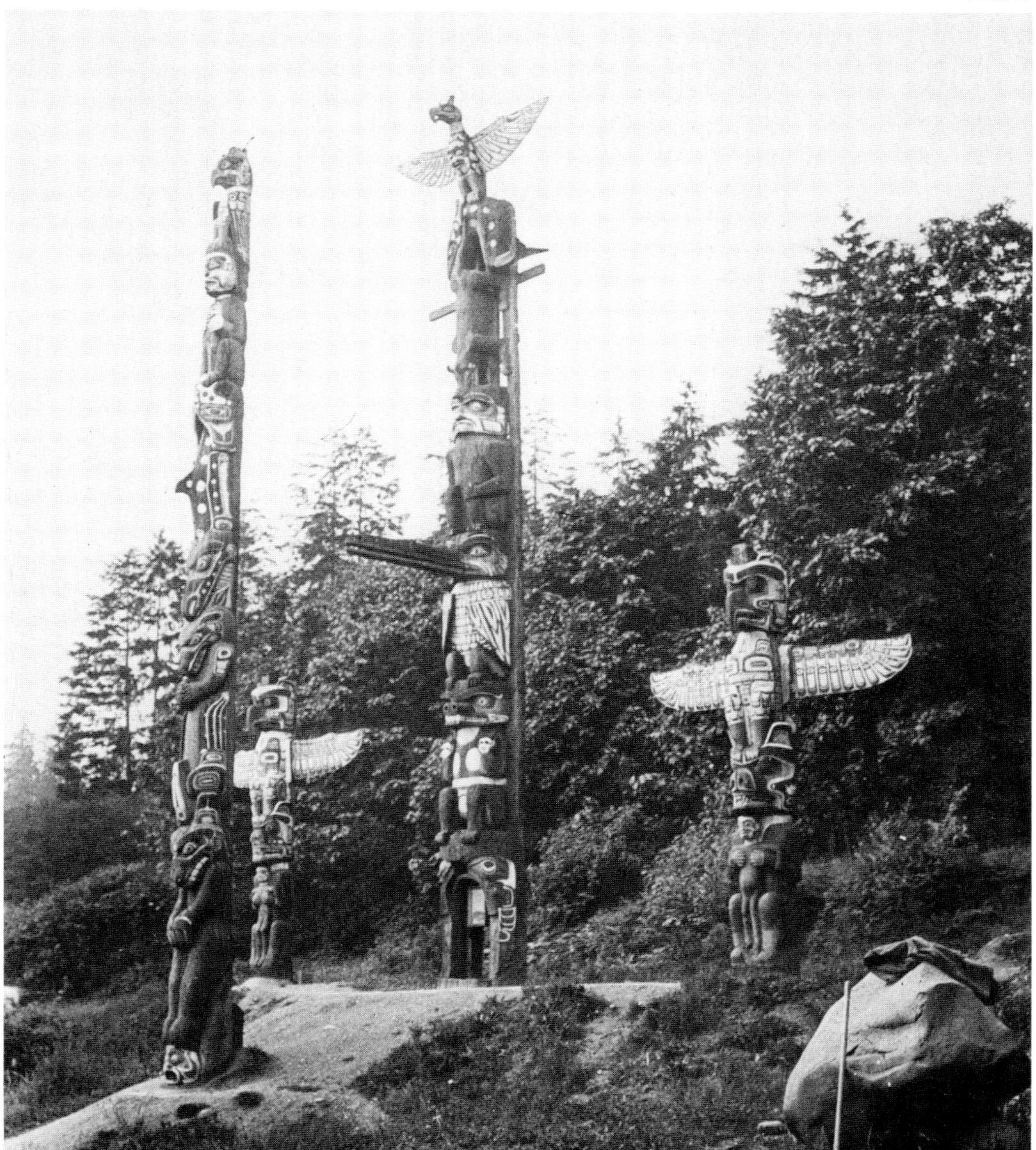

Plate: 42

Plate 42: The totem pole group at Stanley Park. This photo shows the grizzly bear houseposts (background) and the pole of 'Sisax̱o'las' (foreground), carved by Charlie James. The house front of 'WAKIUS' is the central pole—although the large 'entry-beak' of the bottom raven figure is missing .
These poles are shown in the original Lumberman's Arch location approximately one year after the group was acquired from Alert Bay. (Vancouver, 1928. Photo: C.F. Newcombe. Courtesy: B.C.P.M. PN-914.)

Plate 43: A close-up of one of the Thunderbird houseposts. In it's original Stanley Park location at Lumberman's Arch. (Vancouver, c. 1927. Photo: B.C.P.M. PN-14426.)

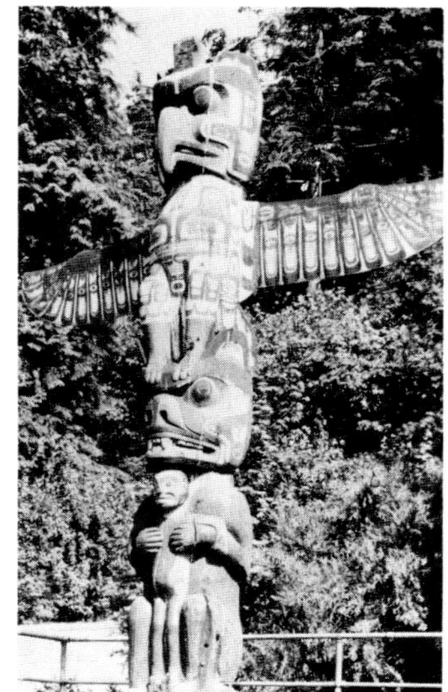

Plate: 43

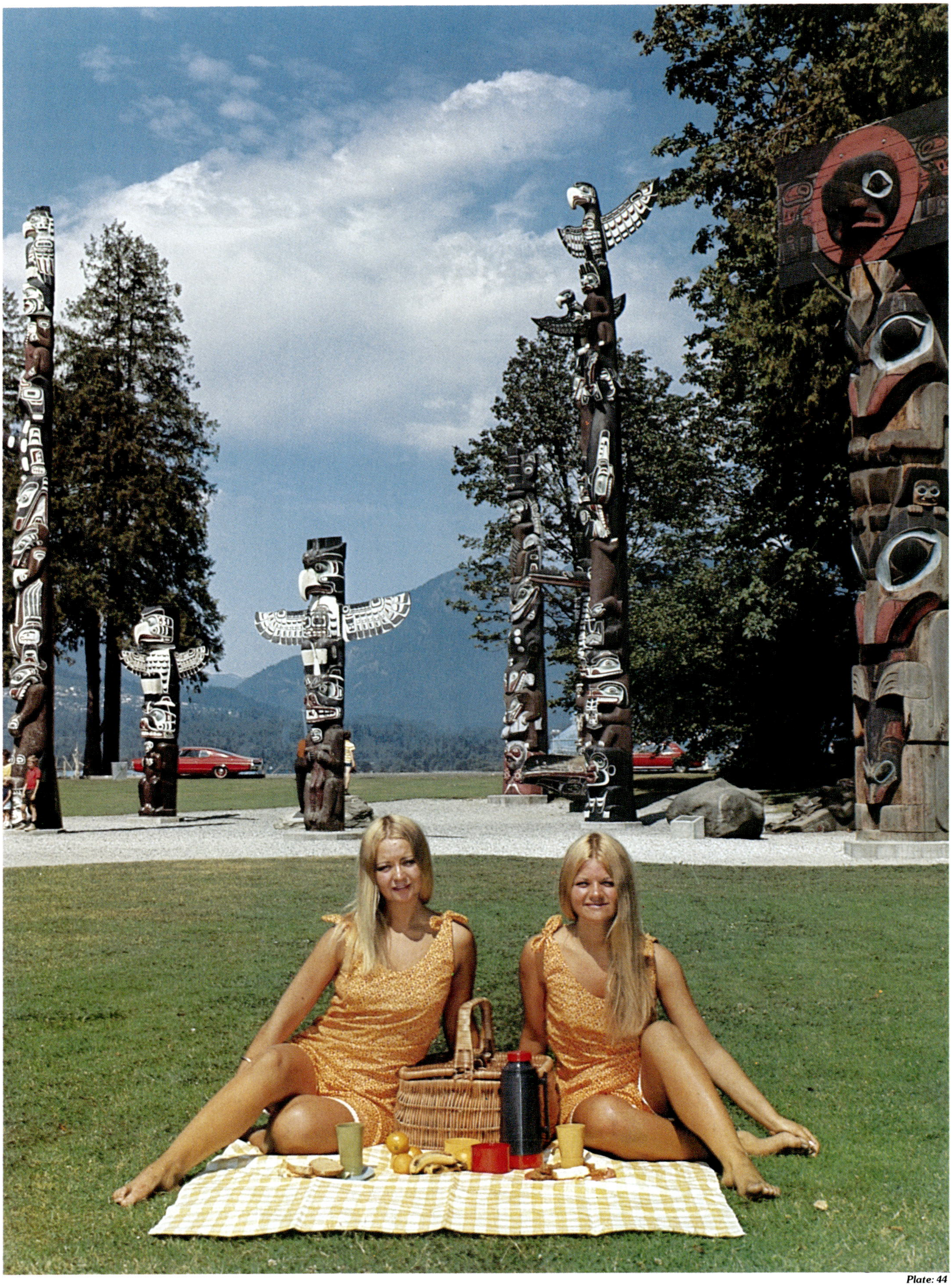

Plate: 44

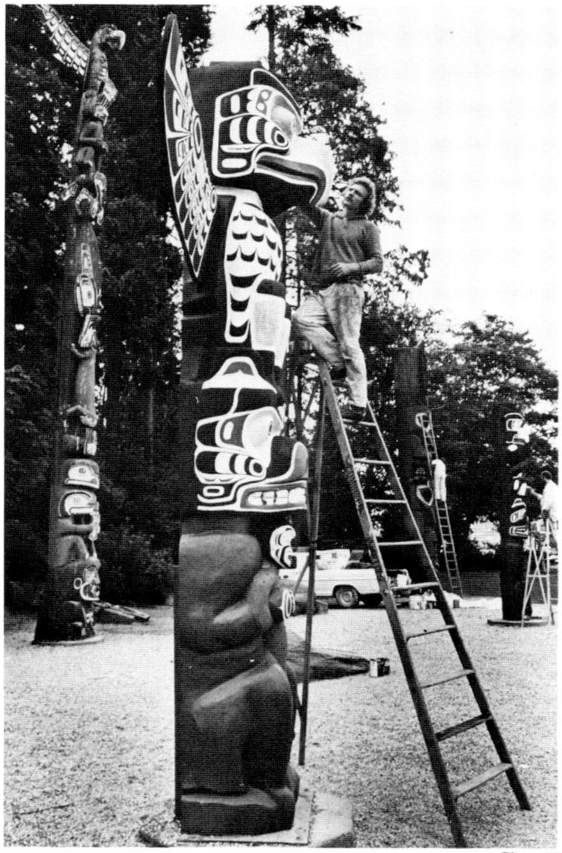

Plate: 45

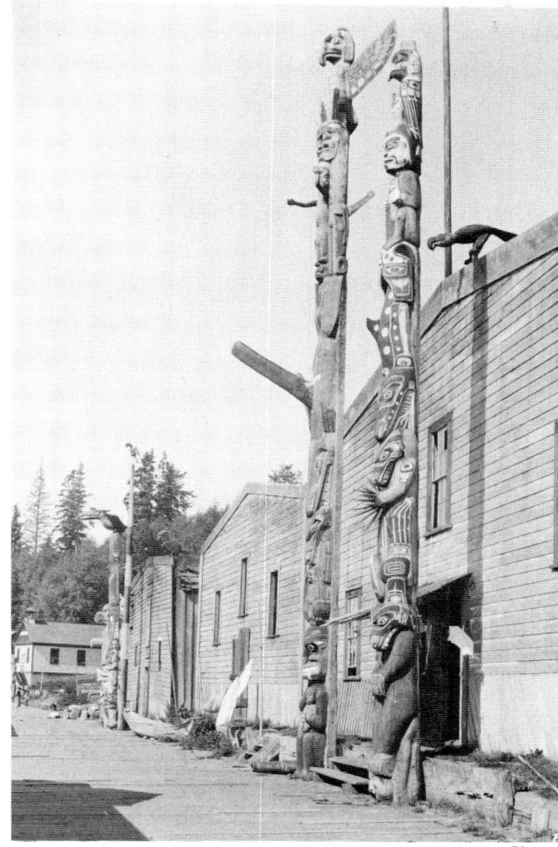

Plate: 46

Plate 45: One of the Thunderbird house posts undergoes its annual repainting. The author recently looked at this pole and mused that Charlie James' crisp adze marks must be blurred and softened under many layers of paint. A closer look revealed that this particular pole was not an original at all, but a fibreglass replica! The 'missing' original was found hiding in storage at the Vancouver Centennial Museum. (Vancouver, 1978. Photo: *Vancouver Sun*.)

Plate 46: The 'Sisax̱o'las' pole is the one to the right of the two tall totems shown in their original positions in Alert Bay. The 'Sisax̱o'las' pole was moved from this location to Vancouver's Stanley Park where it is today. Note the individual spines on the sea urchin—these have been lost over the years and have not been replaced in subsequent restorations. (Photo: N.M.C.)

Plate 44: Too bad Charlie James did not live to see this! A summer picnic in front of the totem poles at Brockton Point, Stanley Park. The poles of 'Sisax̱o'las' and the Thunderbird houseposts are the first three poles on the left. The housepost on the left of the two is a fibreglass replica (see *Plate 45*) while the one on the right is one of the original pair. (Vancouver, date unknown. Photo: Courtesy of Tourism B.C.)

Of the many large totem poles that Charlie James carved during his life, the most famous and widely viewed are three that now stand in Vancouver's Stanley Park. The Stanley Park totems are a pair of house posts and a tall memorial pole and are known as the Thunderbird House Posts and the pole of 'Sisax̱o'las,' respectively.

The Thunderbird House Posts are a pair of totems that were originally made to support a cross-beam and acted as two of four interior posts. That is, they formed a part of the structural skeleton of an old-style communal house. The Thunderbird House Posts were carved by Charlie James around the turn of the century. Their original owner was a Kingcome Inlet chief named 'Tsa-wee-nok.'

Whether these house posts were ever erected at Kingcome Inlet is not known, but some years later—in 1914, these same poles were used as props during the making of a motion picture. The full-length documentary was called 'In the land of the Head-Hunters,' and was written and filmed by Edward S. Curtis, of Seattle, Washington. Curtis' epic was the first such feature film depicting the life of the Northwest Coast people.

Curtis relied heavily on the assistance of George Hunt (mentioned previously), and it was probably Hunt who arranged to have the house posts set up for the filming at Blunden Harbour. The posts were arranged with a cross-beam and were positioned in front of a planked house-end, exactly as would have been the case in an old-style communal dwelling. A critical difference was that this house had no roof or front as Curtis used the bright sun as his Klieg lights!

The entire story of the making of this film is fascinating reading and is presented in detail in a book by Bill Holm and George Quimby entitled 'Edward S. Curtis in the Land of the War Canoes.'

In 1927, the two house posts were acquired by the Art, Historical and Scientific Association of Vancouver, and were erected beside Lumberman's Arch, on the north shore of Stanley Park.

One summer afternoon, in the early Fifties, I walked by Lumberman's Arch with Ellen Neel. She pointed out features of the various poles and she mentioned the Thunderbird house posts. She said they were made by her grandfather before she was born, and had been used in a movie. She said that the owner of the poles lived in Alert Bay and refused to sell the poles, but offered to rent them out instead. I had never heard of Curtis, or his film at that time so it meant little to me.

Ellen laughed as she related how 'Old ——' had boasted for years of the fine bargain he had made. He not only got the agreed-on rental payment, but also a brand new paint job—by Charlie James—paid for by the film maker.

I'm fairly sure that Ellen told me 'Old ——'s' name . . . but try as I might, and even at the urging of Bill Holm, I just don't remember it.

The posts stayed at the Lumberman's Arch site for nearly 40 years, and then were moved to their present site near Brockton Point, in Stanley Park.

Over the years, repainting and minor restoration was carried out by Ellen Neel and later by Doug Cramner and now by Park's Board employees. Only one of the pair that now stand at Brockton Point is one of the original house posts. The other is a fibreglass replica, made when the wooden pole became too badly deteriorated to stand many more seasons. The original pole is currently in storage at the Vancouver Centennial Museum.

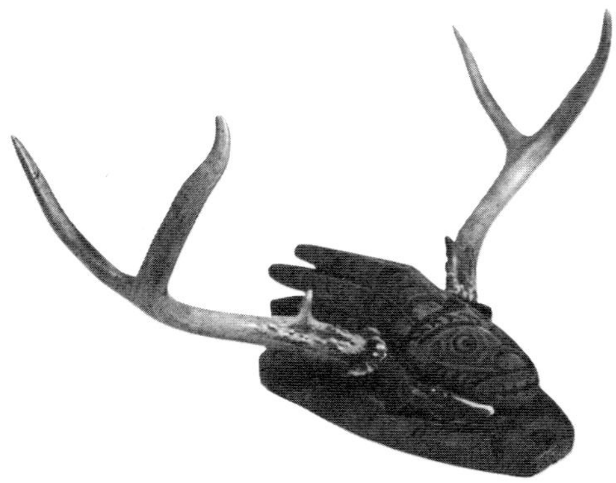

Plate 47: An unusual Charlie James piece. Deer antlers and red cedar, carved and painted. Museum entry card refuses to guess at what it is! W.L. Webber collection. (Vancouver, 1972. Photo: Centennial Museum Vancouver NA-11:29.)

The Thunderbird House Posts are not remarkable examples of James' work, but they have come to represent a typical northwest totem pole in the minds of many people. These two poles have been used for decades by advertising agencies, television stations, tourist bureaus and postcard printers. Line drawing versions are found on drinking glasses, spoons, paperweights, keychains and the whole gamut of tourist kitsch. It is almost incredible the way that these particular poles have popped up in tourist bureau hand-outs—children's school books, encyclopedias—European guide books—Indian lore and craft books and so on.

It is probably reasonable to assume that neither Charlie James nor Chief 'Tsa-wee Nok,' nor even Edward Curtis, had any notion that these particular carvings would ultimately be photographed by hundreds of thousands of tourists and come to be emblematic of a Pacific Northwest Indian 'Totem Pole.'

The large Charlie James pole in the Stanley Park cluster was commissioned by Chief 'Sisaxo'las,' of Kingcome Inlet who later came to live at Alert Bay on Cormorant Island.

The 'Sisaxo'las' pole was erected to tell the story of a mythological ancestor of 'Sisaxo'las,' called 'Siwid.' The 'Siwid' legend and its depiction on the 'Sisaxo'las' pole was explained by Mrs. James Cook of Alert Bay, and is found in Marius Barbeau's field notes for 'Totem Poles,' in an old pamphlet entitled 'The Totem Poles in Stanley Park' by the Reverend, John C. Goodfellow, and most recently in 'Totem Poles of British Columbia' by S.W.A. Gunn: (who was, incidentally, Ellen Neel's family doctor!)

'Siwid' was the son of a Chief—but not given to the adventurous pursuits of the other young men of the village—seeming quiet and almost delicate when his actions were compared to the boisterous activities of the others—his father was greatly disappointed in him and constantly berated him to do 'something great.' One night a raid on the village was averted by an alert young member of the band who sounded the alarm—when the danger had passed, the Chief spoke to his son in a disparaging manner, saying that it should have been he who sounded the warning, rather than the son of a commoner... Siwid was deeply hurt by his father's words and walked away from the sea-village and into the forest—determined to suffer whatever fate would come his way.

After walking a long time, he came to a place where the sea formed a deep lagoon—at the end of a forest-surrounded fiord. He sat by the limpid water and could see a long way into the depths of the unruffled lagoon... while he was watching, he saw a motion deep in the water and the surface became frothed with bubbles and became agitated by an upwelling current. Siwid watched with some trepidation, but moved not a muscle... at length, a great frog appeared on the surface... the sea-frog told Siwid that he was aware of the mistreatment that Siwid had received and asked him if he cared to accompany him to that deep place from which he'd come... Siwid answered in the affirmative and climbed onto the back of the sea-frog.

Siwid travelled far down to the sea bottom, on the back of his unlikely steed, and there he saw all the marvellous creatures that dwelt in the sea kingdom. The sea-frog told Siwid that each of these creatures that he had seen were to be his crests and the crests of his family until the end of time... there were many trials that Siwid was asked to undertake... but, armed with the things that had been given him (his 'długwala' or 'supernatural treasure'), he easily overcame all these obstacles and, after a long time, again came to stand on the shore of his village—when these things were recounted to his tribe and to his father, Siwid stood as a great and powerful man who took the chieftainship when his father stepped down and spent all of his days increasing the greatness of his village among others.

The 'Sisaxo'las' pole stood originally in front of a large communal house at Alert Bay. When it was moved to Stanley Park, it stood there beside the Thunderbird House Posts at Lumberman's Arch and was moved, with them, to Brockton Point. The figures on the 'Sisaxo'las' pole are; from the top down:

Kolus—the young thunderbird—covered with down.

Chief 'TŁA-WUNUM-KOLUS,' an ancestor of Chief 'Sisaxo'las'—the son in his arms subsequently became a Chief—this 'cradling' of the son gave birth to the Kwakiutl custom of the 'cradle' during potlatches.

The Killer Whale—the human face above its head representing the blow-hole.

Sea Otter—shown floating on its back and eating a 'sea egg' or sea urchin.

'Sea Bear'—an amphibious creature who normally lived in the undersea kingdom, but who sometimes ventured ashore.

Chief's head—the open mouth representing a rival who had spoken against 'Sisaxo'las'—and who had been 'pushed down'—to the bottom of the pole.

It is doubtful that one person in ten thousand has ever heard of Charlie James. Yet, virtually every resident of the City of Vancouver has stared at these three works from his hands.

It is said that every large pole has its story—of the carvers, the legends, the people involved or all these things combined. Each story is different, in its own way. The stories are not confined to large cedar monuments, however. Even the small tourist poles and paintings sometimes have a story, either individually or in a collection:

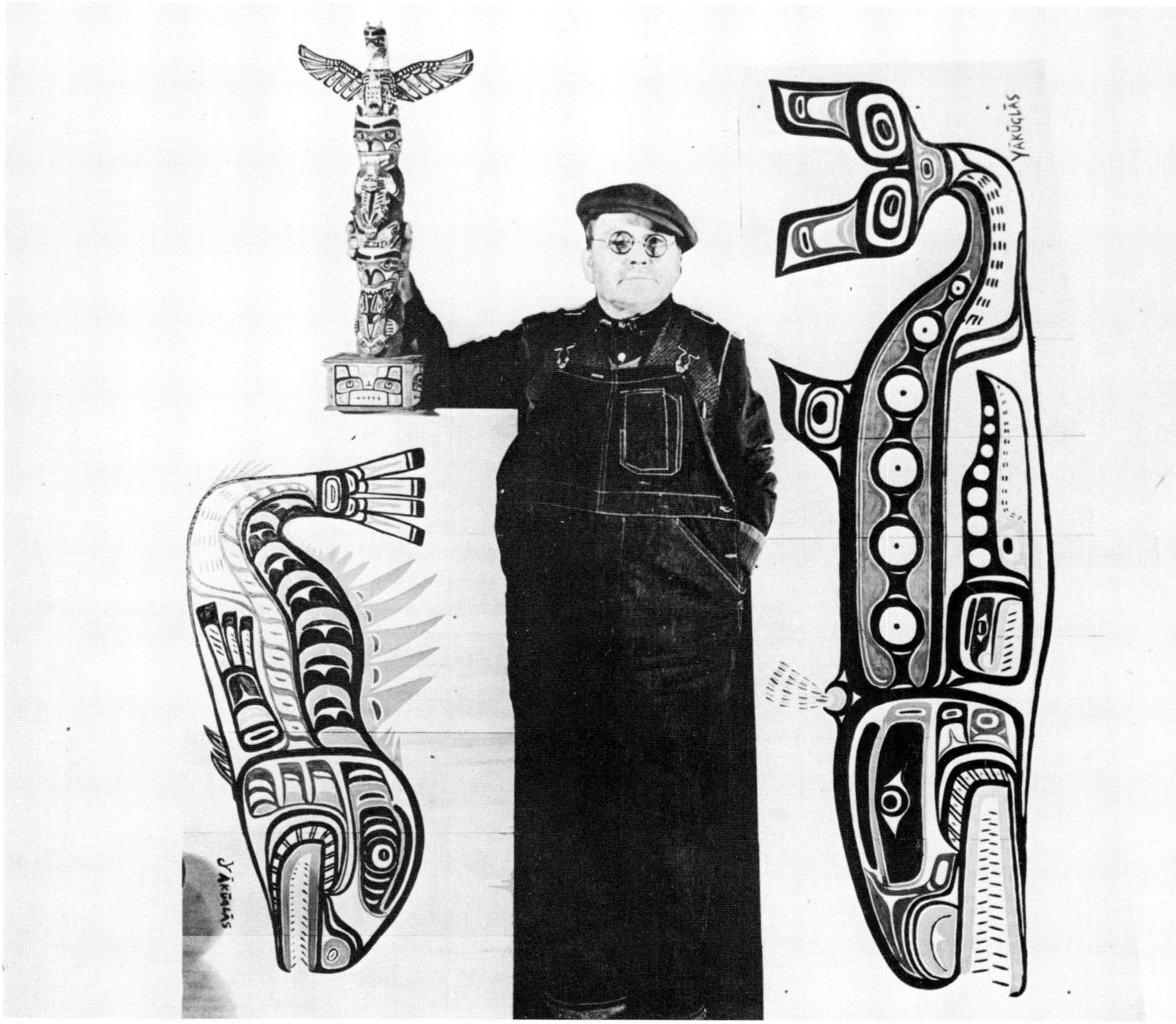

One of the largest collections of this type of Charlie James material is currently in the Vancouver Centennial Museum, near Kitsilano Beach, in Vancouver, B.C. This group of model totems, paintings and boxes was originally donated to the Vancouver City Museum by Mr. William L. Webber, when he retired from business in 1952.

Bill Webber had been a news agent on the Canadian Pacific Railroad for some ten years, starting in 1913. In 1923, with a total capital of $400, he opened a souvenir and curio shop called the 'Scenery Shop' on Hastings Street near the CPR station. Webber spent $65.00 for shelving, out of his meagre capital, and made a display of stationery and second-hand books—his first day's receipts came to the grand total of 25¢.

The second day he sold $2.25 worth of goods and on the third day, the captain of a French ship bought $16.00 in merchandise. An impressive growth record in percentage, if not in absolute dollars!

Webber wanted his little shop to be unique, and once he was in the black on a consistent basis, he commissioned Charlie James to come to Vancouver to decorate the store with carvings and paintings. James and Webber became good friends and while he worked, Charlie James explained what he was doing, and more important, he gave Webber an understanding of what the crest and figures and legends meant to the Kwakiutl people. As Webber's understanding grew, his enthusiasm for B.C. native culture expanded and his shop began to specialize in such work. Around this time, he began a collection of totems and paintings, mostly by Charlie James. Webber regarded Charlie James, and rightly so, as a master in Indian art, and he valued his friendship highly.

As Ellen Neel explained to Marius Barbeau: 'Mr. Webber used to receive him (C.J.) at his home here in Vancouver. He did a lot of work for Mr. Webber, who thinks much of him. I came down (from Alert Bay) with him (C.J.) several times when I was very small. He used to stay in Vancouver two or three weeks at a time.'

When Barbeau showed her a photo of Charlie James, Ellen responded: 'This is a good photo of him when he was working on painted boards for Webber. He is holding a pole in his right hand—the two boards on each side . . . one a whale, the other a cod fish . . . as he used to call it . . . it has a number of fins on the back.'

***Plate 48:* Charlie James. Ellen said of this particular picture, 'A good photo of him when he was working on painted boards down here in Vancouver. He spent several weeks working for Webber. Holding a pole in his right hand, two boards on each side: A whale and a codfish'—as he used to call it.' (Vancouver, c. 1928. Photo: V.M.P.A.)**

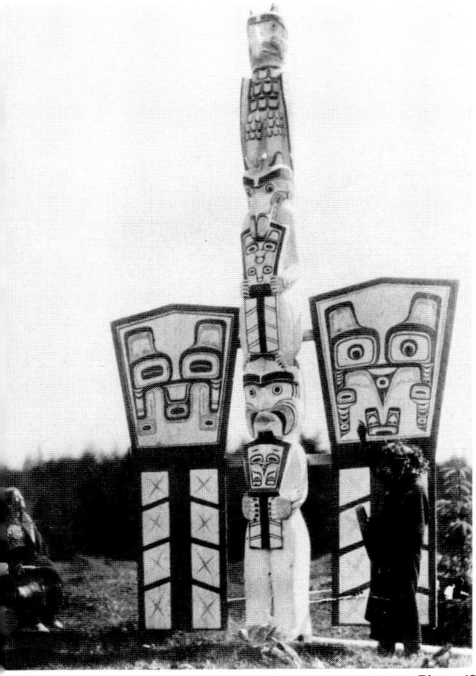

Plate: 49

Plate 49: A graveyard pole and painted boards representing coppers—by Charlie James. This photo was taken in the graveyard at Fort Rupert, B.C., probably by J.B. Scott. This pole now stands at the Port Hardy Airport—a few miles from Fort Rupert. (Fort Rupert, c. 1928/33. Photo: J.B. Scott. Courtesy: B.C.P.M. PN-9535.)

Plate 50: A painted tray by Charlie James. Trays of this sort sold well to tourists and James produced many of them. From the W.L. Webber collection. (Vancouver, 1972. Photo: Centennial Museum Vancouver NA-21:17.)

Plate 51: Painted design board—Charlie James. 'Wolf'. From W.L. Webber collection. (Vancouver, 1972. Photo: Centennial Museum Vancouver NA-42:22.)

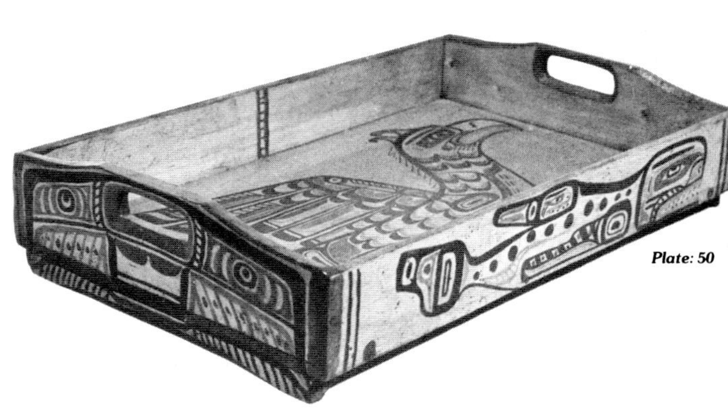

Plate: 50

Plate 52: Design board painted by Charlie James. 'Huxwhukw'—Cannibal bird. From W.L. Webber collection. (Vancouver, 1972.)

Plate 53: A chest of drawers—painted by Charlie James in another version of the Thunderbird. W.L. Webber collection. (Vancouver, 1972. Photo: V.M.P.A. NA-119:5.)

Plate 54: A painted plaque depicts the 'Thunderbird' as the sun W.L. Webber collection.

Plate 55: Charlie James—painted design board. 'Beaver with lightning.' W.L. Webber collection. (Vancouver, 1972.)

Plate 56: Design board painted for W.L. Webber by Charlie James. 'Frog with copper.' (Vancouver, 1972.)

Plate 57: Painted design—'Double-horned Thunderbird' by Charlie James. From W.L. Webber collection. (Vancouver, 1972.)

Plate 58: Painted design board—Charlie James. Museum entry says 'Eagle.' W.L. Webber collection. (Vancouver, 1972. Photos 52, 54-58: Centennial Museum, Vancouver NA-42:15-42:20.)

Webber moved his shop to the 800 block on Granville Street, in downtown Vancouver where it remained as a tourist landmark for nearly twenty years. In 1936, Webber brought out the first edition of 'The Thunderbird, Tatoosh'—a book on totemism. The Charlie James version of the thunderbird became Webber's registered trademark. Webber advertised his shop by printing a miniature booklet of totem designs—which was handed out free of charge.

In all, over a million of these little booklets were given out. Many of the printed designs were simplified versions of Charlie James paintings, although the names given to them, by Webber, were largely in Chinook, an Indian 'Esperanto' or trade language. The designs from Webber's booklet can still be seen (1982) on the placemats of the 'Tomahawk Restaurant' in North Vancouver, B.C., amid the owner, Chick Chamberlain's collection of carvings.

William Webber retired in 1952, selling the Scenery Shop to a book salesman from Toronto, Ontario. Webber's collection of Charlie James' work was donated to the Vancouver City Museum except for one favourite James pole, which he kept for himself. He believed that the thunderbird symbol had brought him good fortune, all his life, and since he was planning to be married at age 72, he kept that one pole for luck!

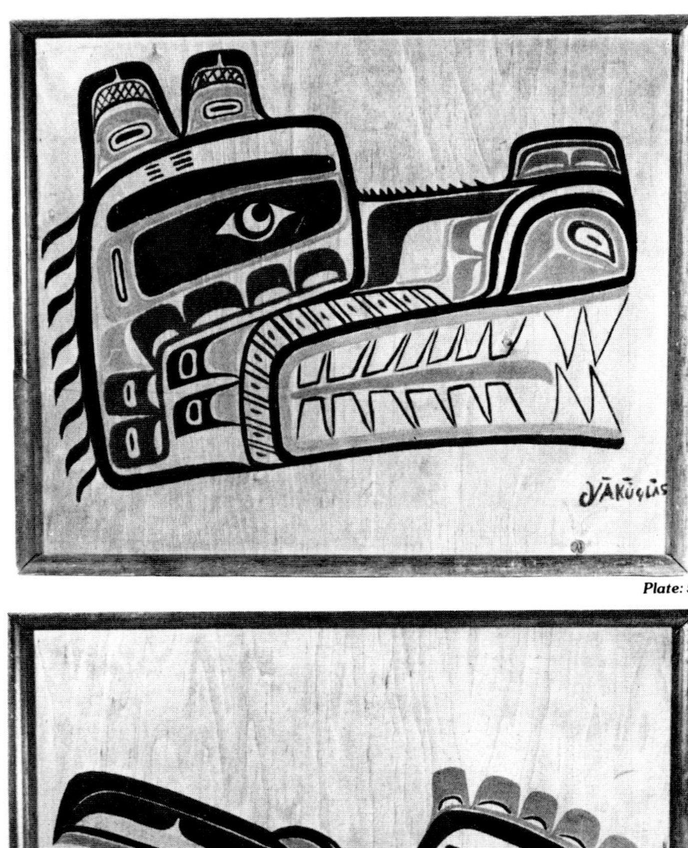

Plate: 51

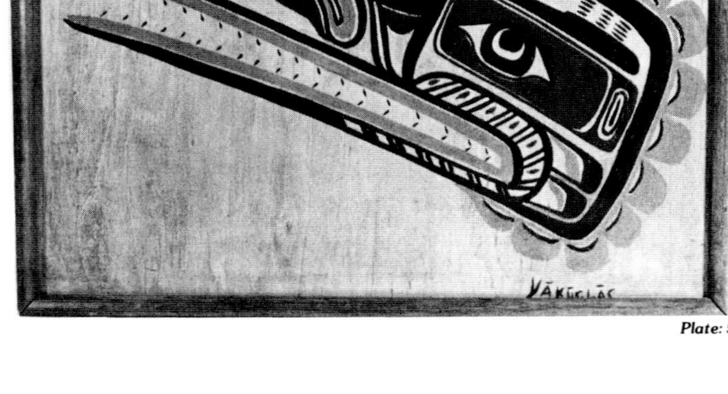

Plate: 52

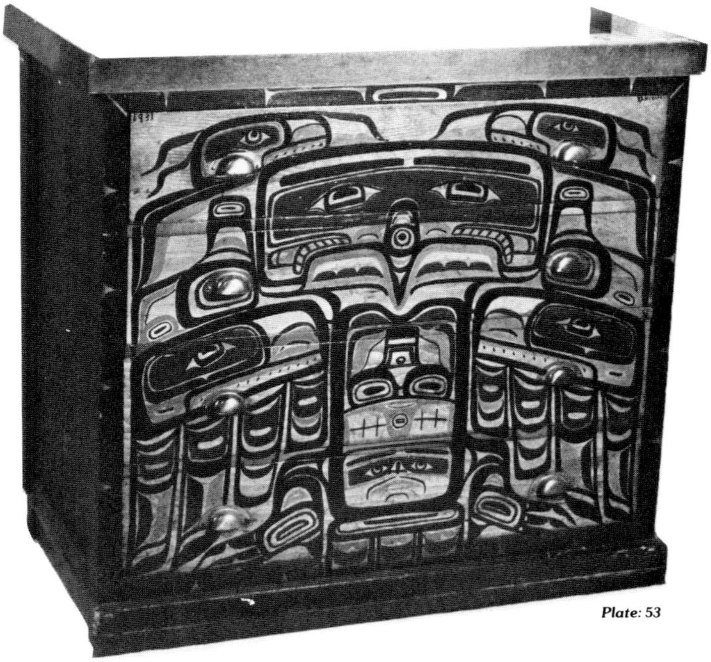

Plate: 53

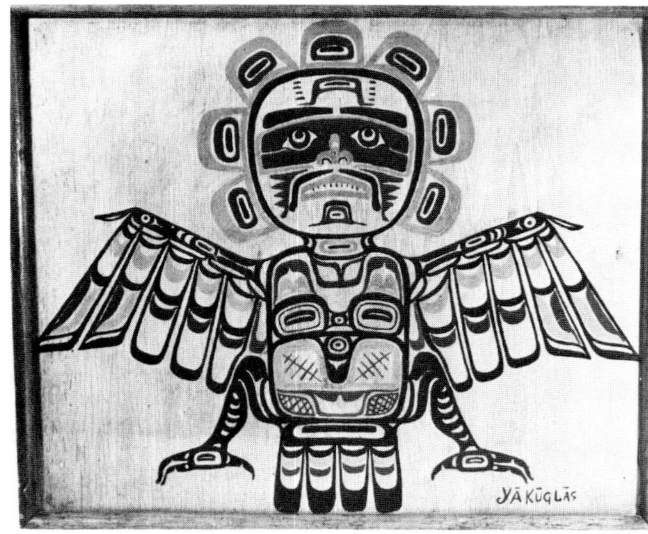

Plate: 54

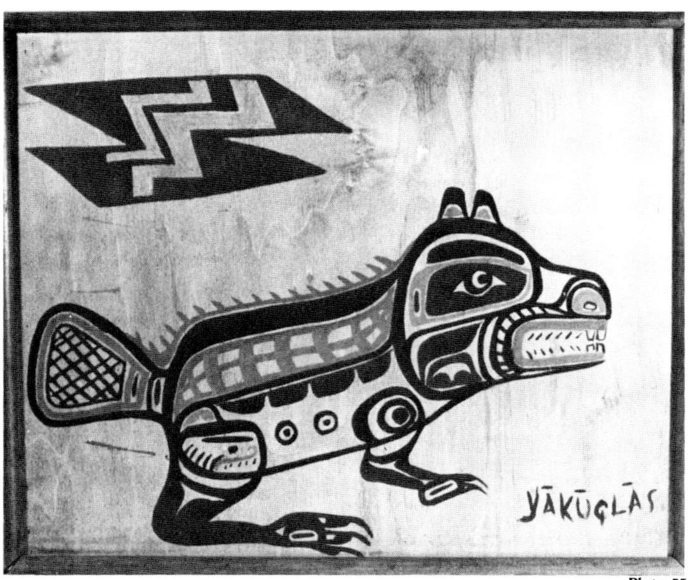

Plate: 55

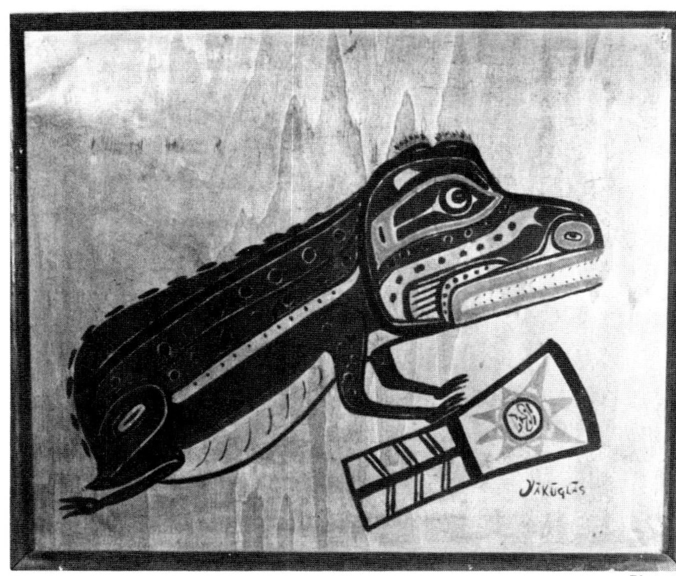

Plate: 56

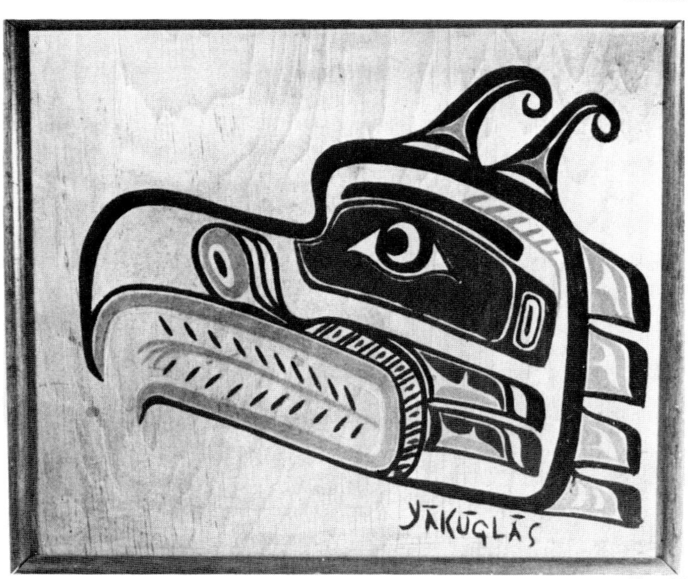

Plate: 57

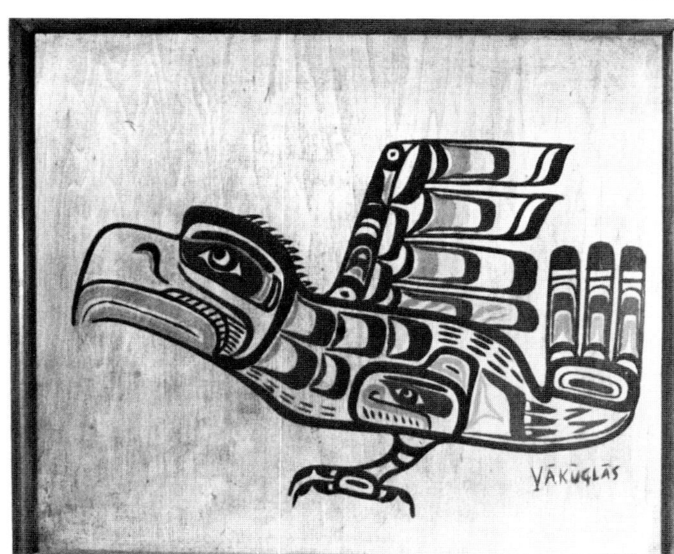

Plate: 58

Plate 59: 'Giant under the Sea, with Fish on his back.' Charlie James watercolour. (Alert Bay, c. 1927. Photo: Author's collection.)

Plate 60: 'Wild man with mask on his face.' (Alert Bay, c. 1927. Photo: Author's collection.)

Plate 61: Watercolour on artist's paper by Charlie James depicting a sculpin or 'Bullhead.' Part of a series of watercolours commissioned by a Vancouver collector, Marie Desbrisay, around 1927. Charlie James grand-daughter, Ellen Neel worked on several of these paintings with him. (Alert Bay, c. 1927. Photo: Author's collection.)

Plate 62: Charlie James watercolour. 'Dancing woman with mask on.' (Alert Bay, c. 1927. Photo: Author's collection.)

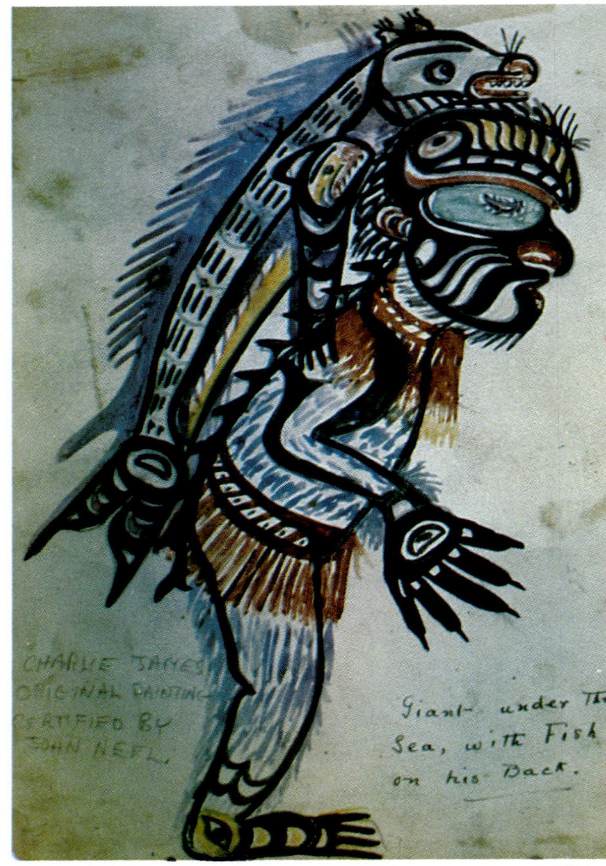

Plate: 59

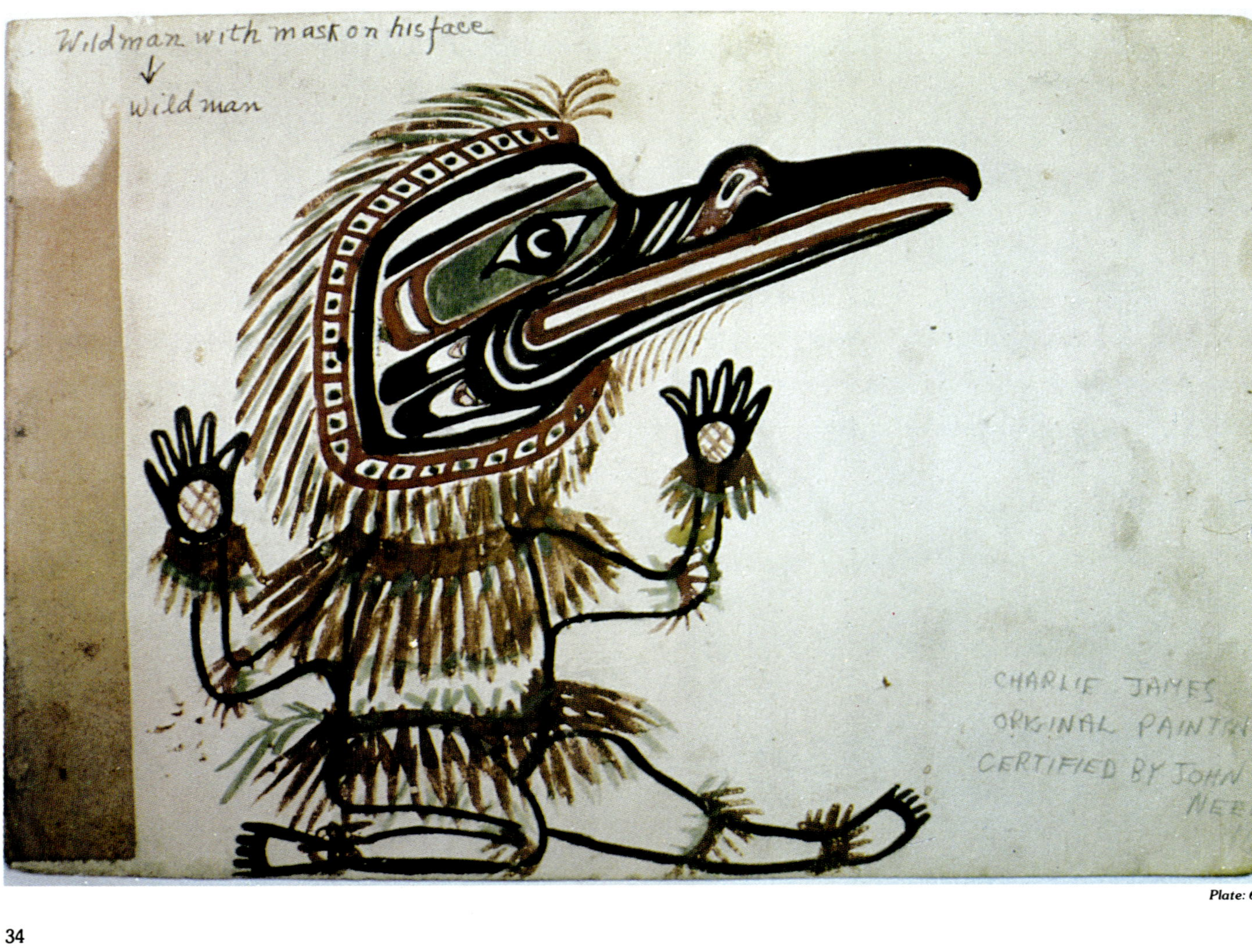

Plate: 60

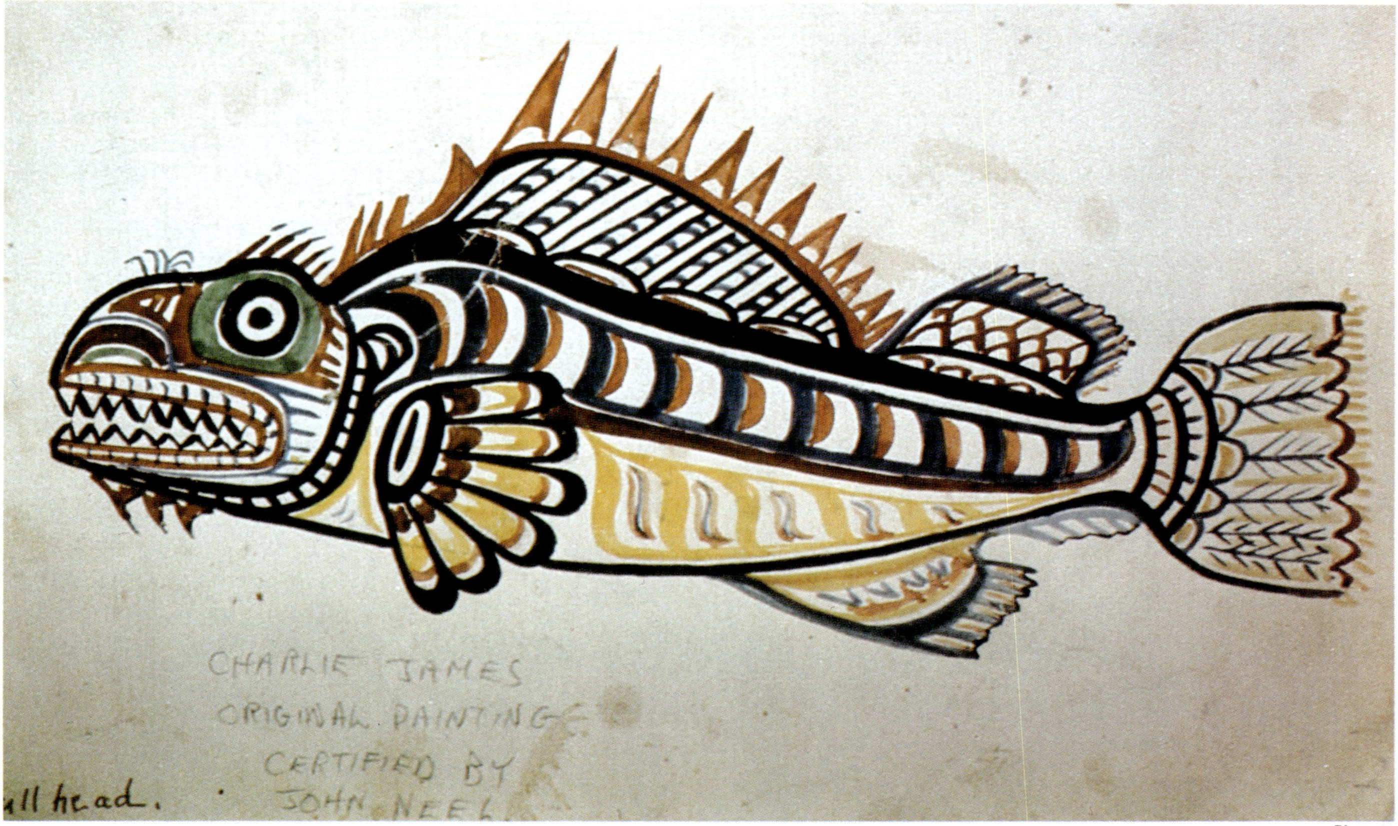

Plate: 61

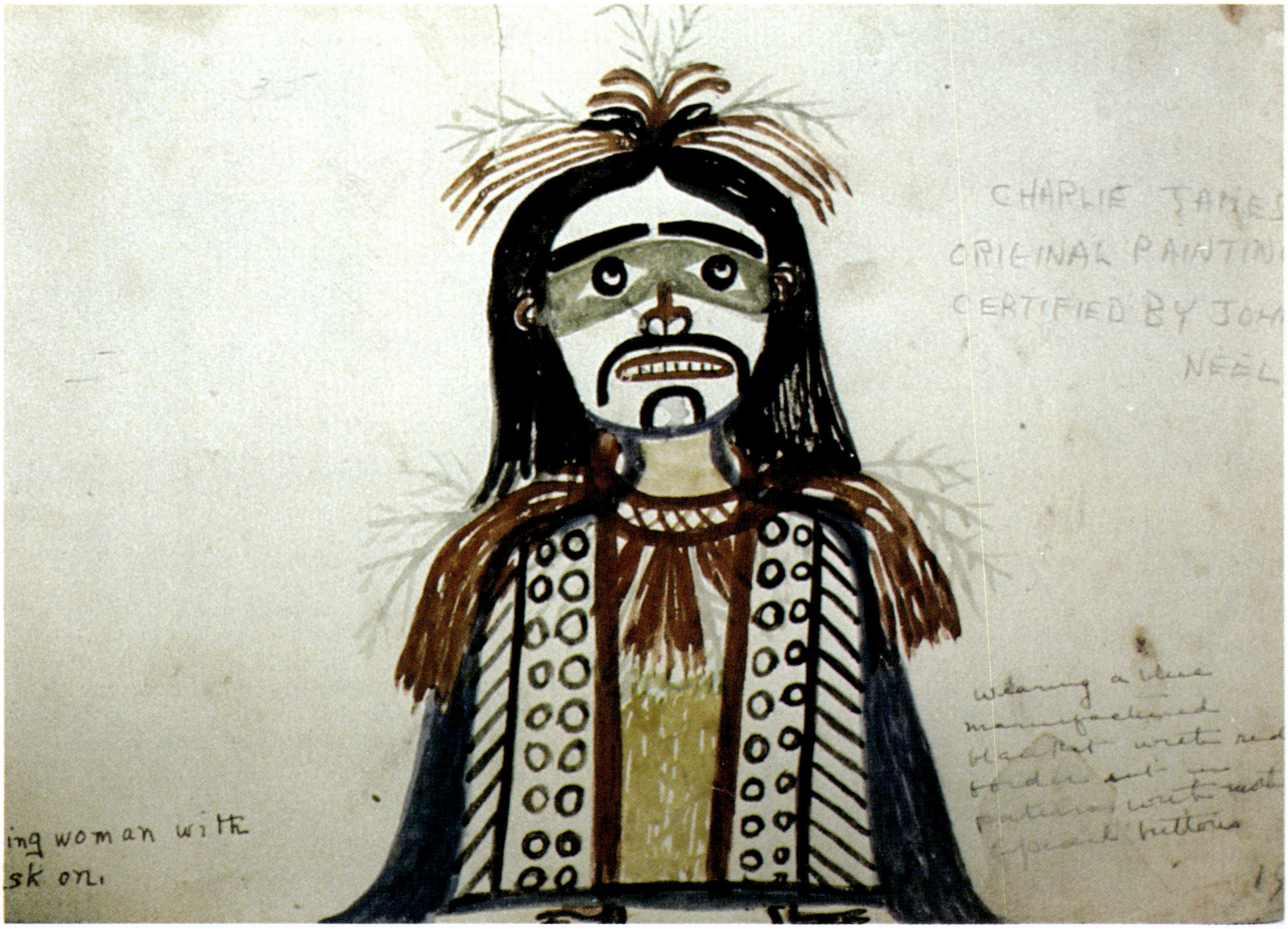

Plate: 62

So, the tourists came and went—some bought totem poles, most did not. Charlie James carved and painted, and life in Alert Bay went on.

Although Charlie James worked in the medium of his forefathers, he was not without addiction to some of the vices of civilization! He loved chewing gum and butter, particularly butter. While his neighbours contented themselves with 'T' łina'—Oolichan grease —'Indian butter'—James demanded the real thing, and often spent a part of his small store of cash indulging this luxury. Ellen Neel said, 'He could eat butter by the pound!' Charlie James' grand passion, however, was the movies or 'picture shows' as they were called. In Victoria, in Vancouver, and even in Alert Bay, he could be found at the movies. He saw the same pictures over and over, and never seemed to tire of them. When Doctor Maudy ran the first picture shows in Alert Bay—Charlie James was there... his daughter, Lucy, used to joke with him and say 'Why don't you just stay there overnight?'

goods, and the imprisonment of those who refused to give up their possessions, can be found from the agent's side in 'Potlatch and Totem,' by William May Halliday, (1939), and from the Kwakiutl people's side in the 1979 publication 'Prosecution or Persecution,' by Daisy Sewid Smith—although the incredible story of the partial return of these items to British Columbia, in 1979, has yet to be published.

Also unpublished, in this connection, is a comprehensive and voluminous report prepared by Marius Barbeau at the behest of the Department of Indian Affairs. This report gave an over-view of the entire potlatch system at that time (1920), with particular emphasis on Section 149 of the Indian Act which made it an offence to potlatch. Although the entire report was prepared for the 'private information' of the Department of Indian Affairs, it is clear throughout where Barbeau's sympathies lay... The Barbeau report is perceptive and in some instances, quite humourous—for example:

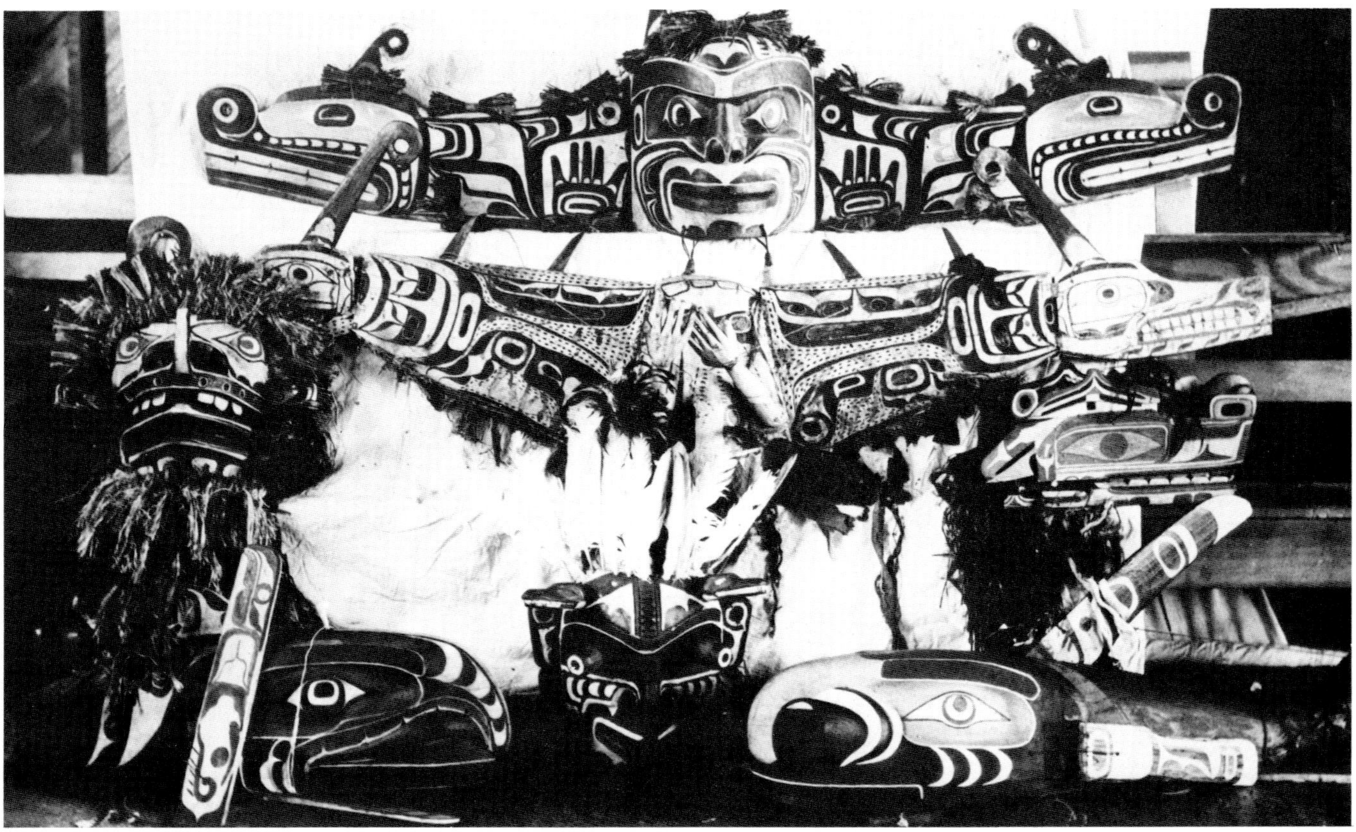

Plate 63: **Part of the potlatch paraphernalia confiscated by Indian agent, William Halliday—Charlie James produced much of this type of ceremonial regalia—although they were in the hands of the commissioning owner by the time the confiscations took place. (Alert Bay, c. 1922. Photo: V.P.M.)**

Somehow, these petty addictions make him seem less obscure and shadowy, and far more real.

James was a retiring person, perhaps because of his self-consciousness over his damaged hand. His name is not prominent in the various treatises on the Kwakiutl potlatch. Although he was not given to the loud self-acclamation of his peers, he was quite heavily-involved in the potlatch system. As an artist, he was required to know the complexities and nuances of use of those items that he created.

Written records of his involvement are sparse. One such record is an inventory of 'potlatch paraphernalia' —pieces confiscated by Indian agent, William Halliday after Dan Cranmer's 'Christmas Tree Potlatch' in 1921.

The story of the confiscation of Kwakiutl potlatch

'When we cease to dress a man up as Santa Claus and tell our children that it is he who brings them presents down the chimney, it will be time to object to an Indian who dresses himself up and tells his child that he is a wolf... about the same time as the Wolf Dance 'Długwala' took place, there was a Bal Masque (masquerade ball) held at Alberni, and the prize for the best portrayed character was given to a white gentleman who impersonated, *and very ably*... a monkey...'

This report, undoubtedly, played a significant role in the Department of Indian Affairs' decision to quietly drop Section 149 of the Act—although it took nearly thirty years to do so.

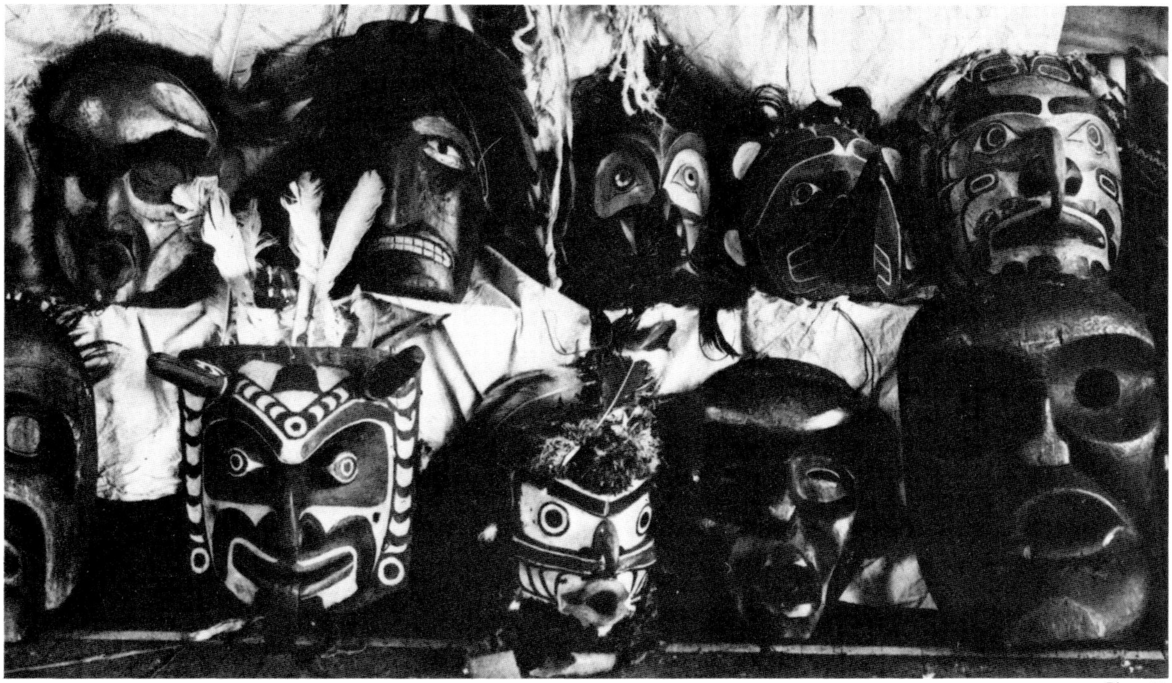

Plate: 64

Plate 64: Over 200 such pieces of potlatch gear and masks were confiscated by Halliday in 1922. Many of these are now on display in new museums at Cape Mudge and Alert Bay—but some of the best pieces were sold by Halliday to the Heye Foundation, New York—see text. (Alert Bay, c. 1922. Photo: V.P.M.)

Plate 65: A Charlie James carving in whalebone. The use of whalebone by James is quite unusual. W.L. Webber collection. (Vancouver, 1972. Photo: Centennial Museum, Vancouver NA-17:8.)

The confiscated material was put on display at Alert Bay and a portion of the collection including a mask by Charlie James, was sold to Mr. G.W. Heye of New York in September of 1922. The sale of this material was without authorization and brought strong censure against Halliday by his superiors. The list of items sold to Heye and the prices paid are:

List of Potlatch Material Sold to Mr. Heye

Jim Naknakim	carving	$1.00	**$1.00**
Harry Mountain	head gear	8.00	**8.00**
John Drabble	2 rattles	4.00	
	1 mask	15.00	**19.00**
Sam Charles	1 head gear	6.00	
	1 fish	20.00	**26.00**
J. Williams	1 gear	6.00	
	1 mask	25.00	**31.00**
Sam Puglas	1 head gear	6.00	**6.00**
Dan Cranmer	1 dance gear	20.00	**20.00**
Billy Assu	1 frog	5.00	**5.00**
Jim Bell	2 shell rattles	1.00	**1.00**
Khomkut	2 snakes	2.00	**2.00**
Amos Dawson	1 bird rattle	1.00	**1.00**
Jumbo Bell	head gear	10.00	**10.00**
Wallace	2 painted boards	8.00	**8.00**
Harry Hanus	1 rattle	2.00	
	1 head gear	6.00	
	1 head band	5.00	**13.00**
John Dick	1 head gear	6.00	
	1 head gear	6.00	
	1 crest	5.00	
	1 cradle	50.00	
	1 mask	5.00	**72.00**
Chas Homeskinis	1 head gear	6.00	**6.00**
Abraham	1 head gear	6.00	
	1 mask	20.00	**26.00**
James	1 mask	25.00	**25.00**
Bond Sound	2 hands	1.00	**1.00**
A. Corrie	fish	10.00	**10.00**
			$291.00

Certified correct: W.M. Halliday

So, it is evident that Charlie James was caught up in the potlatch dragnet and chose to surrender a mask rather than go to jail, a prudent choice, in practice if not in principle!

James made many masks for potlatch use, prior to 1920 and some after, when the potlatch system had gone 'underground.'

A good example of this type of mask is a 'Crooked Beak of Heaven'—in the UBC collection. This mask was featured on the dust jacket of Audrey Hawthorn's book 'Kwakiutl Art' (1979), a newer version of her previous volume, 'Art of the Kwakiutl and Northwest Indians.'

Another Charlie James master work of potlatch hardware is the 20-foot 'grease dish' currently in the Museum of Anthropology—University of B.C.).

Charlie James, 'Dak̲uma' was a fixture of Alert Bay and everyone knew him—at the urging of Mr. Anfield, Charlie James taught the local boys at the residential school the rudiments of Indian Art, over a period of several years. He was a good friend of the minister of the Anglican Church and even though the church disapproved of his involvement in the potlatch system, James' work was much admired.

He travelled extensively, for that time period, and was fondly regarded by all as a sort of regional landmark. What seems to have stuck in everyone's mind, however, was his incredible flair for innovation.

His work *is* different, very different. He introduced many new things that have since become a part of traditional Kwakiutl art.

Ellen Neel once described such an innovation:

'My grandfather used to tell me that he went to sleep in the graveyard behind Cranmer's house, over where the Old Indians died years before. He picked up an ordinary brick before he went to sleep... when he woke up he put orange into his yellow colour until it resembled the brick. His idea of using the orange had never been done before. Before that, they never ate oranges, so they never used the colour. It was original. From then on he always used it.'

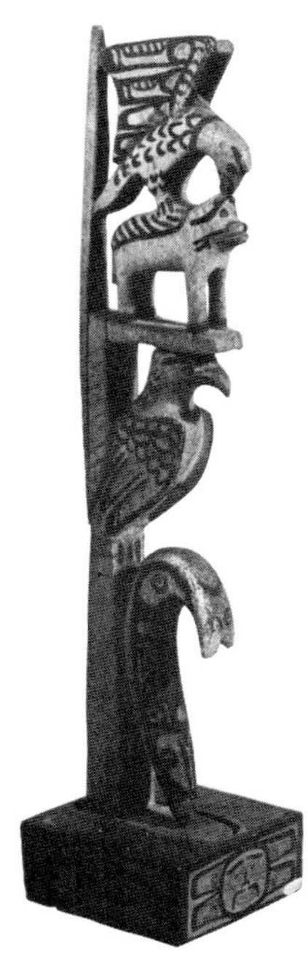

Plate: 65

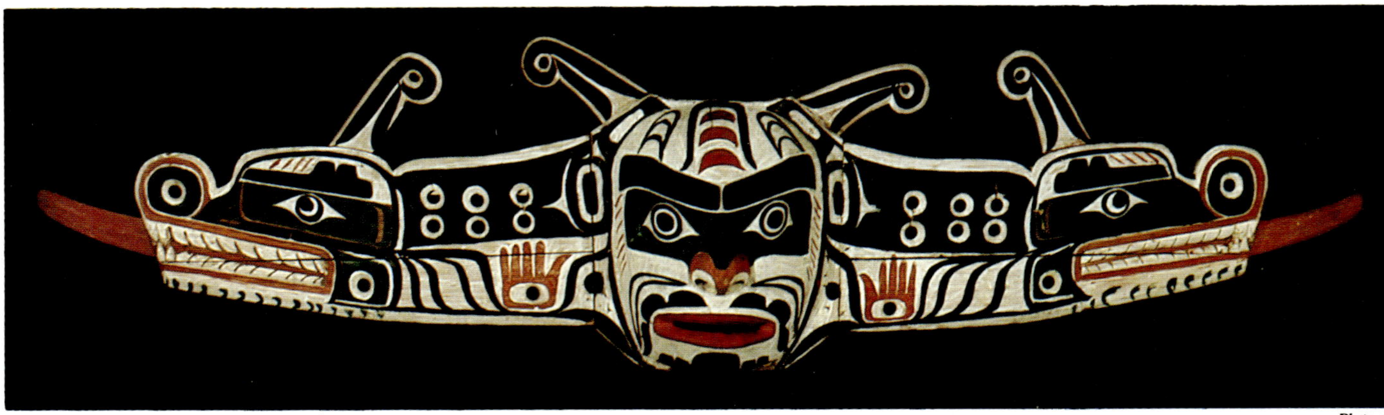

Plate: 66

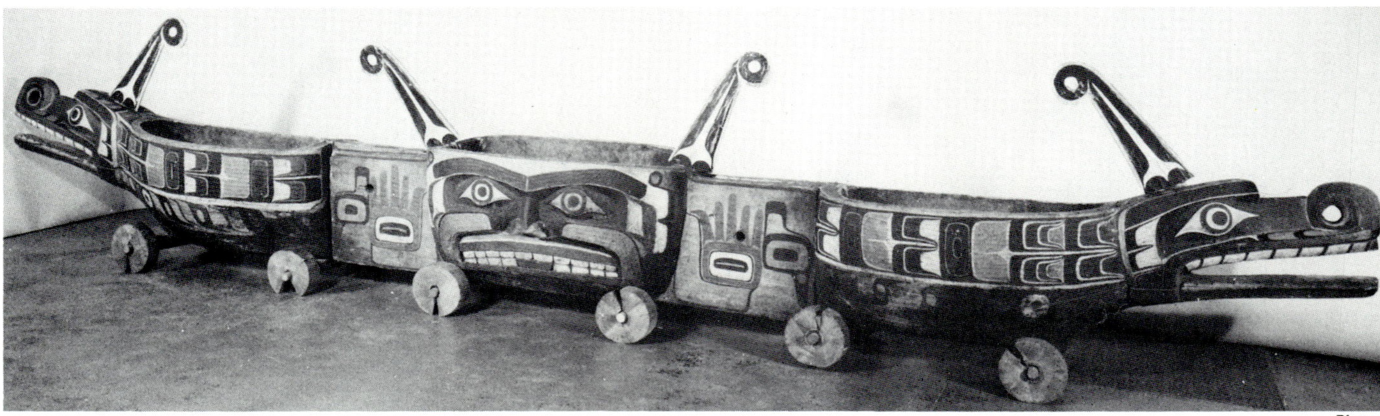

Plate: 67

Plate 66: A large 'Sisiyutł' mask by Charlie James. The 'Sisiyutł,' variously called a 'double-headed snake' or a 'double-headed serpent', is a powerful crest-figure among the Kwakiutl. (c. before 1914. Photo: B.C.P.M. C.P.N.-1954.)

Plate 67: A masterpiece of potlatch art, this 20-foot 'grease' or feast dish was made by Charlie James in 1907. (Vancouver, c. 1950. Photo: Courtesy U.B.C. A-4147.)

Plate 68: Charlie James at Alert Bay, a few years before his death in 1938. James' wife, Sara Nina, shown on left... on his right is a 104-year-old lady who had come to visit James at Alert Bay. (Alert Bay, c. 1936. Photo: Mrs. H. Reid. Courtesy: B.C.P.M. PN-11551.)

This then, has been a very brief sketch of Charlie James, a shy and retiring man. He knew intimately the meaning of what he did. He conveyed it to those who knew nothing of his culture. He was liked and respected and he lived a good life. He was one of those behind the scenes, and when the various chiefs boasted of their power, he sat silent. He knew both worlds well and, by and large, chose the one in which he was comfortable. Those white people who took the trouble to know him, were amazed at the depth of his perception and the complexity of his culture. Now we have only those things that he made, to give us an insight.

In November of 1937, Charlie James was stricken with a respiratory ailment similar to pneumonia. He entered the Mission Hospital in Alert Bay and there, on January the 29th, 1938, he passed away. As the Kwakiutl people say, he 'went home,' to be with his old friends.

He left behind hundreds of carvings scattered throughout the world. He also left behind a new way of doing old things. Through the work of those he influenced, Kwakiutl art was never quite the same.

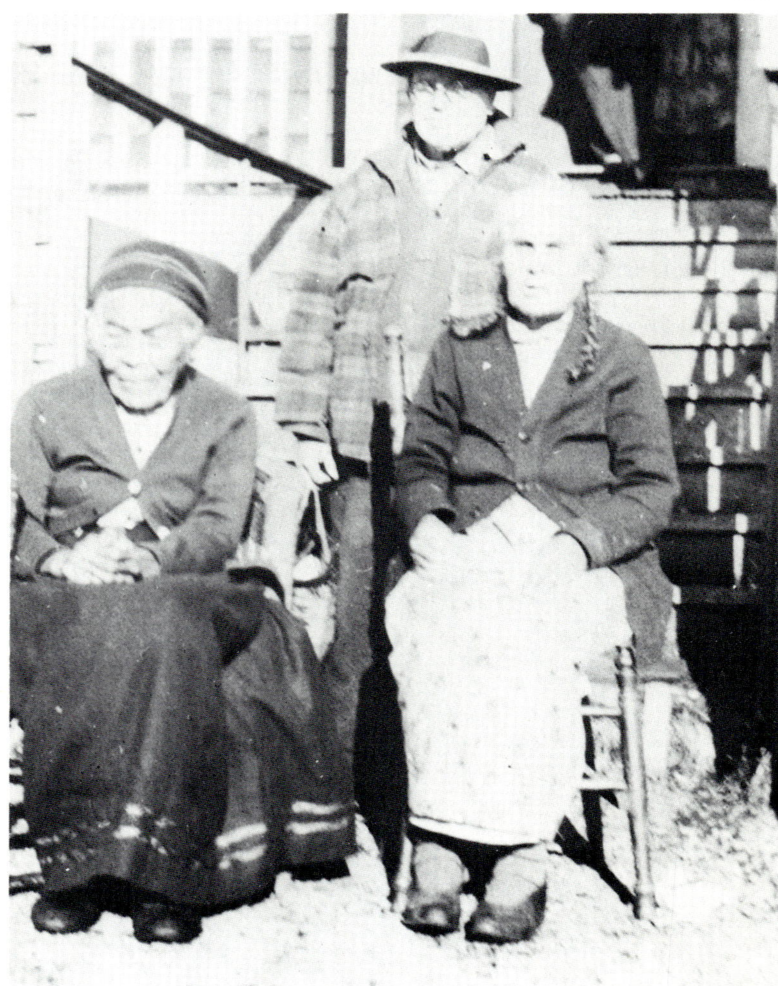

Plate: 68

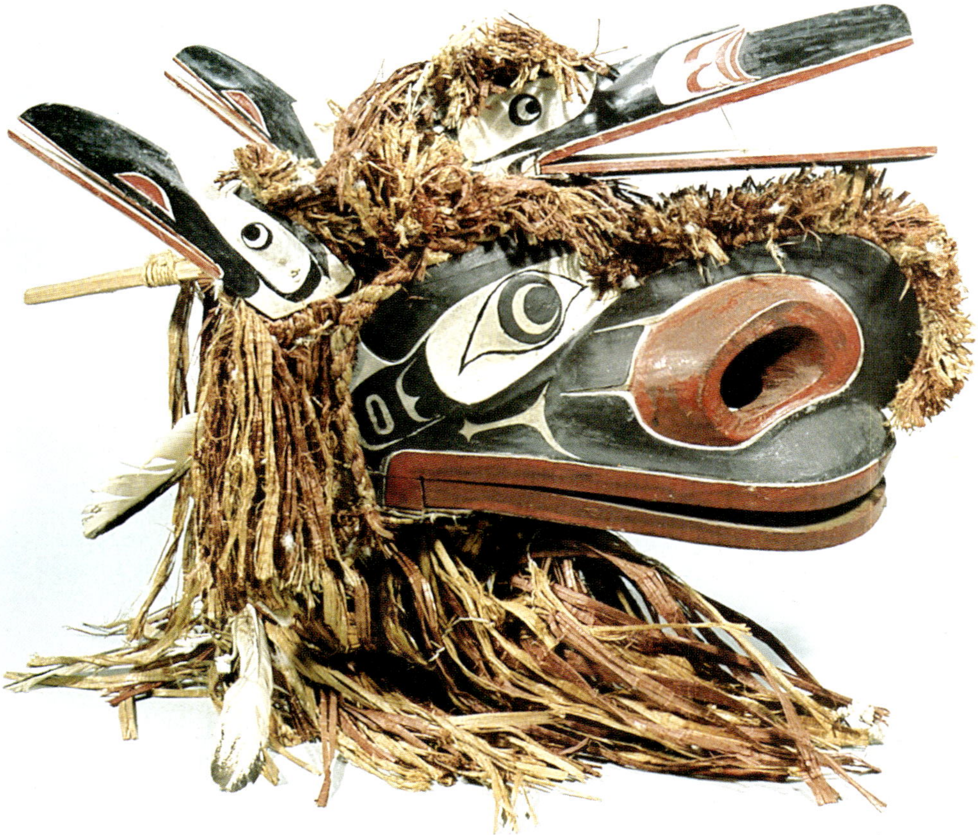

Plate: 69

Plate 69: This mask was carved by Charlie James to assemble some of the mythological bird-like creatures that represent 'the-cannibal-that-lives-at-the-north-end-of-the-world' 'Baxwbakwala-nusiwe'.' (Vancouver, 1951. Photo: Courtesy U.B.C. A—3653.)

Plate 70: 'Shark'—Charlie James watercolour. (Alert Bay, c. 1927. Photo: Aurthor's collection.)

Plate 71: 'Grizzly Bear'—Charlie James watercolour. (Alert Bay, c. 1927. Photo: Author's collection.)

Plate 72: 'Thunder-bird of the Sea'—Charlie James watercolour. (Alert Bay, c. 1927. Photo: Author's collection.)

Plate 73: 'Wild man under the Sea with Fish on its back.'—Charlie James watercolour. (Alert Bay, c. 1927. Photo Author's collection.

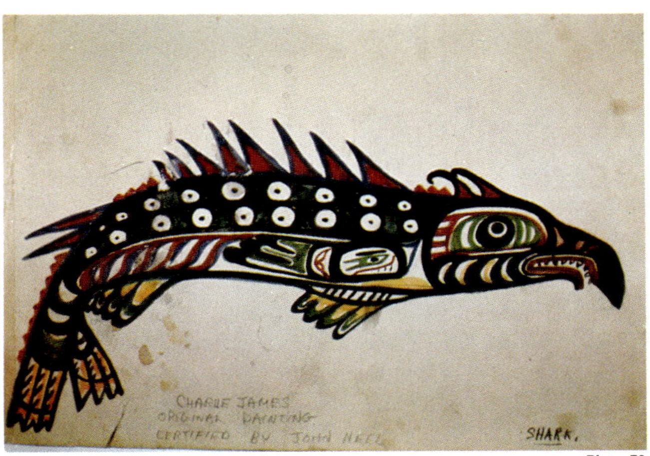

Plate: 70

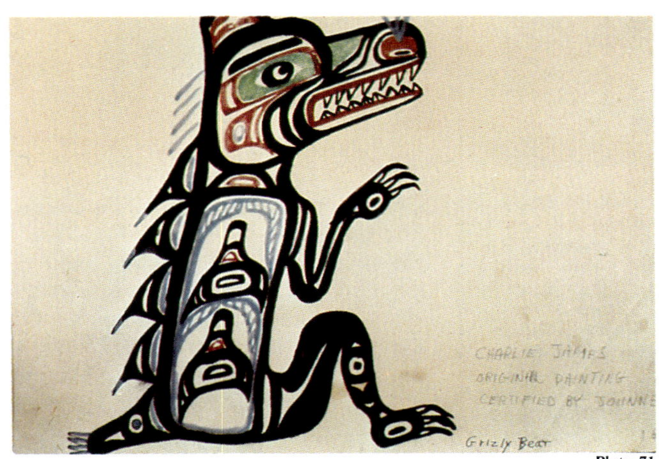

Plate: 71

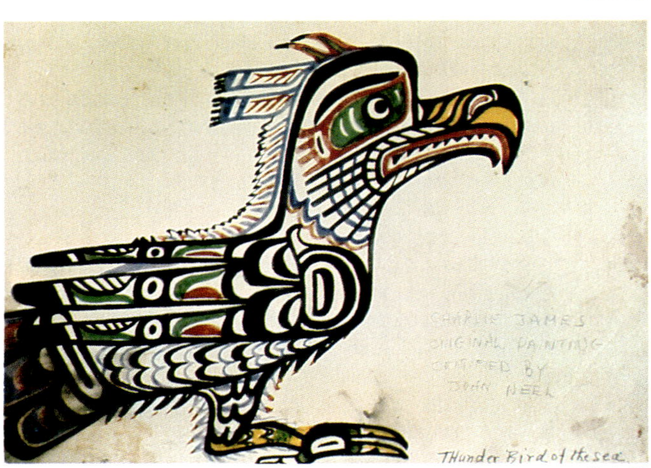

Plate: 72

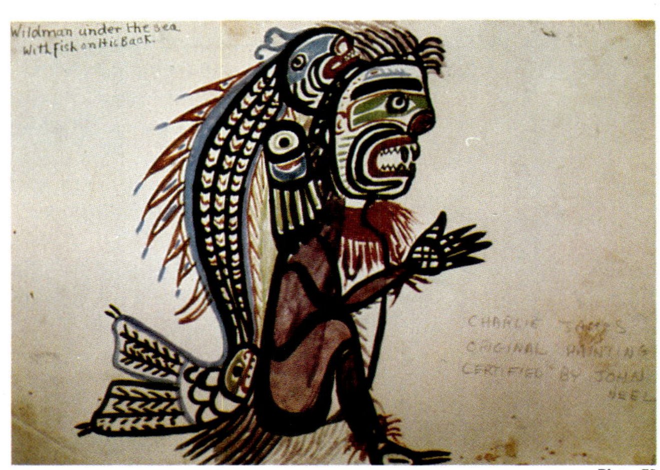

Plate: 73

POSTSCRIPT

After . . .

The Nimpkish Hotel is located on the left knee of 'Yalis' *(Alert Bay). It wasn't always here—it used to be at the other end of town. In 1925 they packed it up, lock, stock and barrel and floated it to this location.*

It was June again and I was back in Alert Bay for the Potlatches. A six-foot dance mask lay across the bed in my hotel room—a 'long beak' or 'Huxwhukw' used in the Cannibal Bird dance—it was scheduled to be used that night in a funeral potlatch and it wasn't finished! I was tired from the potlatch the night before, and the sun outside was inviting, but I got out my paints and brushes and began to do the long vermillon strips of the mouth. The mask looked good—even not quite finished—and the red/orange paint flowed well over the white base coat. The paint was a water base, and when it dried it lost much of the intense colour that it had while wet, but I knew this would be restored by the protective spray of satin lacquer. I finished the painting, and with the bright sun streaming in through the open window, it dried quickly. I spread several sheets of newspaper over the bed, and put the mask on top of them. Shht, shht,—where the lacquer touched it, the dull greyish black leapt into an intense jet black in sharp contrast to the white base coat that formed the background.

A couple of more coats and the mask was done. The hangings made from inner cedar bark and the clipped white feathers in the ruff on top of the head gave it a look quite different from those long beaks hanging in museums. This one was going to be danced . . . tonight.

I held it by the open nostrils in one hand with the back of the mask butted against my stomach and I pulled experimentally on the string-toggle. The beak clapped shut with a satisfying resonance that echoed in a knock on the door.

Amos Dawson stood in the doorway, a drink in his hand. 'My old lady's here with the van . . . if you're finished she can take it up to the long-house with the rest of the stuff.'

'O.K. Where've you been?'

'Just downstairs in the lounge . . . with some friends . . . c'mon down and join us after you get the mask loaded.'

It was pleasant to sip a beer and look out over the water. There were a number of people at the table—some I didn't know and some I did. Gus Matilpi leaned over with his elbows on his knees and asked, 'How's the book coming? . . . you get any new pictures to show us?'

I reached down to the soft-covered briefcase by my chair and pulled out a photo file.

'It's coming pretty good—but slow—you know?—I'm still on the part about Daḵuma (Charlie James).'

'Here's a shot of a pole he did here at the bay that's in Victoria now.'

Gus took the picture—glanced at it and said, 'Sure, I know this one . . . I heard about it a long time ago and then when I was in Victoria a few years ago, I looked for it.' He passed the photo to someone else at the table. 'I asked around and I went to the back of a big church—and they had it in there . . . Jesus, it's a beautiful piece of work!'

The picture was passed around and someone said, 'Hey, this is the same pole that used to be inside Ed Whannock's house!'

Gus shook his head, 'No, it's almost the same . . . but a couple of figures are different . . . but it's so close that it must have been made nearly the same time.'

Amos leaned in close, 'Yeah, I heard the one that old Whannock had was sold to the guy that used to run a floating store . . . I forget his name.' He turned and spoke to an old timer at the next table in rapid Kwak'wala and then turned back.

'He doesn't remember his name either, but he says it was sold for 3,000 dollars. He says the guy lives around Vancouver now, but won't let anyone see the pole . . . don't know why.'

'I'd sure like to see it,' I added, as Don Leo joined the table, 'Just to get a picture of it!'

Don Leo Jonathan was my business partner; a well-known professional wrestling champion—hunter and fisherman extraordinaire, and my best friend.

'Sure, Phil—sure,' Don grinned and winked at Amos.

'Just to get a picture. I'm sure you wouldn't want to buy it or nothing like that!'

'Well,' I defended weakly, 'It's sure as hell worth a lot

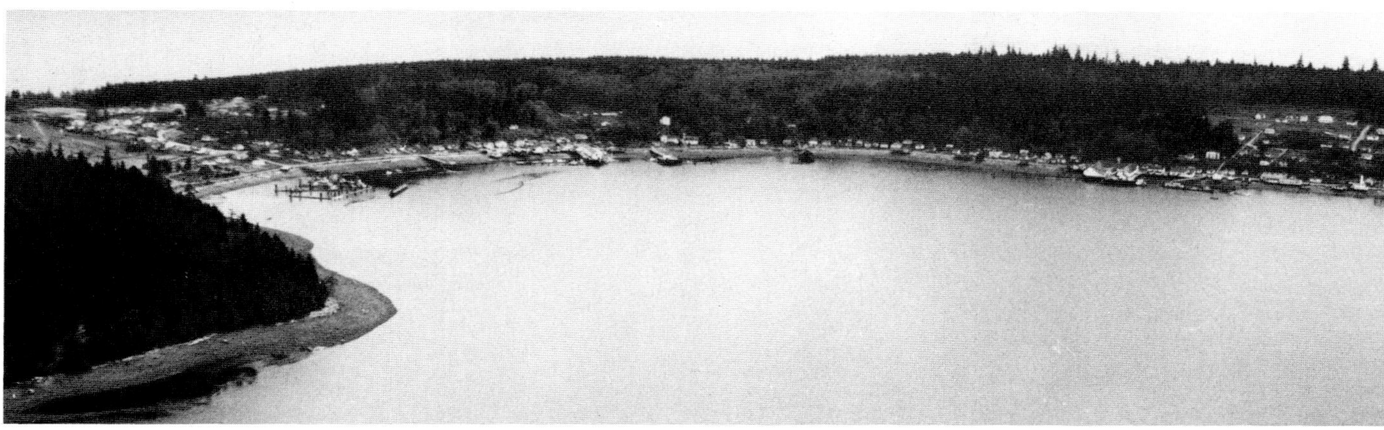

Plate 74: **Cormorant Island and the village of Alert Bay, B.C.—'Yalis'—from this little island came some of the finest carvers and artists in the Pacific Northwest. (Alert Bay, no date given. Photo: Tourism, B.C.)**

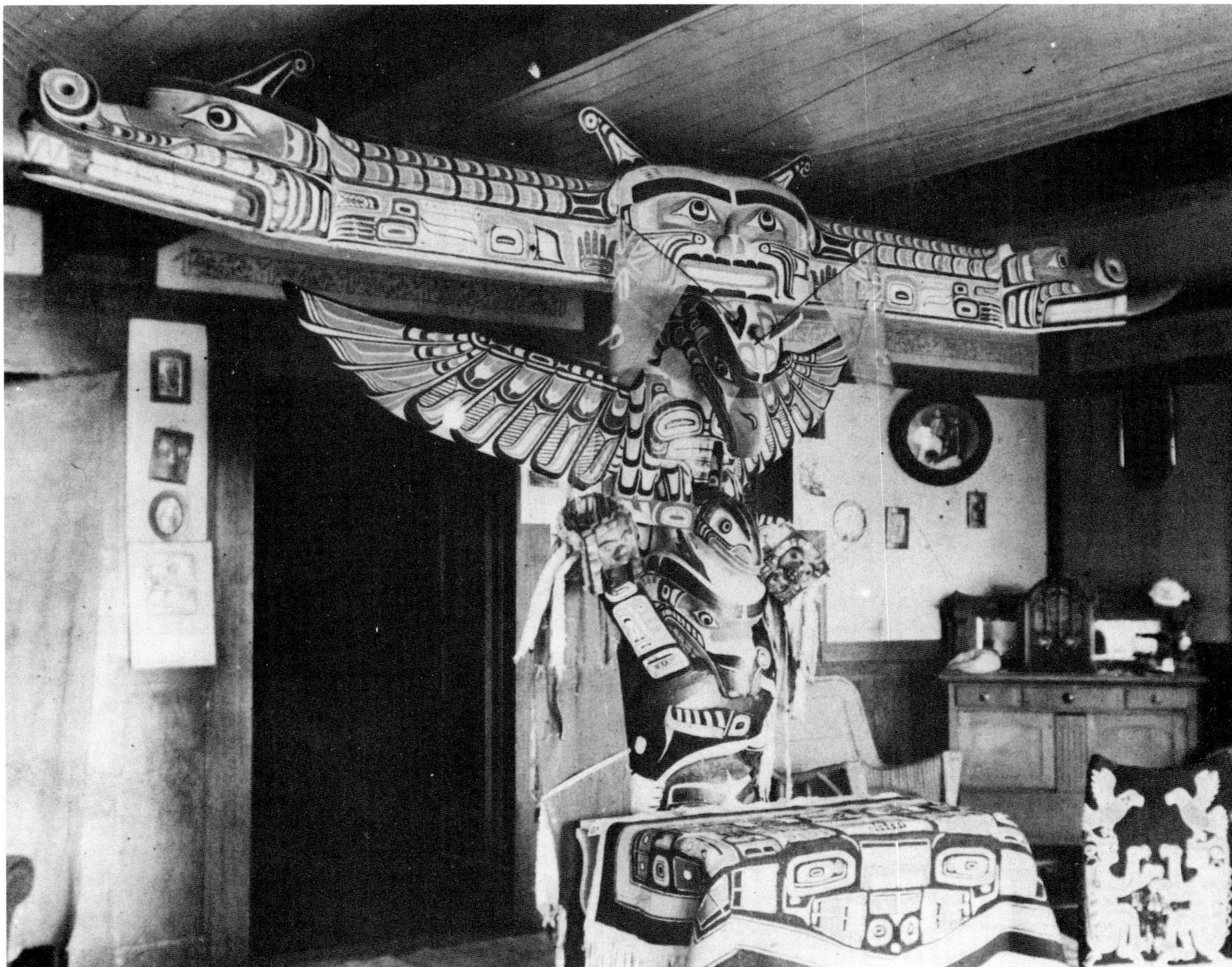

Plate: 75

more than 3,000 bucks.' A number of people were watching the by-play at our table—attracted, no doubt, by the presence of Don Leo Jonathan. When you are over six-and-a-half feet tall and weigh 350 pounds, it's hard to be inconspicuous! The old man at the next table had been following our conversation, his eyes bright, his head darting from side to side, to better hear what was said. When the conversation lulled, the old man leaned closer and tapped me on the knee. He held his left hand up with the middle fingers curled and only the thumb and little finger erect.

'Dak̲uma—he only got one hand—hah!... but he was the best one!' The people at our table nodded in agreement, and I nodded my head to concur.

Later when I got back to Vancouver, I tried to find the owner of the Charlie James pole... with no success. I did find a picture of it though, in old Ed Whannock's house. Looking at the picture, I thought back to the conversation at the 'Nimpkish'. Charlie James died nearly a half a century ago, and yet people talk of him as though he were still around. He obviously left quite an impression!

... And how did the potlatch and my long-beak go?... I shamelessly offer it as one of the illustrations in this book, because I'm proud of it; and because the ability to carve and paint this mask came through Ellen Neel, from her grandfather, Charlie James.

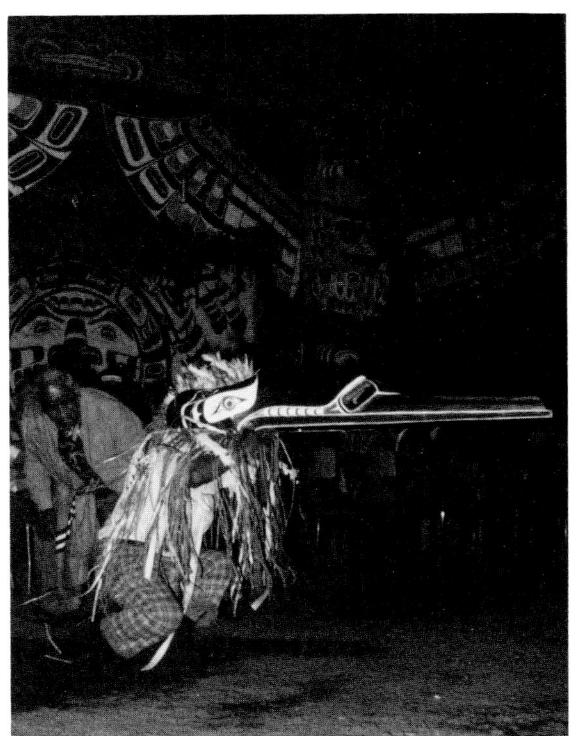

Plate: 76

Plate 75: A view of the Charlie James pole inside Ed Whannock's house. The double-headed snake or 'Sisiyutł' beam crest above this rather cluttered totem, is also by Charlie James. This photo was taken by Mr. Nelson Smith, who was called in to repair a radio—(the radio can be seen on the cabinet in the right rear of the photo). He was startled to find an entire totem pole in the room. (Alert Bay, 1937. Photo: Mr. N. Smith. Courtesy: B.C.P.M. PN-11838.)

Plate 76: A long beak or 'Huxwhukw' carved by the Author. Elsie Williams' Potlatch in honour of her late husband. (Alert Bay, 1979. Photo: Author.)

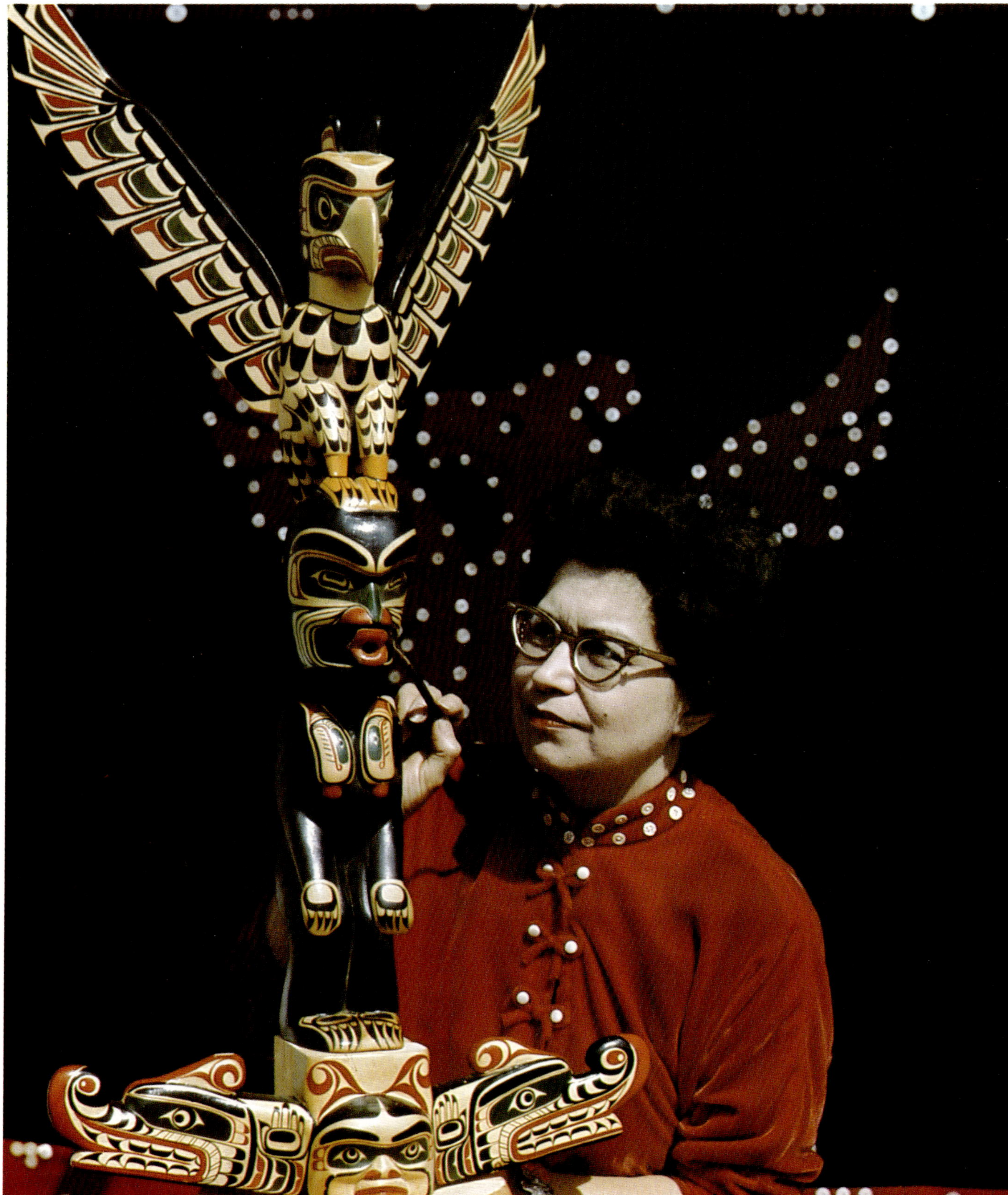

Plate: 77

Ellen Neel
Part 2

Ellen May Neel was born on November 14, 1916, at Alert Bay, British Columbia. She was a member of the Kwakiutl tribe and she was an artist. She lived for forty-nine years and she died on the evening of February 3, 1966.

Ellen's name in the Kwak̓wala tongue of the Kwakiutl people was K̲aK̲aso'las—meaning that 'people came from far away to seek her advice.' The name was an apt one, and she spent the major part of her life living up to it. She was a kind and generous person and she found humour in the bleakest situations. She had time for everyone, even pestering youngsters.

The Hastings Street bus let me off a half a block or so from the corner of Glen Drive. It was early in the morning, but already sunny and warm—kind of a typical 'summer-holiday' day. I stopped for a minute on an overpass and looked into a junk-yard full of squashed cars and huge piles of something that looked like a giant's knitting (I later found out that these were surplus anti-submarine nets). I could see the harbour a few blocks down the hill from me and the mountains behind. It was in the early nineteen-fifties, and I was very young. It felt awfully good to be out on my own on a day like this.

The house surprised me. It was green and white and pretty run down—like most of the other houses surrounding it. I don't know exactly what I was expecting—not an old-style plank house, surely—but a twelve-year-old kid expects his heroes (or heroines, for that matter) to have achieved a little more style, I guess.

I knocked on the door and shrugged myself into shape, trying to look both solemn and intelligent. The door swung open and my composure was somewhat shaken when I saw a little girl in pyjamas peering owlishly up at me through thick glasses. A voice called, 'Who is it, Bitty?' I cleared my throat nervously as a middle-aged woman came to stand beside the little girl. 'Are you Ellen Neel?' I squeaked. Her rollers bobbed as she nodded her head, obviously mystified. 'Well, I'm Phil Nuytten, and I want to learn how to carve totem poles.'

***Plate 77:* (Photo: Jim Ryan.)**

Actually, Ellen's potlatch name, 'K̲AK̲ASO'LAS' was seldom used. Instead, the people called her 'ELLEN-AH'— simply the English name 'Ellen'—'Kwakiutlized,'

Ellen Neel's father was Charles Newman. His name was 'NULIS' in the Kwakiutl language. Charlie Newman was the son of James Newman, an American seaman, and his mother was a Kwakiutl woman called 'GAUTHILAS.'

Ellen's mother was Lucy Lilac James, and she had the Kwakiutl name 'LALAXS'A'. Lucy James was the daughter of the noted carver, Charlie James—also called 'YAK̲UDŁAS,' or to his friends, 'DAK̓UMA,' and Sara Nina Finlay, called 'NA̲GEDZI' or 'K̲UMIG̲A.'

Ellen attended St. Michael's Residential School in Alert Bay, and gained her early education there. She spent much of her free time with her grandfather, Charlie James, learning the rudiments of the Kwakiutl sytle of Northwest Coast Indian art. It wasn't an easy task. Ellen said,

'He used to draw out a design and then make me copy it over and over again. When my lines wavered, he would draw over them. He said I had to learn to do it his way. Sometimes I would cry. There was so much to learn. These drawings here—they were made when I was only ten or eleven years old—most are my grandfather's but some are mine. This one (*Plate 81*) is the Thunderbird-under-the-sea... he has something like scales on... you can see my lines underneath and then where he went over top to show me the right way. He had dozens of variations of the thunderbird and he called each one differently according to the pattern of the painting and carving.'

By the time she was twelve or so, her work was good enough to be sold to the tourists that stopped at Alert Bay en route to Alaska. Her mother was ill much of the time and her grandfather, Charlie James, took care of her. She, in her way, took care of him.

'I was the only one close to him in those days and I was always there. He used to have gatherings at the

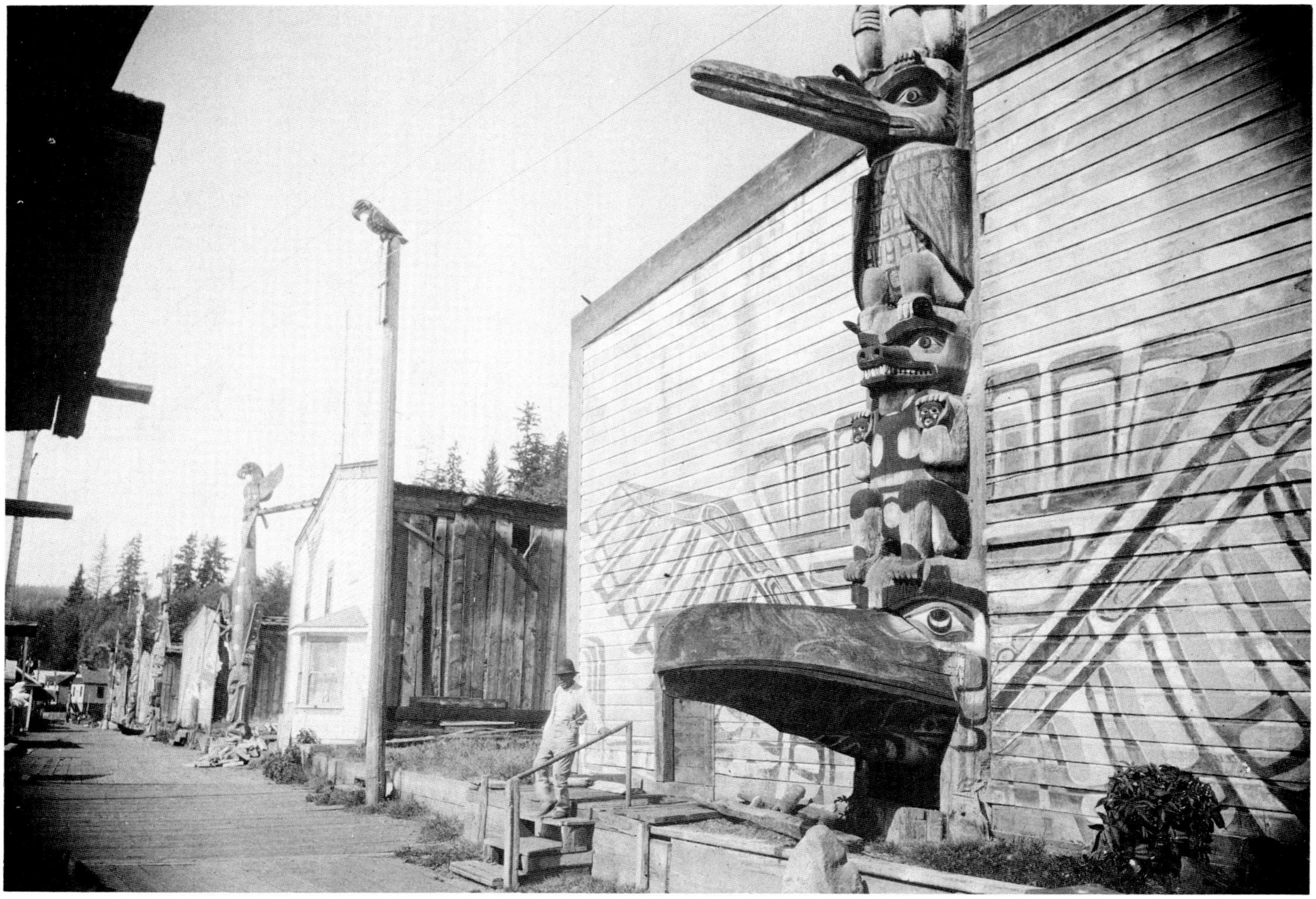

Plate 78:: **The house of Chief 'Wakius'. Ellen Neel was born in this house—it was one of the last old-style houses left in Alert Bay, at that time. (c. 1916. Photo: National Museum, Ottawa.)**

house and I remember all the dishes that I used to wash. Spruce and Mungo Martin would come to stay whenever they were in Alert Bay. Spruce had nine or ten children and he would come with his whole family and stay for days! When they came the house was full and I had to sleep on the floor and I didn't like it much. But, someone had to cook and clean everything. My grandfather was interested in the potlatch and it was important to him that good care was taken of friends and relatives.'

Although records of the Department of Indian Affairs say otherwise, Ellen Neel was only half Kwakiutl. Charlie James and Sara Nina, her grandparents on her mother's side, were both descended from marriages of Indian/Europeans and were half white. Her paternal grandparents, James Newman and Gauthilas were, respectively, white and Kwakiutl. Both her mother, Lucy Newman, and her father, Charlie Newman were half white.

Although the children of white parentage were not as readily accepted in the village (it probably was then as it is now. It matters little what your actual parentage was, only whether you looked 'white' or 'Indian'), Ellen was accepted. Her grandfather, Charlie James, was well known for his carving. Ellen spoke both Kwak'wala and English with equal facility and she carved and painted in the old styles.

Ellen was gawky and a little homely when she was very young. As she grew older, her awkwardness fell away. She left school when she was 18 and at the age of twenty-one met Edward Neel. Ted Neel was a clever, handsome, young white man, and had been somewhat of a hell-raiser. At fourteen he ran away from home and survived by his wits and glib tongue.

He was prone to the continual bending of the law, with the inevitable result that it broke at the thin spots. His Mormon family had immigrated to Lethbridge, Alberta, from the state of Utah. The spelling of 'Neel' is an unusual one, and perhaps Ted Neel was speaking the truth when he jokingly said he had 'modified it' during a period when it seemed particularly appropriate not to use his correct name.

Ted Neel's high-rolling lifestyle came to an abrupt halt when he was surprised somewhat beyond the letter of the law with the usual result.

After he served his time, he arrived at the coastal village of Alert Bay, determined to avoid further skirmishes and in possession of a trade—sheet metal working.

Neel was a minor sensation at Alert Bay. He easily secured a job as a salesman and was successful. He was young, handsome, and 'had been around.' Even the old people had to grudgingly admit that they liked this extroverted newcomer and admired his ready wit and obvious intelligence.

He was ranked as an eligible candidate for marriage—a prize catch. When he chose Ellen over a host of other very willing possibilities, tongues wagged furiously. When Ellen and Ted set up housekeeping they provided juicy gossip for the locals.

Dave Neel was born in 1937. Ellen and Ted Neel were formally married in 1939 and Ted Jr. and Bob were both born in that same year. While Ted Neel had a decided

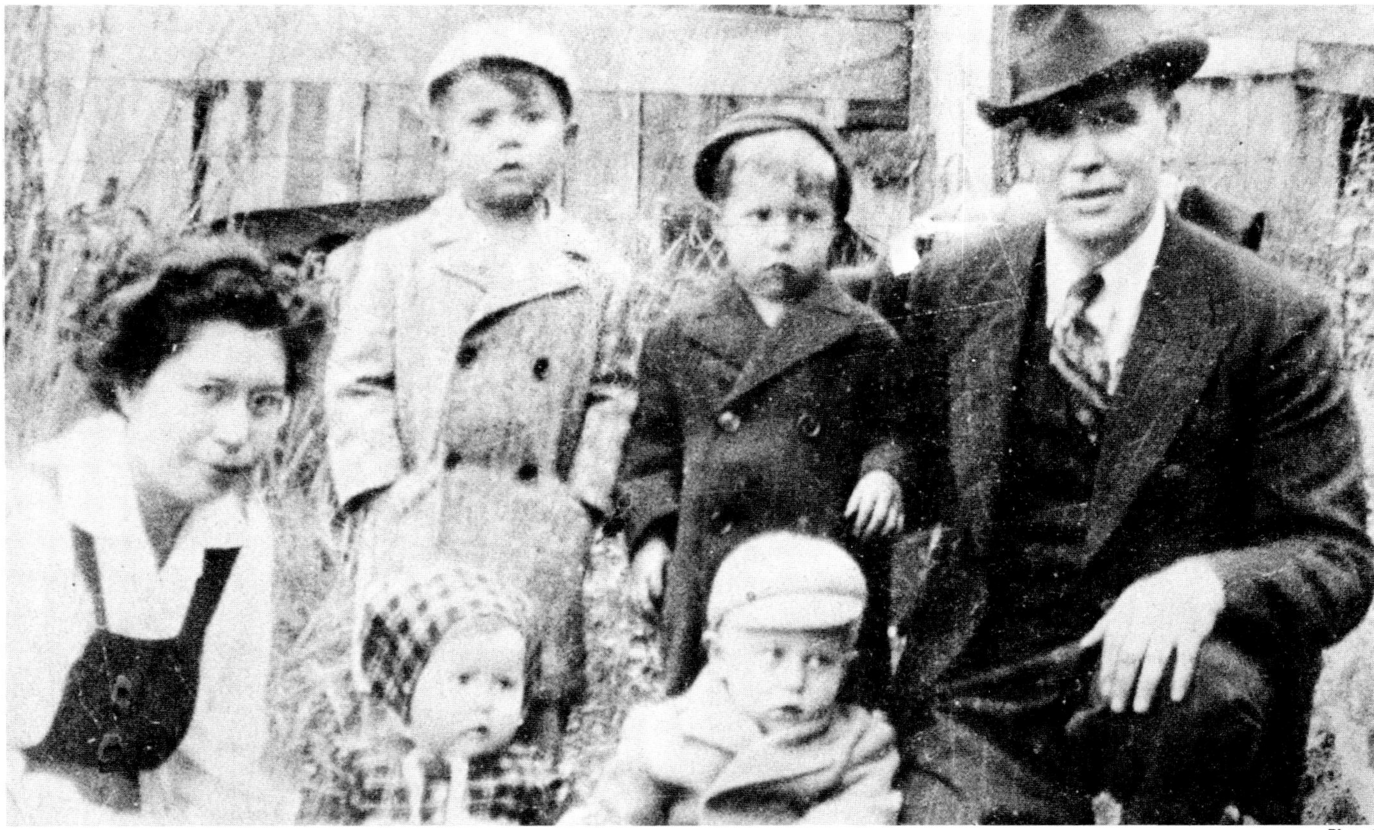

Plate: 79

Plate 79: The Neel family shortly before moving from Alert Bay. From left to right, rear: Dave, Bob and Ted Sr., front: Ellen, Cora and Ted Jr. (c. 1942. Photo: Neel family.)

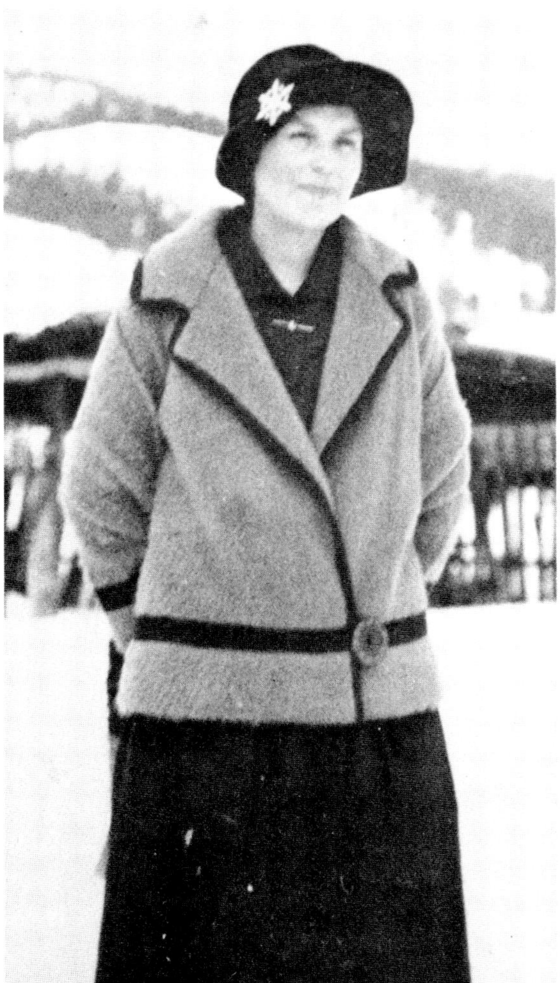

Plate: 80

flair for selling, he also possessed a good manual skill as a tinsmith and sheet metal worker. There was a demand for routine sheet-metal products such as stove pipes, flanges, ducting and the like, and a small consistent business in custom-made articles of copper and brass. In 1943, the Neel family moved from Alert Bay to Vancouver, B.C., and Ted operated a small sheet metal shop. In 1941, Ellen gave birth to a daughter, Cora. In 1942, another daughter, Theo, was born and in 1945, her third daughter, Pamela, arrived.

Vancouver, B.C., to Ellen was a huge city—exciting—intimidating. She made friends easily, though, and between raising her children, keeping house, and extending hospitality to visiting friends and relatives, the time passed quickly. Ellen still carved after her marriage, and sold a few pieces—but most were made as gifts for friends, and as she said, 'to keep her hand in.'

The Neels lived from one pay day to the next. There was usually enough, but never any extra to put away. In 1946, the relative contentment of the Neel family was shattered. Ted Neel suffered a serious stroke—the first of a series of strokes that were to impair his health for the rest of his life.

During his convalescence, Ted and Ellen faced the facts; Ted was partially incapacitated and they had a large young family to feed and clothe. Ellen turned to the one economic possibility that seemed to make sense—Indian art.

It was an obvious choice. Ellen had often spoken of how easily her totem poles had sold to tourists at Alert Bay and how the work of her grandfather was always in

Plate 80: Lucy Newman (nee James) 'Lalaxs'a'—Ellen Neel's mother. Photo taken in Kamloops, B.C. (c. 1925. Photo: Neel family.)

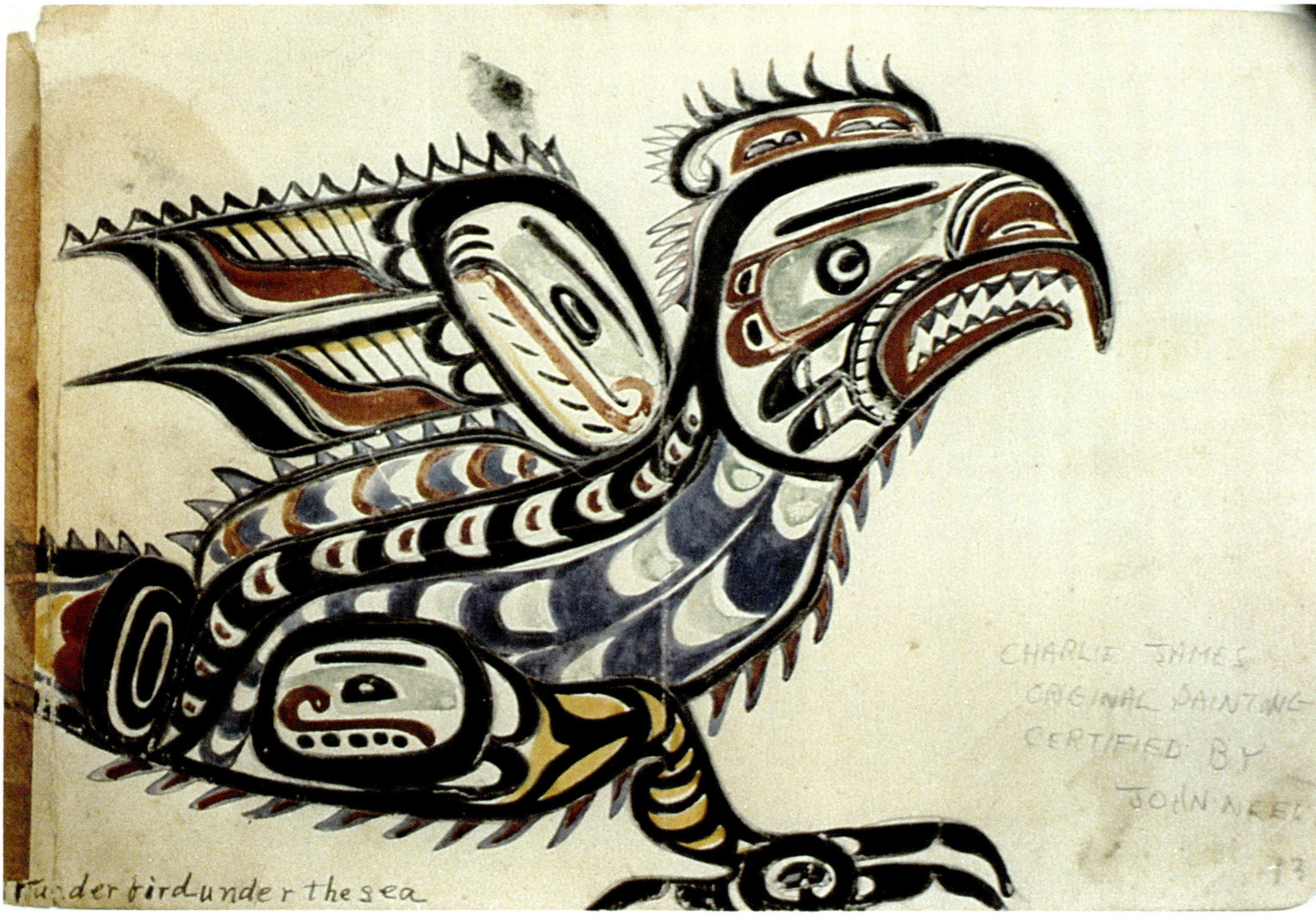

Plate: 81

demand. Prior to 1946, Ellen had produced a few good pieces every year. Even Ted was impressed at the prices that some of them brought from collectors, but there were uneasy questions. Could it be done on a fulltime basis? Was there enough demand to make it an economically viable venture? How could Ted help, with the double handicap of poor health and no formal training?

They talked to some collectors, contacted some curio dealers and the answers were encouraging. They decided to go ahead. Ted was adamant; he'd had enough exposure to business practices to know that the project was doomed unless it could be put on a sound business basis. A part-time home-handicraft set-up was out. If they were going to give it a real try, it would have to be an all out effort. Ted had been a salesman and fairly successful one. He was skilled with his hands, as a tinsmith, but no amount of fast talking or mechanical training could make him an artist. That was Ellen's department.

It was settled. Ted would handle sales, the buying of materials, the rough preparatory work on the large pieces, keep the books, and generally promote his wife's talent. Ellen would design, carve and paint.

If things got tough, Ted could go back to work at his regular job on a part-time basis.

By most standards, they should have failed dismally. But, surprisingly, they at least survived at their new venture. It should be remembered that although Ted had set himself up as the business head and general manager, the 'new' business was anything but new to

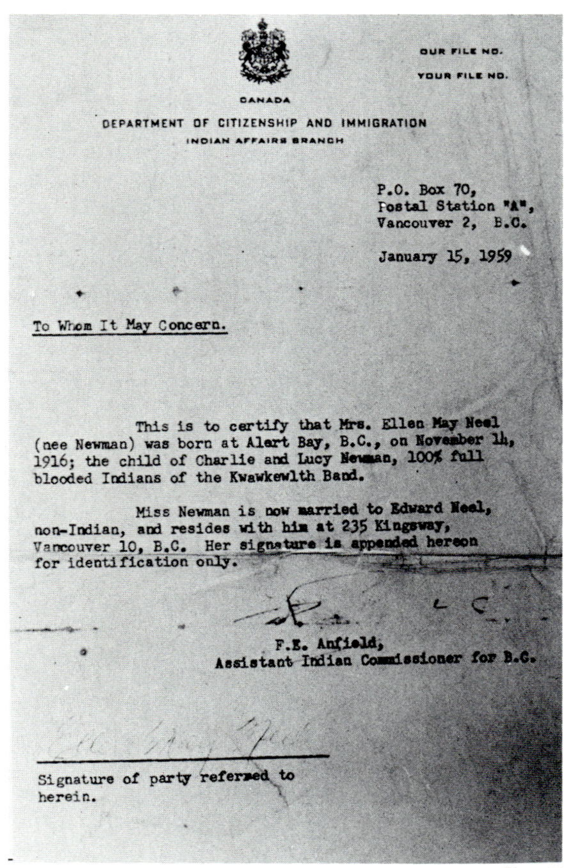

OUR FILE NO.
YOUR FILE NO.

CANADA

DEPARTMENT OF CITIZENSHIP AND IMMIGRATION
INDIAN AFFAIRS BRANCH

P.O. Box 70,
Postal Station "A",
Vancouver 2, B.C.

January 15, 1959

To Whom It May Concern.

This is to certify that Mrs. Ellen May Neel (nee Newman) was born at Alert Bay, B.C., on November 14, 1916; the child of Charlie and Lucy Newman, 100% full blooded Indians of the Kwawkewlth Band.

Miss Newman is now married to Edward Neel, non-Indian, and resides with him at 235 Kingsway, Vancouver 10, B.C. Her signature is appended hereon for identification only.

F.E. Anfield,
Assistant Indian Commissioner for B.C.

Signature of party referred to herein.

Plate: 82

Plate 81: **A drawing/painting of the 'Thunderbird under the sea' by Ellen Neel and Charlie James. These drawings were made in 1927, when Ellen was learning the rudiments of North-west Coast Indian art. (1927. Photo: Author's collection.)**

Plate 82: **A letter from Indian Affairs certifying that Ellen is '100%' full-blooded KWAWKEWLTH (one of the many spellings of Kwakiutl). (Vancouver, 1959. Photo: Courtesy Neel family.)**

Ellen. She had been well-trained by her grandfather and could turn out fine work when the time and sale price warranted. Good work on a near-production basis and at least acceptable work on a production basis. It was obvious to everyone that Ellen was skilled, warm and charmingly articulate. What was obvious only to her close friends was that she was also ambitious and fiercely determined to succeed.

It was around this time she told a close friend, 'By God, one day they'll know my name!'

Ellen was determined, but lacked the ruthlessness of the fanatic. She was blessed, or cursed, with an egopiercing sense of humour that quickly saw through the pretentions and minor pomposity—even her own.

The Neels used their small supply of cash to purchase raw materials—yellow cedar, paint and some additional tools to supplement the few that Ellen had brought with her from Alert Bay. They lived on Powell Street in Vancouver, and their home was converted into a combination studio-workshop and store.

Ted laid out his 'trap line'—the constant round of souvenir shops, curio dealers and department stores. Just about anywhere, in fact, where totem poles could be sold. Ellen settled down to carving and painting. She designed a range of tourist poles that could be produced in reasonable time but still carried the earmarks of condensed authenticity and bore her own distinctive style. Ted helped with the household duties and Dave, by this time, was old enough to mind his younger brothers and sisters. Somehow they worked it out, and the work sold at least well enough to afford a subsistence.

A milestone in these first few years came in the person of Harry Duker. Duker was a colourful character, a self-appointed, one-man publicity agent for the City of Vancouver. Tall, trim and cheerfully witty, he had retired from a successful business in 1928 and decided to devote himself to volunteer work and attracting tourist business to the 'evergreen playground'. Vancouver had owned the appellation 'Totemland' for years and Harry Duker formalized it by the formation of the Totemland Society. The society was dedicated to publicizing the City of Vancouver to people abroad, with particular emphasis on the 'Totemland' aspect. Duker was active in numerous civic societies and on many committees—but this one became his pet.

Ellen was commissioned to design an insignia for the Totemland Society and she came up with a concept that became known as the 'Totemland Pole'. The pole was topped by a thunderbird, then a globe of the world with the geographic features of the B.C. Coast prominent, and a kneeling figure representing the first man. Duker was delighted!

Harry Duker was 90 when I asked him about the formation of the Totemland Society. He was a little hard of hearing, but as cheerful and enthusiastic as the last time I'd talked to him, almost twenty-five years before.

'Sure I remember you. You were the youngest member of the Totemland Society—a quiet little guy then!

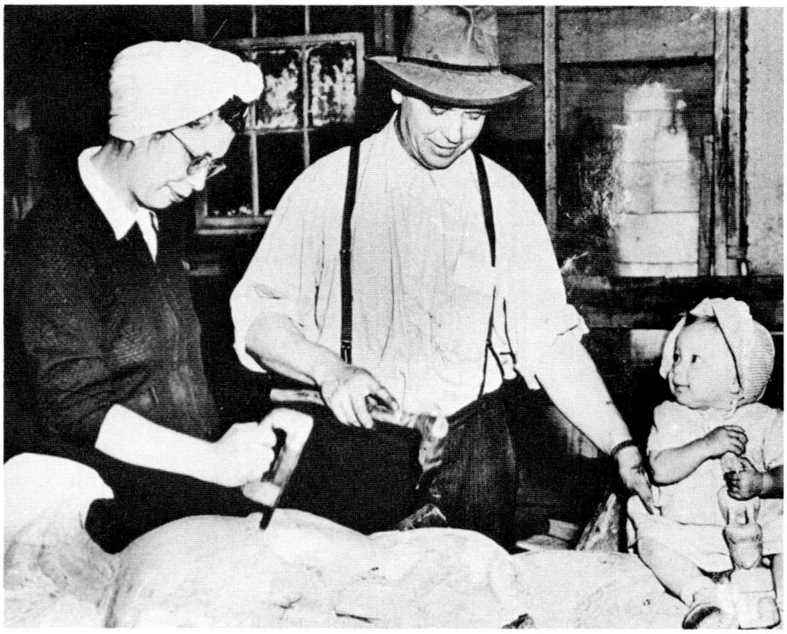

Plate: 83

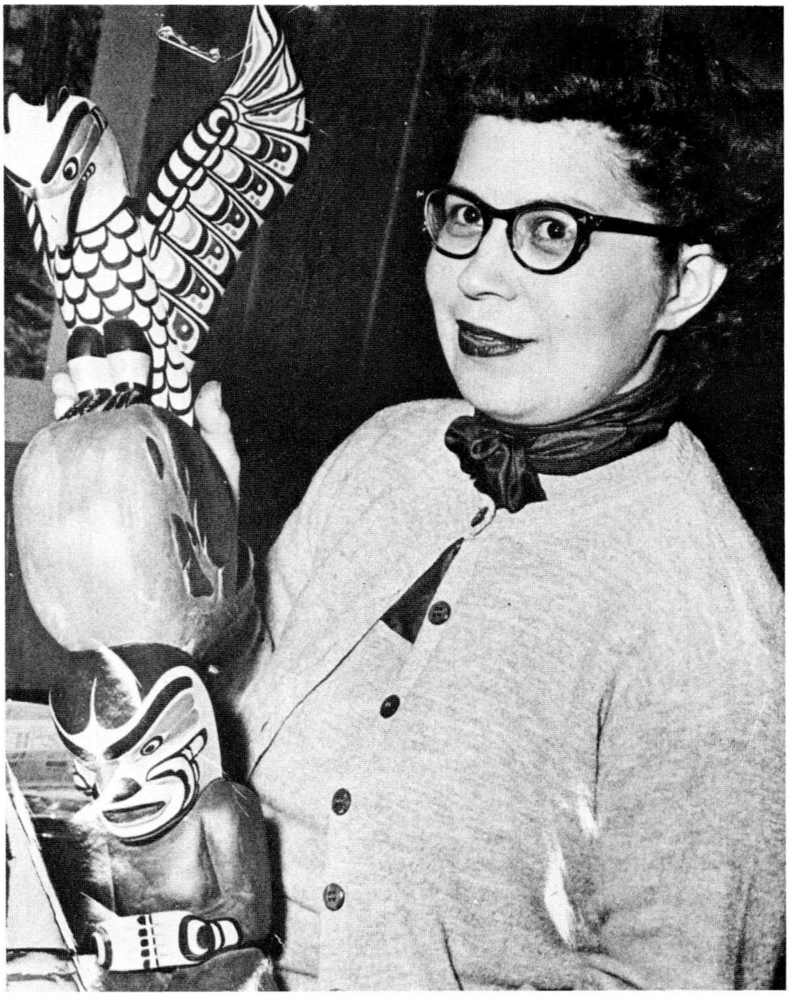

Plate: 84

Plate 83: **Ted and Ellen work on a 12-foot totem in July of 1948. Year-old Bitty watches and plays with, appropriately, a totem pole. (1948. Photo Vancouver Sun.)**

Plate 84: **The 'Totemland' design is chosen as the official emblem of the Totemland Society of British Columbia. Ellen Neel looks pleased with the decision. (Vancouver, 1950. Photo: Vancouver Sun.)**

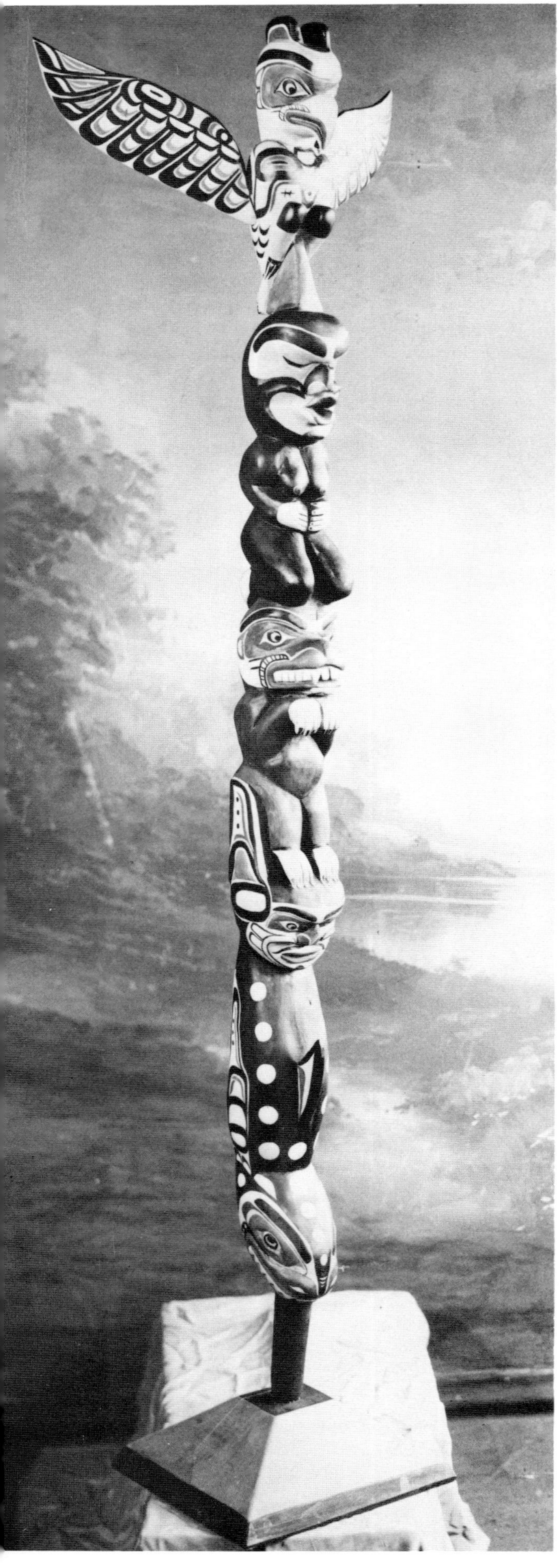

Plate 85: **'Talking stick' carved by Ellen Neel and presented to the people of Australia as a gift from the city of Vancouver by Mayor C.E. Thompson, April, 1950. Marjor J.S. Matthews, City Archivist explained in a note to the archives file dated May 26, 1950: 'When I first met Ellen Neel it was in the Mayor's office, City Hall. The ceremony was the presenting to him—to take with him to Australia as a gift—a symbol of British Columbia, and a totem pole had been selected. It was of wood, cedar, supposedly about five feet or a little more high and standing on a base of wood.**

'A number of chiefs headed by Chief William Scow of Alert Bay, were gathered in the Mayor's office (they were the chiefs of the Native Brotherhood of B.C.) Mrs. Neel was an invited guest. The formalities and the bestowing of the honour of Chieftian ship upon his worship Charles E. Thompson, with the Indian title 'Hya-pene-ulth,' supposed to mean something like 'he who looks after others.' Then the totem pole was formally handed over.

'Strangely, of all present of Indian blood, Mrs. Neel was the only one not asked to speak. She is the mother of six children, a very bright, vivacious lady who would adorn any company.

'Afterwards . . . next morning . . . it was arranged for the totem pole to be taken in a taxi by Mrs. Neel to W.J. Moore Photo Studio, where it was photographed.' (Vancouver, 1950. Photo: W.J. Moore. Courtesy: City Archives, Vancouver.)

'The Totemland Society? Gosh, that was a long time ago! You see, Charley Thompson—he was the Mayor of Vancouver then. Charley went on a goodwill tour to Australia. He took some small totems and a talking stick. You know what a talking stick is? Okay, well, when he got back he said all they talked about in Australia was the totems and the talking stick. He'd made a present of them to the City of Sydney.'

'I guess this was about thirty years ago. Anyhow, when he got back, he called a bunch of us together for a luncheon over at the old Terminal City Club. He talked about his tour and said he figured we were missing a bet. We should use the name Totemland more often and pursue that aspect of the city's attraction for tourists.'

'I got up and said, 'Well Charley, if you want to do something about it—like forming a committee or something, we had better elect a secretary right now and start taking some notes or minutes.' Charley said, 'O.K. Harry, you're elected!' Duker chuckled, 'And I wound up as secretary from then on!'

'And the Totemland totem? After I got to know Ellen, we asked her to design something for us. Gee, she was good at that sort of thing. We used to give them away, you know, and everybody was really impressed. She did a beautiful job!'

A photogravure of the pole became the main feature of the Society's letterhead and Ellen worked with a silkscreening studio to produce the screens to allow this and other designs to be put onto textiles—teeshirts, placemats, ties and scarves. A silk tie with the Totemland pole emblazoned on it became Duker's personal trademark, and he was seldom without it. Duker pushed hard for the Totemland Society and almost every prominent visitor to Vancouver went away with a Totemland tie and, if they were particularly important, a model Totemland presentation pole carved by Ellen Neel.

It was Harry Duker who arranged for the Neel family to begin carving in Vancouver's Stanley Park. Nothing elaborate, just permission to sell poles in a good tourist area. A large boost to the family's economy. Perhaps permission is the wrong word. There was nothing official, only the verbal assurance that the rules against commercial vendors would be waived; that Parks Board officials would look the other way. After all, it was not really a commercial thing—more like a display of native crafts, wasn't it? If they sold a few to the eager tourists—so what? Unfortunately, opinion was divided on the Parks Board, with the result that it became a small, continuing issue. It was obvious to the Neels that their 'permission' wouldn't last forever, but it was foolish not to take advantage of it while they could!

The Neels set up a tent and a large table displaying finished carvings. Ellen would carve and paint while Ted acted as the pitch man in an almost carnival atmosphere. They had fun, in those summer days and more importantly, sold a lot of totem poles.

In 1947, the well known Canadian anthropologist and ethnographer, Marius Barbeau, called on Ellen at her home in Vancouver. He was seeking information on Charlie James, preparatory to doing a monograph on her famous grandfather. Ellen talked and Barbeau made copious notes in his curious field-shorthand. He asked questions about data he received from other informants around the Alert Bay area. Ellen confirmed or gently denied and explained. Much of the information found its way into one of Barbeau's many scholarly works entitled 'Totem Poles'. When I recently had the remaining shorthand notes transcribed, it was impressive to read the amount of detail that Ellen passed to Marius Barbeau. Her knowledge was sought by a foremost expert; tourist poles were beginning to sell consistently. Things looked brighter. The year was rounded out by the birth of her seventh child, a daughter that she named Theresa, but who was, almost immediately, nicknamed 'Bitty'.

In the spring of 1948, Ellen Neel was invited to be the guest speaker at a Conference on Native Indian Affairs to be held at the University of British Columbia. She was asked to address the subject of Indian art and its potential commercial market. Ellen and Ted worked feverishly to build up an inventory of carvings to display at the conference, since it could provide a degree of exposure that would be difficult to match. At the same time, Ellen worked on her speech, how best to tell others just what was in her mind. How to explain the excitement she felt! Her enthusiasm came through well at the conference, and a local Vancouver newspaper carried the following article:

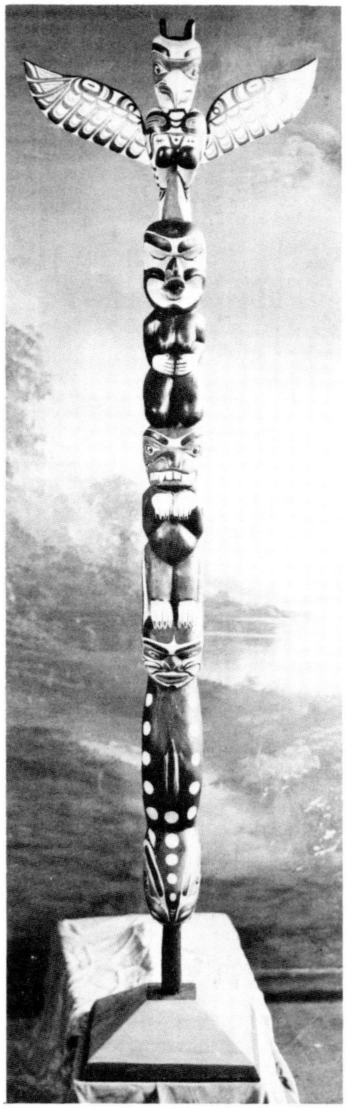

***Plate 86:* Another view of 'talking stick.' (Vancouver, 1950. Photo: W.J. Moore. Courtesy: City Archives, Vancouver.)**

Woman Totem Pole Carver Loves Art

Vancouver Province, April 3, 1948.

Mrs. Ellen Neel, a native of Alert Bay, is probably the only woman totem pole carver in the world. Today, in a tiny former store at 359 Powell St., she and her husband, Edward are striving to develop and further Indian art and so, revitalize the native culture.

'Oh, I'm so excited,' she told friends at the opening session of the conference on Native Indian Affairs at UBC's Acadian Camp. 'Dr. McKenzie (President of UBC) just bought my polished pole and it's the first polished totem that I've ever made!'

Crowds admired Mrs. Neel's display of colourful, authentic Indian carvings. Her greatest effort, towering over displays of native art in UBC's Brock Hall, is a brilliant nine-foot totem pole...

'It took me six weeks of steady chipping with an adze,' she said, 'and then there's all the carving and sand-papering and the final painting. My children all want me to become famous,' she grinned. 'They think that if I were famous, we'd have lots of money. They keep saying, Mummy, when will you be famous?'

From relative obscurity to the beginnings of recognition in just a couple of years. Things were looking up! Portions of her address to the conference held at UBC communicate something of her feelings, her ambitions and that she cared deeply about what she was doing.

UBC Address

'During the time that I've been selling some of my work and in the course of meeting some of the people who deal in Indian art work, I have come across some very odd ideas concerning it. When I was asked to speak at this conference, I saw a golden opportunity to present my side of the picture.

The point of mine, which I shall endeavour to illustrate, deals with the idea that efforts should be confined to the preservation of the old work. This idea is a great fallacy where the art of my people is concerned! If our art is dead, then it is fit only to be mummified... packed into mortuary boxes, and tucked away in museums!

To me, the art is a living symbol of the gaiety, the laughter, and the love of colour of my people—a day-to-day reminder that even we had something of glory and honour, before the white man came. Our art continues to live, for not only is it part and parcel of us, but can be a powerful factor in combining the best part of Indian culture into the fabric of a truly Canadian art form.

When the white man came, he brought with him saws, axes, hatchets, steel chisels and knives—paints in brilliant white, red, green and yellow. There was no involved question of propriety—as to whether the new tools should be used... rather, they were seized on, avidly, and with startling results!

The golden age of totem art had arrived—totems sprouted at every village where formerly there had been but few—chiefs vied with one another in the giving of potlatches, making work for artists who flourished and plied their trade. New forms evolved... in short, the art was a living art. New techniques were adopted, new materials incorporated, new ideas were welcomed and used. I can find no instance where an idea, a material, or a tool was not used simply because it had not been used before.

Unfortunately, then began a period in which this growing and living manifestation of my people's artistry was partially destroyed. Because of the economic, religious and other factors too numerous to mention at this time, an attempt was made to suppress the potlatch. The suppression of the potlatch emasculated the creative ability of the whole nation. The production of art was so closely coupled with giving of the potlatch that, without it, the art withered and almost died.

Were it not for the interest created by the tourist trade, the universities and the museums, we would no longer have any of our people capable of producing this art.

We are gathered here at this conference to attempt to bring about, among other things, a resurgence of the creativity of the native people. I strongly emphasize a point and, here, make it also my plea;

IF THE ART OF MY PEOPLE IS TO TAKE ITS RIGHTFUL PLACE BESIDE OTHER CANADIAN ART, IT MUST BE A LIVING MEDIUM OF EXPRESSION!

We, the Indian artist, must be allowed to create. We must be allowed new and modern techniques... new and modern tools... new and modern materials. For, in every instance, creative capacity has increased, following the discovery and use of better materials. I don't mean that we should disregard the old, only that we should be allowed the new.

I'd like to take the time to briefly examine some of the problems that I've encountered in attempting to produce my work.

In my family, carving was a means of livelihood. My grandfather was Charlie James—the famous 'Yakuglas'. He carved for over forty years. To his stepson, Mungo Martin, he taught the rudiments of his art... and we, his grandchildren, were literally, brought up amongst his work. Totems were our daily fare, they bought our food and furnished our clothing. There was no problem of sale, since his work was eagerly sought after.

Now the situation is different. Curio dealers have so cheapened the art in their efforts to profit, that I doubt if one could find a single household where the authenticity of the art is important to them. I have strived, in all my work, to retain the authentic, but I find it difficult to obtain even a portion of the price necessary to do a really fine piece of work.

This being so, it's difficult to blame my contemporaries for trying to get enough from their work to live on... though I believe they are wrong in cheapening their heritage. Certainly, great work could be produced by the native people, if a true appreciation of their art could be instilled into the general public. Only when there is an adequate response to efforts to retain the best of our art, will it be possible to train the younger generation to appreciate their own cultural achievements.

As far as applying this art to everyday living... I believe it can be used to stunning effect on tapestry, textiles, sportswear and in jewellery. Many pieces of furniture lend themselves admirably to Indian designs. Public buildings, large restaurants and halls have already begun to utilize some of this art. We need only to have some sort of an organization to which architects, builders and manufacturers could go to guarantee authentic products. Both my husband and myself stand ready to contribute... we have plans and are willing to share.

I strongly believe that the Indian people, as a whole, would gladly share... if only the dignity and honour of their personal crests could be preserved. And so, we look confidently to the future... to bring a fuller, a better, a more dignified existence to the Native people of Canada. I personally, look forward to being a part of the movement which brings these things to pass.'

Ellen Neel,
April, 1948

The effect of Ellen's plea was dramatic. Far from falling on deaf ears her voice was heard by a number of people who believed in what she said, and, more importantly, some of these people were in a position to help out. A few months after the UBC conference, the 'Native Voice', (an 'Indian' newspaper, and the official organ of the Native Brotherhood of B.C.) reported in part:

ELLEN TO TEACH INDIAN ART

Native Voice, 1948.

A matter of great importance to the Native people of British Columbia has recently taken place in Vancouver. At the recent conference on Indian affairs held at the University of British Columbia, it was repeatedly pointed out that the native people would much prefer an opportunity to help themselves.

Such an opportunity has recently been given to our Ellen by the Board of Park Commissioners of the City of Vancouver, B.C.

Realizing that perhaps more tourists go to Stanley Park than to any other single area in British Columbia, and to the tourists, Indian art is perhaps the greatest drawing card in the province. The Parks Board moved with commendable speed after the conference pointed the way. Appointing Mr. Rowe Holland as committee of one to interview Mrs. Ellen Neel, the Parks Board set in motion the machinery to give Indian artists an opportunity to sell their work in Stanley Park.

In an agreement with Ellen and her husband, Edward, both formerly of Alert Bay and more recently from Vancouver, the Board of Park Commissioners have placed at their disposal a large workshop in Stanley Park.

This shop is located at Third Beach, just a stone's throw to the site of the Pauline Johnson Memorial.

Here among the towering trees, with the sound of the sea waves gently lapping and in a place where native people may have held their potlatches, eaten their barbequed salmon and steamed clams since time immemorial, Ellen and her husband will make the first effort to conscientiously attempt the resuscitation of the Old Indian Arts.

As soon as volume will allow, there will be an opportunity for other artists to work with them and an attempt will be made to interest the younger people in this part of their heritage.

To Ellen, this opportunity is a challenge and a great responsibility.

This was a busy year for Ellen and Ted and their young family. The business had been named 'Totem Art Studios' and events were happening briskly around them. That summer, Ellen and her young sons worked on a large pole at the Pacific National Exhibition. The giant annual fair held in Vancouver. Thousands of people watched daily as the pole took shape and a small card proclaimed that the work was being done by 'Ellen Neel and the Totem Carvers'. A young girl from eastern Canada, asked Ellen about the pole and, as Ellen explained the meaning of the crest figures and how the tools were used in carving, the crowd drew closer to hear.

When she had finished, the young girl asked hesitantly, if she could have Ellen's autograph. Ellen took a pen out of her pocket and glanced about for a piece of paper. Impulsively, she reached down and picked up a fragrant cedar chip. 'Better than just an autograph. You can take a piece of the pole home with you.' She signed the large chip with a flourish. Before the fair closed, Ellen Neel had signed hundreds of 'totem pole chips' for the demanding crowds. On the last day of the PNE, the Neel family arrived in the morning to find that a large rosette and ribbon had been pinned to the still unfinished totem. The exhibition judges had given it the sculpture award.

As the Neels had hoped, orders came in as a result of the Pacific National Exhibition display—primarily orders for small batches of tourist poles from various souvenir shop proprietors—but also some commissions for good, carefully done pieces. For example, a

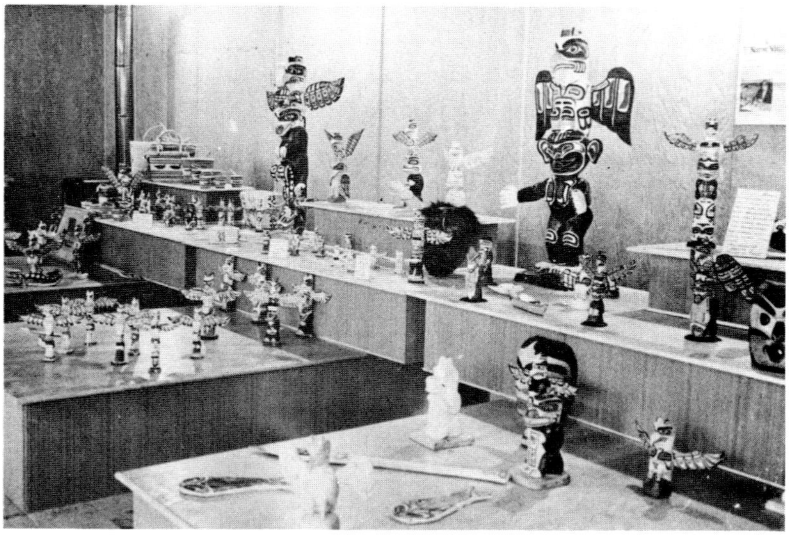

Plate 87: **Part of the show-room at Ferguson Point in Stanley Park. (Vancouver, c. 1949. Photo: Courtesy Neel family.)**

model pole was commissioned by a director of social services in the province of Quebec. He ordered it as a gift for a friend, a monk in France whose monastery held a fine art collection from around the world.

In the fall of 1948, Totem Art Studios completed a 16-foot thunderbird totem. The large pole with outstretched wings was carved for the Alma Mater Society of the University of British Columbia as a gift from Ellen and Ted Neel.

The presentation ceremony was carried out in the centre of a football stadium to an enthusiastic crowd of over 6,000 fans, there to see the UBC 'Thunderbirds' football team play. The presentation was made by Chief William Scow, of Alert Bay, President of the Native Brotherhood of B.C. He wore full ceremonial regalia and when he spoke to the crowd, he said in part:

'On behalf of Ellen and Edward Neel and with the full consent and approval of our tribal council and our people, I present this totem to the Alma Mater Society of this University. I give you also the right to use the name 'Thunderbird' for your team. This is according to

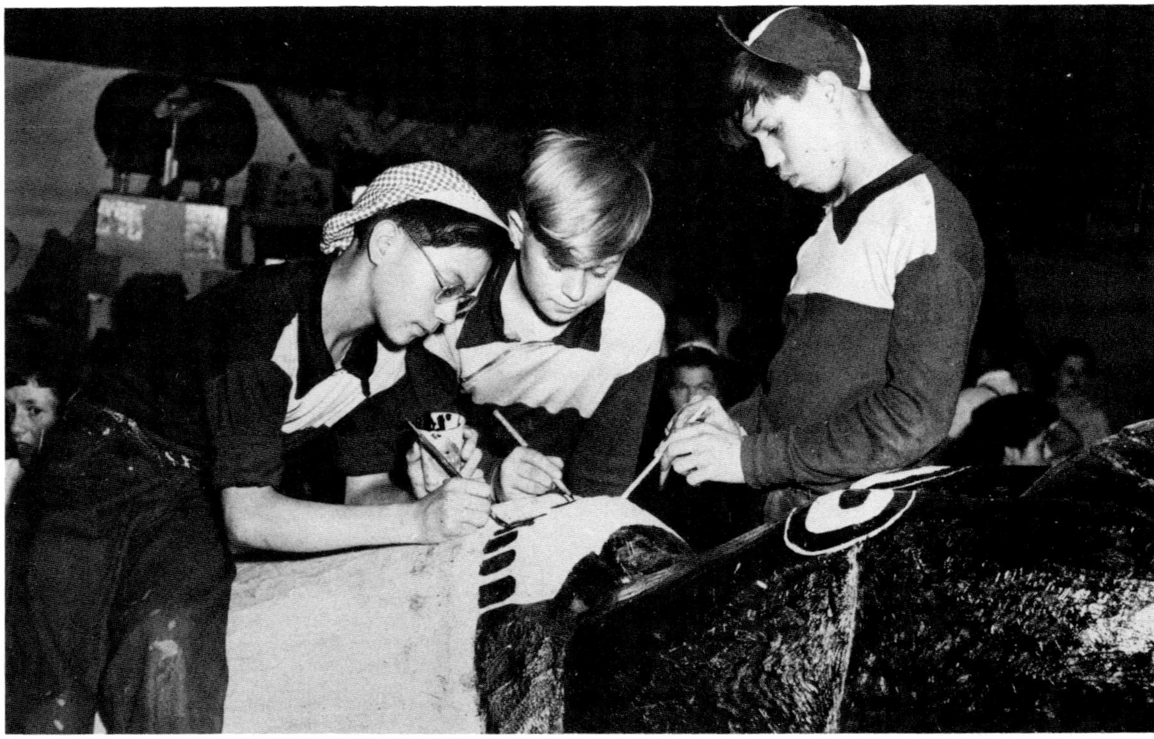

***Plate 88:* The boys work on a large pole at the Pacific National Exhibition. Left to right: Dave, Bobby and Ted Neel. (Vancouver, 1948. Photo: Courtesy Neel family.)**

the laws of my people and (the use of the name) is therefore legal for the first time. The totem has been carved for you by our two best tribal carvers. It has a long and an honourable history, a totem of which your team has every right to be proud. It is yours now, and if you follow the precepts accepted with it, you cannot fail.'

Ellen later said, 'Both Ted and I wanted the university to have a real totem, one given directly from the native people and one to which they have the rights under the old customs.' The University of British Columbia had given her a chance, earlier in the year, and Ellen picked this appropriate method of showing her appreciation.

That summer, Totem Art Studios was contracted to begin restoration of a group of old Kwakiutl totem poles for the Department of Anthropology, University of B.C. After lengthy discussions with a committee comprised of Professor Hunter Lewis, Dr. Harry Hawthorn, and Professor Geoffery Andrew, Ellen agreed to undertake this formidable task—with some misgivings. The summer was 'tourist season' and even though the restoration project would enhance her reputation in the academic world, it wouldn't put much in the way of food on the table. Economics dictated that the family should concentrate on carving at the Stanley Park workshop during the summer, but Ellen agreed to spend at least part of the summer on the restoration project.

Ellen worked hard that summer and the results were impressive. She tackled the restoration of four large poles from Fort Rupert; a frontal pole depicting the raven and thunderbird, a house post showing a bear holding a human head, an eagle crest pole, and finally a pole carved by her grandfather, Charlie James.

It must have given Ellen a good deal of pleasure to work on a pole carved by her grandfather, and this was a good one. It was carved about sixteen years before Ellen's birth. The figures were: a human at the top, thunderbird, Sisiyutł, man holding a copper, and a raven. Charlie James carved it when he was a young man, at Fort Rupert, and half a century later, his granddaughter worked to repair it.

Once into the restoration project, two things became apparent; the tourist sales in Stanley Park were suffering badly; and patching up old decayed poles was an incredibly difficult job to do properly. There was only so much that could be done with decayed wood, and even after an entire area was replaced and repainted, it was still, obviously, a patchwork job.

Before long, the idea of copying the old poles evolved. Leave the damaged, decayed originals in the condition that the years had brought on them and replace them with new poles, exact to the last detail, that would be as the originals were when they were first carved. This process would have the advantage of leaving the old university owned poles in their original condition for later study by scholars as well as providing poles that could be erected in select areas for the enjoyment of the public.

Dr. Hawthorn was first to point out that many of the old poles in advanced stages of deterioration in various villages could then be salvaged before they finally crumbled back into the forest soil. In the past, the various museums and universities had purchased them from disinterested families or simply taken them away from abandoned villages. With the Native people's ever-growing awareness of the fragility of their heritage, they would no longer allow the few tangible pieces of evidence to be removed and squirreled away in dusty storage sheds. But, if they were offered replicas—new, handsome poles that would last another half century at least—then surely the band councillors would consent to the removal of the originals.

The new plan was enthusiastically embraced and it only remained to find the funding and get started. The scheme was a sound one and any carver would be proud to be involved in such a worthwhile project, but it presented a problem to Ellen Neel. She was a carver, but more, she was an artist. She wanted to turn out

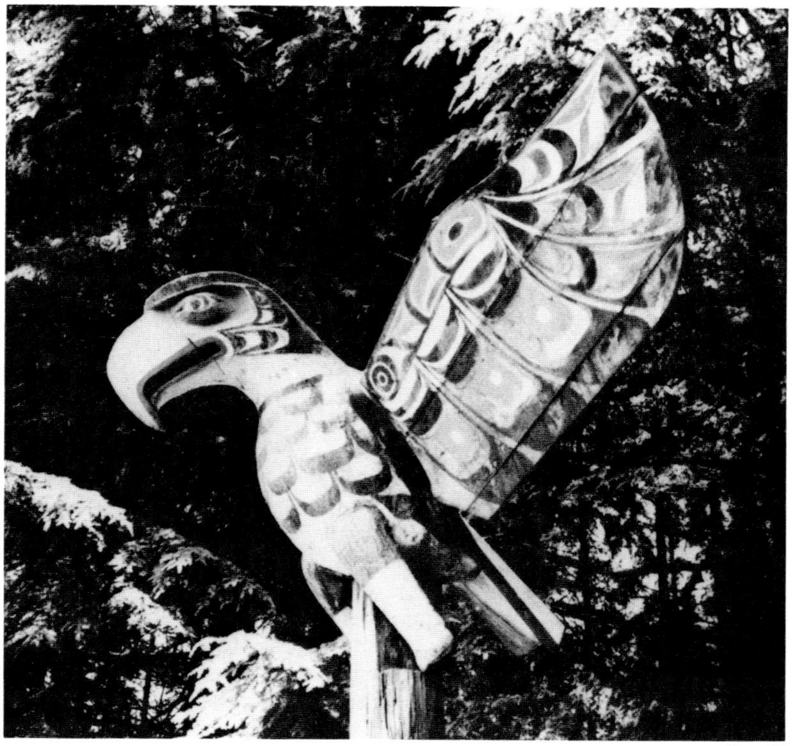

Plate: 89

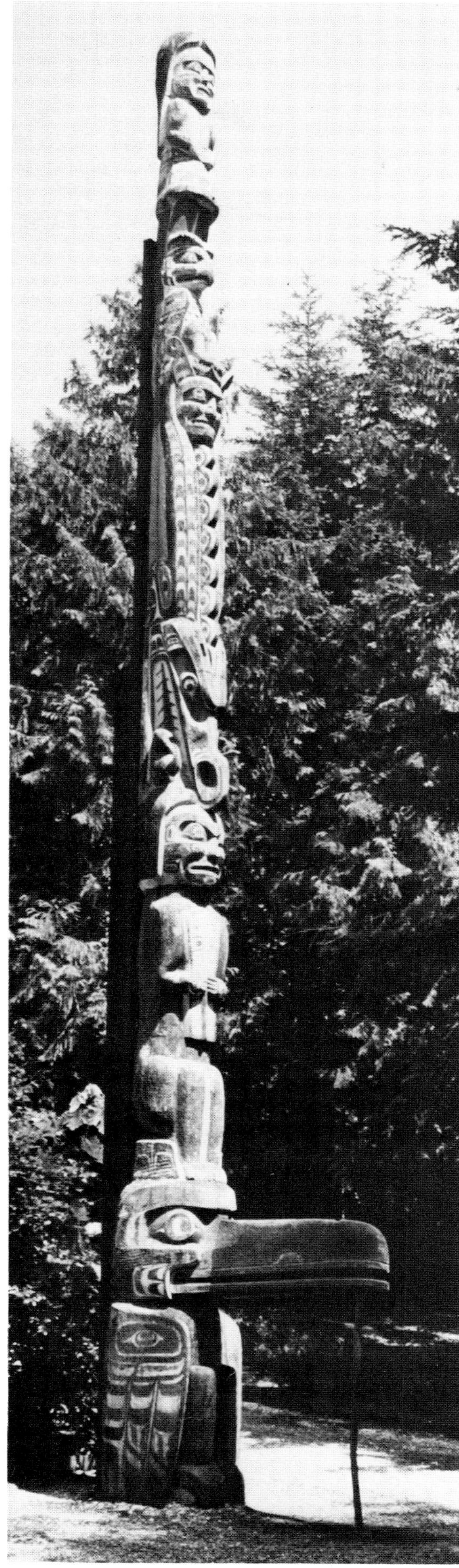

Plate: 90

Plate 89: A 'Kulus' or young Thunderbird crest figure from Fort Rupert. This pole was purchased for the University of British Columbia by Marius Barbeau, in 1947. Originally located at Fort Rupert. The restoration work of Ellen Neel is evident in the painting of the wings. (Vancouver, c. 1960. Photo: Courtesy U.B.C.)

Plate 90: A carving by Charlie James—carved around 1900 and subsequently restored by Ellen Neel and Mungo Martin. Shown at Totem Park, U.B.C., Vancouver, B.C. (Vancouver, 1950. Photo: U.B.C.)

new, original work that would bear her name and allow her particular art style to continue to develop. As she had passionately stated the year before, Ellen didn't believe that the efforts of an artist 'should be confined solely to the preservation of the old work'. If she agreed to undertake the resoration and duplication project, it would be a full-time job.

Her growing list of other commitments would suffer, the exhibitions that were desperately needed to bring her work before the public would be neglected. Yet the art was still speculative, in spite of a growing appreciation, whereas the UBC project promised a steady income, albeit, a meagre one.

More importantly, the restoration work should be done, and it should be done by both an artist and a skilled craftsman. If Ellen believed any of the things that she had been saying, over the past few years, she had to agree that the work should go forward. But—to whom should it be entrusted?

The dilemma resolved itself when they talked to her uncle, Mungo Martin, who was visiting Ellen at the time. They asked him if he would be interested in taking over Ellen's work at UBC. Interested? He was delighted.

Trained in the same school as Ellen, he was a master carver of large poles. In the forties he had found less and less demand for the application of his skills and had been forced to turn his hand to other methods of earning a livelihood. To have the opportunity to work again in the field of his choice: Yes, he would be glad to stay in Vancouver.

The decade of the fifties was an important time for the Neel family and for Totem Art Studios. A time in which many of the early goals would be achieved and replaced by new challenges.

In the spring of 1950, Ellen was commissioned to handle the decor of the foyer for a new hotel at Harrison Hot Springs, B.C. The project was a significant one to Ellen. It marked the first time that she could plan the integration of her traditional carvings within a decidedly contemporary setting. A number of detailed sketches were made and the final designs were enthusiastically approved by the hotel owners. Then came the time consuming work of translating the drawings into finished pieces. The final assembly was quite formidable, comprising two eleven-foot totem poles, two four-foot totems and a total of sixteen smaller decorator pieces. All of these were skillfully blended into the ultra-modern surroundings.

The opening was a tremendous success and people pressed around Ellen, eager to praise her and congratulate her on her work. Ellen was delighted, of course, although she tempered her delight by remarking that her efforts would probably vanish in a couple of years with a change of owners or a change in the hotel's motif. A realistic appraisal perhaps, but on this particular point, she was wrong. Her work was still there a quarter of a century later.

During that year, Ellen was active in a number of areas not connected with Indian Art. In the late summer of 1950, she became the first native woman to hold office in a major political organization. She was elected to the executive board of the Vancouver Centre Liberal Association—a support group for one of Canada's strongest political parties. By all accounts, she handled her duties well, finding time among an ever-growing list of art commissions, tourist poles, Totemland presentation poles, silk screens, and designs for future lines.

In the fall, Ellen's work was represented at an exhibition held at the Montreal Museum of Fine Arts (in the eastern Canadian province of Quebec). Two pieces, a traditional Kwakiutl dance mask and a more contemporary totem were well-received and resulted in several orders.

In 1951, Totem Art Studios carved a pole that was shown on national television in the United States. The pole was carved under commission from the Vancouver Tourist Association and presented to Robert Q. Lewis during his television programme 'The Show Goes On'. Lewis was an avid collector of totem poles and the presentation made in New York added, as he put it, 'the finest piece to my collection'.

Shortly after this, Ellen produced another small pole that was particularly intricate and well finished. It was presented as a wedding present to Lord and Lady Selkirk in London, by some Vancouver friends.

1951 was a relatively quiet year (in terms of major efforts). As well as the commissions mentioned, Ellen also had her work exhibited at an international trade fair in Toronto. The Neels had hoped that the success of the hotel foyer design the year before would attract other interior design assignments, but none materialized.

Perhaps it was this levelling of activity that prompted Ellen and Ted to make a fairly drastic change in the following year. They decided to stop carving at the Ferguson Point workshop in Stanley park and use it strictly for summer sales. The decision was primarily economic. Ferguson Point was an idyllic setting and a good place to sell finish products, but it was hardly an efficient set-up to produce carvings in any quantity. The key was quantity.

The large poles and the commissioned pieces brought a good feeling of pride and built Ellen's reputation as an artist, but the lowly tourist poles, the 'idiot sticks' as some experts disparagingly referred to them, paid the rent and put food on the table. While the market for good carvings at high prices was unpredictable, the market for a complete line of souvenir poles was increasing. The prices were low, but the market was there. If they could increase production—double or triple it—then Totem Art Studios would become a commercially viable business. It would allow volume ordering in advance of the tourist seasons and keep everyone busy during the normally slow winter months. To Ted Neel fell the responsibility of convincing the various tourist shops to place firm orders for given quantities of poles prior to the season in which they would be sold.

To get these vendors to commit to stocking a number of pieces was a difficult job. To accomplish it, Ted had to promise low prices, good quality and guarantee a reliable, consistent supply.

Ellen's job would be to design a line of poles in various sizes, ranging in height from six inches to eighteen inches. The degree of complexity and quality had to increase as the poles got to the larger sizes, yet the smallest to the largest should be identifiable as the same basic pole. Three alternate bottom figures were to be used, each with a thunderbird on top; Dzunuk̲̓wa (wild woman of the woods), the killer whale and the bear.

All the poles were complete with out-spread wings on the thunderbird, a base and a small decal on the back explaining the origin of the pole. The small poles were very simple, with no detailed features and simple, stylized painting. The large poles were carefully done with a prominent hooked beak on the thunderbird, carved nose and mouth on the Dzunuk̲̓wa (or 'Noona' as it was dubbed by the Neels) separated jaws, fully carved recurve on the whale's tail, and the like.

The painting was carefully done on the larger poles—not the same degree of intricacy as the commissioned pieces—but the same amount of care and precision.

A good reason to believe that the time was right to produce a large number of low cost poles was the capacity and abilities of Ellen's sons. The youngest, thirteen and the oldest, well into his teens, were good carvers. They would do the bulk of carvings up to the finish sanding and Ellen would do the painting, a skill at which she excelled. Dave Neel could carve nearly as well as his mother by the time he was twelve or so, but no one could touch Ellen when it came to painting.

The Neels had been living on Glen Drive for several years and while most of the carving had been done at Stanley Park, they had a small area of the basement cleared for carving at home in the winter. Ted located a wood-working shop a few blocks from the house. It was vacant and boasted an enormous band saw, several other power tools and a large loft where the finished poles could be sprayed with lacquer. It was ideal. The Neels rented it as an integral part of the 'go-commercial' scheme. A larger area was cleared in the basement of the Glen Drive house. All the scrapbooks, boxes of junk and large, partially-completed pieces were pushed to the side, and the basement became the focus of carving.

The morning that I knocked on the door and told Ellen that I wanted to carve totem poles, was the first of many, many summer mornings that I would race up the block and pound on the door, and then stand there flushed and out of breath. Theo and Cora would usually still be sound asleep upstairs, but Bitty was generally skittering around the house while the old man (even Ellen called Ted the 'old man') would be sitting at the dining room table, reading the paper. The boys would be just finishing breakfast, or already in the basement, carving.

That basement was probably the greatest basement in the whole world! The smell was always the tang of freshly cut yellow cedar—cool and acid and in sharp contrast to the warm, lingering smells coming from the kitchen above. The basement was full of totem pole blanks (the band sawn pieces of wood that would become totem poles), partially completed carvings, poles with the beaks broken off (a constant hazard), boxes of pole patterns, other boxes with woven cedar bark sticking mysteriously out of the seams, big poles, small poles, dance masks, old carvings, totemistic paintings, knives, adzes, chisels and galvanized wash tubs with bright yellow blanks floating in them.

It must have taken me three months to explore every corner of that basement. I'd be filled with resolve to poke through everything but I'd always get side-tracked looking at old scrapbooks or perhaps spending a half hour examining a Charlie James carving. I guess, in reality, it was a dark and gloomy old basement. It had a dirt floor and a liberal layer of dust over everything outside the small carving area, but I believed it was the most fantastic treasure house that anyone could ask for. Can you imagine turning over a stained, grimy plank only to find the other side held a beautiful carved thunderbird, with every line and cut precise. Mungo Martin showing one of his great-nephews the art of incised carving.

Mungo's nephews, Ellen's sons, 'the boys'. Dave, the oldest, Ted and Bobby. Nice guys! Kind to me, patient beyond belief for young men, artistic, talented and always humourous. They walked a path of responsibility for the work that had to be done, but took countless side forays in the wild undergrowth of growing up. The oldest was only a few years older than me, but at that time of life a few years are nearly light years. They were becoming young men and I was still a kid, but what a pleasure it was then and over the years, to learn with them and from them, and to discover some new things together.

Early in 1953, the Neel family completed a large totem pole under commission from a museum in Copenhagen, Denmark. The pole was eleven feet high and comprised a Thunderbird with outspread wings, a seabear, a killer whale and a sculpin at the bottom. The influence of the teachings of Ellen's grandfather, Charlie James, was evident both in the selection of figures and method of handling them, the killer whale twisting sinuously around the pole and the bulbous head of the sculpin forming a natural base. The pole was dispatched by ship and everyone relaxed when it was safely on board.

In 1953 Ellen's great-uncle Mungo Martin gave a potlatch to dedicate an old-style house that he had constructed at Thunderbird Park in Victoria, B.C. (The details of this dedication are given in a following chapter).

Mungo had assumed his most important name—'Nakapankam'—by this time, but he was still called 'DATSA' (grandfather) by Ellen Neel and her family. It was 'DATSA' who insisted that Ellen's children be given proper names at his potlatch, in the Kwakiutl fashion.

Plate 91: Ellen puts finishing touches on an 11-foot totem destined for a museum in Denmark. Pole was commissioned by a Danish shipping firm for a new museum's international collection. (January, 1953. Photo: Vancouver Province.)

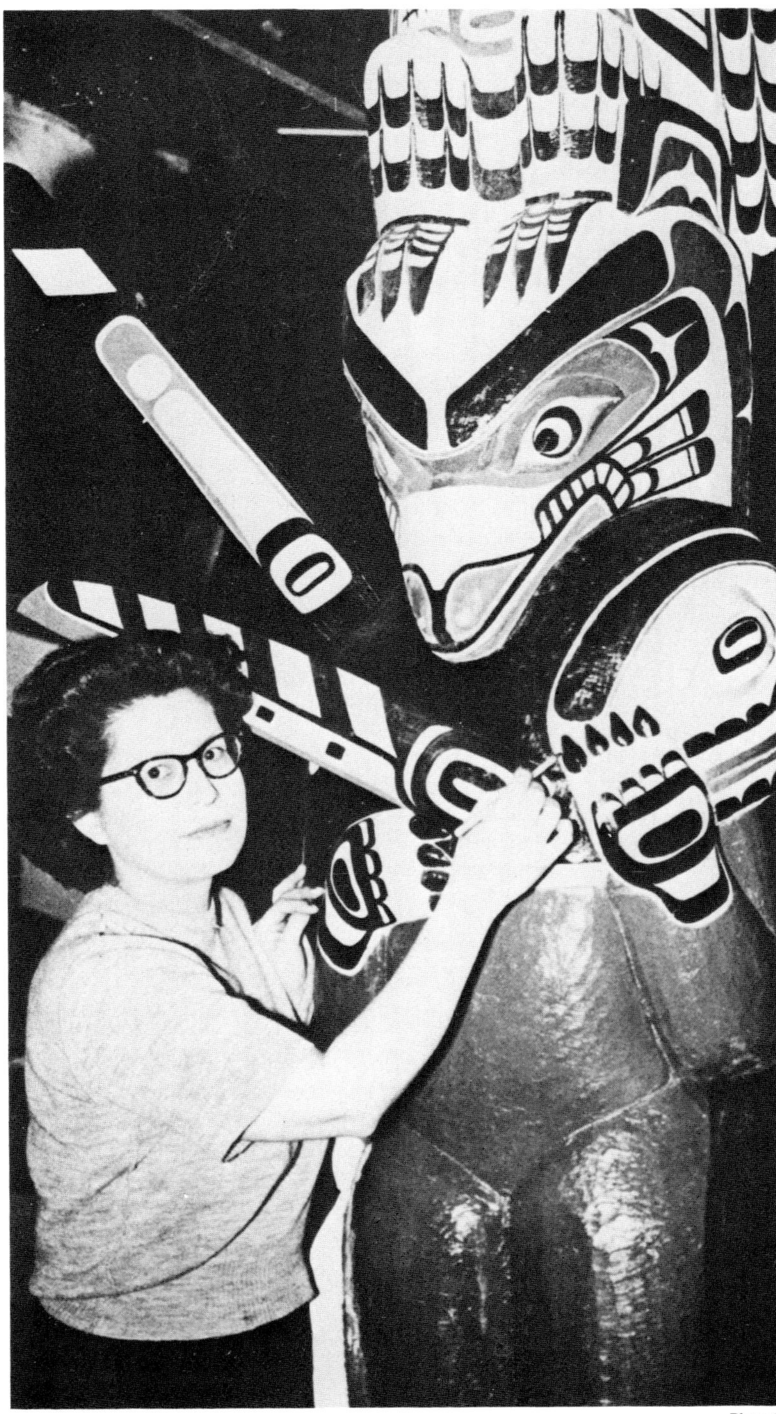

Plate: 91

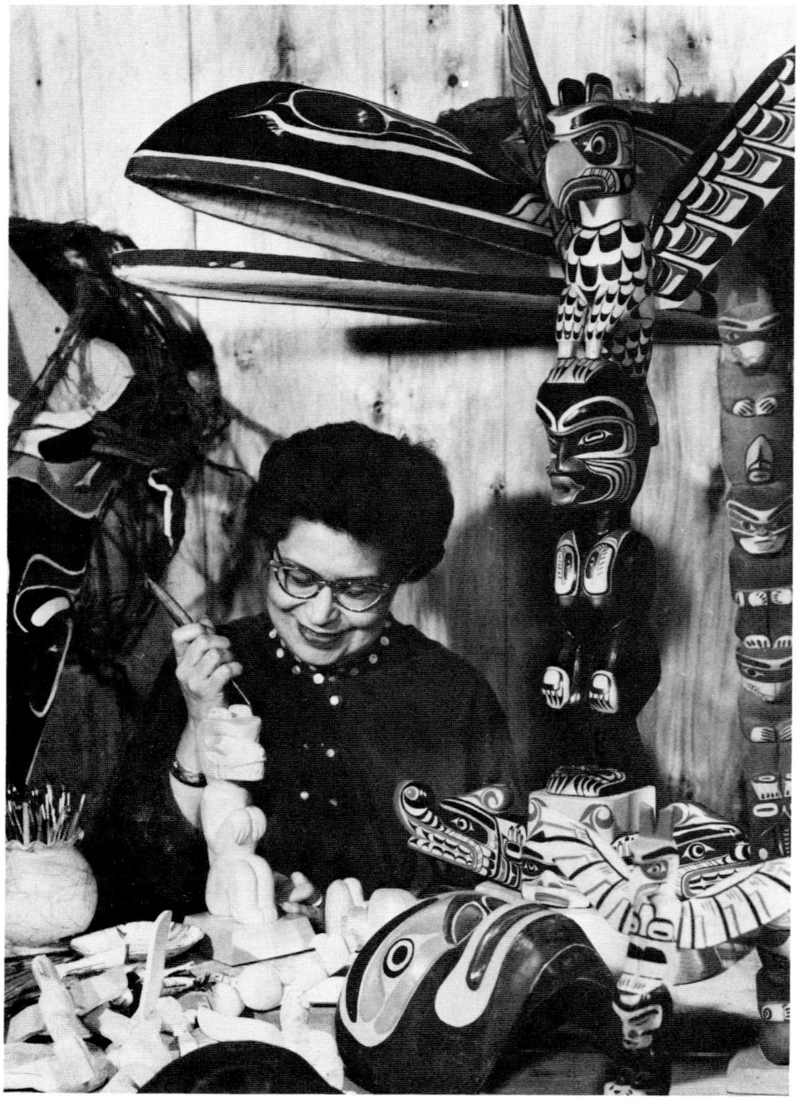

***Plate 92:* Ellen works on a bear figure. Note the large commissioned pole on Ellen's right. The degree of detail on the Thunderbird and Dzunuk̲wa is evident. The smaller pole in the lower right of the photo is also a Thunderbird and Dzunuk̲wa, but was designed for the low-cost, tourist market. (Photo: Jim Ryan.)**

The affair was exciting for the Neel children; watching the various masked dancers, the 'wild man' and particularly when it came time to receive their names. Mungo spoke in Kwak̓wala and gave a brief history of each name as he bestowed it. Dave Neel became 'T'łat'ła̱ła̱'wis'. Ted Neel was called 'Mas'ma̱wisag̱a̱me". Bobby got 'X̱ix̱a'niyus'. Bitty was named for her greatgrandmother 'Na̱gedzi'. Theo was named after her grandmother, Ellen Neel's mother, 'Lalaxs'a' and, finally Cora Neel was called 'K̲wa'xa̱lal'. Ellen wrote these names down in one of her ever-present little memo books... and as the formal oratory progressed, Ellen scribbled snatches of translations about 'the legend of the beginning of our family, in the time before the flood'—the pencil notes now give no clue whether 'our family' pertained to a direct lineage or the Kwakiutl people in general. All in all, it was quite an evening, but then... back to the tourist poles...

The efforts to produce a uniform line of tourist poles had been quite successful and the retail price list and illustrated product description of Totem Art Studios was mimeographed and sent out to interested customers across the country. Essentially, it consisted of a limited selection of figures for the cheap souvenir poles, a greater selection of available figures in the more expensive poles and masks, and a flat rate per foot for large to full-size totems.

Some examples from the Totem Art Studio's brochure:

Totem Poles

1. Thunderbird and either: bear, whale or Dsonogwa (wild woman) complete with wings and base—in white pine.
Size: 3/4"×3/4"×6 1/2" .... each $2.25

2. Totemland totem—small size. Thunderbird, earth, man. Complete with wings and base—in white pine.
Size: 1"×1 3/8"×8" O.A. .... each $4.50

3. Spread winged Thunderbird and bear totem.
Size: 2"×2"×10 3/4" .... each $7.20

4. Spread winged Thunderbird and Dsonogwa (wild woman of the woods).
Size: 2"×2"×12" .... each $9.00

5. Spread winged Thunderbird and Dsonogwa with human head between.
Size: 2"×2"×14" .... each $10.80

The following are very well made totems in yellow cedar, with the wings swept back 15 degrees and upward 20 degrees. They are painted, then lacquered so that they can be handled, a very fine piece of art work.

6. Thunderbird and either: grizzly bear, sea bear, whale, Dsonogwa, beaver or sea otter.
Size: 2"×2 3/4"×12" .... each $25.00

7. Thunderbird and either: grizzly bear, sea bear, whale, Dsonogwa, beaver, sea otter or Totemland pole (Thunderbird, earth, man).
Size: 2 1/2"×4"×16" .... each $40.00

Masks

Flat-back masks, for wall decoration, flat-backed either stained or natural wood grain.

8. First man or Dsonogwa
Size: 6"×7 1/2" .... each $14.40

9. As above, but curved back
Size: 7"×8 1/2" .... each $18.00

10. First man or Dsonogwa
Size: 8"×10" .... each $31.80

11. Grouse mask
Size: 8"×10" .... each $36.00

12. Fool dancer
Size: 8"×10" .... each $36.00

13. Thunderbird
Size: 8"×10" .... each $36.00

14. West wind
Size: 10"×12" .... each $40.00

Painted Masks

These masks are made of red cedar, curved back, painted with an overall coat of off-white, then painted in the old colours of red, green, yellow, brown, grey and black.

15. Either: First man, Dsonogwa, West wind, Grouse, Fool dancer, or Thunderbird.
Size: 10"×12" .... each $50.00

Large Poles

16. **Specification:** All poles carved in Western red cedar. *Type A*—is fully carved, painted with

a base coat of white, then finished in traditional colours. *Type B*—fully carved but left natural as to ground, then painted in traditional colours. *Type C*—fully carved then all detail such as teeth, eyes, claws, etc. carved in, wood stained and varnished.

Prices per lineal foot—all types.

Square timber size	Price/ft
6″×6″	$40.00
8″×8″	$55.00
8″×10″	$60.00
10″×10″	$66.65
12″×12″	$80.00

17. **Yellow cedar totems:** *Type D*—fully carved, painted in traditional colours onto the natural wood, (a beautiful light beige in colour) then varnished or lacquered. Wings of thunderbird swept back and up at an angle of 45 degrees. All details carved in before painting—various figures available.

Overall height	Price each
14″	$30.00
16″	$40.00
18″	$50.00
21″	$65.00
24″	$80.00
32″	$120.00
36″	$150.00

Note that all sizes increase in square lumber size as they increase in height. Price is based on bulk, and is actually figured on the same formula as the larger poles.

That was the totem pole business in 1953-1954. Calculating prices and putting out a professional brochure was one thing; getting sales was quite another. The sales for the month of June, 1954 consisted of 39 small tourist poles for $113.90 and one set of carved table legs for $125.00—for a total of $238.90. That was considered not a bad month!

In 1954, the family took stock and made out an inventory of all the pieces in the house at 348 Glen Drive, in the display room at Ferguson Point, and those pieces loaned to various displays, museums and clubs. The inventory was quite large. Over a thousand small tourist poles; about 200 in the larger sizes; 1 carved paddle; 7 carved ashtrays; 1 man-in-smoke-hole; 2 sets bookends; 4 rattles; 14 masks; 1 carved Indian seat; 1 chief's staff; 4 house posts; 2 lamps; 1 whale portal; 1 model house frame; and 1 set carved table legs.

I worry about those table legs... since the inventory was taken after June, what happened? Didn't the customer like them? Were they never picked up? Does that mean that June sales were actually only $113.90... or perhaps, flushed with the success of selling a set—another set was carved for inventory! None of the kids remember now. It was too long ago.

The inventory came to a grand total of $5,872.11. In the late spring, Ellen was commissioned to carve a five-

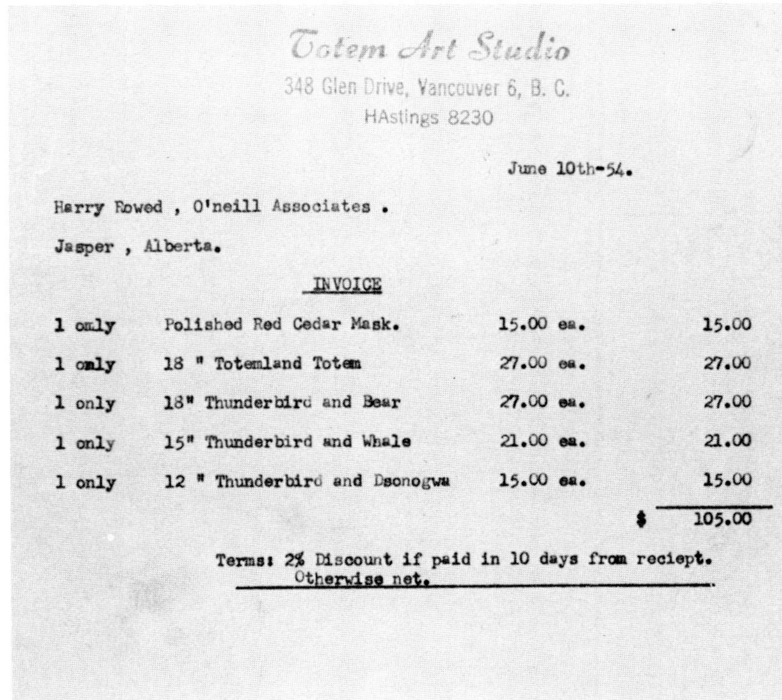

Totem Art Studio
348 Glen Drive, Vancouver 6, B. C.
HAstings 8230

June 10th-54.

Harry Rowed , O'neill Associates .

Jasper , Alberta.

INVOICE

1 only	Polished Red Cedar Mask.	15.00 ea.	15.00
1 only	18 " Totemland Totem	27.00 ea.	27.00
1 only	18" Thunderbird and Bear	27.00 ea.	27.00
1 only	15" Thunderbird and Whale	21.00 ea.	21.00
1 only	12 " Thunderbird and Dsonogwa	15.00 ea.	15.00
		$	105.00

Terms: 2% Discount if paid in 10 days from reciept.
Otherwise net.

***Plate 93:* The 'tourist pole' business in 1954. A sample invoice from Totem Art Studio. (Vancouver, c. 1954. Photo: Courtesy Neel family.)**

foot totem for a group of Boy Scouts in Welshpool, Wales. Donor of the pole was Senator W. Rupert Daves, a Canadian newspaper publisher from Kingston, Ontario and an honourary officer in the Clive Company of Boy Scouts. The thunderbird pole with a wing span of five feet was shipped nearly 6,000 miles from Vancouver, and crossed the Atlantic on board the liner *Empress of Scotland*. The newspapers enthusiastically described Ellen as 'famed totem pole carver' and 'attractive Indian native'.

A few weeks later, Dave Neel made the papers. There was a picture of him putting the finishing touches on what was billed as 'the world's smallest totem'. It also carried a miniature likeness of the famous comedian, Bob Hope, and it was presented to Hope when he appeared in Vancouver. Dave was sixteen at that time, and unquestionably a skilled carver and painter.

Special pieces like those two, helped break the threat of monotony but after the clippings had been pasted into the scrap book... it was back to the basement, and back to the tourist poles. No one complained though, things were going well, and besides, it was kind of fun... carving in the basement.

The boys were paid on a piece-work basis by Ellen and the old man. Every day after school, and on weekends they worked on tourist poles ranging from 'ten centers', six-inch poles completed in a few minutes to 12-inch poles that were worth a dollar a piece for roughing out. One of my proudest moments came the first time a couple of my poles got included in with the general output and the old man grudgingly handed me a dollar. I promptly used it to buy a family-load of double-scoop ice cream cones from the dairy across the street. Dave said, 'Jeez, old man, give the kid a couple of bucks. He musta done five whales this morning.' The old man fixed him with a baleful eye and said, 'Yeah, so you can con him out of it? Besides he probably ruined 10 blanks before he even finished one.' By the time the exchange got further I had already scuttled off to the basement to make myself inconspicuous.

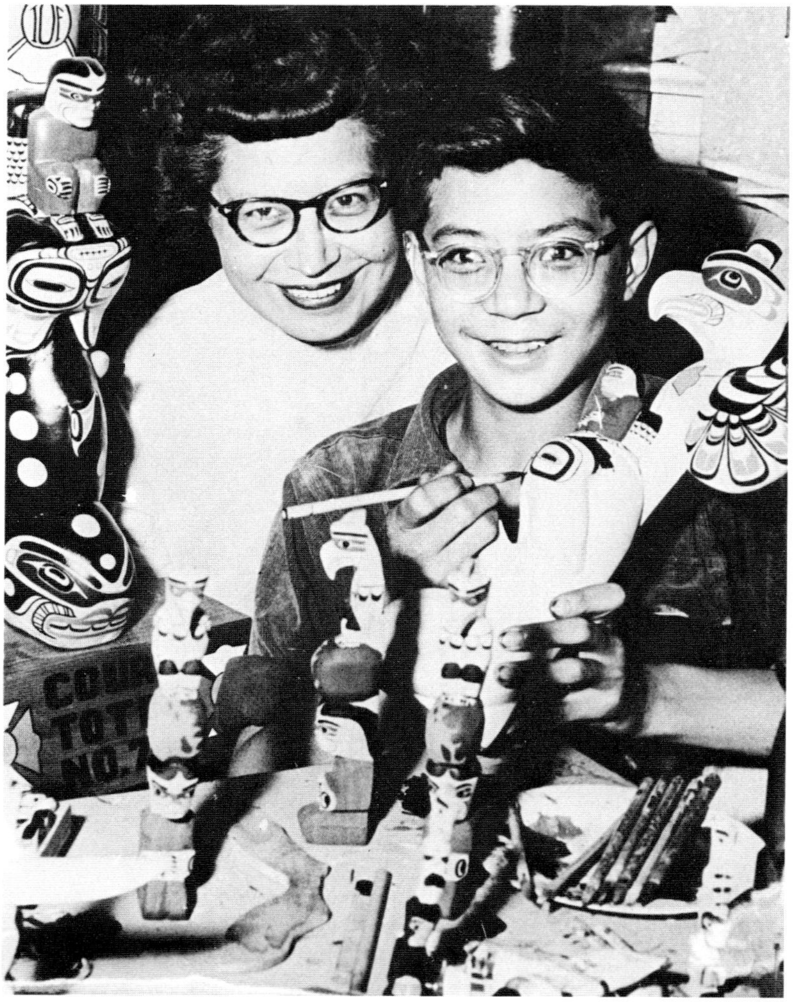

Plate: 94

Plate 94: Ellen and Dave Neel, August, 1953. Dave is painting a pole commissioned by the International Order of Foresters—another, similar pole for the Foresters is shown finished, on the left. (Vancouver, 1953. Photo: Vancouver Sun.)

Plate 95: 'The world's smallest totem'—or so they said! This miniature pole was carved by Dave Neel for presentation to comedian Bob Hope and bears Hope's 'ski-jump' likeness on the bottom figure. (Vancouver, 1954. Photo: Vancouver Sun.)

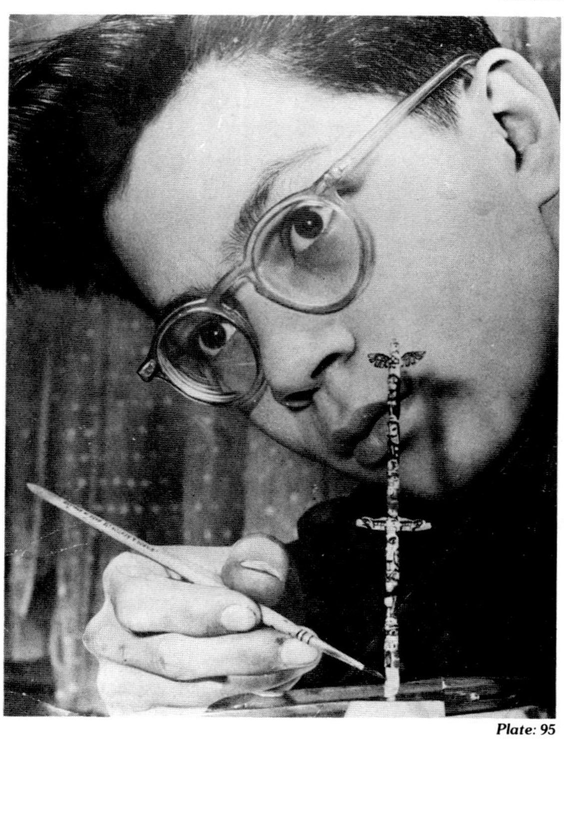

Plate: 95

Once the sweet smelling poles were roughed out they were taken to a rented wood-working shop a couple of blocks away for sanding. This was done on wheels that alternated brushes with flaps of fine sandpaper held in slots. You had to press hard on a rough area to sand it smooth, but the form stayed intact.

Then the poles were brought back to the house and Ellen would paint them. Occasionally, Cora and Theo would help on the tourist poles, but Ellen most often did the better pieces herself. Saucers with dried tempra-colours lay around the living room and Japanese lettering brushes were everywhere.

I would sit curled up on the couch sketching patterns, colours and combinations in my dog-eared notebook and asking Ellen questions—all kinds of questions. Her humour was generally good, except perhaps, early on Saturday mornings, and most of the questions were answered seriously. It was quite easy to unfocus your eyes and have the living room melt into a community house of long ago, particularly with the yellow cedar smell in the air and Ellen's soft voice describing how she had sat with her grandfather, Charlie James, learning her art.

It was art. No question about it. Certainly the tourist poles were bread and butter, but there was usually one or two commissioned pieces, and those were beautifully done. Dave did the roughing after Ellen had drawn it out and he would sometimes finish the carving while she supervised or Ellen would finish the fine carving herself and then do the painting.

Since the tourist poles were standard figures it was a real treat to watch something different—a whale man or a sea otter, come to life in intricate detail.

Often there would be the large 'Totemland' poles to do. This pole bridged the gap between traditional totem forms and a free expression of artistic creation. It depicted the thunderbird giving the world to the first man. It's a beautiful pole but I've often wondered if Ellen had her tongue in her cheek as she solemnly described how 'Kwa̱nkwa̱nxwa̱lige" the great thunderbird, gave the land mass of British Columbia to 'Bagwanam', the first man.

When asked if this pole was traditional or of an old design, she would blithely say it was an 'idea' pole or represented a concept, or translated an old legend. She laughed a lot about the Totemland poles, but I noticed that the large ones received a level of care in the carving and painting that was generally reserved for the best.

The Totemland poles were carved in much the same fashion as other poles commissioned by individual collectors and perhaps they can best provide a clear example of the specific procedures. The steps to produce a finished 'Totemland' pole were, in sequence:

Layout

The figures are laid out on a block of yellow cedar. Sometimes a cardboard template was used, but usually the figures were simply drawn free-hand, in soft lead pencil. A surrounding line was drawn, adjacent to the line of figures, to indicate the bandsaw cut. The position and depth of the side cuts were also drawn on the block.

Bandsaw Blank

Note that the bandsaw contours are located on the profile of the pole only. The side cuts are straight lines with no attempt made to delineate any contours. The position and depth of the side cuts are critical; too deep and the narrow sections of the pole will be too thin and weak; too shallow and the pole will appear blocky.

Roughing

A wide chisel is used to remove side wood to the depth of the side cuts. The form of the finished pole is determined at this stage and it is surprising just how much of the pole is completed with the chisel alone.

Carving

The finish carving was carried out in two stages, overall whittling to the the final form of the figures and detailed finishing, such as the thunderbird's 'horns' or in this case, the hands of the man. Note that the carving knife is pulled towards the carver for best control. Carving away ('pushing') is usually done with the thumbs of both hands steadying the knife. Carvers do cut themselves occasionally, but usually in 'carving away' because of the difficulty in controlling the blade in this position.

Sanding

The 'Totemland' poles were all sanded to satin smoothness. The face of the human is protected during sanding to avoid smoothing out the detailed facial cuts. Ellen Neel and other artists like the look of the carved pole, with minimum sanding, but the customers emphatically disagreed, and wanted everything sanded—to a point where sanding was often carried out to excess (in my opinion!).

Wing Preparation

The wings were cut from a tapered piece of yellow cedar—tapering from approximately ¼″ where they joined the body of the thunderbird, to about 3/16″ thick at the wing tip. The thick edge of the wing was cut at a 45 degree angle and dowel blocks installed by gluing and nailing. The dowel blocks were individually made to fit into mating holes drilled into the back of the thunderbird's 'shoulder' and positioned so that the wing swept upwards and outwards from the slight flat area left for this purpose, on the sides of the thunderbird's 'shoulders'. The result was a snug fit with no wobbling, yet the wings could be removed for transport, by simply pulling straight outwards on them. On all the Totemland poles, the fitting of the wings was a fine piece of craftsmanship.

Fabricate Base

The base was a simple block of yellow cedar with a screw hole drilled through it. The screw hole was deeply countersunk with a larger bit to allow access to the screw head. The base of the pole was hand-drilled to proper size to accept the threaded portion of the screw and a daub of glue was smeared on the base of the pole to prevent it from swivelling should the base screw loosen. (Sometimes a nail was driven in, in place of the screw, depending on how much time was available and who was installing the base!)

Painting

Painting was carried out using water colours and Chinese or Japanese lettering brushes. The colours were: black, vermillion, 'Indian' yellow (an orangish or deep yellow), viridian green and brown. The 'ocean' portion of the world was painted a lighter green, made by adding a little white to the viridian green. The chest of the thunderbird was painted with a simple feather design. Ellen sometimes used her crest, the Killer-whale, on the chest of Thunderbirds, as she had been taught by her grandfather—and as he sometimes did. But, on other pieces, not on the Totemland poles. The design is laid out very lightly in pencil, before painting and any pencil-lines not covered by paint can be removed later by a soft gum eraser.

Lacquering

The poles were given several coats of clear high-gloss lacquer for two purposes: to protect the water colours and to bring back the intensity of the dried paint. When the water colours dried they became much more pastel than they appear in the wet state. The lacquer brought the intensity back so it resembled enamel.

The 'Totemland' pole, as mentioned previously, is not a traditional Kwakiutl pole—although the Thunderbird and man figures are traditional and are shown in classic position. It was made to represent British Columbia—'Totemland'. Hence, the world globe and the northwest coastline. But more importantly, it was designed to be 'read'. The recipients of these totem poles most often wanted to know the 'story' the pole tells. It is pointless to explain the figures represent only crest figures or, more rarely, participants in a legend, story or event—not the event itself. So the Totemland pole was designed to bridge that gap. The thunderbird, its powerful wings spread in flight—grasping the world in its talons and lowering it onto the back of mankind, depicting 'The thunderbird giving the world to the first man'. This is highly visual and makes sense. Not dear to the hearts of purists, perhaps, but this is what Ellen was talking about when she spoke of the freedom to expand.

Totemland poles were designed for presentation to visiting dignitaries and celebrities since the poles were representative of 'Totemland'. One celebrity to whom Ellen enjoyed presenting her work was prima ballerina, Maria Tallchief. Maria Tallchief was the star of the Ballet Russe de Monte Carlo. To Ellen's delight, she was also the daughter of a full-blood Osage Chief from Oklahoma. They talked for hours at the Stanley Park shop and later, Ellen officially presented her with a Totemland pole, a gift of the City of Vancouver.

Plate 96: Dave Neel lays out a 'Totemland' design on a block of yellow cedar. (Vancouver, 1953. Photo: Vancouver Sun.)

Plate 97: Band-sawing laid-out block for 'Totemland' pole. (1979. Photo: B. Johnson.)

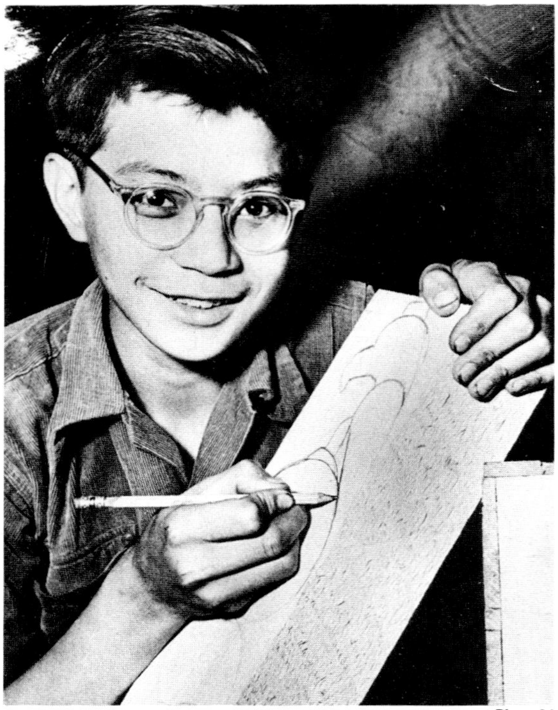

Plate: 96

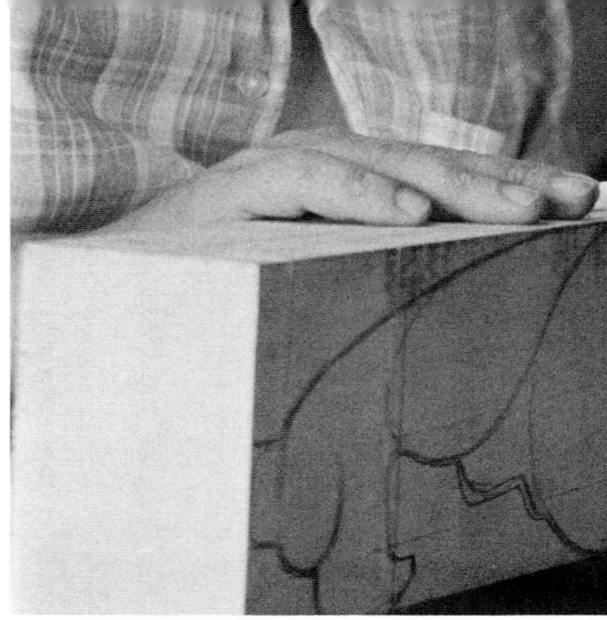

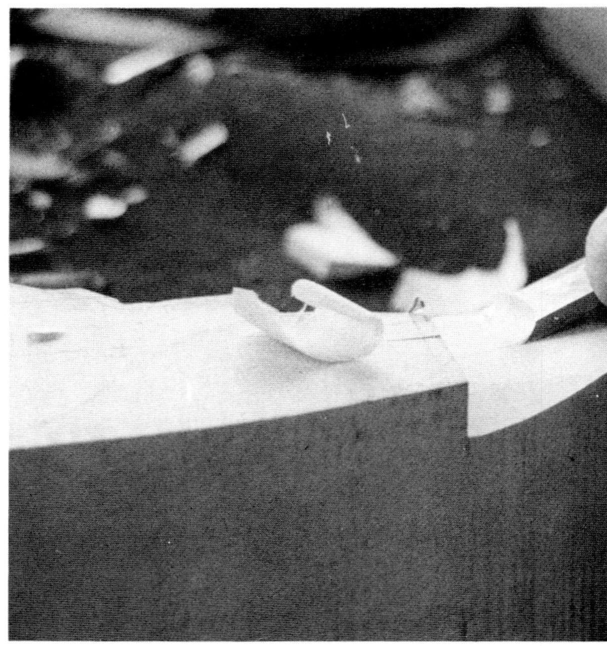

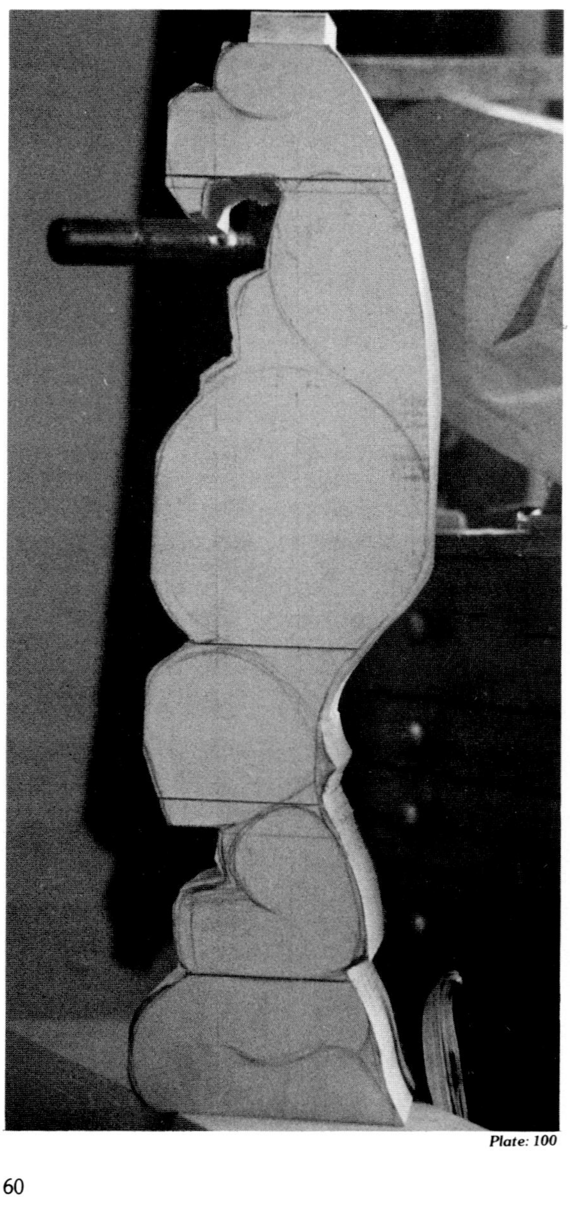

Plate: 100

Plate 100: 'Totemland' pole sawn out. In this stage it is called a 'blank.' (1979. Photo: B. Johnson.)

Plate 101: Detail carving. In this case, of the human figure. Note that the author pulls the knife towards him, rather than away. (1979.)

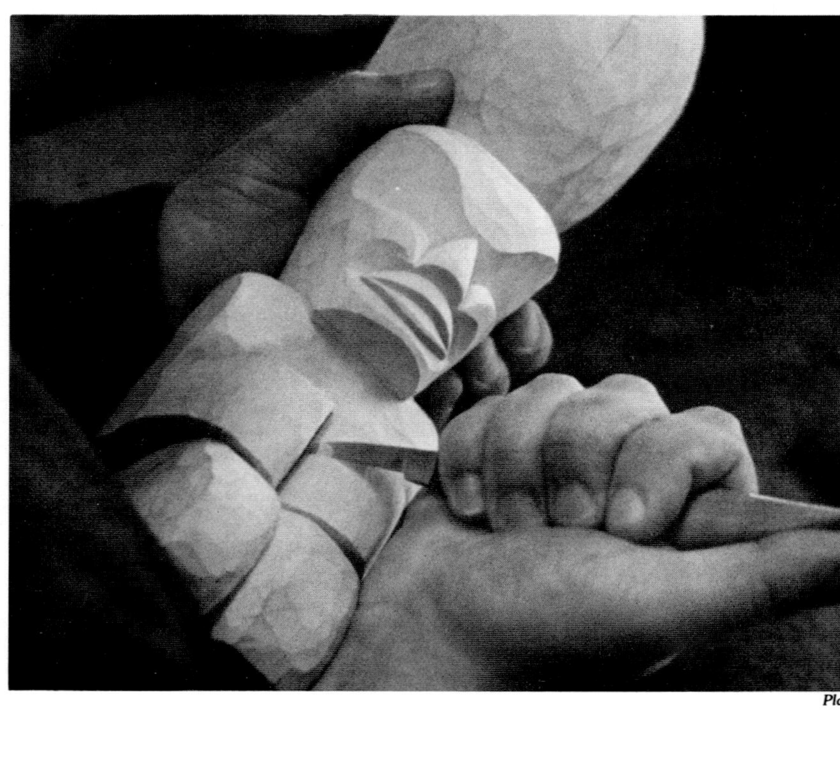

Plat

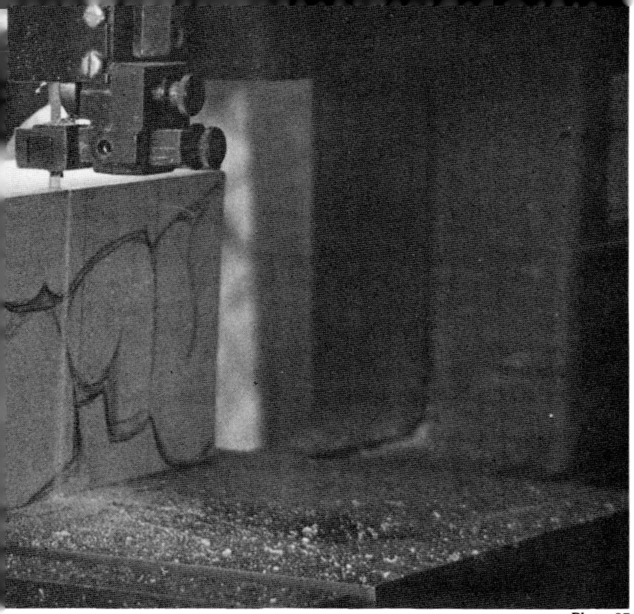

Plate: 97

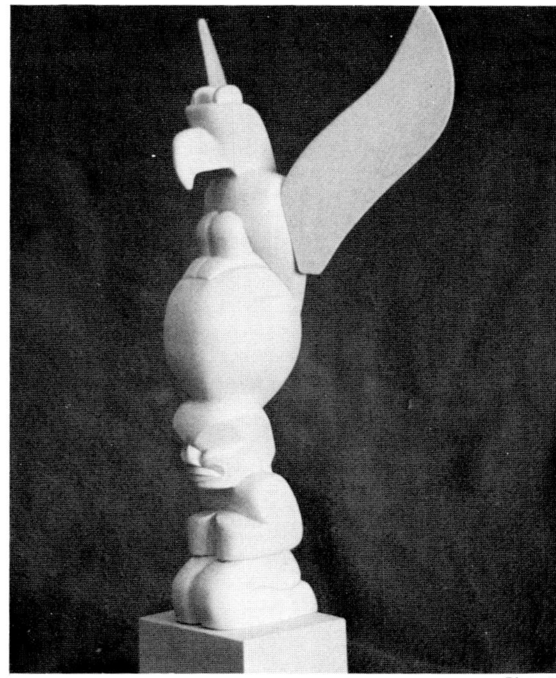

Plate: 98

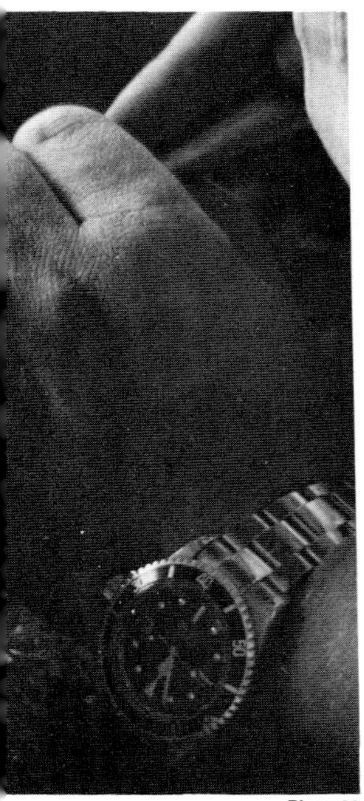

Plate: 99

Plate 98: Sanding. Once all detailed carving is completed, the entire pole is sanded to a smooth finish. (1979. Photo: Author.)

Plate 99: Roughing. The 'Totemland' pole is cut roughly to form with a wide chisel. (1979. Photo: B. Johnson.)

Plate 102: Finish carving. The totem is finished by whittling to remove the blocky planes left by the chisel. (1979. Photo: Author.)

Plate 103: 'Totemland' pole. Start of painting. (Vancouver, 1979. Photo: Author.)

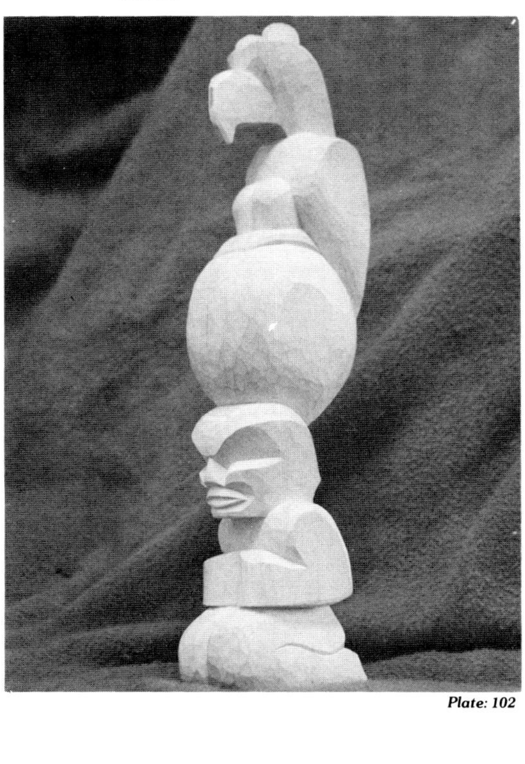

Plate: 102

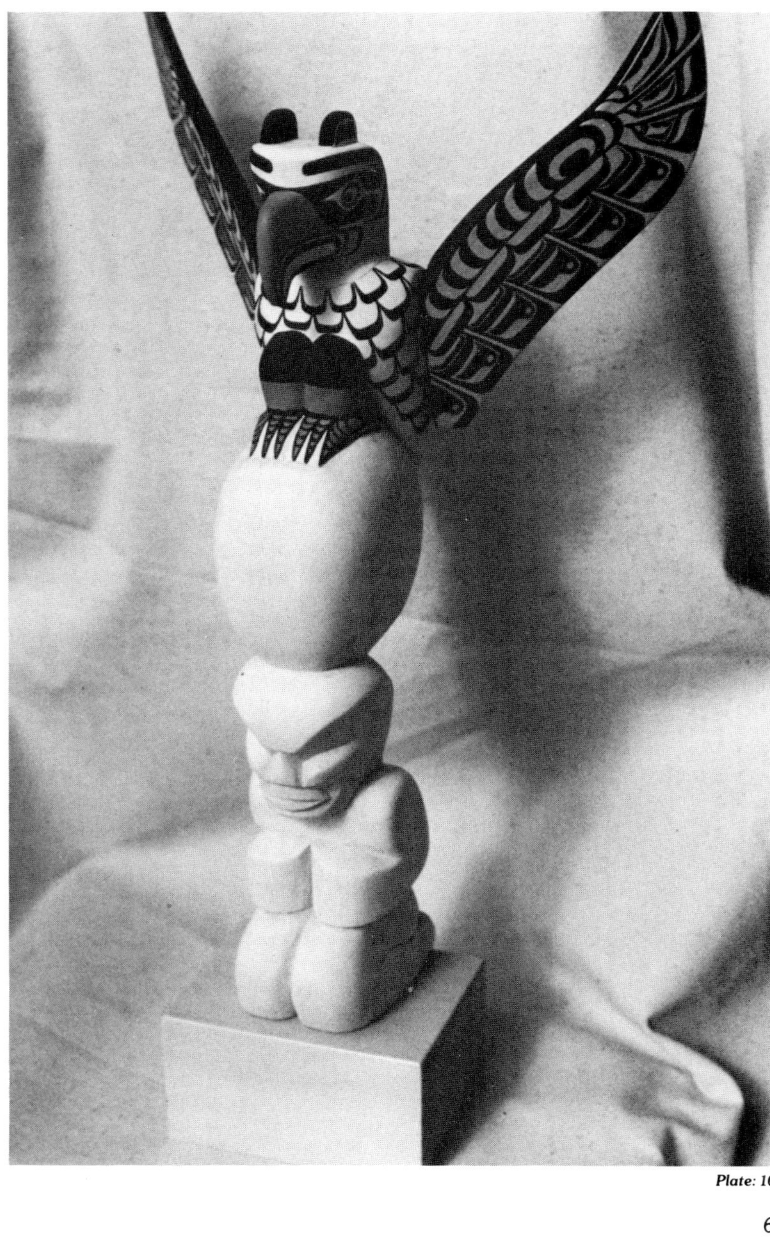

Plate: 103

The green and white house on Glen Drive witnessed a constant stream of friends and visitors. Relatives from Alert Bay would often make it their headquarters while visiting Vancouver, and you could tell by the laughter amid the excited bursts of Kwak̓wala, that Ellen was catching up on news from the Bay. Visitors from up the coast also brought 'care packages' in the form of oolichan oil or grease, smoked salmon, seaweed, and a special treat—wind-dried halibut.

Ted and Ellen Neel had an assortment of friends. They ranged from writers like Reg Ashwell, columnists like Mamie Malonie or Paul St. Pierre, artists such as Mildred Valley-Thornton or Bill Reid, to some of Ted senior's shadier acquaintances who had now, of course, 'gone straight' as the old man said, with a wink. Ted and Ellen were involved in politics, as advisors to various civic groups, and prominent in the International Order of Foresters—and that meant even more visitors. The few native artists that made their living from carving could often be found there having a cup of tea or a beer. Jimmy-John, a noted Nootka carver, would drop by while he was in Vancouver demonstrating carving at the Hudson's Bay Company, and Mungo Martin, Ellen's uncle, was a frequent visitor.

It was a treat if I happened to be there when Mungo Martin showed up. He never said much to me, but I could stand by inconspicuously and watch as wood turned to art in his hands. I remember that he once spent a whole afternoon carving an incised front for a box, perhaps a foot square.

Dave followed his movements and cuts and turned out a passable copy. After his great uncle had gone, Dave cut two side boards and a bottom, nailed his copy on one end and Mungo's work on the other. He sanded it smooth and said he was going to stain it and sell it to Lambert Potteries (they bought a lot of odd-ball stuff—single figures, beaver bookends, etc.). He never did, though—months later the box sat on a shelf in the basement with rust stains from the nails discolouring the yellow wood. I really wanted that box, but didn't have the nerve to ask Dave for it because it was 'saleable' and that meant big money—perhaps ten or fifteen dollars!

Dave was as generous as he could be, with his time and his talent and more often than not, with some piece he was working on. He'd say, 'here kid, you can use this for a model' or, 'first time I ever tried smoking a pole 'stead of staining it—you kin have it, if you want' or, 'I've been working on narrow headed whales, like Mungo carves. Here, give it a try.' But, finished poles were like cash—money in the hand—and once one of the boys had finished carving a pole, it had been sanded, painted, the wings put on, base attached and sprayed with clear lacquer, it no longer belonged to an individual in the family. It was part of the pay cheque! Playing with practise pieces was one thing, 'special' figures carved as a favour was another, but you didn't give away finished poles—a near inflexible rule.

One Christmas I turned up with a present for the Neel family—a totem pole. I'd purchased it retail from the Hudson's Bay Company, reasoning that anybody who was an expert in the field would love to own another well known carver's work (in this case, Jimmy-John's). The old man unwrapped it, looked at it, and the whole place broke up! When the old man finished laughing, he wiped his eyes and said dryly, 'Just what we needed, a totem pole.'

Amid another round of laughter, I tried to explain my logic and wound up red-faced and not a little indignant. Bobby was laughing so hard he could hardly squeeze out the words, 'Guess... what... we... have... for... you kid!' I joined in the third explosion of merriment when Cora produced an 18-inch 'Noona' pole.

Riding back home on the bus I was touched when I looked at the pole. It was fully finished, ready to sell—'cash in the hand' from a family who could ill afford to pass up any cash crop at all. 'It was probably meant to go out with that shipment back east,' I thought. 'Oh well, maybe they can send out that Jimmy-John pole instead!' The bus driver turned around and glared at the noisy kid, killing himself laughing at the back of an otherwise empty bus.

Ellen was always busy—but never too busy to offer assistance to anyone who asked. The April 1955 issue of 'The Native Voice' printed a copy of a letter they had received:

TRIBUTE TO ELLEN NEEL
The Native Voice, Vancouver, B.C. Canada
March 22, 1955

Attention: Mrs. Hurley

Classic art, like classic music, earns the proud distinction of being 'classic' only because it is fine enough to endure beyond the changes in customs, times, habits, and the whims of man.

Standing like a bullwark against decadent assaults of 'modern' art is that of the Totem of Northwestern America. It is the essence of American art, and it had been as true and steadfast to its principles as is the compass needle to the north. The carvers and painters of the British Columbia totem poles as worthy descendants of those early pioneers in that art, for art it is, in the fullest sense. They have refused to deviate from the inspirations of their predecessors, and wisely so. Among the foremost of them stands Ellen Neel of the Kwakiutl tribe. Her work is supreme. She has refined and made more beautiful the designs and patterns of old, so skillfully that none of their authenticity has been lost. This makes the truly great artist.

When we determined to place a bit of genuine American Art at the Boy Scout cabin in Bronxville, New York, a totem pole was chosen as being the most representative. None of us had any previous experience in such an undertaking and although we had, in Marius Barbeau's books, enough of the designs to go ahead with carving, we had no pattern of colour, nor any knowledge of what combination of animals and birds could be made without going counter to the laws of totem.

In our dilemma, we turned to Mrs. Ellen Neel of Vancouver. She came to our rescue with the kindness and understanding, the assurance that goes with ability, and the hearty co-operation that could only be given by a lovely person. To her goes whatever credit is due a modest, but sincere effort to follow where she showed the way. The photos that accompany this letter indicate the results achieved, made possible by the great help given up by Mrs. Neel. The only time we erred (in painting the sun, shading from deep crimson at the edge, the brilliant yellow at the centre) was when we departed from her colour pattern.

We who made the totem pole, as well as the Boy Scouts, present and future, will ever be grateful to the peoples of British Columbia who continued the art of Totem and to Ellen Neel, who is so ably continuing its faithful reproduction.

Sincerly,
Harrison Wright
Kenneth Russel
Ronald McLeod
Nelson R. Perry
New York, U.S.A.

A little flowery perhaps, but the sentiment comes through—Ellen was never too busy to help. Her friends often asked 'where do you find the time?' At least a part of the answer lay in the fact that Ellen was very well organized! Each day she noted the things to be done, articles to be picked up, people to see, shopping lists... all in 3-inch by 5-inch bound notebooks. Some of these notebooks still exist, today crammed with notes, long vanished telephone numbers and the minutiae that comprises a person's life. When thumbing through them, one has to admire her energy!

Tuesday

See or phone Harold Lando
Phone Dr. Gunn — Vegetable broth powder
Call at Hudson's bay — Whole wheat
Bank—Pills—Vitamin C — Wilson Duff 4:00 pm
Materials for silk screen—Behnsen Silk Screen Supply.
Mrs. Knight
L.A. 2.2309—3-foot pole of grandfathers. She has.
Velvet $1.35 yard—36"—538 Seymour.
1 doz blue
1 doz white for cabin craft
1 doz beige (need to be packaged and whipped edge)
Nylon chiffon for Mabel

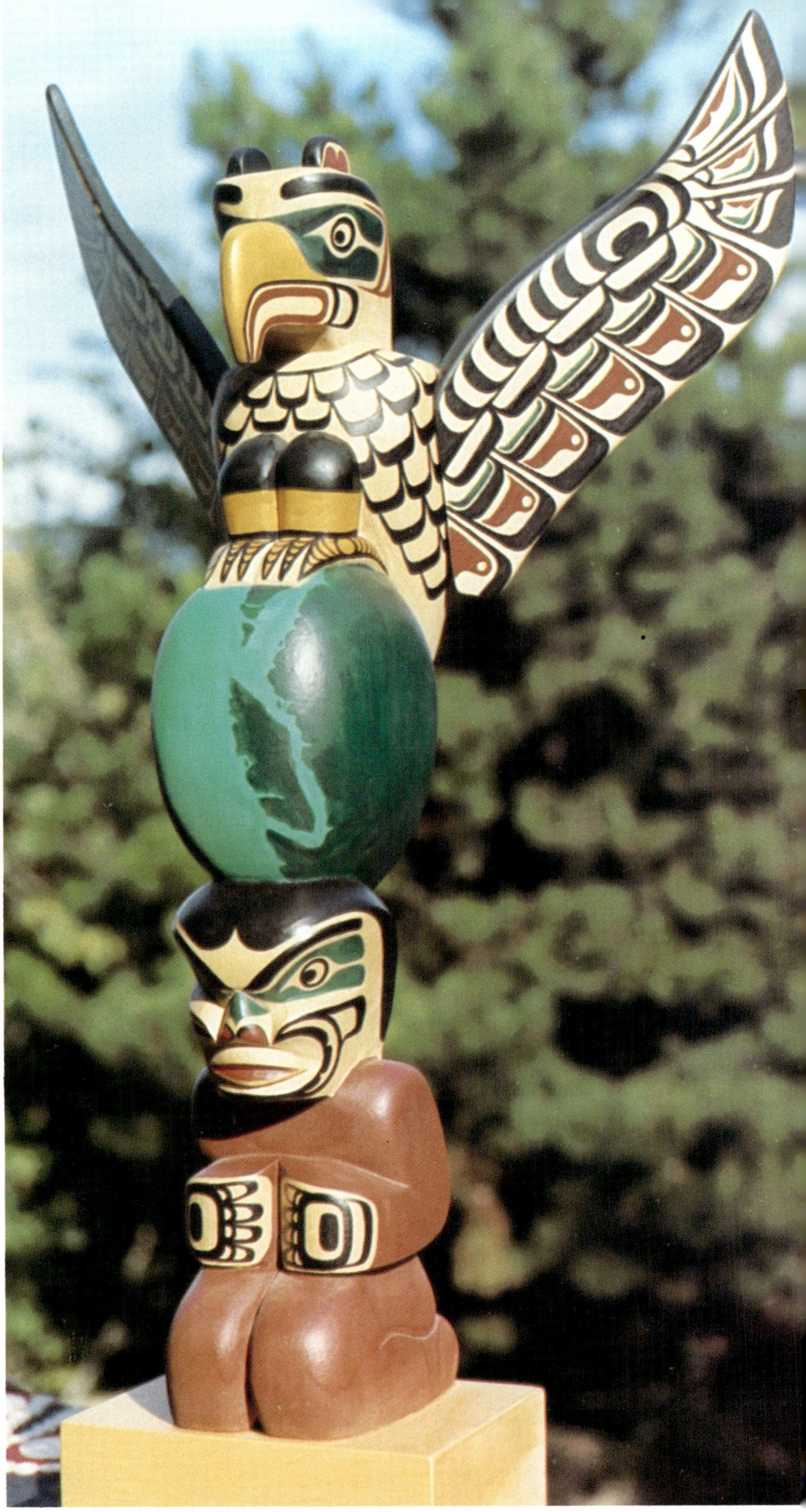

Plate 104: **The completed 'Totemland' pole. Note the B.C. coastline on the globe of the world... a succinct way of saying that B.C. was 'the whole world.' (North Vancouver, 1981. Photo: Author.)**

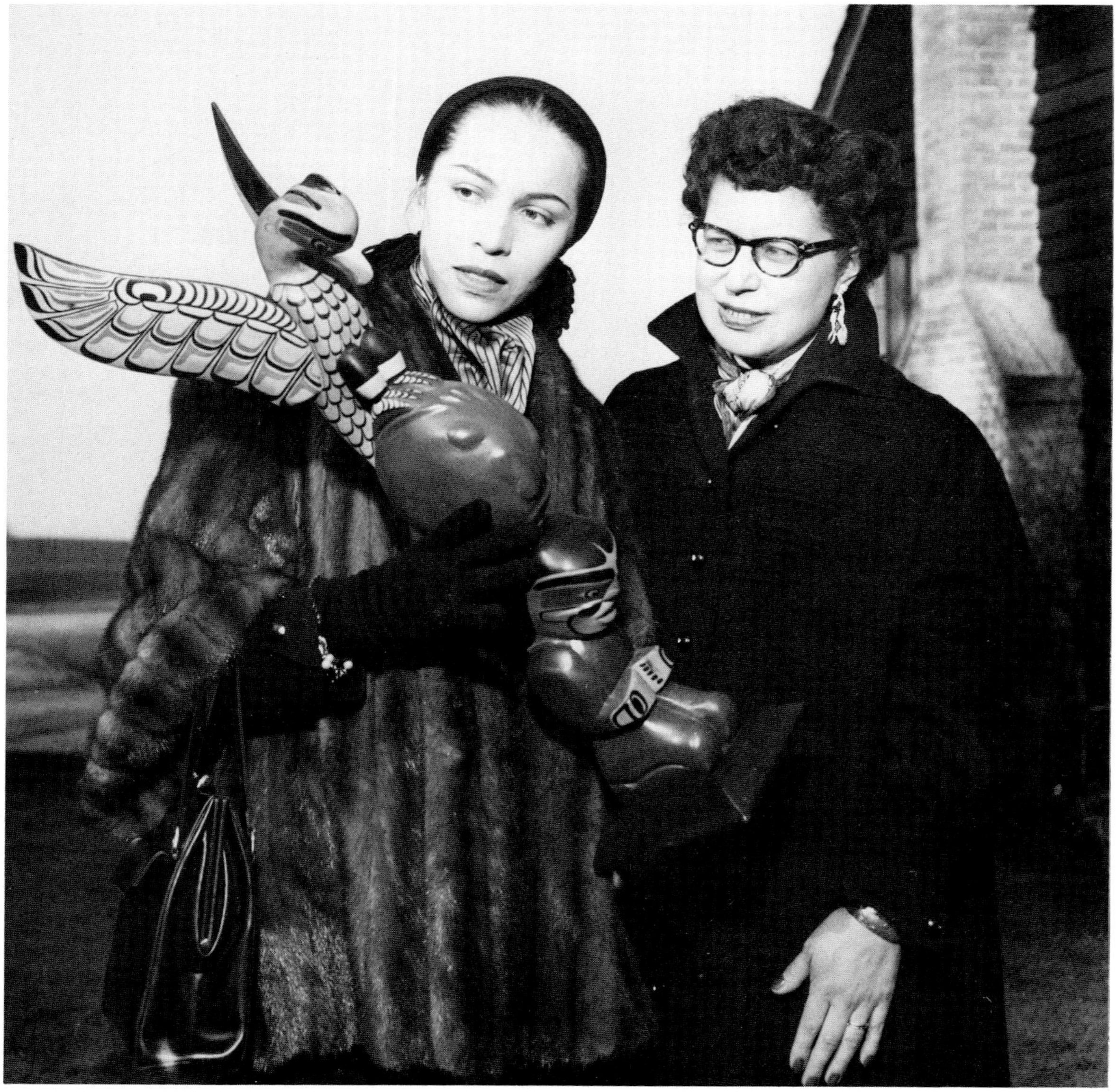

Plate 105: **Ellen Neel on the right, presents a 'Totemland' pole to Prima Ballerina, Maria Tallchief. (Photo: Vancouver Public Library.)**

March 25th

take cleaning in Write for Designing & Making
See Dave Lambert Hand-wrought 'Jewellery'
New Design Gallery Joseph Shoenfelt $4.95
Buy green & white paint
Buy meat—vegetables
Buy candy for kids
Wedding present
Phone Margaret

Do

Haida Replicas by Queen Charlotte Enterprises —Victoria
Call Bill Reid about this
'Picasso—50 years of his art 'Barr Cedar Hill Road—Kiwanis Bldg. 2 blocks left Oakcrest Dr. 3rd house—Tuesday lunch 12:30
Benzendrex inhaler
Helen Kent—Radio Stn. CFRN—C.P.R. Bldg. 10:30 a.m.
Dinner 4 p.m. Doghouse—Winnifred Mather
Bus to pick up girls
Look at clothes
Cora Bra—Jr 34, Waist 24, Hips 35
Theo Bra 32—Waist 25

That spring, Ellen and her family took on a major project: five full-sized totem poles for the Westmount Mall, a new shopping centre in the City of Edmonton, Alberta. The poles were carved in a shed erected near the sales room at Ferguson Point, Stanley Park and when a photograph of the project appeared in the Vancouver Province newspaper, it was captioned 'Family co-operation' and showed the entire family working to meet an August deadline to coincide with the opening of the Shopping Centre.

It was a good summer, but it was the last summer that the Neel family worked together.

I was doing the research to find out what had happened to these poles in Edmonton, when I received a call from David McCoy. He explained that he was Cora's son, Ellen's grandson, and that he lived and worked in Edmonton. His mother had called him and told him about the research that I was doing and asked him to call me. He explained that the poles were scattered, that the local Lions Club had three of them, one was at a high school and only one remained at Westmount Mall. He went on to say that the three at the Lions Club had been repainted by members of the club and the other two were badly in need of repainting, preferably by someone who knew what they were doing. He sounded bright and articulate and he was very excited over the prospect of a book about his grandmother. He asked many questions and was obviously quite delighted and interested. I promised to keep in touch and thanked him for his trouble.

After I hung up, I pulled out the 'Family Co-operation' photo—a sharp 8″ × 10″ glossy—and looked at it. There was Bitty perched up on the big totem pole, and beside her was Cora, also perched on the pole. Cora was about 14 years old then and I had just talked to her son, a young man in his twenties, about that same pole. That totem pole was still standing in Alberta with every adze cut the same as it was in that summer of 1955. But how everything else had changed—all of us.

Plate 106: 'Family Cooperation' was the caption of this photo, when it appeared in a local British Columbia newspaper. The Neel family working to complete a series of poles for Westmount Mall, a large shopping center in Edmonton, Alberta. From left to right: Theo, Ellen, Dave, Ted Sr., Bitty, Cora, Bob, and Ted Neel. (Stanley Park, Vancouver, 1955. Photo: Courtesy Vancouver Public Library.)

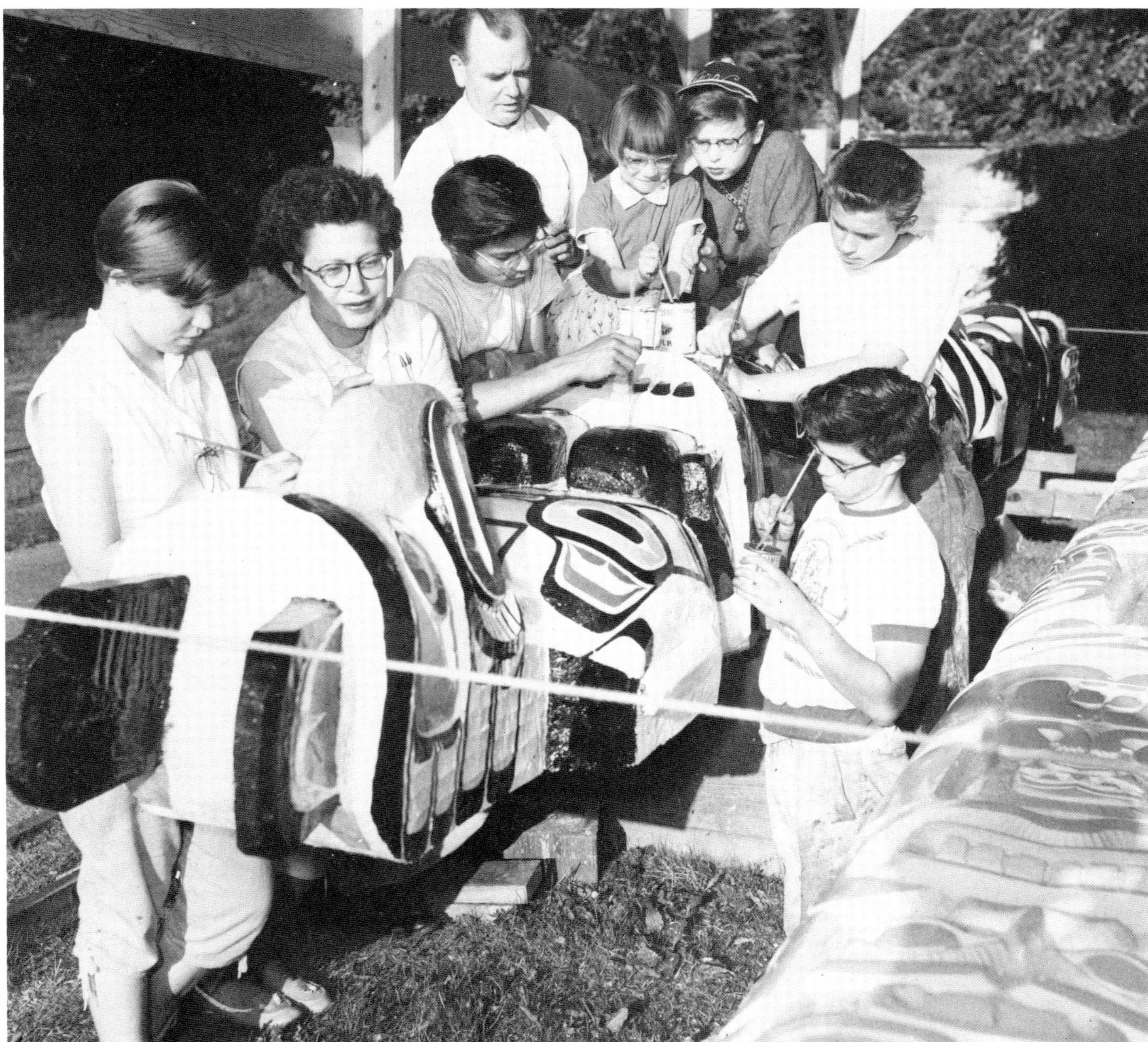

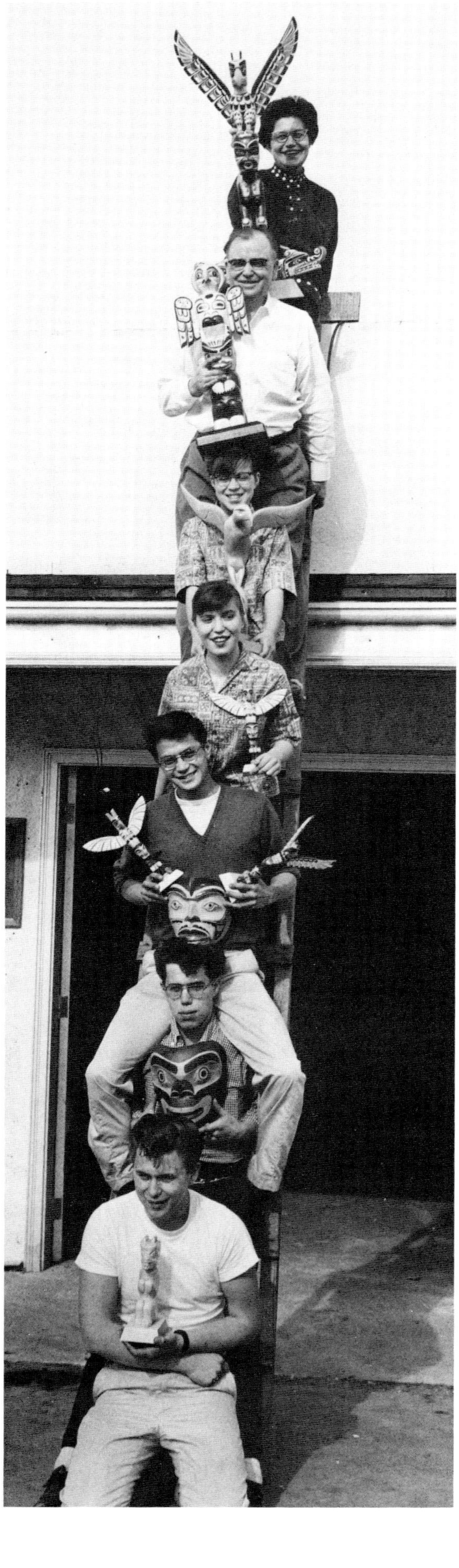

***Plate 107*: This photo was captioned the 'Neel Totem' when it appeared in a Canadian National news magazine in 1959. From top to bottom, the 'totem' figures are: Ellen, Ted Senior ('the old man'), Bitty, Theo, Dave, Ted Jr. and Bob Neel. (White Rock, BC, c. 1959. Photo: Jim Ryan.)**

The Neel family moved away from the little green and white house on Glen Drive, where there had been some bad times, but so many good times and so much laughter.

When they were moving, Ellen asked me if I wanted the big 'grease dish' beside the house. It was a huge piece, some seven feet long and represented a wren with the back hollowed out to hold oolichan oil. Ellen explained that it was an old piece and she'd like to keep it, but simply had no place to put it. I'd asked her about it many times and now it was mine, if I wanted it. The problem became apparent immediately; I couldn't move it. It was jammed between the basement wall and a concrete retaining wall that ran up ten feet to the sidewalk above. Years of rain had run off the roof and poured through the rain gutters directly onto the dish. It was thoroughly waterlogged and probably weighed in excess of a thousand pounds. I was frantic. How to move it? I tried levering it out with two by fours. No luck —it wouldn't budge.

Every chance I got, I was on the bus, over to Glen Drive and worried away at that dish like a terrier with a bone. Finally, weeks later, I talked my father into giving me the money for a tow-truck, by promising to forego weekly allowances forever. He drove me over to Glen Drive to view what I was proposing to spend his money on and when we turned off Hastings Street, my eyes almost started out of my head—the house was gone and so was my grease dish. I raced around to the neighbours, but they knew nothing past the fact that the house and the one beside it had been levelled to make way for a new building. Everything had been bulldozed into dump trucks and taken away. On the way home, I silently handed the tightly crumbled bills back to my father. He seemed surprised at the depth and intensity of my disappointment.

The Neel family settled in at 2405 Antrim Street in South Burnaby. Dave Neel made the newspapers again, in April of 1956, by winning first prize in a community arts council contest. His carving of a thunderbird surmounting a pair of comedy/tragedy masks, symbolic of the theatre, earned him top place over a large number of contestants. Dave had learned his lessons well and approached his designs seriously.

Dave left home in 1956 to establish his own studio and pursue carving as an individual artist, rather than a member of 'Ellen Neel and the Totem Carvers.' Cora left home in 1957 and Bob Neel followed two years later. The 'kids' were growing up fast and leaving the nest.

In 1959, the Neel family lived in White Rock, B.C., and were planning a move to Aldergrove, B.C. A pictorial layout appeared in a Canadian news magazine entitled 'Totem Poles are her business.' A photo captioned 'The Neel Totem' had the whole family standing at various positions on a high stepladder, seeming to form a human totem pole. Dave showed up for the photographs and they were all there except Cora. Bitty was featured holding a large 'Dzunuk̲wa' mask up over her head as she puckered her lips in imitation of the mask.

A number of photos were taken by Victoria photographer Jim Ryan, showing the family in various poses as well as a squence that was meant to illustrate the various steps in carving a small 'tourist' pole. When the article finally appeared, it was seen by a senior director of the Stratford Society in Stratford, Ontario. He contacted the Neels and arrangements were made for Ellen and Ted Neel to travel to Ontario and demonstrate the carving of a full-size totem pole, during the Stratford Summer Festival. The Vancouver Province Newspaper carried the following article on May 9th, 1960.

B.C. CARVERS WILL MAKE TOTEM POLE AT STRATFORD

Stratford, Ontario (C.P.) a five-ton tree trunk from the forests of British Columbia is to arrive here in a few days to be carved into a 22-foot totem pole during the festival.

The two British Columbia Indians who will carve the totem in the West Coast Exhibition during the summer festival arrive early in June. One is Mrs. Ellen Neel of White Rock, granddaughter (sic) of 80-year-old Mungo Martin of the Kwakiutl tribe who is considered the greatest living totem pole carver. The other is Bill Reid of Vancouver—a member of the Haida Tribe.

Ellen and Ted completed the move to Aldergrove just one day before leaving for Stratford.

In January of 1980, Bill Reid and I were having lunch at a restaurant in North Vancouver, and I asked him about Stratford. He looked puzzled and I explained the about the clipping from the Vancouver Province, in 1960.

'According to the newspaper, you were supposed to go . . .' Bill chuckled, and said, 'If everything was done according to the newspapers, *all our lives would be a lot different . . . I don't recall anything about Stratford, and I sure as hell wasn't there . . .'*

So much for newspapers!

The pole that Ted and Ellen carved at Stratford was to be 22 feet in finished length. It was commissioned for presentation to a collector near Ann Arbor, Michigan.

Although the Stratford Shakespearean Festival was largely given over to the performing arts, the additional features caused as much interest among the viewers as the traditional portion of the festival. Among these attractions was a large display of Northwest Coast Indian Art which came largely from the National Museum at Ottawa: an exhibition of Emily Carr paintings depicting totem poles and B.C. Coast villages on loan from the Vancouver Art Gallery's Carr Collection, and, of course, totem pole carving as demonstrated by Ellen and Ted Neel.

The West Coast exhibit was arranged to give the spectators of the festival a feel for the rain forest beauty. The National Film Board of Canada's colour film called 'The Loon's Necklace' played continuously and the forest sounds mingled with the muted Indian dance music.

A viewer standing in front of the large Emily Carr canvasses that showed huge forests and small villages could faintly hear the movie sound track and could smell the fresh-cut cedar as Ellen carved.

Far more genuine interest was displayed in the totem pole carving, than either Ellen or Ted had ever experienced at any other exhibition. Ellen had carved large poles in front of crowds on many occasions, but here it was different. Totem poles were 'old hat' to most B.C. residents, but here in Ontario the various displays combined effectively to culminate in Ellen's work. They were a graphic example of the 'living art' she had often spoken about.

Newspaper reviews were excellent, but these were different than what the Neels had come to expect. There was no mention of 'Indian Princess Carves', or 'dying art revived', but rather the reviewers made statements like:

'The success of the Indian display is the most remarkable (of all the exhibits)—the general public may fear that it is another of those affairs that are dull for anybody but an anthropologist or, worse still, an affair with a silly awe of anything primitive. Don't believe it. A lover of sculpture would question whether the old Indian civilization was primitive. I saw figures which could make some modern sculptors look like poseurs.'

And:

'Mrs. Ellen Neel, of Vancouver, and her husband, Ted Neel, are the human focal points of the arena shows.'

And:

'Ellen Neel, in charge of the carving of the 22-foot totem being carved during the festival, is a direct descendant of Indians who specialized as carvers, for the Indians had their recognized master artists as well as their general craftsmen.'

Perhaps the comment that summed up Ellen and Ted's feelings over their reception at Stratford was one made by an art critic who said that their participation brought a sense of quality to the Stratford displays.

Young Theresea 'Bitty' Neel handled much of the public relations work associated with Ellen and the Old Man's work at Stratford. Bitty was seventeen years old then, but through the many displays and exhibits that she had been a part of, she had learned to feel comfortable with media representatives. She gave interviews to radio stations, television stations and the hordes of journalists that were ever present. That summer, the Canadian Broadcasting station did a one-hour interview with Bitty. She explained the significance of the Stratford project, gave some family history and related some legends and stories that she had learned from her mother and from Mungo Martin. At Stratford, she gave guided tours of the Northwest Indian exhibit and trained other guides to do likewise. All in all, she had a marvellous time! Years later she remarked 'That was, for me, the *summer that was.*'

In due course the project was completed, the festival ended and Ellen and Ted packed up to come home to B.C. Ellen later said, 'It almost seemed like a mistake to leave. We got several good pieces to do and so many people wanted us to stay for a while. They were really

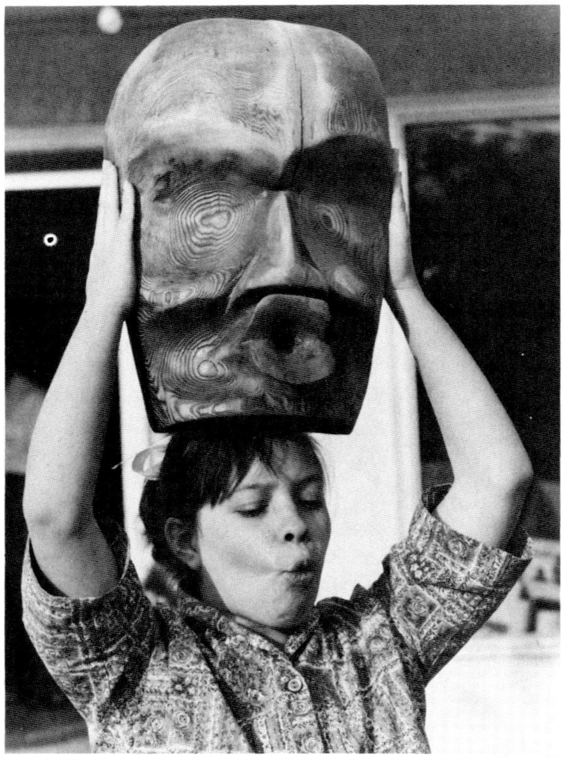

Plate: 108

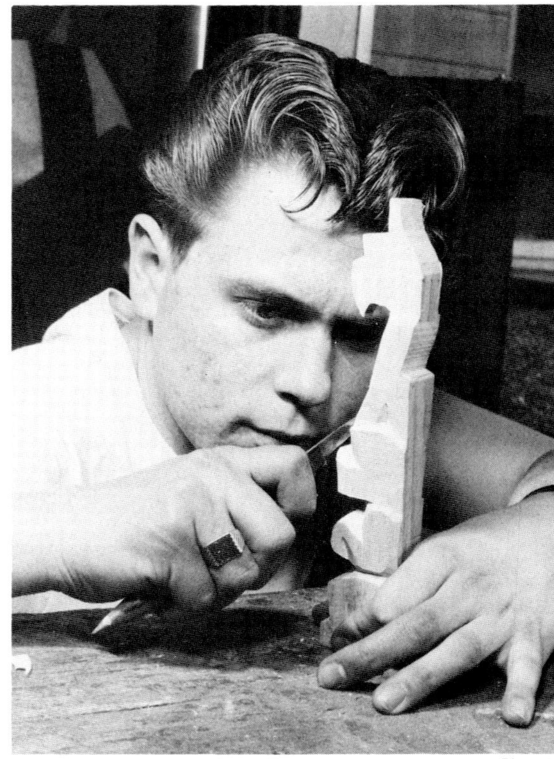

Plate: 109

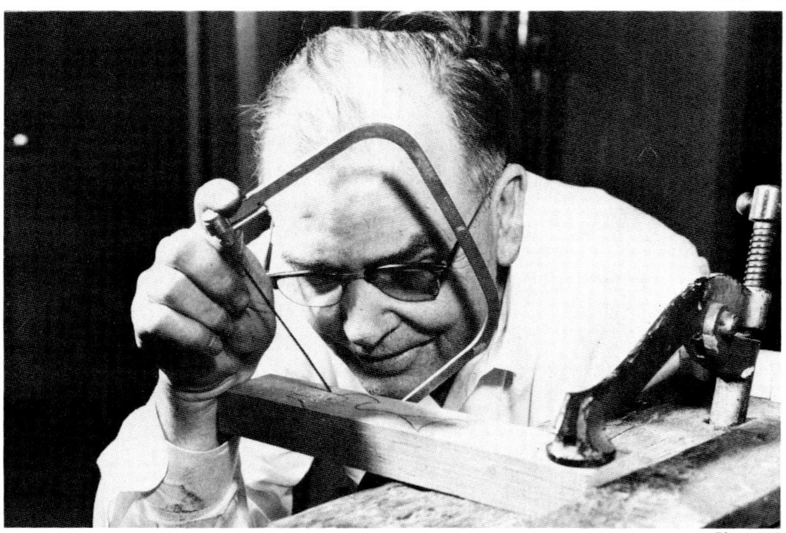

Plate: 113

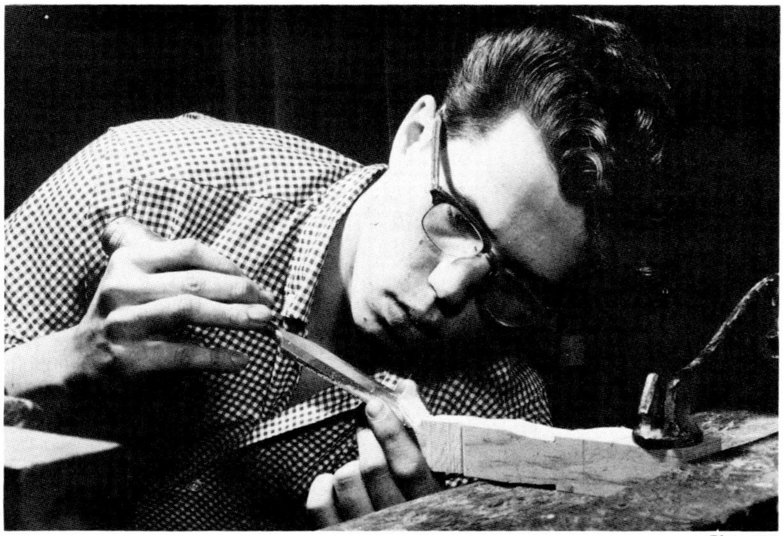

Plate: 112

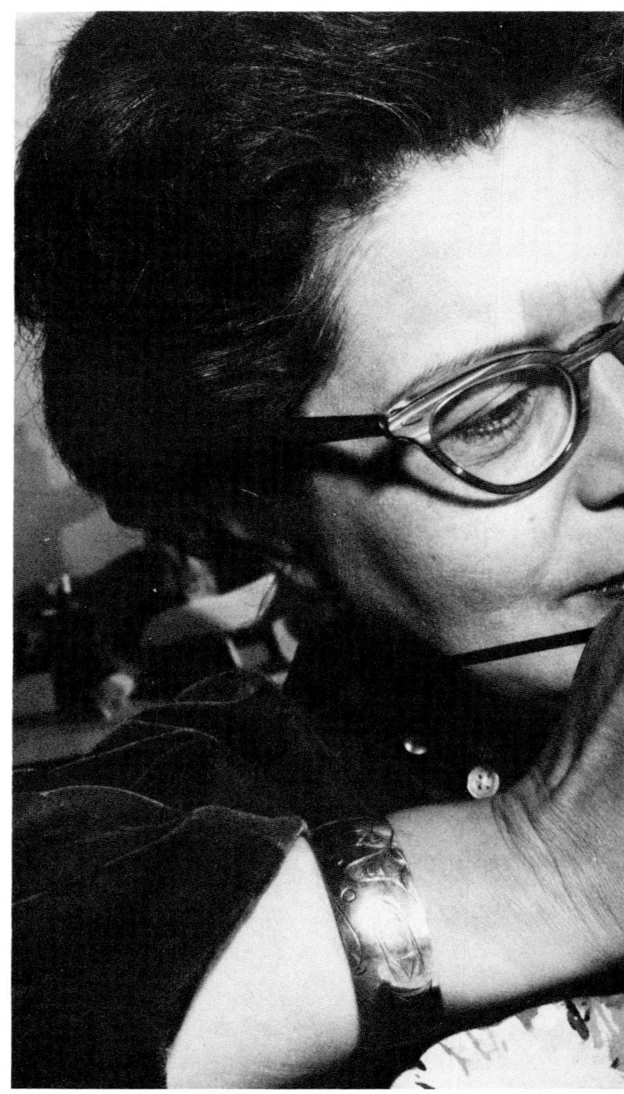

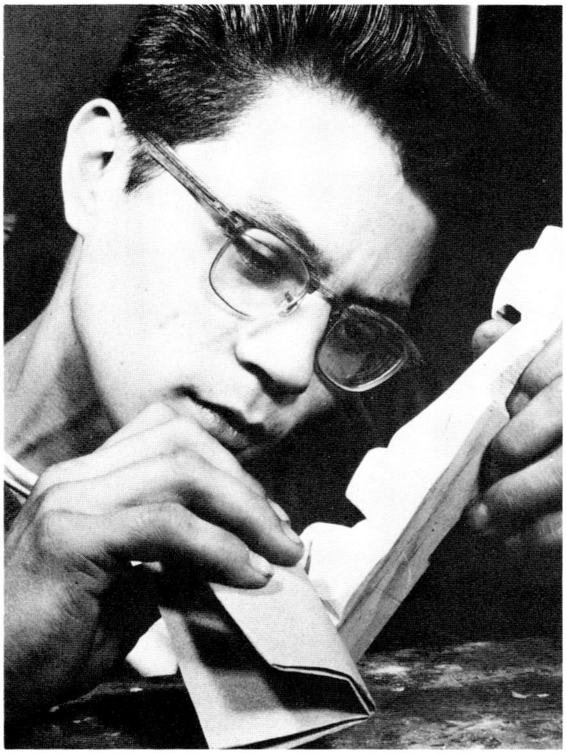

Plate: 110

Plate 108: Bitty Neel puckers her lips in imitation of the giantess 'Dzunuḵwa.' The large cedar piece was carved and burned to expose the wood grain and was destined to become a decorator piece for the restaurant of the Hudson's Bay Company store in Vancouver, B.C. (c. 1959. Photo: Jim Ryan.)

Plate 109: Bob Neel continues the tourist pole example—the blocky planes left by the chisel are smoothed by whittling and small contour details added, ie: the triangle cuts to delineate the Thunderbird's legs, and the bear's paws in a 'begging' position. (c. 1959. Photo: Jim Ryan.)

Plate 110: Dave Neel shows the final step before painting a tourist pole—the finish sanding. Although this was shown as done by hand, it was most often actually carried out with a powered 'flap-sander.' (c. 1959. Photo Jim Ryan.)

Plate 111: Ellen finishes the 12-inch tourist pole by painting. The crest on the chest of the Thunderbird is a very much simplified version of the killer whale crest—used by herself and her grandfather Charlie James. (c. 1959. Photo: Jim Ryan.)

Plate 112: Ted Neel Jr., shows the start of the 'roughing-out' on a tourist pole—a wood chisel is used to rough-out the figures from the band sawn blank. (c. 1959. Photo: Jim Ryan.)

Plate 113: This illustration and the four previous plates, show the steps in the production of a typical 12-inch 'tourist' pole—the outline is marked with a template and sawn out. Ted Sr., is shown with a handsaw, although this stage was most often done with a power bandsaw. (c. 1959. Photo: Jim Ryan.)

Plate 114: 'Happiness is a totem pole!'—particularly one that has been sold. Theo Neel shown with one of the many possible versions of the 'Thunderbird' and grizzly bear. (White Rock, B.C., c. 1959. Photo: Jim Ryan.)

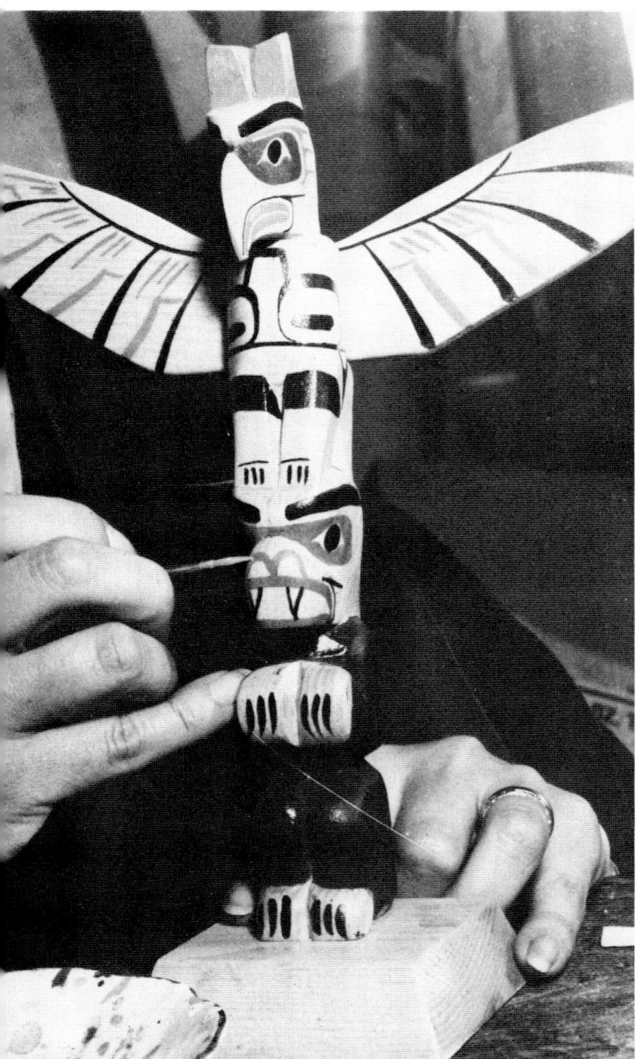

Plate: 111

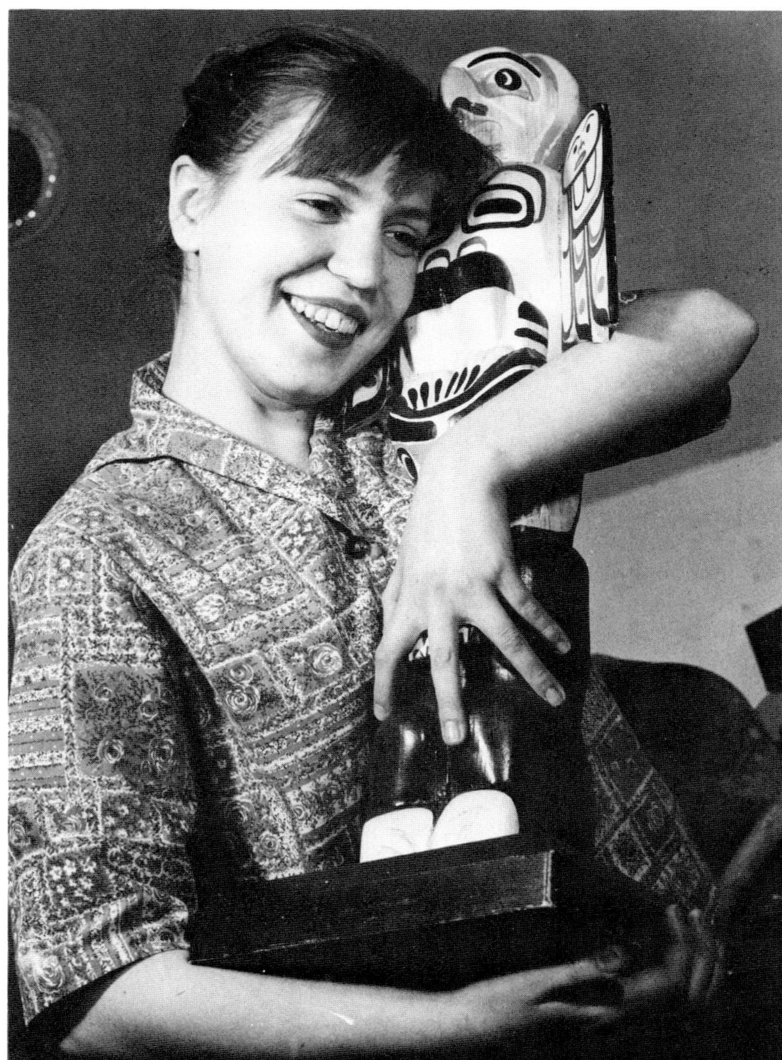

Plate: 114

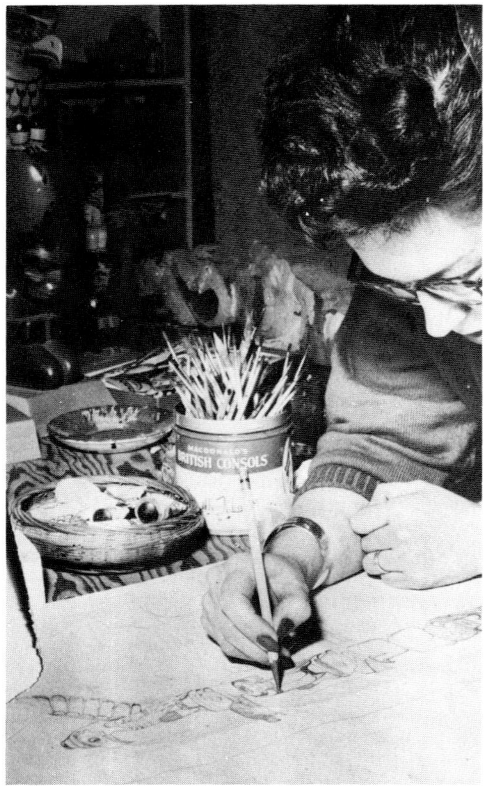

Plate 115: **Ellen works on a pole design. She invariably did careful lay-out drawings before tackling a big pole. (Stratford, Ontario, c. 1960. Photo: Courtesy Neel family.)**

interested and enthusiastic. Maybe we should move and set up shop!'

When Ten and Ellen returned from Stratford to the studio in Aldergrove, Ellen launched straight into a new project—the design and completion of the O'Keefe Conservation Trophy. This trophy was to be awarded to the B.C. club that had the most worthwhile conservation project for the year. Ellen's health had been poor for the past year or so and now it was compounded with problems with her eyes. She worked alone on the conservation trophy and curiously, chose to use a northern style carving rather than the Kwakiutl style for which she was known.

Ellen finished the trophy, despite a sojourn into the hospital and set about to design a piece that had been commissioned while she and Ted had been working in Stratford.

In 1961, Ellen had continually recurring bouts of illness and she was very tired. Theo left home that year and of the Neel family, only Ted Sr., Ted Jr., Bitty and Ellen remained at home. The 'Old Man's' health had also deteriorated and with Cora, Dave, Bob and Theo gone, it was hard to make ends meet. Ted Jr., who now used his middle name, 'John', to avoid confusion with Ted Senior, did the best he could but he could make infinitely better money as a commercial fisherman and often left during the fishing season.

In September of 1961, Ellen and the Old Man suffered a blow that they never really recovered from. Dave Neel, Ellen's oldest son, died as a result of a car accident in Washington, U.S.A. The shock and dismay at Dave's death was not confined to the Neel family. All those with an interest in Northwest Indian Art were stunned. Perhaps Maisie Hurley summed up the feelings of many when she wrote in 'The Native Voice':

> Gla-Gla-Kla-Wis is gone. David Neel, son of our famous British Columbia totem pole carver, Ellen Neel, died on Sunday, September 10, following a car accident in the United States.
>
> He was the great-grandson of the famous old-time Native carver, Charlie James, whose totems are recognized throughout the world as among the greatest creations in this art form.
>
> With his great-grandfather and his mother as inspiration and guide, Gla-Gla-Kla-Wis, at 24, had emerged not only as a fine carver in his own right, but as a painter, his art always reflecting a deep love of his Indian heritage.
>
> Somehow, words cannot convey our feelings of grief.
>
> David left a young wife, Norah, 19—and a son, David—16 months, his dear parents Ellen and Ted, four sisters and two brothers. We extend our deepest sympathy to them in their great and untimely loss.

To Ted and Ellen and the rest of the Neel family, things could never be the same. Ellen finished the piece that had been commissioned at Stratford; a huge single eagle figure destined to adorn a summer house in Quebec. It came out well, but in the blurred snapshot of it in the family album, Ellen's usual smile was gone.

They had another order to complete-a five foot pole for a Japanese landscaper in Seattle. Ellen and Ted walked the beaches at Steveston, B.C. for several days looking for a suitable cedar log to carve into the five foot pole. It must have been sad to see them walk together and talk about Dave.

The Neels' economic burdens grew heavier as Ellen's health declined. The Old Man was bedridden much of the time and could offer only limited help. Orders still came in, but Ellen was hard put to fill them. It took her longer and longer to complete even single poles, and larger orders for small tourist poles had to wait until Ted Jr. was home to do the bandsawing and roughing-out. The quality of the work began to deteriorate and even the intricate painting in which she had taken such pride, began to be replaced by daubs only suggestive of what had been before.

Many old friends tried their best to help. Harold Lando of Lando's Furs continued to buy single poles and odd lots from both Ellen and 'John' Neel even though the quality was not what he had come to expect. Dave Lambert, of Lambert's Potteries bought what he could.

Mrs. Millie Ryerson, who operated a gift shop in Toronto, returned to Ellen the full retail price that she received for Ellen's work. But, it was still not enough and Ellen worked longer and longer hours each day, trying to keep the rent paid and food on the table. Her health demanded attention, but there just wasn't the time to take care of herself properly-nor was there money.

Ellen and the old man talked of moving to Stratford, where her work had been so well received, but such a move to a new business would require financing and enthusiasm and strength-and they no longer had any of these things. Ellen's friends pressured her to seek help from the government. Surely, they argued, there's something available for one who had done so much for tourism, and for British Columbia; some sort of stipend or grant that will let you rest, get good medical attention, get back on your feet and go forward.

In 1963, Ellen was forty-six years old. She was a well-known artist with much fine work behind her and greater work ahead-given the opportunity. In the fall of 1963, Ellen took the suggestion of her friends and put together an application to the Canada Council for a grant. She was candid in her application, outlining her problems and why she needed the assistance and what she hoped to do in the future. As background she sent copies of dozens of articles and clippings-all glowing warmly with enthusiasm and praise. 'Don't worry', her friends assured her, 'they give grants to hippies and derelicts to do the stupidest things. You'll see. They're just looking for a chance to really help someone that deserves it.' Ellen waited anxiously for a reply. Perhaps her friends were right-maybe she should have applied sooner.

In November, 1963, she received the following response:

THE CANADA COUNCIL

Patron: Rt Hon. Vincent Massey—C.N.
Chairman, D.E. Woldon; Vice Chairman, Gerard Filion; Director, A.W. Truman.

Ottawa, Ontario

Mrs. E. Neel
5591 Otter Road
R.R. 3, Aldergrove, B.C.

Dear Mrs. Neel:

Thank you for your letter of November 16, and for the accompanying pages describing your background and your work. The officers of the council have looked over your request and I have regretfully to tell you that this cannot be considered under Category 10 of the scholarship programme. If you would like to enter one of the competitions you are free to do so, but unfortunately competition 4A for senior artists is already closed for this year and competition 4B is open only to candidates of more than 35 years of age. You may thus have to wait until the next round of competitions.

I should like to add that while we sympathize with the difficulties in which you find yourself, due partly to your husband's sudden illness, the Council has from the beginning refused to give grants on compassionate grounds or related to the means of the applicant. It was decided that this was too difficult and too private an area for the Council to become involved with. As a consequence our grants are given according to merit and as the result of competitions. I am sorry to have to send this reply which is not helpful to you and I hope you may be able to find somehow the help you need.

Yours sincerely,
Julia Osborne
Assistant Supervisor
Scholarship Programme

One of the children who was home at the time said, 'Mom just sat there, with that letter in her hands, not saying anything.'

In the early spring of 1964, I was working up the B.C. coast near Port Hardy, B.C. I had chartered a large halibut boat and was diving every day to locate and inventory undersea beds of abalone—a shellfish delicacy that commanded high prices in the Orient. The weather was rough and the water was cold. I looked forward to going south—particularly since we planned an overnight stop at Alert Bay.

We tied up next to the Nimpkish Hotel and I walked over to the 40-K taxi stand and asked if Bob Neel was on. 'Sure—he'll be back in a few minutes.' I hung around and waited and looked down the road. Alert Bay hadn't changed much. Bob saw me standing there and his cab screeched to a halt.

'Jeezus—Phil—what the hell are you doing here?' We went downstairs for a beer at the Nimpkish and I plied him with questions. How was everybody? Where was everybody? I hadn't seen Ellen for several years and the rest of them for even longer. Bob said, 'C'mon—leave your beer, I got a surprise for you. Let's go over to the Harbour.' We drove the short distance to the Harbour Inn and went in and sat down. The waitress had her back to me and I was in the process of admiring the shape of that view when she turned around—it was Theo!!

Bob had to go and pick up some fares and Theo and I sat and talked.

I caught up on the news. Ted had taken a few weeks off from Vancouver to crew on a commercial fish boat. Cora was married and raising kids. Ted would be back in the Bay in a few days. I shook my head in amazement! Ellen and the Old Man had made the big move from Alert Bay over twenty years before—all the kids had been raised in Vancouver, yet here they were—back in Alert Bay with the instincts of homing salmon!

And what of Ellen and the Old Man? Theo told me the many problems and I felt sad and helpless. Ellen had taken her time to help so many people and done so much, and now no one seemed interested. I promised Theo that I would go and see Ellen when I got back, although at that time, I could offer little more than moral support.

When I had to leave, Theo hugged me briefly and said, 'It's good to see you. You remind me of good times and there haven't been too many, lately.'

I went to see Ellen and I was shocked to see how sick she looked. We talked for a while and I bought several small poles—ostensibly as gifts for friends. She looked curiously at me and said, 'You're getting lazy, Phil, you should carve these yourself.' It was evident that things were not the best, but I had no way of knowing just how bad they were.

In 1965 John Neel worked long hours along with his mother. The market was poor and even though they could sell a few totems here and there, it was nothing like previous years where orders for several hundred small poles at a time were not unusual. In one frantic

Plate 116: Bob Neel presents a totem pole to the host of the television production 'Flashback.' (February 27, 1966. Photo C.B.C.)

Plate 117: Ellen and the boys at White Rock, B.C.—shortly before the move to Aldergrove. Left to right: Dave, Ellen, Ted Jr. and Bob. Ellen is holding the Neel copper in this photo, posed for Victoria photographer, Jim Ryan. (White Rock, September 1960. Photo: Jim Ryan.)

Plate 118: Perhaps the last photo taken of Ellen Neel. She is shown with her son, John Neel (Ted Jr.), as she worked on a canoe model. The effect of illness shows clearly . . . but she kept on working as long as she was able. (Photo taken late 1965. Photo: Courtesy Neel family.)

Plate 119: Ellen working on the central figure for the O'Keef Conservation Trophy. Note that carving is being done in Northern style. (Aldergrove, 1960. Photo: Courtesy Neel family.)

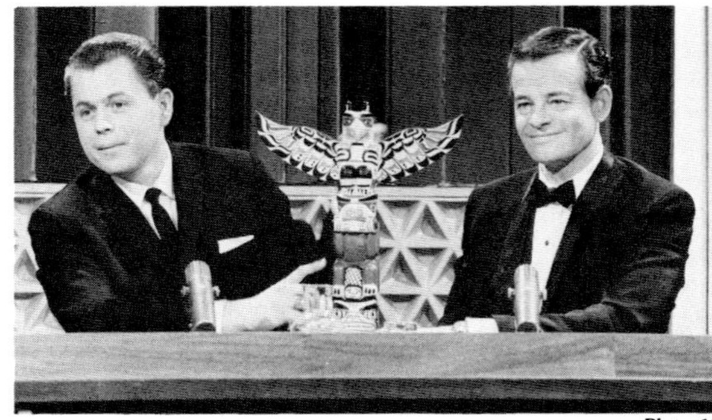

Plate: 116

Plate 120: Ellen's silver bracelets. The top bracelet is a Haida piece from the Queen Charlotte Islands, while the bottom one is from Bella Coola, B.C. Ellen was seldom seen without these bracelets and Bill Reid remembers repairing the Bella Coola one when it cracked from long use. Ellen's daughters Cora and Theo now proudly wear them. (Vancouver, 1979. Photo: Author.)

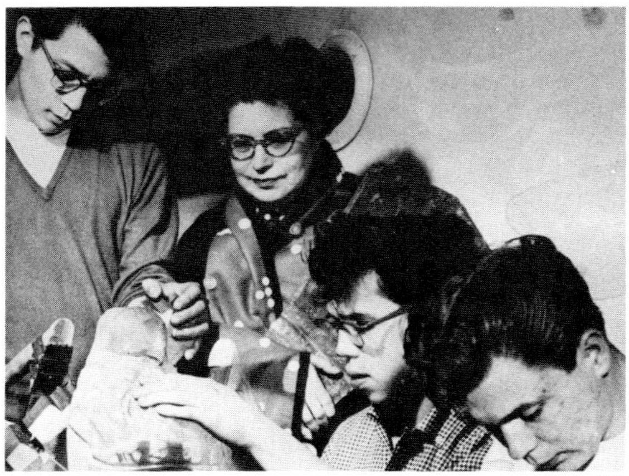

Plate: 117

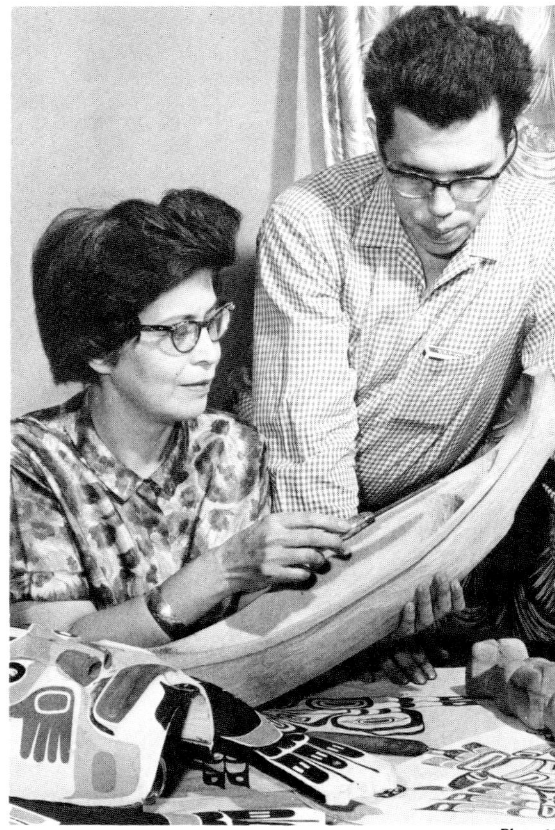

Plate: 118

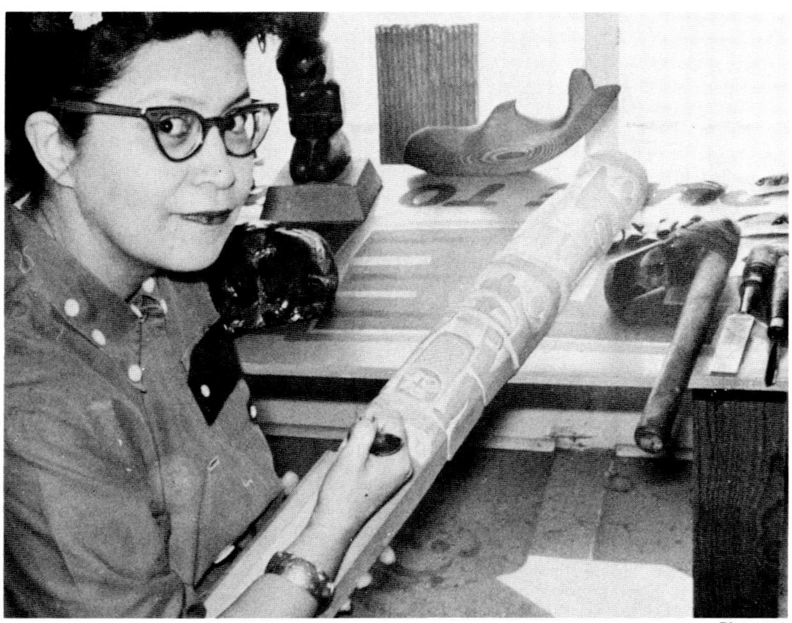

Plate: 119

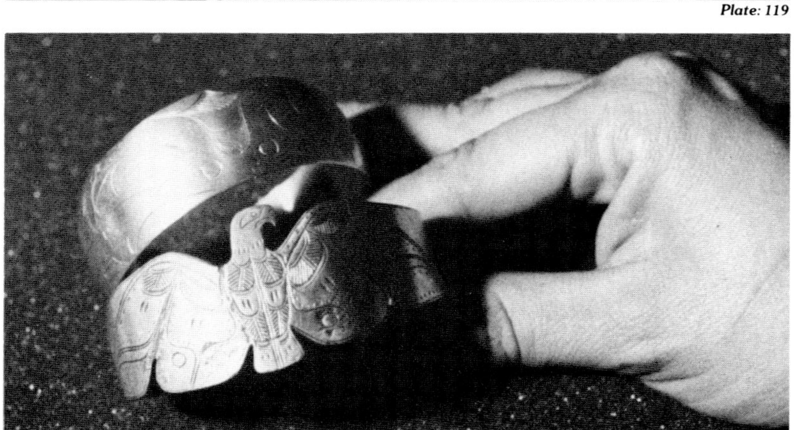

Plate: 120

period, the whole family had turned out 5,000 small poles to fill a Hudson's Bay cross-Canada order. But, that was years in the past and things were desperate now.

When Ellen's health prevented her from doing production work, she and her son worked on carving copies of a Charlie James totem that Ellen had brought with her from Alert Bay years before. John was not good enough to paint with either Ellen's or Charlie James' skill, so he wisely let well enough alone and sold them unpainted. Ellen signed these poles, hoping to capitalize on whatever fame she had left, even though the quality was not the best. In addition to these tourist poles, John carved masks and plaques and sold them as he could.

When things got really tough, John Neel began selling off the 'curios' that Ellen had brought with her from Alert Bay. They had some small value to collectors, particularly the Charlie James pieces. One by one the original water colour paintings went, paintings that had been done by Ellen and her grandfather decades before. Ellen had kept them all those years. Collectors bought them, but insisted on 'certification' note by John Neel—for $5.00 each.

These paintings were great examples of Charlie James flamboyant style.

Then the Charlie James poles that Ellen had kept as reference pieces went, one by one. Next, the small items accumulated over the years—the hooked rug with the thunderbird design, the elbow adzes and 'D' adzes and several of Ellen's sketch books—bit by bit disappeared.

Theo was working in Vancouver at that time and was giving her mother and father every spare cent that she could afford, as well as making payments on some long outstanding debts incurred by Ellen and the Old Man. Theo was furious at 'John' for selling off these old pieces, but she had to admit that the need was very real. You could get credit at the corner grocery store, but you had to pay cash for prescriptions.

One that she wouldn't see sold was the family 'copper'. This 'copper' had come down from the Newman family and Theo took it to her apartment to safeguard it. But John got it, and left her a funny little note saying he had 'burgled' her, but that he wouldn't sell the copper—only borrow on it—because they really needed the money and the copper was all that there was left. John got $30.00 on it.

All the family were upset over these items being sold, but it was hard to stay mad at their brother. He was staying home and carving to help support Ellen and the Old Man, while the rest of them were out in the world, building their own lives.

That's how Ellen's story ended. When you get to rock bottom, there's no place else to go.

Ellen re-entered Vancouver General Hospital in January, 1966. She had been looking forward to a trip east to be a guest on the Canadian Broadcasting Network's Television show 'Flashback'. She was proud to have been invited and she keenly wanted to go but it was obvious that she was gravely ill. Bob Neel went in her place and did an admirable job. When Bob appeared on nation-wide television on the night of February 27, 1966, it was hard for him to smile for the cameras because his mother was dead.

Ellen Neel died in Vancouver General Hospital during the evening of Thursday, February 3rd, 1966.

The following days brought newspaper articles such as 'Famed Indian Wood Carver Dies at 49'; 'Carver Ellen Neel Mourned'; 'Reknowned B.C. Carver Dies'; and a host of others. Everybody was sorry and genuinely so, but only a few knew the real tragedy of the previous few years. Paul St. Pierre, wrote in the Vancouver Sun Newspaper on February 26th, 'Two years ago, hemmed in by financial difficulties, she finally made application to the Canada Council for a grant. She was rejected. The next half-vast poet who gets a Canada Council Grant might spare a thought for this talented, independent, hard-working, Indian woman.'

The Canadian artist, Mildred Valley-Thorton said of her friend, Ellen Neel, 'I admired her as a woman and honoured and respected her as an artist—she was a most self-sacrificing woman who kept her family through her art. She was gentle and kind, and loving in every way as an individual. She was,' Mrs. Thorton said, 'a great credit to Canada and to her own people.'

The list of tributes and testaments offered over the following weeks was impressive. But Ellen's last wishes asked little, as Ellen had, in her life. She asked only that her remains become part of those places that she had loved.

Harry Brown, one of Ellen's closest personal friends chartered an aircraft and scattered a part of her ashes over Johnston Strait, the mouth of the Nimpkish River, and the Cluxewe River, near Port McNeill. The rest he returned to Alert Bay for burial.

So, she became a part of the sky, the forest, and the sea, in the land of Kwakiutl, whose culture she had spent her life transforming into objects of power and beauty.

Gone home to Alert Bay—where her most fitting eulogy is the memory of her laughter.

POSTSCRIPT

After . . .

'Daiyu' Dick stood by the microphone at the end of the communal longhouse, waiting for the crowd to quieten. Some of the old people in the crowd hushed the young ones loudly and two singers hit their batons against the drum-log for silence. I stood beside 'Daiyu' and he put his hand on my shoulder. He waited 'til all was quiet and then began to speak into the microphone, in Kwak'wala—quietly at first, then louder. He spoke in rapid bursts, with pauses as he looked around at the people. The pauses obviously served as emphasis to his words, but I understood little of what he said. I wore a band of cedar-bark around my forehead, symbolic of the sacred season and the alder smoke from the central fire stung my eyes.

'Daiyu' switched to English for the benefit of those that didn't understand his earlier words and repeated what he had alread said. He took his hand from my shoulder and gestured around the room. 'Look at him,' he said, pointing at me, 'so you know him. We Mamalilikala adopt this man into our tribe and we give him the name T'ła̱xwsa̱m*—Red Snapper—one of the kings of the undersea world.' He put his hand back on my shoulder and spoke directly at me, but loud enough so everyone could hear. 'You used to be a white man. Now you are an Indian. Now you belong to us.'*

I shook his hand and made a short thank-you speech. I don't remember exactly what I said. I kept it short because my eyes were wet—probably from the alder smoke. I went back behind the dancers' screen where Wayne Alfred and Emma Tamilin were getting ready to dance in my honour—Wayne as 'my' Hamatsa and Emma to calm him with motions of a cradled 'copper'. I stood behind the screen and Tony Hunt, Simon Dick and Amos Dawson came over to congratulate me. When the others drifted away, Amos said quietly, 'Too bad Ellen Neel couldn't be here. She would have been proud.'

I wish she could have been there.

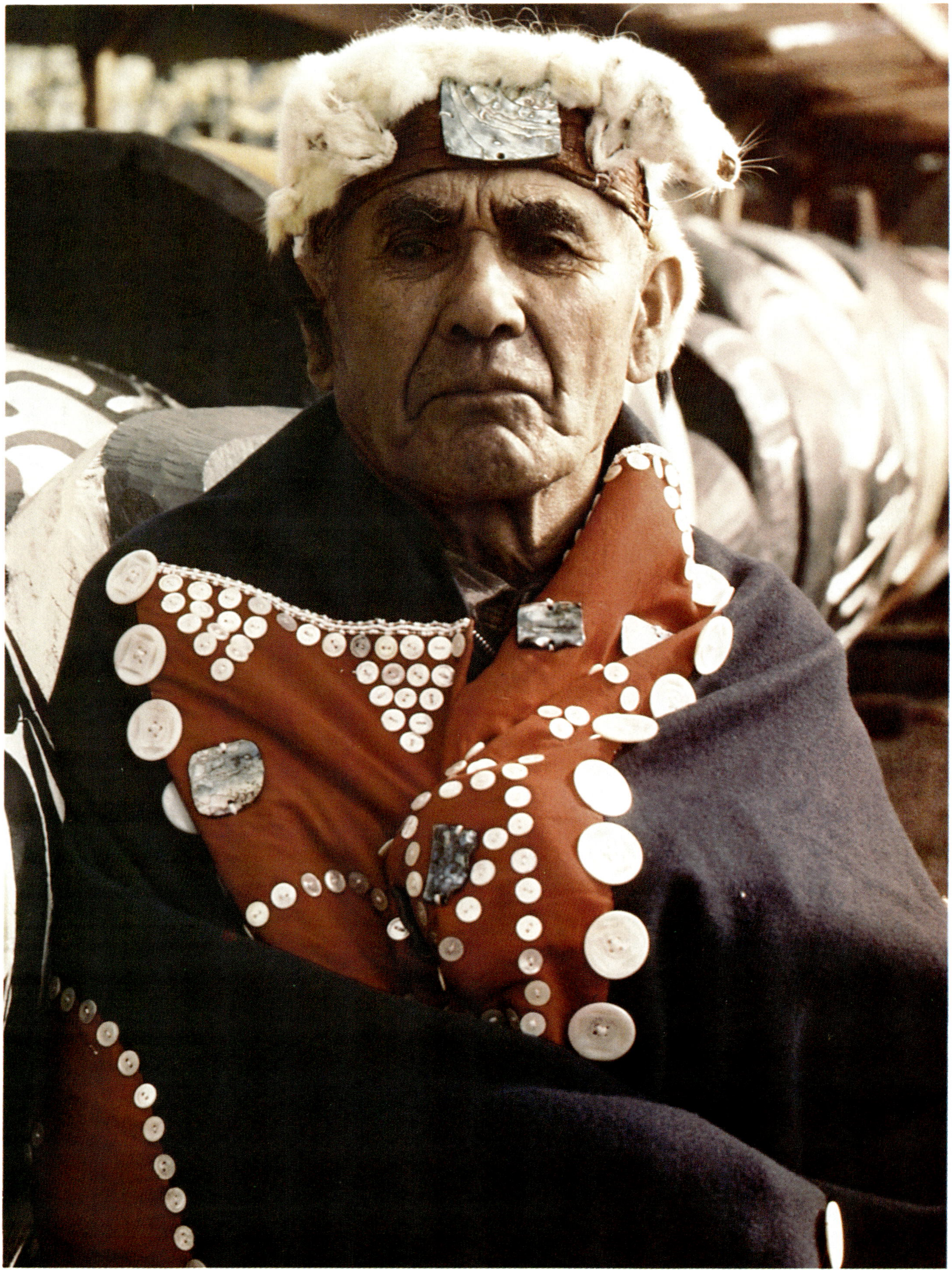

Mungo Martin
Part 3

Mungo Martin was born in the coastal village of Fort Rupert, B.C. around 1880 or 1881. The exact year is uncertain, since his birth was not registered... but, it was in the spring when his family was preparing for the trip to Knight Inlet, for the oolichan run. Mungo used an 'official' date of April, 1884, although he believed himself to be several years older.

He was a noted carver—learning the rudiments of this skill from a paternal uncle, and the mastery of it—from his stepfather, Charlie James.

Mungo Martin lived a long, useful and interesting life... and he died in his sleep, at seven a.m., the morning of August 16, 1962, at Victoria, B.C.

Mungo's mother was Sara Finlay 'NA̲GEDZI', and his father was a member of the 'GWATSINUX̲W' tribe, from Gilford Island, whose name was 'YAX̲'NUKWA̲LAS'—although he was called in English, just 'Martin'.

Mungo's father, 'YAX̲'NUKWA̲LAS' moved to Fort Rupert, B.C. after most of his band had been massacred by a raiding party of the Bella Coolas. In Fort Rupert, 'YAX̲'NUKWA̲LAS' met and married Sara Finlay and it was there that Mungo was born. A member of the 'GWATSINUX̲W' on his father's side and a member of the 'WALAS KWAKIUTL' (or 'real Kwakiutl') on his mother's side.

When Mungo was born, the year was not recorded—usual in that generation—but Mungo estimated his birthdate from the great Seattle Fire of 1889, which he saw when he was a boy of nine or so, and from other people of like age and known birthdate.

It is said that when Mungo was a baby, his mother wished that he might be a fine artist and singer. She asked a noted carver named 'YAK̲UDŁASA̲ME' for his advice... he plucked two lashes from each of the baby's eyelids. These lashes, the carver combined with porcupine guard hairs and tied them all into a paint brush. 'YAK̲UDŁASA̲ME' used this brush so his skill would be transferred to Mungo.

Mungo had an uncle who was a good singer and song-maker and Mungo's mother asked that uncle for help in ensuring that he would have a special musical talent. This uncle placed Mungo inside a box-drum, while it was beaten softly to a traditional song... four times in four days... This happened, Mungo said, when he was just a little boy. Later, his grandfather on his mother's side, taught him to sing. Twice each day he would practise... and, young Mungo Martin learned to compose songs from an old man named 'UMX'ID'.

By the time Mungo passed into manhood, he was a skilled singer and song-maker and, at least, a reasonable artist.

As Mungo grew into a young man, he received no formal schooling, except for a brief period when he was about ten years old. That came about when he used a loaded rifle to attempt to club a raccoon in a trap. The raccoon had to be considered the victor, since Mungo had managed to shoot himself in the leg during the skirmish. His parents took him to Alert Bay to the doctor. While he was there, they enrolled him in the residential school.

Mungo hated it. His injured leg made it difficult to play with the other boys and demonstrate his physical skills, and he had no academic skills to show. Accordingly, Mungo made his getaway as soon as he could. This was accomplished by talking a relative into giving him a boat ride back to Fort Rupert. As Ellen Neel put it, 'His mom was really mad, but everybody was glad to see him... he was supposed to go back, but somehow, he just never did.'

Mungo Martin's father, 'YAX̲'NUKWA̲LAS', died when Mungo was in his late teens, or very early twenties. Sara Martin then married Charlie James and James took Mungo and his two brothers, Spruce and Herbert, as his stepsons.

Having Charlie James as his stepfather was a fortunate turn of events for Mungo. James was only five or six years older than Mungo, but already a skilled carver of some reputation. Because of their closeness in age, Mungo and Charlie James enjoyed a relationship closer to 'pals' than father and son. From Charlie James, Mungo learned to master the real skills of designing, carving, and painting—skills that Mungo

Plate 122:
Photo: Jim Ryan.

Plate 123: Mungo Martin as a small boy. Photographer and exact date unknown. (Fort Rupert, c. 1890. Photo: American Museum of Natural History Neg: 11621.)

Plate 124: Mungo Martin (second from left) dressed as a member of the 'Nul'mal' or 'Fool' society—although the term 'Fool Society' sounds rather clown-like, in English, this group is an important and powerful part of the Kwakiutl potlatch hierarchy. The older boy is Mungo's brother, Spruce Martin. The squatting figure is Peter Pascaro and the man on the extreme left is Charlie Wilson. Figure on the right is unidentified. (Fort Rupert, c. 1894. Photo: Smithsonian Institute.)

Plate 125: Mungo Martin's 'Raven of the Sea' pole on 'totem row' in Alert Bay. This is the pole carved for Chief John Drabble, 'A̲'walaskan̲is' around the beginning of this century. This photo from the City Archives, Vancouver, has an annotation by Major J.S. Matthews, Archivist: 'Indian totem poles, Alert Bay, British Columbia, circa 1910. Stood along the village beach. Carved with stone hammers and stone chisels, and painted with natural pigments mixed in fish oil.' Mungo would have been amused with this description! (Alert Bay, c. 1910. Photo: A.M. Wastell album. Courtesy: City Archives, Vancouver IN.N. 51P103.)

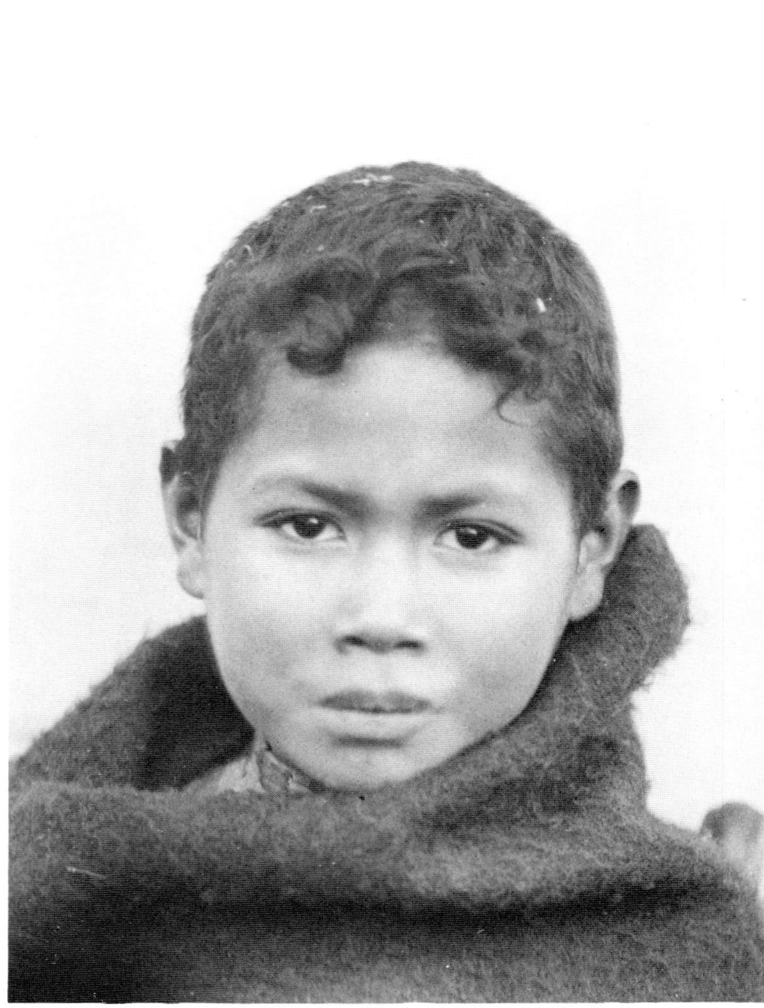

Plate: 123

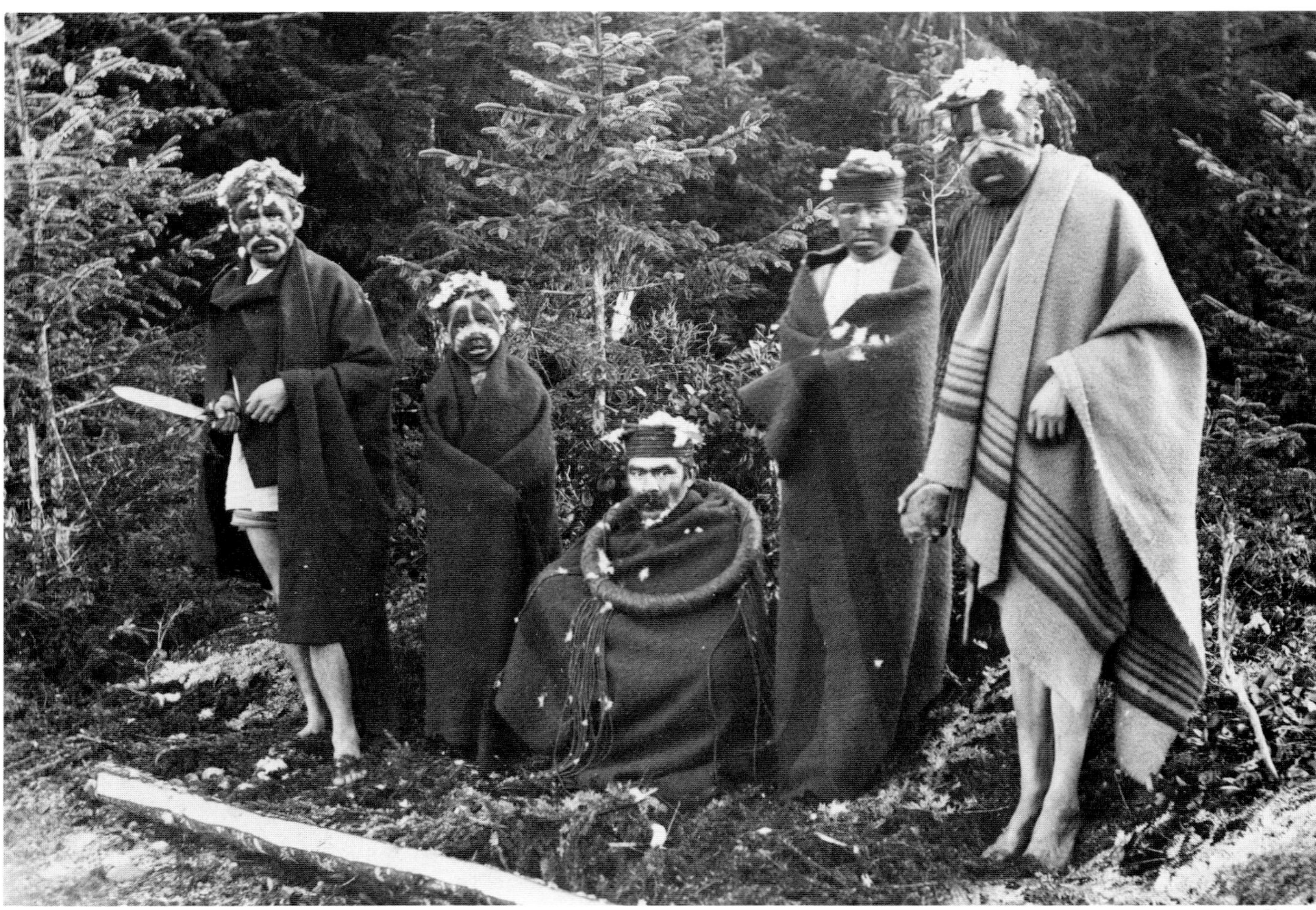

Plate: 124

thought he already possessed until he watched his step-father! James also taught him to read and write—not in English, but in a phonetic transcription of the Kwakiutl language originated by Reverend Alfred James Hall (of Fort Rupert, and later, Alert Bay).

Mungo assisted Charlie James in the carving and painting of many of the totem poles, masks, and other potlatch objects that were in demand at that time. One of the first major poles that Mungo was commissioned to do was for 'KWAKSILANUKUMI', John Drabble, (also called 'A̲'WALASKA̲'NIS',) of Alert Bay—shortly after the turn of the century. The 34-foot pole was called the 'Raven of the Sea', and it was erected at a potlatch where the names and social ranking of the nephews and nieces of 'KWAKSILANUKUMI' were given. This pole was acquired from John Drabble's widow in 1947 and taken to the university of British Columbia, where Mungo restored it, nearly half a century after it was originally carved. Obviously, the original owner valued it highly, since Mungo was paid $350.00 to carve it. The pole was acquired by UBC for $500.00—all those years later.

When the pole was completed, there was a second commission to carve and paint a house-front for a man named 'K̓UMUGWE'. The house-front was done in the figure of a killer whale and the painting was arranged to have the mouth of a killer whale carving form the front door of the house. When Mungo needed advice on design or technique, James was there.

Mungo and Charlie James made numerous trips together, while James was demonstrating his carving or selling tourist poles. 'Wandering', Ellen Neel called it. These were good times for Mungo. He and James travelled to Victoria, and to Vancouver, then back to Fort Rupert, and later back to Alert Bay.

When Charlie James died at the beginning of 1938, Mungo was the logical person to take over his work, but there had been little real market for carving skills since the final Potlatch prohibition in 1921. Mungo tried his hand at numerous trades, but finally settled down to salmon fishing and the small amount of carving for which there was still a demand.

Mungo Martin was married early in the century to one of the daughters of Sarah Constance Smith and David Hunt (son of previously mentioned George Hunt). Mungo had a daughter, Lucy, and a son, David. Later, when his first wife died, he married Sara Constance. Everyone called her 'A̲BAYA̲'A'—meaning 'mother of all'.

'Abaya'a's' formal name was 'TŁAK̲WAGILA̲'OG̲-WA'—meaning 'copper-maker woman,' and her father was a Chief of the 'ŁAWITSIS' (Turnour Island) band—named, in English, SEAWEED Smith, and in Kwak̓wala... 'SIWIDA'NAKWALA' and 'G̲WIK-SISA̲LASA̲ME''. 'A̲baya̲'a's' mother came from TSAWATI... Knight Inlet. This union with 'Abaya'a' was to continue all of Mungo's life.

So Mungo fished, made songs and sang at the 'secret' potlatches and did some carving. His life progressed in that fashion until 1948-49, when he was called to the University of British Columbia to take over the totem pole restoration programme from Ellen Neel. Since that commission proved to be pivotal in Mungo's life, it is worth giving a brief background to the restoration project.

In 1947, the Hon. E.W. Hamber, Chancellor of the University of British Columbia donated monies to purchase existing totem poles, repair them, and bring them up to a condition suitable for display. A committee was set up, under Professor Hunter Lewis, and, as explained earlier, Ellen Neel was contacted to begin restoration work. When Ellen no longer felt she could carry out the work, Mungo Martin took over. A valuable record of this early effort comes to us in the form of a report drafted by Hunter Lewis, Chairman, Totem Pole Committee, October 30, 1951, which said in part:

'In marking the annual report of the Totem Pole Committee, I did some gratuitous and probably superfluous work. I thought that there should be, in the President's office, a permanent record containing as much detail about the totem poles as possible. Consequently, I appended to the report, a section headed 'Details of Totemic Collection'.

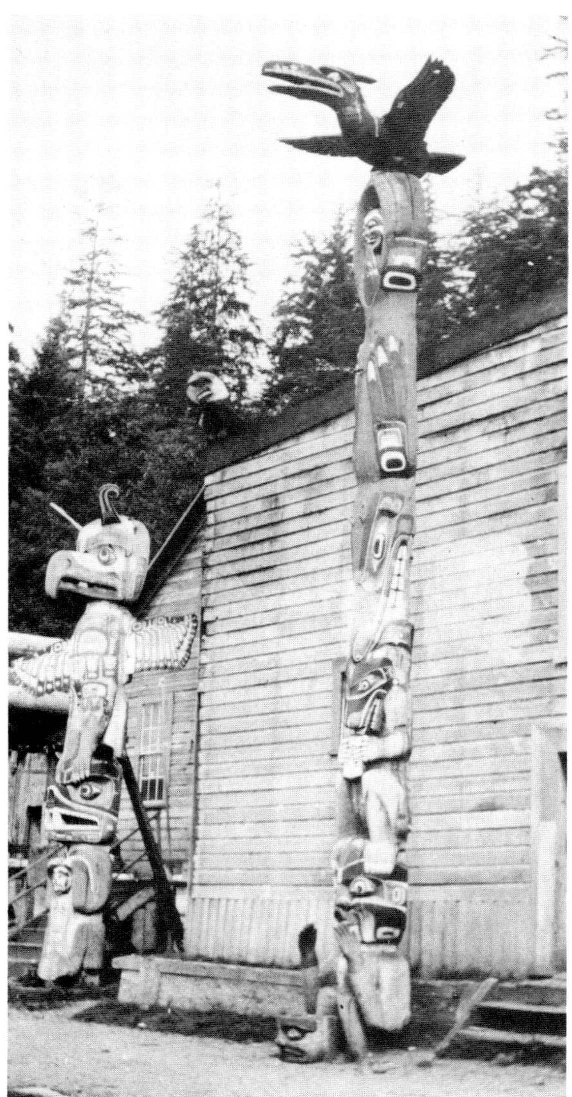

Plate: 125

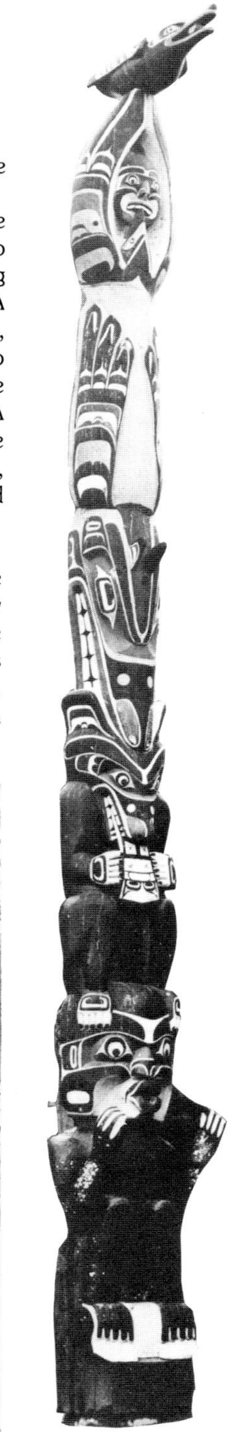

***Plate 126:* The 'Raven of the Sea' pole. Mungo regarded this as his first real commission. Shown after restoration in Totem Park, University of British Columbia. (Date unknown. Photo: U.B.C.)**

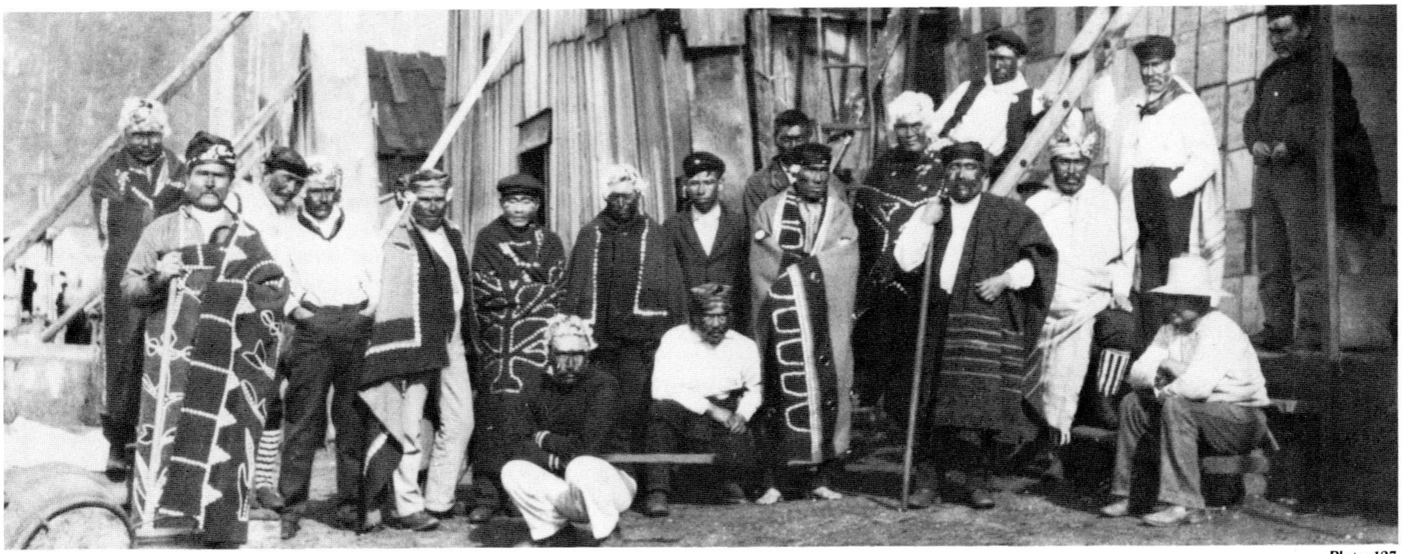

Plate: 127

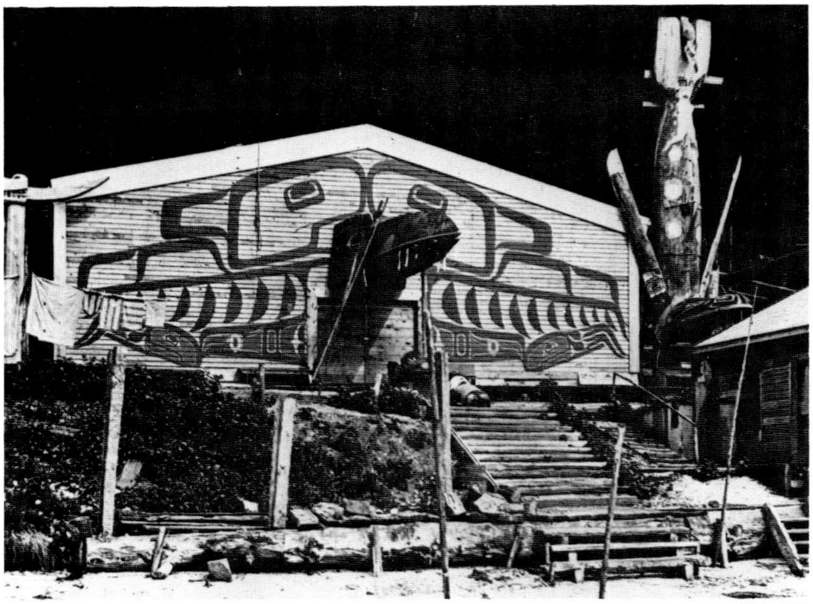

Plate: 128

Plate 127: A potlatch group at Alert Bay.
The chief in the left foreground is 'Siwida'nakwa̲la,' a chief of Turnour Island. This man was Mrs. Mungo Martin's —'A̲baya̲'a's' father. (Alert Bay, c. 1901. Photo: C.F. Newcombe. Courtesy: B.C.P.M. PN-254.)

Plate 128: A community house at the village of 'Gwayasdums,' Gilford Island. The large pole to the right of the house was carved by Mungo Martin at the end of his first decade as a commissioned carver (about 1910). Originally intended as a house-front pole, the giant whale figure would have had the guests entering through the open mouth. The added pieces making up the whale's head, pectoral fins and the small raven figure perched between the tail flukes—show the influence of Charlie James' teaching. (Gilford Island, c. 1917. Photo: C.F. Newcombe. Courtesy: B.C.P.M. PN-42.)

Plate 129: Potlatch paraphernalia at Alert Bay, 1914.
The large 'Sisiyutł' mask shown immediately in front of the door was carved by Charlie James and is shown in more detail in *Plate 66*. The second figure from the left is Mungo Martin, holding an elbow adze and carving knifes. Mungo was in his early thirties when this photograph was taken, and his surroundings bear out his intimate involvement with the ceremonial life of the Kwakiutl. (Alert Bay, 1914. Photo: W.M. Halliday. Courtesy: B.C.P.M. NA-2777.)

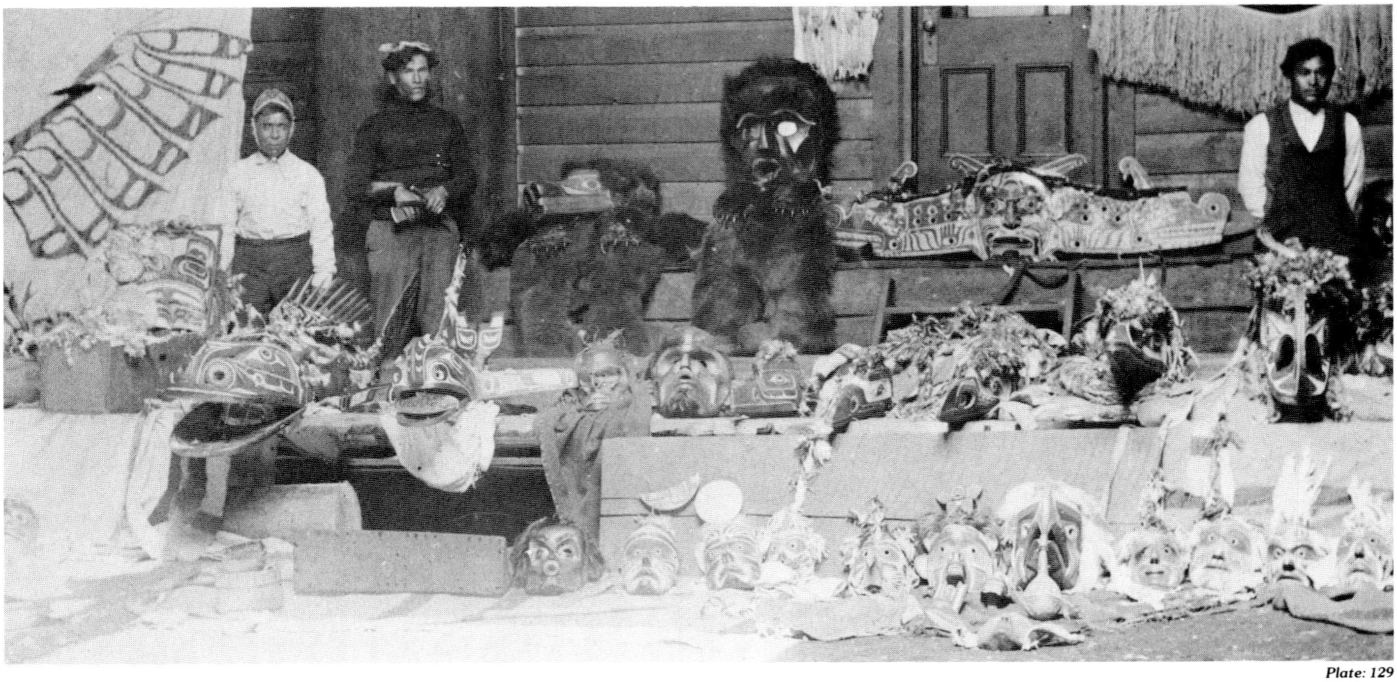

Plate: 129

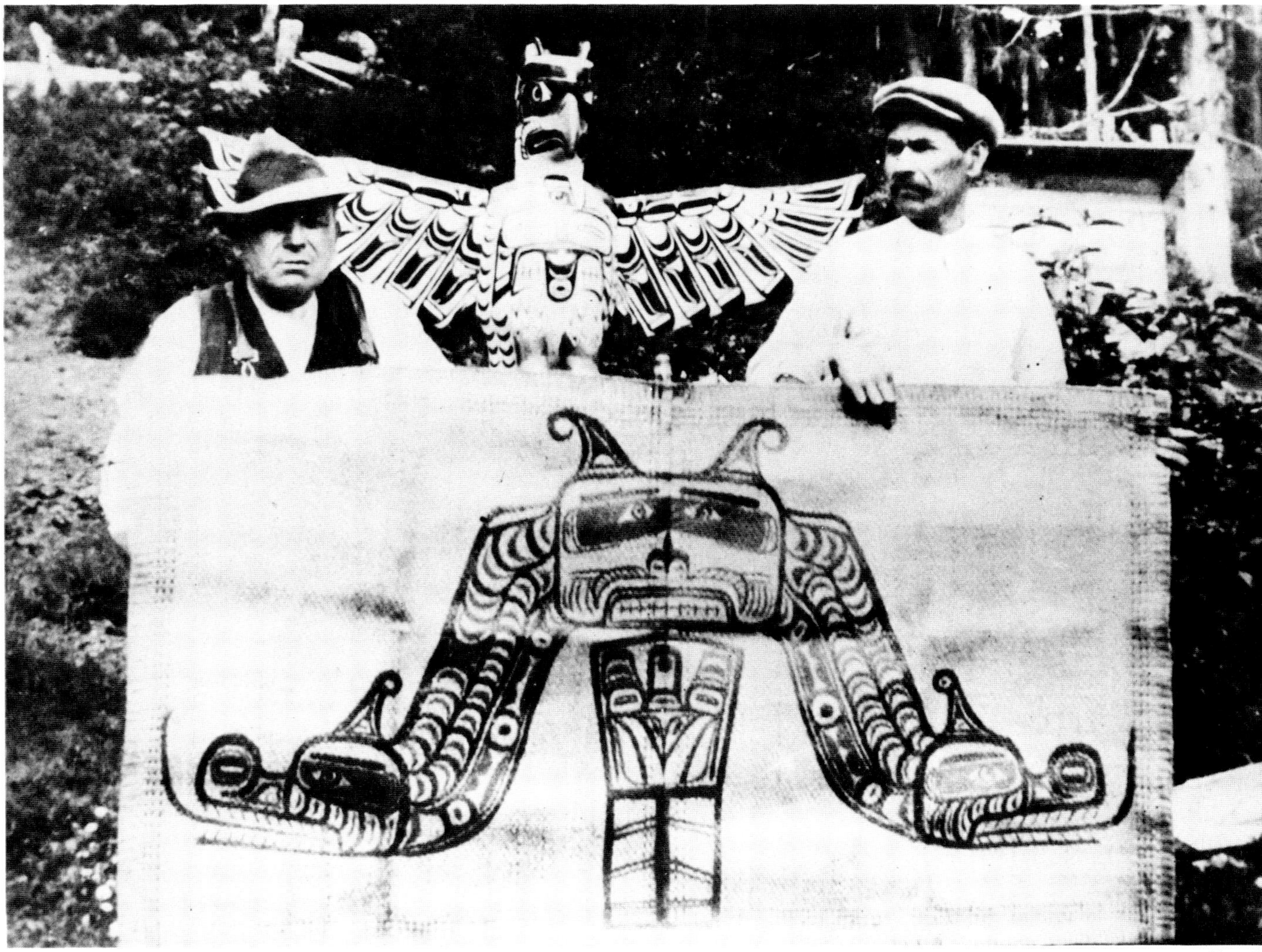

Plate: 130

'With funds from a grant to be devoted to museum and other anthropological purposes, Dr. Hawthorn was able, during the present year, to employ Mungo Martin at the University. During this period, Dr. Hawthorn has had him carve two original totem poles.'

'Of these poles, it has been decided to keep at least one and to investigate the possibility of selling the other to some institution. If the pole is thus sold, the money received for it will be applied toward securing a pole of other than Kwakiutl origin.'

'The Committee is indebted to Dr. Hawthorn for his generous assistance. In consultation with him, it was felt that though it should be securing poles from other tribes, Mungo Martin's presence on the campus was too valuable, in many other ways, to be dispensed with. In addition, there is no other carver at present, known to the committee, whose skill is known to equal that of Mungo Martin.'

The Committee in 1950-51, comprised: Professor Hunter Lewis (Chairman), Dr. C.E. Borden, Dr. Ian McTaggert-Cowan, Dr. H.B. Hawthorn, Professor F.M. Knapp, Mr. J.D. Lee, Mr. K.P. Caple, Chancellor E.W. Hamber, President N.A.M. MacKenzie, Professor G.C. Andrew.

So, the mid-point of the century found Mungo back in business, employed to restore old poles, duplicate some unrestorable ones, and carve new ones. How did it compare to salmon fishing? To quote a letter signed by N.A.M. MacKenzie:

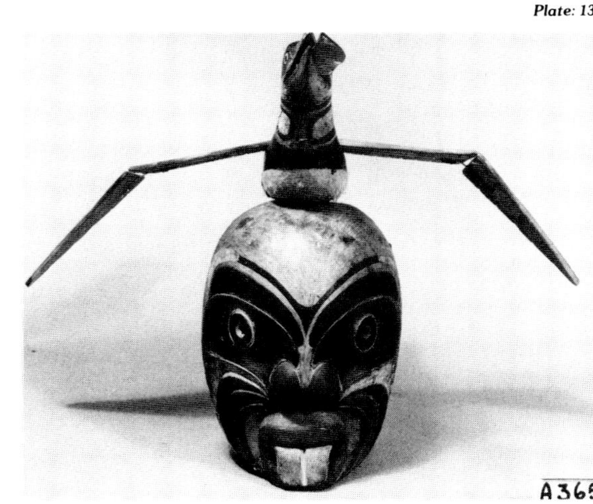

Plate: 131

Plate 130: **Charlie James (left) and Mungo Martin (with mustache). Ellen Neel described this photograph to Marius Barbeau as 'another photo of (Charlie James)... with Mungo Martin. Behind them, a Thunderbird which he (C.J.) made for a grave at Alert Bay. In front, a cedar mat with a painting of a 'Sisiutl' and a copper'—no date given, but probably around 1915. (Alert Bay, B.C. Photo: Courtesy City Archives, Vancouver IN-P-121.)**

Plate 131: **A 'pugwis' or Merman mask— carved by Mungo Martin for ceremonial use in 1911. The bird surmounting the Merman is a loon that will act as the Merman's guide while he is above the water. The mask in currently in the U.B.C. collection. (Vancouver. Photo: Courtesy U.B.C. A-3659.)**

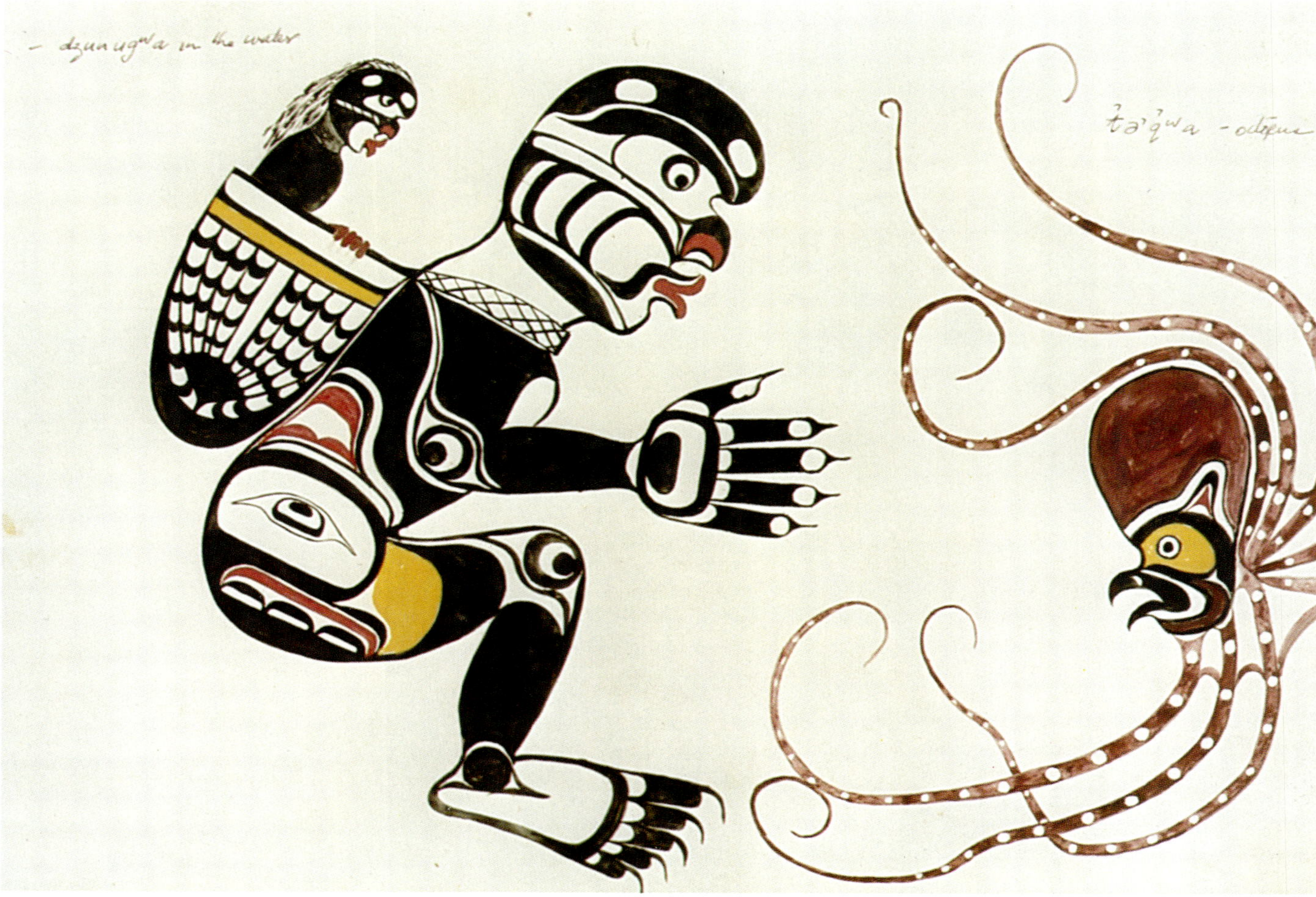

Plate 132: **A water-colour painting of the 'Dzunuk̲wa-under-the-sea' or 'Dzunuk̲wis'—in confrontation with a Pacific octopus . . . commonly called the 'devil fish' or in Kwakwala 'Tagwa.' The subsea version of the wild-woman-of-the-woods (Dzunuk̲wa) obviously shares her surface counterpart's habits . . . note the child-stealing basket on her back. Painting by Mungo Martin. (Vancouver, 1950. Photo: Courtesy U.B.C. A-9045.)**

'The Board granted authorization to employ Mr. Martin for a period of five months at a total expenditure, for labour and poles, of $1,850.00'

Considering inflation, it was not quite as good as the $350.00 that Johnny Drabble paid Mungo to carve the 'Raven of the Sea' pole, but then money wasn't everything to Mungo and the opportunity to use his considerable skills might never come again.

Those things about Mungo Martin that are well-documented come from this time and later. In full detail, they could fill several volumes this size.

In addition to his skill as a carver, Mungo represented an unprecedented ethnographic opportunity; to have this man—his incredible memory and his crisp authority on matters KWAKIUTL—amid those scholars who tried hard to understand a culture as foreign to them as the sea-dreams of dolphins.

To those who viewed him, Mungo was a gaunt old Indian whose seamed and lined face spoke of his life outdoors. He wore the clothes of a fisherman and the soft slouch hat of the thirties. His English was rudimentary and he seemed impatient—stumbling in a language ill-suited to his tongue. Everyone called him Mungo—even small children, so there is no disrespect intended in calling him by his first name.

To the Kwakiutl people, he was 'DATSA', an endearing name meaning 'grandfather'. His highest formal name was 'NA̲KA'PA̲NKA̲M', a potlatch chief 'ten times over'.

By all accounts and by all measures—he was an exceptional man.

Mungo was happy in his work at U.B.C., and he displayed his pleasure. Audrey Hawthorn, who spent much time with Mungo during his stay at U.B.C., was moved to write in 1951 a single page describing how he worked.

'Mungo Martin is about the most creative person I have ever known. To watch him over a period of time is an experience.

'To begin with, he is 62 plus, and works all alone, all day, in the totem pole shed, drawing, carving, chipping, sawing, axing, using a knife cleanly and clearly, in a pure, steady line. I think if we can indicate the variety of techniques in our movie of him, it will be a revelation, how many techniques one person can absolutely master. In any case, the totem poles are going to be magnificent, and he himself feels them to be his best.'

'While he is working, he sings a song, sometimes under his breath, sometimes aloud. If a passerby comes along, he stops them and explains the song. Usually, it is the song of the figure he is doing. Sometimes it is the song through which this character was introduced. Sometimes, it is a work song. But, he explains it, perhaps sings the song at length, in a clear voice. If the audience is an anthropologist with a notebook, he says, 'Put that down, Hawthorn. Got that down?' And waits. Usually the explanation involves a dance step, and a cry, as well. He does this.

'There is in no way, a chance to knock off work—it is an integral part of thinking and creating, and he goes back to work with the same steady stroke and the same song emphasizing the rhythm.'

'After an 8-hour day, he goes back to Acadia Camp, where his wife is. From then until 2 or 3 in the morning,

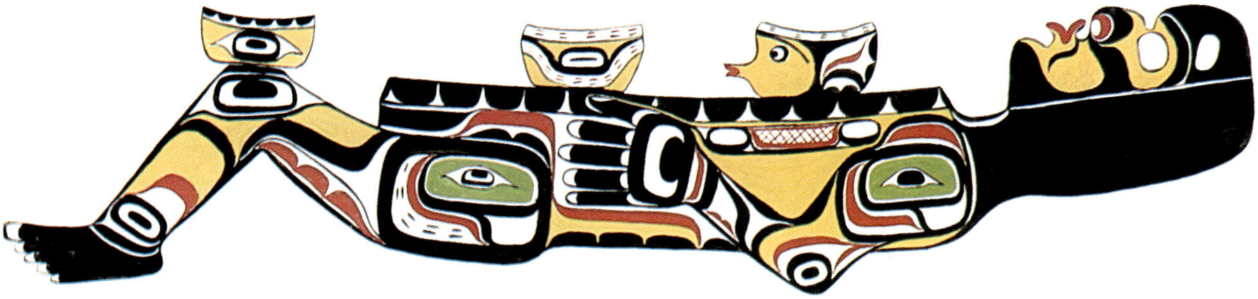

Plate: 133

the two of them are busy.

'Abayah embroiders (blouses, little dresses, scarves—all gifts, or knits—Kwakiutl designs on Indian sweaters).'

'Mungo carves small model poles, very often amusing little figures, like two whalers throwing a harpoon at a small whale, harpoon attached to the whaler by a tiny woven cedar line—or he paints. This is a new departure for him. It started when he went into the hospital for a check-up and we gave him a large pad of paper and a box of paints. (He doesn't read.) When he came out of the hospital a week later, he had a pad full of very fine Kwakiutl drawings and paintings of legendary figures, masks, dancers, etc. These, I feel, I should get published. They are just unusually fine. In any case, he now paints any surface. His walls are covered with paper plates! They are excellent for they have a round space already designated and a round frame. So there they are.'

'He and Abayah sing as they work, and stay up till all hours. When we come at 10:00 they have a whole group of new things to show us.'

'Sometimes, they go to Ida Halpern's to tape record some of Mungo's songs, in which case, with a glass of whiskey, they sit all evening, singing, beating time with a stick, laughing and explaining, between songs.

'Or, they come to our house and listen to ethnological records from other places, this being a highly-competitive and stimulating thing. One night Mungo sang us a Navajo song he had learned from an uncle who had learned it at the St. Louis World's Fair, 1904. Once, he sang a song about Geronimo going to fight the Kaiser, and the Prince of Japan entered into it somewhere. I think he said this was Navajo too!'

Plate 133: **Watercolour painting of a 'Dzunukwa' 'grease dish'—used primarily for serving oolichan oil at potlatches. The kneecaps, navel, and breasts of the giantess are represented by separate dishes—while the face is removable to expose another oil cavity. By Mungo Martin. (Vancouver, 1950. Photo: Courtesy U.B.C. A-9055.)**

Plate 134: **A watercolour painting of a 'Pugwis'—variously called a 'Merman or man-in-the-sea. This 'Pugwis' has the large buck teeth, similar to beavers, that help identify it. The confrontation appears to be with a sculpin or spiny rock fish. By Mungo Martin. (Vancouver, 1950. Photo: Courtesy U.B.C. A-9050.)**

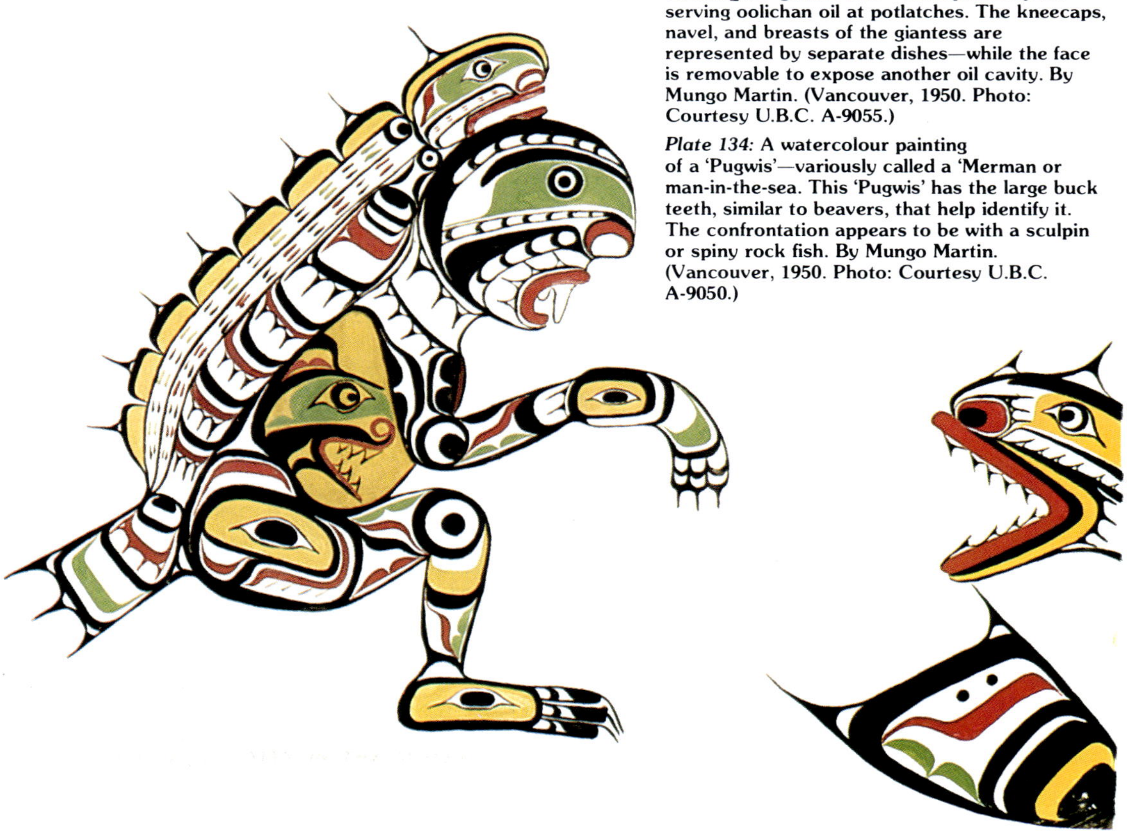

Plate: 134

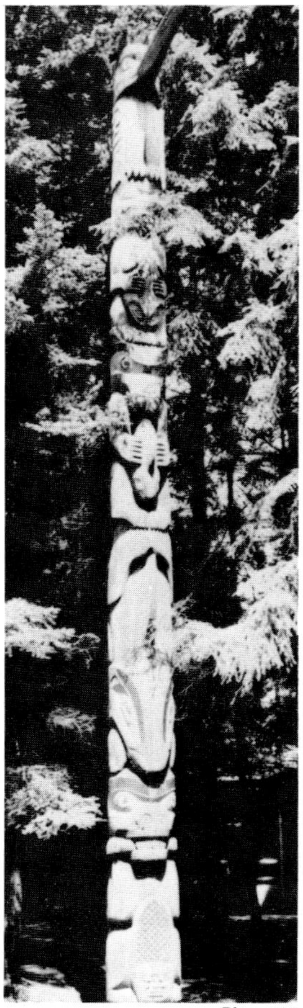

Plate: 135

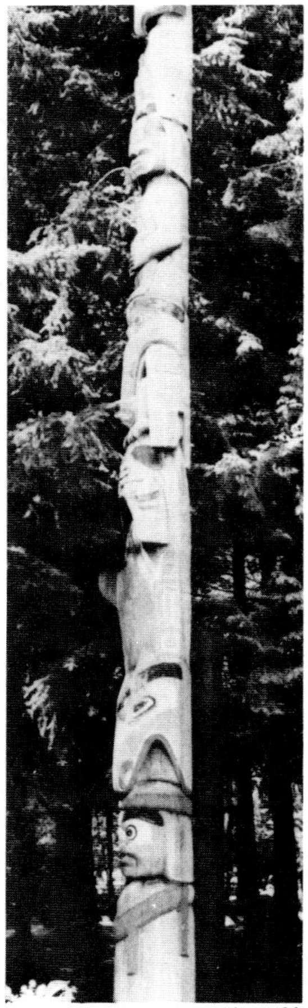

Plate: 136

Plate 135: **A pole carved by Mungo Martin in 1951, at the University of British Columbia. The pole contains some of the crests that Mungo was entitled to depict. From top to bottom; a 'Huxwhukw' or 'Cannibal Bird;' a chief; a bear; a killer whale; and the bottom figure shows the beaver. It was this pole that is shown in a 16 mm colour film produced by U.B.C. showing the stages of carving—from raw log to finished pole—and entitled 'Making a Totem Pole' (available from Instructional Media Centre, U.B.C., Vancouver, B.C.) (Vancouver, 1951. Photo: Courtesy: U.B.C.)**

Plate 136: **A totem carved at U.B.C. in 1951, by Mungo Martin. Audrey Hawthorn describes it as: 'Totem pole of Chief Kalilix—to commemorate the head of his (Mungo's) family line, who obtained the privilege of being served first at Potlatch feasts.' The figures are; Thunderbird; an ancestoral chief; a raven; a killer whale; and another chief. (Vancouver, 1951. Photo: Courtesy U.B.C. A-50040.)**

When Mungo Martin worked at U.B.C., he often visited Ellen Neel's house. That's where I first met him and remember thinking that he looked like an old man, which, of course, he was.

He would look around the living room and almost grimace visibly when he saw dozens and dozens of small tourist poles ready to go to be lacquered. But then his face would wrinkle in a smile when Ellen showed him a good piece commissioned by a collector, or perhaps destined to be given to a visiting dignitary.

Once, he was handling a pole, about 18 inches high, with a top figure of the 'hawk/man as the sun'. He took it over to the window to view it better in the bright sun and when he had finished his scrutiny, he looked over at Dave Neel and nodded several times. Dave flushed with pride. A compliment could hardly come from a more authoritative source.

I took the bus out to the University of British Columbia to watch Mungo work on the copying of old poles from distant villages. There were dozens of tourists already there when I arrived. They were snapping pictures and exclaiming over the carefully measured adze cuts. Mungo worked, oblivious of the crowd, staring for a long time at the curve of an elbow or the mask of an eye, before a few strokes brought symmetry with the side already done. I was fascinated with his tools. The smaller elbow adzes and the 'D' adzes were almost fragile compared to the ones I'd seen in the Neels' basement. The shaft of the elbow adze, in particular, was carved thin where it joined the blade mount and the length of the handle was slightly curved. Whether carved that way, or bent from long use, I couldn't tell.

When he changed to the 'D' adze, it fit snugly in his right hand and he steadied himself against the horizontal pole with his other hand. The unhurried beat of the blade against the soft pink wood was mesmerizing and the uniform chips lifted in a jagged roll and fell away, leaving long fluted areas.

Mungo's deftness, borne of long practice, was impressive, but the versatility of the tool itself was amazing. Mungo used it in short, chopping strokes—always at an angle to the surface, both vertically and horizontally. He held the handle in his left hand and pushed with his right, making the adze do the work of a conventional plane. He even used it gripping tightly in both hands and pushed it downwards across the edge grain—and it functioned as a chisel.

The wood of the handle was a smokey, honey colour, with the smooth patina of much use. The blade was razor sharp. I didn't feel it, but from the way it cut cleanly across the grain, it must have been. It looked razor sharp. I squatted for a long time in the sun—amid the tourists coming and going—and watched. When my legs became cramped, I sat cross-legged on the ground with my face in my hands and my elbows resting on my knees. When the angle of the sun had become shallow, I painfully got up, stretched my legs and prepared to hike over to the bus stop. Mungo looked at me, as I dusted the grass and needles from my legs, and said, 'How's your carving going?' I, like Dave Neel the week before, flushed with pleasure. 'Gonna do a big one,' he patted the unfinished pole, 'sometime?' Several of the remaining tourists looked at me with respect and I mumbled something like, 'I hope so.' Then made my getaway, red-faced, but grinning from ear to ear.

On the way home, I mentally kicked myself over and over for not expanding the conversation. A dozen intelligent replies to Mungo's brief query sprang to mind, but, as always, far too late. I thought to myself, 'Well, I may be shy, but, dammit, I'm determined!' The fact of Mungo's brief recognition and few kind words were a soothing balm in the abrasion of self-examination.

Naturally, the next time I was carving at the Neels, I cornered Dave and talked to him about making an adze. 'Yeah, I could use a new one myself, kid. C'mon over on Saturday and we'll work on it—but you need a blade. So do I, for that matter.'

My mind raced and I thought, 'A blade—where the hell do you get an adze blade?' Dave saw the blank look on my face and laughed, 'What we need is the leaf spring out of a car. Put the arm on your old man for a couple of bucks and go to some car wrecker. You should be able to get one for just about nothing.'

Early Saturday morning I sat on the curb in front of a junkyard near the Neel's house. The same junkyard with the 'giant's knitting' that I'd observed on my first trip there. When the owner finally opened the front door, yawning and scratching himself, I made my needs known.

'What kinda car?'

I shrugged, 'Any kind.'

'Well, do you need the shackles or the mounts or what?'

'Just a leaf spring,' I replied.

'Well, then I gotta cut the shackles with a torch and chisel the binder straps off to get just one leaf. Cost you three bucks.'

My heart sank.

'Or you kin have the whole bundle for a buck.'

I wrapped my heavy, grease-covered prize in a piece of newspaper and again made my getaway. This time, however, my red face was from exertion, not shyness!

I proudly presented it to Dave and his response was not unexpected, 'Jesus, kid, you got enough for twenty blades, but how are we gonna get them apart?' We finally went over to the rented shop and Ted Neel and I held the heavy object in position while Dave started the power grindstone and directed us how to hold the spring bundle to cut it in several places. Much grunting and complaining later, we had two pieces, perhaps five inches long, cut from the bundle.

Ted looked at the grindstone and observed that the old man was '...gonna be pretty unhappy...' because we'd rounded both corners off the stone. 'In fact,' Ted further observed, 'I think I'll go back to the house. You guys said an hour or so, but you're gonna be here all afternoon.'

Some further grinding, interspaced with dipping in water and we had two blades ground out. 'O.K. kid, I saved a good piece of oak and I'll bandsaw out a couple of handles. You do want a 'D' adze, right?' I reflected back on Mungo Marin's 'D' adze rhythmically producing that fluted finish and I nodded affirmatively. Dave drew out the shape on the two by six plank end and said:

'See, I gotta cut through the handle, to cut the center out 'cause there's no other way to get the band saw blade in.'

'Can't you take the blade off the saw?'

My query was met by a look of disgust.

'No, the blade's one loop. Even if you drill a hole you can't get it in 'cause the saw blade's all one piece. Don't worry though, I'll cut through it right at the back corner of the 'D' where your thumb goes and we can countersink a screw into it and it'll be O.K.'

I shook my head, 'I don't want a screw in mine, I want it all one piece.' Dave looked even more disgusted and said, 'What do ya wanna do, carve the centre out?'

'Uh-huh, if I have to.'

'Fine,' said Dave, 'You know so much about it, you make your own handle.'

'Nope,' I observed, 'you said I get the leaf spring and you'd make the adze. Just remember, that's a piece of my leaf spring you're planning to use in your adze.'

Dave laughed and punched me on the shoulder, 'O.K.,' he said with a grin on his face, 'you own the blades, you hold the cards.' He drilled the centres out of both handles and we hand-carved them smooth. While Dave was sanding them on the flap sander, he admitted that it probably was better in one piece.

We went back to the house on Glen Drive and spent the balance of the afternoon fine-honing the roughed-out blades. When the blades were finished, the butt ends of the blades were snugged up against the step, cut for that purpose and bound tightly with black electrician's tape.

'Well,' I thought, 'my anti-shyness resolution has already paid off!'

'O.K. Dave, now show me how to use it.'

Dave smiled slyly and said, 'Aha, my stubborn little friend. That wasn't part of the deal. You want to learn how to use it, it's gonna cost you!' Noting my crestfallen look, he said, 'Christ, kid, just kidding you,' as he got out some cedar slabs and we proceeded to try the adzes. They worked fine. The resulting finish didn't look much like that of Mungo Martin's, but to me, they worked just fine.

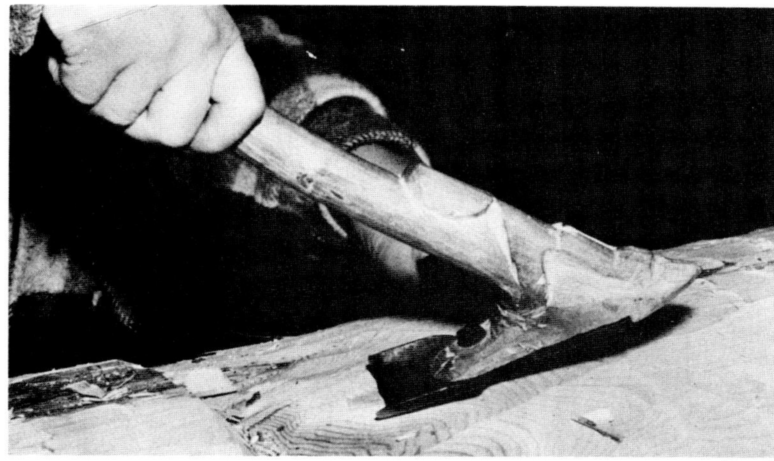

Plate: 137

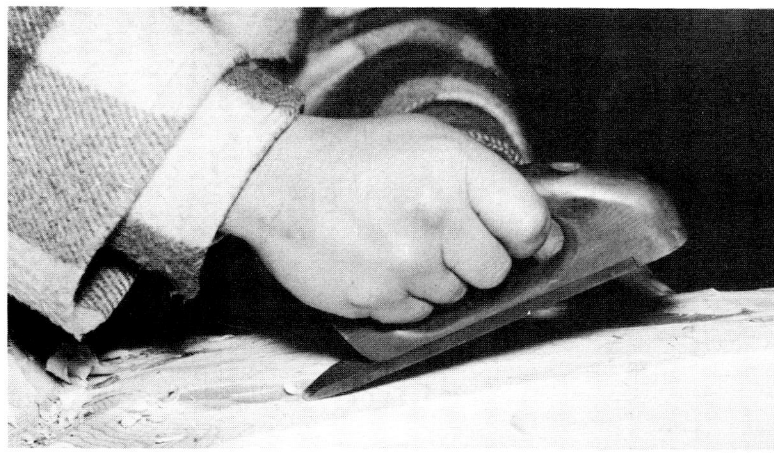

Plate: 138

***Plate 137:* One of the tools of the trade. David Martin demonstrates the use of an elbow adze or 'Kendalayo.' This one has a feature copied from a shipwright's adze—a curl at the edges of the blade to prevent tearing while cutting cross-grain. David Martin was the first to use this type of modified adze. (Thunderbird Park, Victoria, 1956. Photo: Victoria Daily Colonist.)**

***Plate 138:* David Martin demonstrates the correct position of the 'D' adze—in Mungo's hands this simple tool became a marvelous precision instrument. (Thunderbird Park, Victoria, 1956. Photo: Victoria Daily Colonist.)**

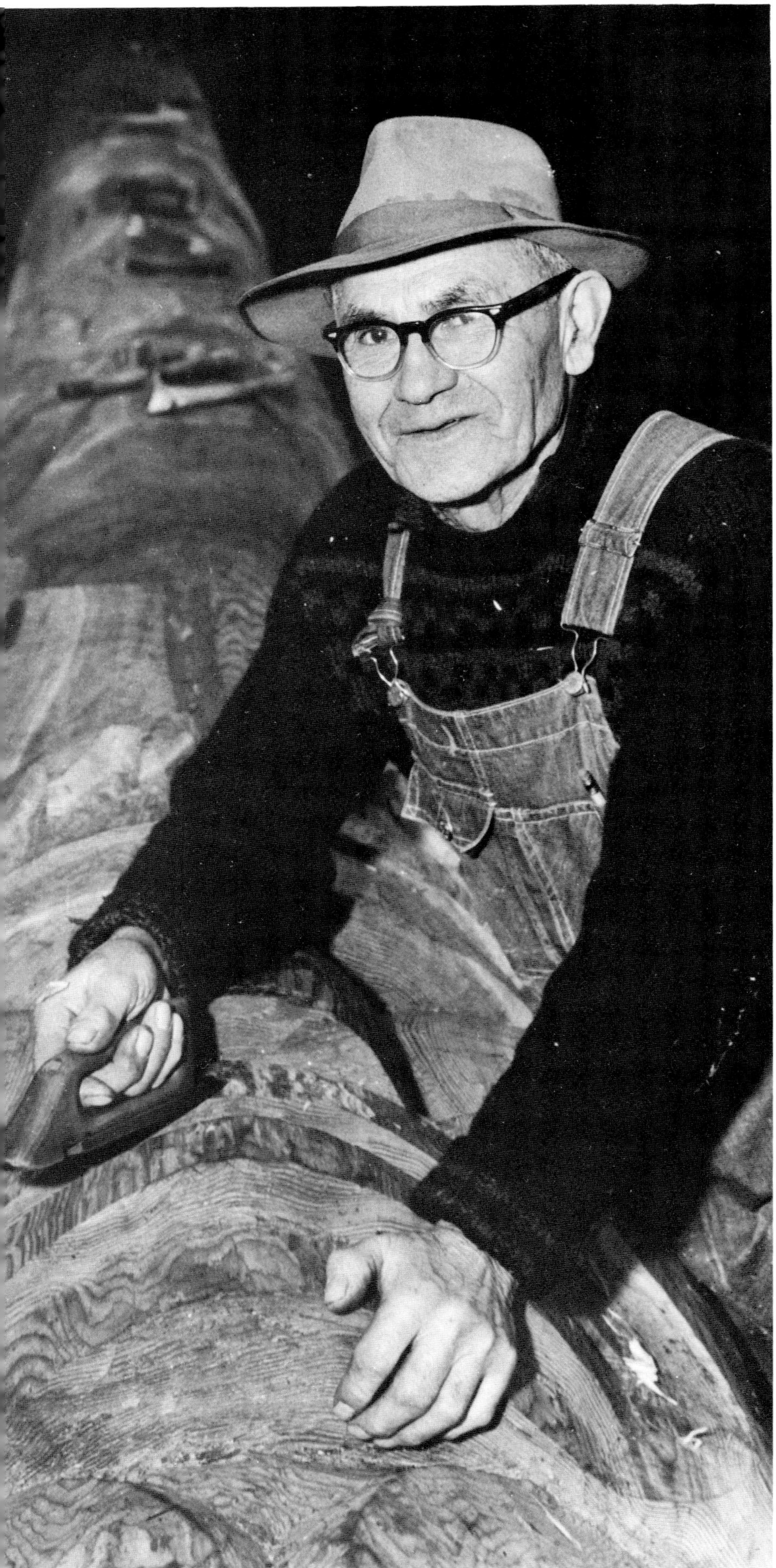

***Plate 139:* Mungo Martin, Chief 'NA̱KA'PA̱NKA̱M.' Master carver, remarkable man. (Date unknown. Photo: Jim Ryan.)**

During the period of 1950-1951, Mungo carved several new poles. One contained the crest figures that he, as a Chief of Fort Rupert, was entitled to depict. The top figure is a 'HUXWHUKW'—also called the 'Cannibal Bird'—an important figure of the 'HAMATSA' or Wild Man Society. This creature was one of the several representatives of 'BAXWBAKWALANUSIWE',' 'The cannibal that lives at the north end of the world.' The second figure is that of a chief, shown wearing a blanket and cedarbark neck and head rings.

Below the chief is a bear and below the bear, a killer whale. The bottom figure is a beaver, shown in the typical pose of chewing a stick held between upright paws.

The other new pole was carved to represent the figures of Mungo's family history. The thunderbird is carved on top, an ancestoral chief below him and below the chief, a raven. The killer whale is shown next and another ancestoral chief forms the bottom figure.

These poles were made to join several of the poles that Mungo had already restored and a group of others that, collectively formed 'Totem Park' at the University of British Columbia.

Totem Park was originally conceived in 1947 by Professor Hunter Lewis and the committee previously mentioned. It was designed to show Kwakiutl, Haida, and other tribal examples of totem carving in a natural setting, surrounded by ethno-botanic flora (the important plants used for a variety of purposes by the original people of the northwest coast).

When Marius Barbeau visited the west coast of Canada in 1947, he located a number of significant carvings at various coastal villages and negotiated for their purchase. A sum of money to acquire these poles for the proposed Totem Park, was made available by Mr. Eric Hamber. Two of the poles were purchased by the U.B.C. Alma Mater Society, and later, more funds were forthcoming to complete further purchases, cover shipping costs, and provide a place for storage.

It was the goal to restore two complete villages of two tribes prominent in the northwest—the Kwakiutl and the Haida—along with individual displays from other tribes.

In November, 1949, the University of British Columbia made available a plot of land some three acres in size. In this area, the program of restoring old poles and carving new ones went ahead, under Mungo Martin.

As Audrey Hawthorn mentioned earlier, Mungo participated strongly in other phases of identifying, explaining, and recording the culture of the Kwakiutl. He worked closely with Audrey and Dr. Harry Hawthorn at U.B.C., and once the machinery for purchase of potlatch material was set in motion (largely grants from Dr. H.R. MacMillan and Dr. Walter C. Koerner), Mungo showed a strong interest in seeing these things properly identified.

Audrey Hawthorn said:

'Mungo visited the museum frequently to see what had arrived during the week. At the height of the flow of materials, wooden crates, old trunks, sea-chests and cardboard boxes came in by every ship from the north. Addressed to the University, to Mungo Martin himself, and to a number of other addresses, these reached their destination with the help of a wonderfully understanding post office.

'Mungo awaited the unpacking with keen interest. Being a full participant in the ceremonial system, he recognized many individual pieces and identified almost all of them with assurance. He gave both the Kwakiutl name and a translation, based on his clear comprehension of the use and background of the piece. He was concerned that his words not be wasted.'

Every couple of weeks Mungo and Abaya'a would go to the home of Dr. Ida Halpern to record Kwakiutl songs. Dr. Halpern received her PH.D in Musicology from the University of Vienna in 1938, and was teaching at U.B.C. Over a several-year period, Mungo recorded one hundred and twenty-four songs for Dr. Halpern. A number of these songs were subsequently published in New York in an album entitled 'Indian Music of the Northwest Coast'.

When approached by other chiefs for having given away his songs, Mungo responded:

'I was a sick man when I started to sing for her. Now after the years singing, I sang myself back to health and am well again!'

Dr. Halpern was fond of pointing out how well-developed and sophisticated was Mungo's musical sense. He used to accompany her occasionally to symphony concerts and she said:

'His criticisms of our music were pertinent, unconsciously, he showed fine discrimination, preferring the best-known conductors.'

Richard Oman wrote of Mungo's musical interest (and his sense of humour) in an unpublished course-end thesis.

'Once, while he was at the University of British Columbia, Harry and Audrey Hawthorn took him to a symphony concert. All through the performance, Mungo stared at the bald head of the conductor. When the concert was over, Mungo turned to the Hawthorns and said, 'What a waste of a bald head. I could paint a beautiful frog on it!' *(A. Hawthorn interview, March, 1975.)*

There is no question that Mungo was a remarkable man with a great mental store-house of cultural knowledge. It was during these years at U.B.C. that he came to appreciate the importance of recording and preserving what he knew—an appreciation that turned into determination, and lasted throughout his life. It made Mungo much more than just a totem pole carver.

In 1952, Mungo Martin and his wife left their cottage on the university campus. Totem Park was well underway and the U.B.C. group simply had no funds to continue to employ Mungo. There was little time to be despondent, however, for all the many people that had come to know Mungo and appreciate his skill would not let him rest long. There were new, exciting plans for Mungo, as explained many years later by the Chairman of the 'Totem Pole Preservation Committee' in this quote from a *Memorandum on Totem Poles* dated October, 1978:

'We overspent our budget even before the Totem Park was finished as planned. Although Mungo was about seventy, it seemed a pity not to continue to use his abilities, as they were completely unique. We wanted to get some other carvers trained and continue the work of production. With the Provincial Museum, (Victoria) therefore, we set up a 'Totem Pole Preservation Committee', and we persuaded the Provincial Government to start supporting the program of duplication, repair, new carving and training—at Thunderbird Park in Victoria, B.C. This has gone on since 1952 and its output has been considerable. At least three younger carvers have had some training and two of them have become competent, one of them being perhaps, as good as Mungo himself.'

In March, 1952, a handsome article outlining Mungo's work at U.B.C. was published by the magazine 'Beaver'. The article was well written by Audrey Hawthorn and illustrated with a half dozen photos, but by the time the article appeared, Mungo was no longer at U.B.C. He had gone back across Georgia Stait to the Island where he was born. This time, however, he took up his residence on the other end of Vancouver Island, in Victoria, B.C., over two hundred miles south of Fort Rupert.

For the second time in a few years, Mungo Martin was back in business! It was good, in Victoria. The press liked him, ethnographers and anthropologists were ecstatic, the people of Victoria respected him and welcomed him—and the tourists loved him!!! In August of 1952, a local newspaper featured an article which said, in part:

INDIAN CRAFTSMAN PRESERVES B.C. TOTEMS

'Mungo Martin is a combination reference library and an Indian Burke's Peerage. He also makes totem poles—at present he is working for the Provincial Government, in Thunderbird Park, carving copies of the totem poles and other Indian Art displayed there. These native pieces of wooden statuary which are exposed to the weather, are beginning to rot. After Mungo and his son, David, have duplicated all of them, the originals will be stored under cover until the Provincial Museum has room to exhibit them.

The Martins were brought down from their home at Fort Rupert, near Port Hardy on Northern Vancouver Island, especially to do this job, which is expected will take them about three years. Not only is it appropriate to have native Indians carve these replicas of their ancestors' craftsmanship, it is doubtful if any others could be found capable of doing the job. All the carving is done with small hand-adzes, which were made by the workmen themselves, and differ in shape from the ordinary adze.

The B.C. Coast Indians had quite an involved culture long before the white man arrived, but they didn't have a written language. So, they had to find some way of keeping records of their history. Certain individuals with exceptionally good memories were given this job. They remembered who had the right to sing certain songs and what totem belonged to which clan, etc. Mungo Martin is the official 'rememberer' for his tribe.

For the next three years, Victoria will probably be the only spot in North America where one can see the practise of an art that was old when Columbus discovered the continent. Moreover, it is being done in the same manner, with the same instruments, by the descendants of some of the original practitioners. Captain Vancouver may have gazed at practically the same sight that tourists are taking pictures of, this summer.'

In 1953, Mungo tackled a formidable project and one dear to his heart. In a large space cleared next to the totem carving shed at Thunderbird Park, he planned to build an old-style Kwakiutl house. The house was to be a reduced-scale version of one erected by his uncle 'Chief NAKA'PANKAM', nearly a century before, in Fort Rupert, B.C. Mungo knew the design well, since he had been born in that house. Mungo had, in 1953, the highest name to which he was even distantly entitled—the name 'NAKA'PANKAM' meaning 'ten times over'. With the name, as he explained, came the right to use the same housepost crests, on his new house, as had been used on the original one.

Mungo was emphatic about one point—that this would be more than just a free copy of a Kwakiutl house. It was to be the house of 'NAKA'PANKAM', of the Mamtigila clan of the Kwakiutl tribe. It was to be Mungo Martin's house. It would be built correctly—(with some steel and concrete concessions to permanence!). Its building would be documented and it would be dedicated or opened with a potlatch.

To Mungo, the potlatch was one of the most important parts of the entire enterprise. He was proud of what he had done towards ensuring the survival of the Kwakiutl culture—the endless hours with ethnographers and anthropologists; the miles of recording tape; the dozens of songs, the labourious expanation of cultural concepts that he understood so well, but found difficult to explain clearly. All of this he had done.

The only fitting manner to make his peers acknowledge his accomplishments was in the old way. 'You Chiefs, this is what I have done. This is what I claim for my children and my children's children. These things I say publicly.' Yes, the potlatch was the thing!

In some ways, the idea of a potlatch in the old manner was an innovative concept. Since the jailing of prominent Kwakiutl chiefs in 1921-22 for participating in the prohibited potlatches, the whole system had gone 'underground'. In attempting to explain their actions, the old chiefs had spoken eloquently, to those that would listen, that 'a strict law bids us dance'. But an equally strict law, called Section 149 of the Indian Act, sent them to jail for dancing.

By 1953, the law prohibiting the potlatch had been quietly dropped from the revised Indian Act, but the old people remembered and they wondered at Mungo's temerity in announcing this potlatch. Potlatching had gone on, certainly, over the previous thirty years, but quietly and clandestinely. Now it was to be done in downtown Victoria, in the shadow of the Parliament Buildings that still held records of the old trials and sentences.

The Provincial Museum people assured Mungo that there was no problem. Some, notably Wilson Duff and Michael Kew, helped arrange the details. But many of the old people were not quite so sure. It was inexplicable that it had ever been wrong—but people went to jail and their families suffered. Why was it okay now?

The house that Mungo, his son David, and his son-in-law Henry Hunt laboured to build, is worth describing in detail.

The house was to be named. Old 'NAKA'PANKAM' owned two important house names, and Mungo chose one for this house. He would call it 'WA WADITLA'. That name means 'He orders them to come inside'. In other words, the owner was so powerful that he could order any passerby into his house, to be his servant.

The carvings on the houseposts that support the main beams would be the same as the original house of 'NAKA'PANKAM'. The back houseposts have the cannibal bird, 'HUXWHUKW' at the top and a grizzly bear holding a child, at the bottom. The front houseposts have the Wild Woman of the Woods, 'DZUNUKWA', on top and a grizzly bear holding a copper, below. These figures represent the crests of one of the clans to which 'NAKA'PANKAM' was related—directly or by marriage.

For example: The cannibal bird, 'HUXWHUKW' was the main crest of the Gi'Ksem clan (or 'NA'MIMA') of the Kwakiutl proper (or 'Walas Kwakiutl or 'Ft. Rupert Kwakiutl'). The wife of old 'NAKA'PANKAM'

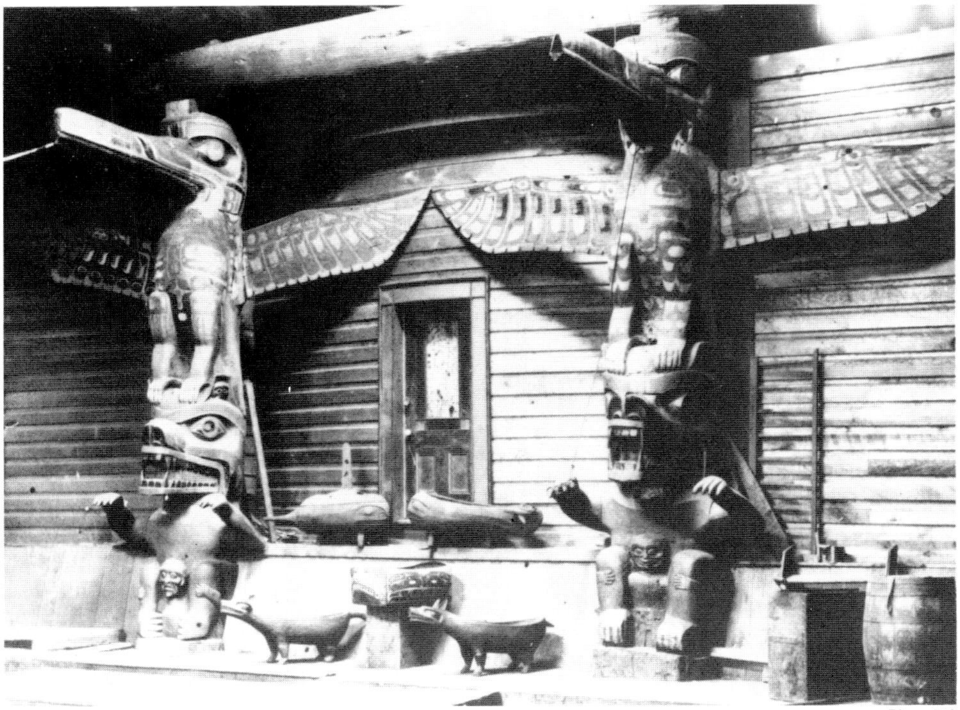

Plate: 140

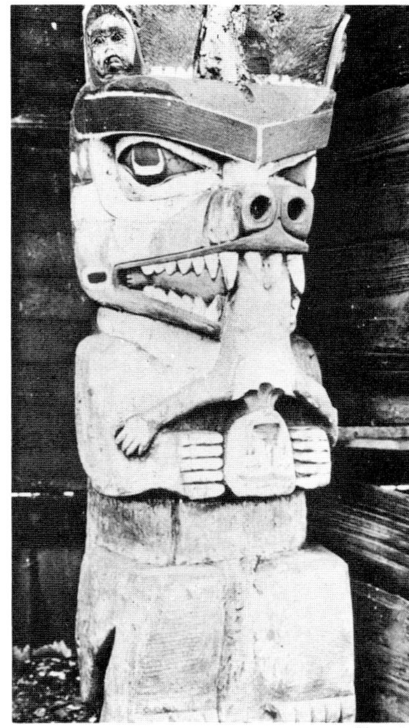

Plate: 141

belonged to this clan and so did Mungo Martin. He said at that time he was the only man left in that clan.

The 'HUXWHUKW' figure has a story of origin which says, briefly:

At the beginning of time, the original ancestor of the clan was named Gi'Ksem, and he lived in the area now called Gold Beach, at the mouth of the Nawhitti River. At dawn one day, he heard strange noises and was surprised to see a large totem pole rising out of the ground. All of the figures on the pole were alive and each made its own noise or cry. The totem pole had the 'Huxwhukw' on top, then the whale, eagle, seal, fur-seal, beaver, and finally, a man. The man spoke to Gi'Ksem and told him that this would be his 'KIS'U' (crests, privileges, etc.), and that he and his descendants could use the figures as their crests and the 'cries' in dancing.

The tradition goes on to tell the story of the various exploits of Gi'Ksem and traces out his descendants.

The grizzly bear is the crest-figure of a different clan to which 'NAKA'PANKAM' was related through his parents. The original ancestor of this clan had the supernatural ability to transform himself. He had been a bear, and then by removing the bear skin, he became a man and took the name 'YAXTLAN'. His previous name had been 'WA'LIBUI' (Bully). His descendants formed the 'WA'WALIBUI' clan and have the grizzly as their crest.

The 'DZUNUKWA' came to 'NAKA'PANKAM' through a grandparent of the 'KWIKSUTENUK' Tribe of Tribune Channel, B.C. Their story of origin relates to a fisherman who accidentally harpooned a 'DZUNUKWA' while spearfishing. He took the dead 'DZUNUKWA' back to his village and split the body open to use as a feast dish. From that time his descendants have used the 'Wild Woman' on their totem poles and feast dishes.

The huge painting on the front of Mungo's house was often referred to as a 'Killer Whale', but is was designed to be 'TSEE'AKIS'—a supernatural sea-creature shaped like a sculpin and variously called a 'bullhead,' a 'rock cod' or similar.

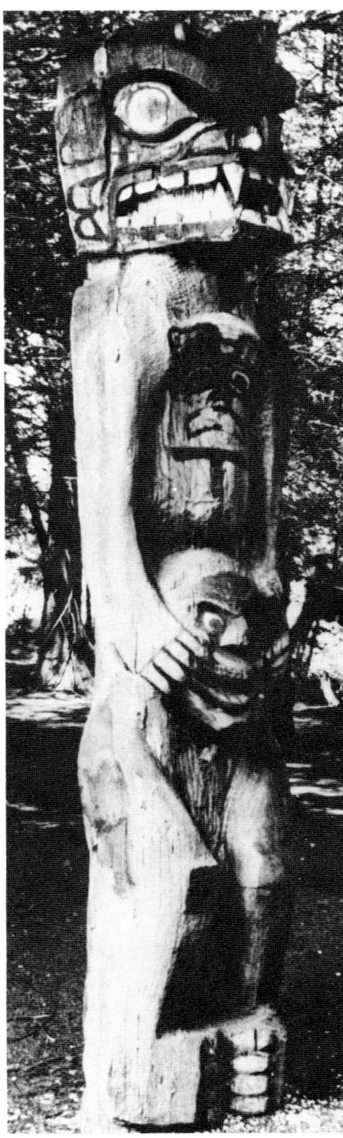

Plate: 142

Plate 140: A pair of houseposts at 'Memkumlis' (Village Island), similar to the rear houseposts of Mungo Martin's house at Thunderbird Park, Victoria, B.C. The figures represented are the same, but the style is much different. Note that the beaks of the 'Huxwhukw' and the arms of the grizzly bear are articulated and will move in unison when operated from the back of the pole. (Mamalilaculla, B.C., 1912. Photo: C.F. Newcombe. Courtesy: B.C.P.M. PN-29.)

Plate 141: One of the original houseposts of Chief 'Naka'pankam' at Fort Rupert. This was the house in which Mungo Martin was born . . . and he chose these same figures for his house at Thunderbird Park, albeit in a slightly different arrangement. (Fort Rupert, c. 1900. Photo B.C.P.M. PN-14208.)

Plate 142: A bear figure in the U.B.C. collection. This figure was collected in Fort Rupert by Marius Barbeau, in 1947. Note the similarity to the bear houseposts of Mungo Martin's house in Thunderbird Park. (Vancouver, 1951. Photo: Courtesy U.B.C. A-50036.)

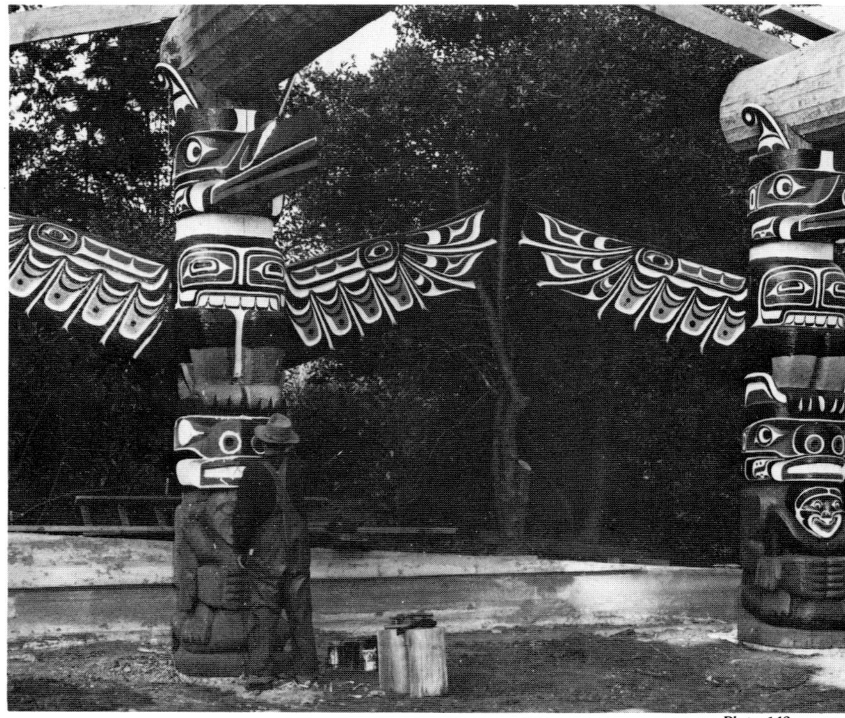

Plate: 143

Plate 143: The rear houseposts of 'Wawaditla' are up and Mungo does the painting. The top figures are the mythical cannibal birds call 'Huxwhukw', while the lower figures represent the grizzly bear holding a child. (Thunderbird Park, Victoria, 1953. Photo: Tourism, B.C. 7137.)

Plate 144: Mungo works on the front houseposts for 'Wawaditla' while David Martin (rear) uses a double-bitted axe to remove the sapwood from a cedar log. The figures of the front houseposts will be the 'Dzunuḵwa' on top and a grizzly bear holding a potlatch 'copper' below. Mungo is using an elbow adze on the lower jaw of the grizzly bear. (Thunderbird Park, 1953. Photo: Tourism, B.C. 7504.)

Plate 145: Mungo Martin, left, and his son David, are obviously pleased with what they are doing . . . and look forward to erecting the finished communal house 'Wawaditla'. Mungo has his hand on the nose of the giantess 'Dzunuḵwa' that will form one of a pair of front houseposts. (Thunderbird Park, Victoria, 1953. Photo: Tourism, B.C. 7506.)

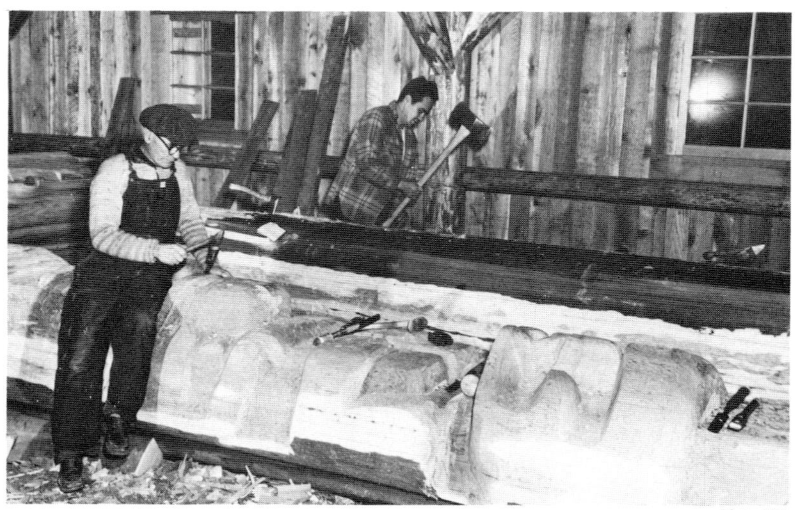

Plate: 144

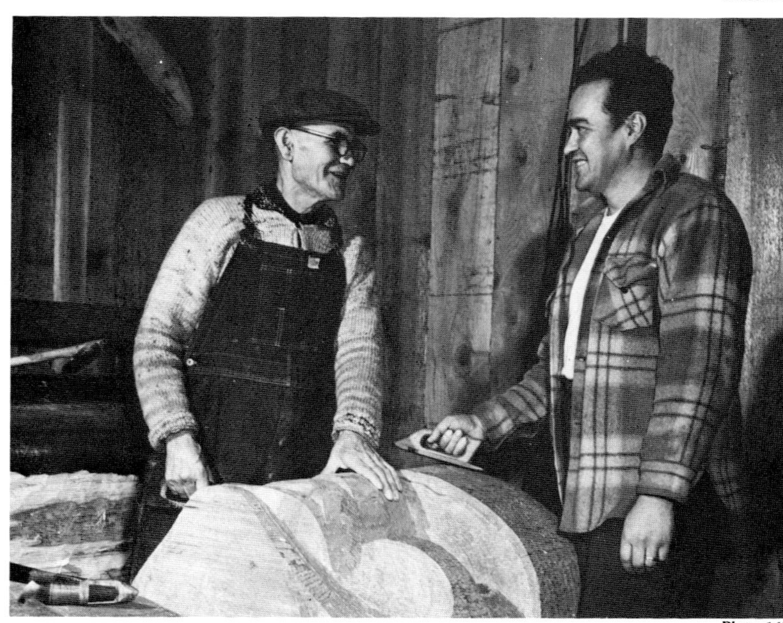

Plate: 145

The design was originally used on the house front of a chief called 'KWAXSISTALA' who lived in the village of 'Galakwis'. The design is representative of the 'DA̱'NAXDA'X̱W' tribe of the Kwakiutl, from the Knight Inlet area. 'KWAXSISTALA' was a distant uncle of Mungo's and Mungo thereby claimed the right to use the painting.

Outside the house of Mungo Martin was one feature not found in the original dwellings of 'NAḴA'PA̱NKA̱M' or 'KWAXSISTALA'—a huge heraldic totem pole, with figures carved by Mungo to represent all of the Kwakiutl tribes, by showing the main crests of four of them: 1. the 'A̱'NA̱'EYTŁA̱LA' 2. the 'NAK WAX-DA'X̱W' 3. the "NA̱MG̱IS' 4. the 'WALAS KWA-KIUṮL.'

The top figure on the pole is 'TSOONA', the Thunderbird, a crest of the 'A̱'NA̱'EYTŁA̱LA' tribe. The original ancestor of this tribe was the Thunderbird, who became a man. His son returned to the sky to control thunder and lightning. The next two figures represent the 'WA'WALIBUI' clan of the Kwakiutl and depict 'WALIBUI' as grizzly bear and below as 'YA'KTLEN', a man.

Below 'YA'KTLEṈ' is 'T'SAWI' the beaver, a crest figure of the "NAḴWAXDA'X̱W' tribe of Blunden Harbour. The bottom figure shows the wild giantess, 'DZUNUḴWA' holding her son 'T'SIL'WALAGAME"—a Nimpkish clan claims the Dsonoqua as their crest. According to their tradition, a man hunted the 'DZUNUḴWA' because the creature was stealing fish from his family's drying racks. After capturing the 'DZUNUḴWA' he became fond of her and ultimately married her.

Their son was 'T'SIL'WALAGAME"—half man and half 'DZUNUḴWA'—who became the founder of this Nimpkish clan.

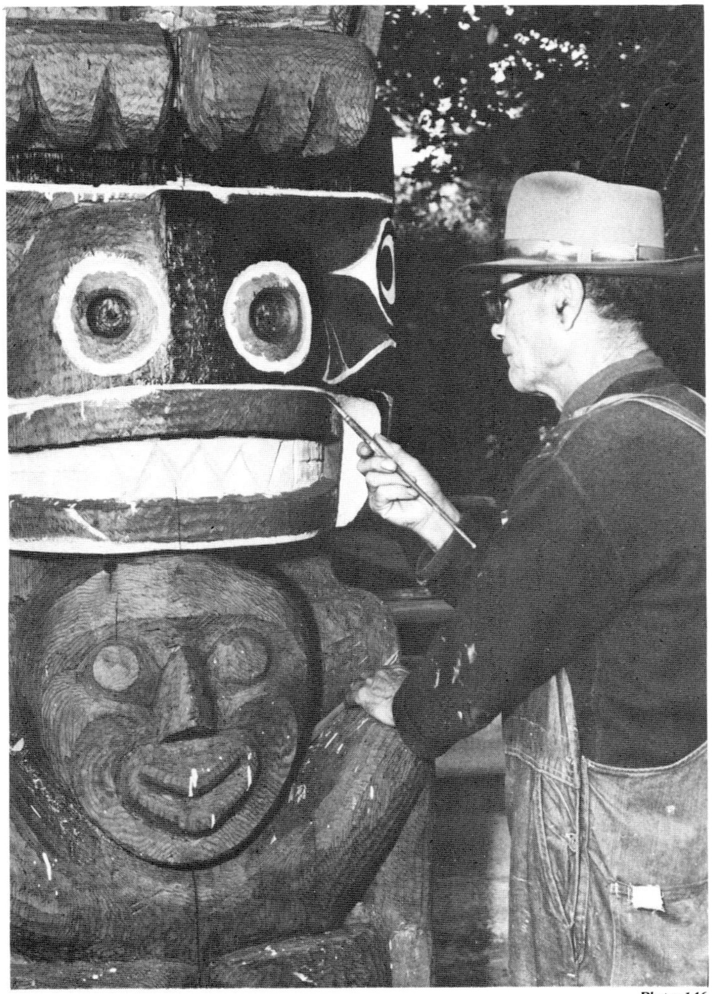

Plate: 146

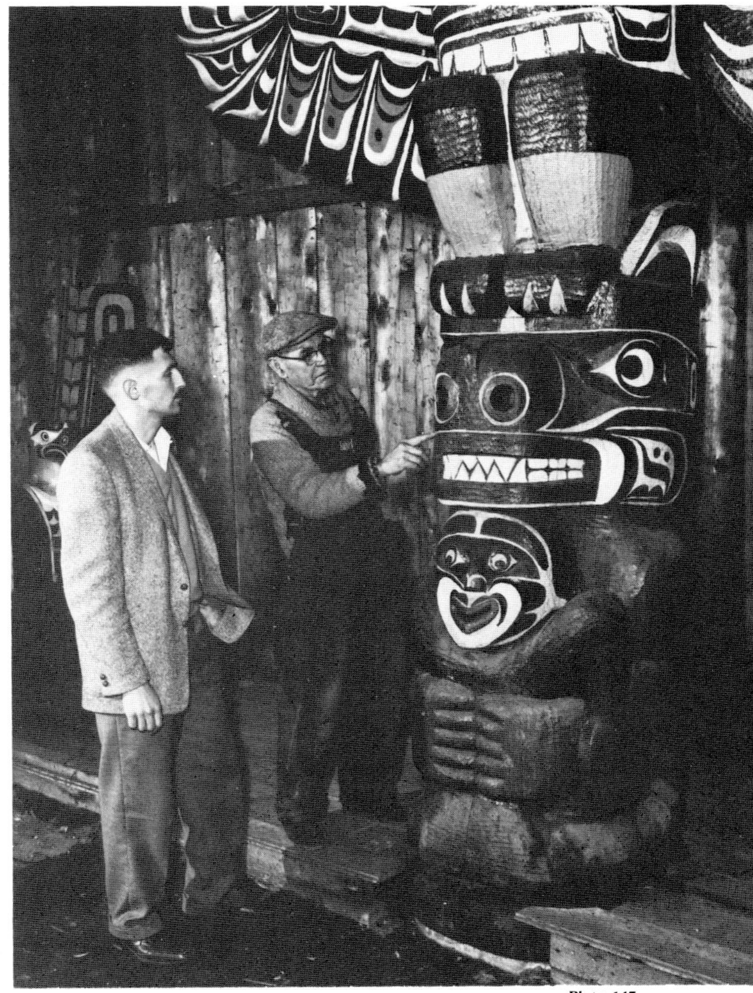

Plate: 147

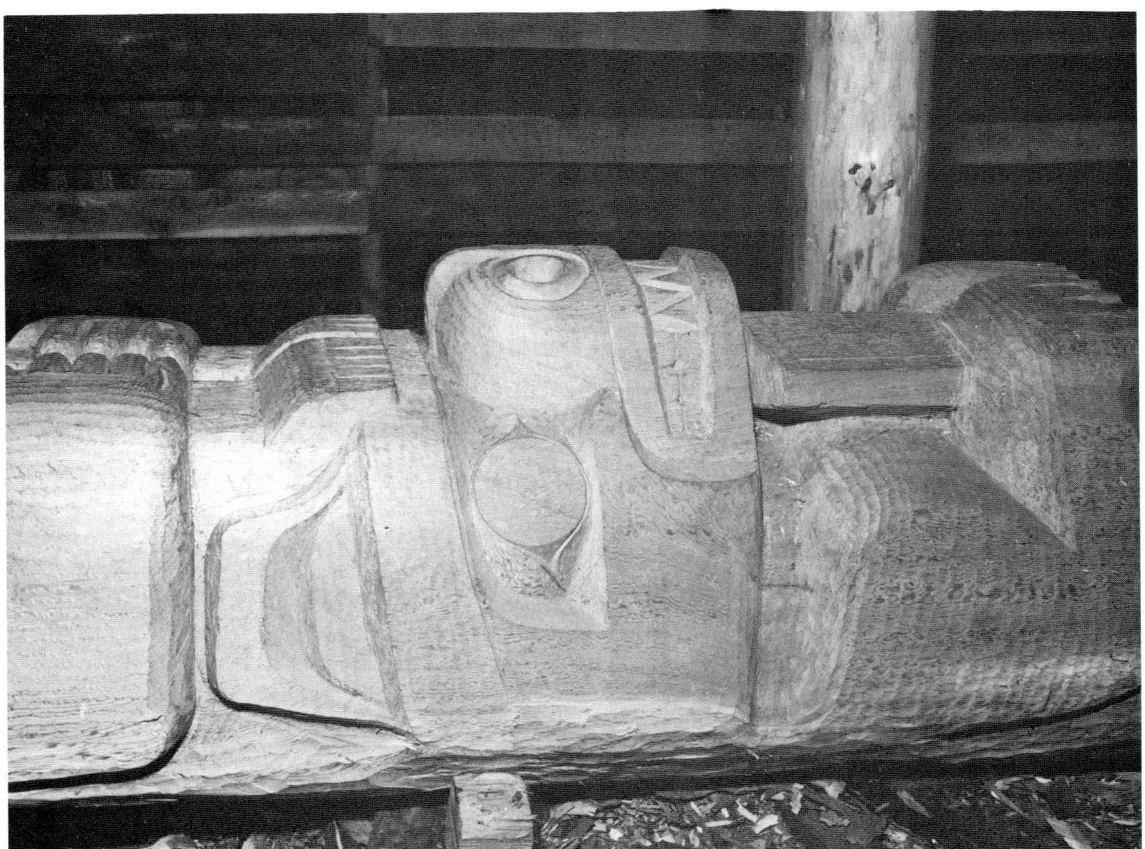

Plate: 148

Plate 146: A closer view of the painting on the rear houseposts. Mungo does not give the entire pole a base coat of white, but paints those areas which will remain white slightly larger than the area of the over paint. (Thunderbird Park, Victoria, 1953. Photo: Tourism, BC.)

Plate 147: One of the pair of rear houseposts inside 'Wawaditla'—Mungo's house at Thunderbird Park. Mungo points out features of the grizzly bear holding a child to Michael Kew. (Thunderbird Park, Victoria, c. 1953. Photo: B.C.P.M.)

Plate 148: One of the front houseposts of 'Wawaditla' after 'D' adzing. Shown is the head of the grizzly bear clutching a 'copper' to his chest. (Thunderbird Park, Victoria, 1953. Photo: Tourism, B.C.)

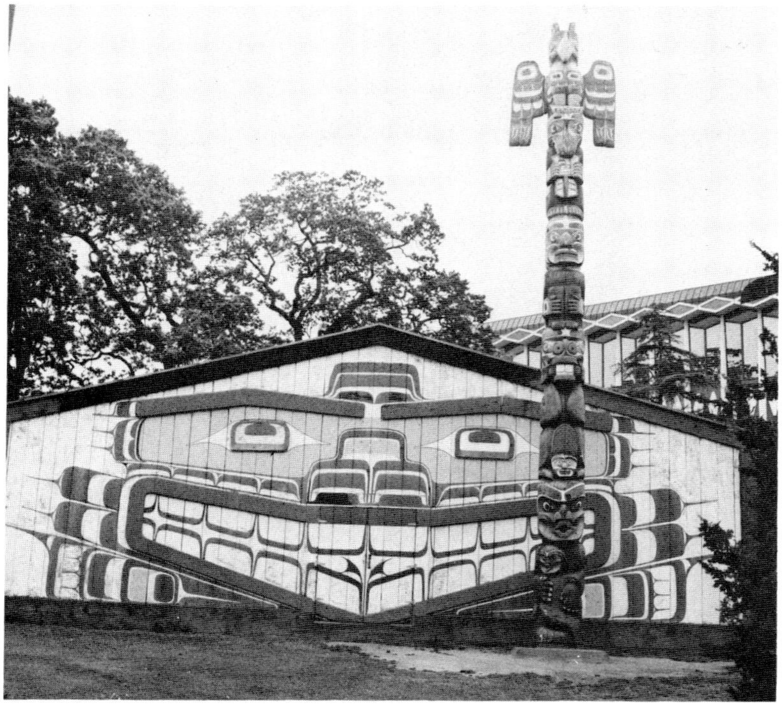

Plate: 149

Mungo and his assistants worked steadily on the house 'WA'WADITLA', throughout 1953. As the summer progressed, the hours became longer as the pressure to finish increased. They *had* to finish on schedule. Invitations had gone out months before, both official and by word of mouth, since time was required for the dancers to prepare their regalia; for the old people to collaborate with Mungo on the selection of songs and names for relatives. All the minutiae of a big occasion. Concurrently, Mungo worked on the masks to be used in the opening potlatch.

Finally, the house was finished and the date for the potlatch was set. It was decided to carry out the potlatch in three versions. The first day for native people and a few white 'good-friends' and researchers. Then a night for white people 'by invitation only', and lastly, a brief run-through for the general public. The potlatch was tacitly referred to as the 'opening ceremonies' and the program read:

PROGRAM OF EVENTS

Monday, December 14th, 1953

Ceremonies, banquet and masked dances. For Indian guests only, by invitation.

Tuesday, December 15th, 1953—8 p.m.

Formalities

Host's speech of welcome ..... Mungo Martin
Interpreter .. Daniel Cranmer, Alert Bay, B.C.
Passing out of souvenir cedar bark headbands.

Ceremonies and Dances

Yathla—the cradle ceremony
.... Mungo Martin and others

This ceremony, called 'rocking the baby' belongs to the Martin family and is being performed for Miss Dorothy Martin.

Dances of the Ha'Matsa
.... David Martin and others

The Ha'matsa (David Martin) dances first, then the masked figures (the Ha'matsa spirits)

Plate 149: **Mungo Martin's house. The various figures are explained in the text. (Thunderbird Park. Photo: Andrew Niemann. Courtesy: B.C.P.M. PN-13195-10.)**

Plate 150: **The wild giantess 'Dzunuk̲wa'—the bottom figure of the heraldic pole in front of Mungo Martin's house in Thunderbird Park. (Thunderbird Park, Victoria, c. 1980. Photo: Author.)**

Plate 151: **Detail of the 'Dzunuk̲wa's' son 'T'sit'walagame'—half 'Dzunuk̲wa and half human. Mungo has captured the apprehensive, half-fearful look on the small one's face as he looks back from his mother's arms. (Thunderbird Park, Victoria, 1980. Photo: Author.)**

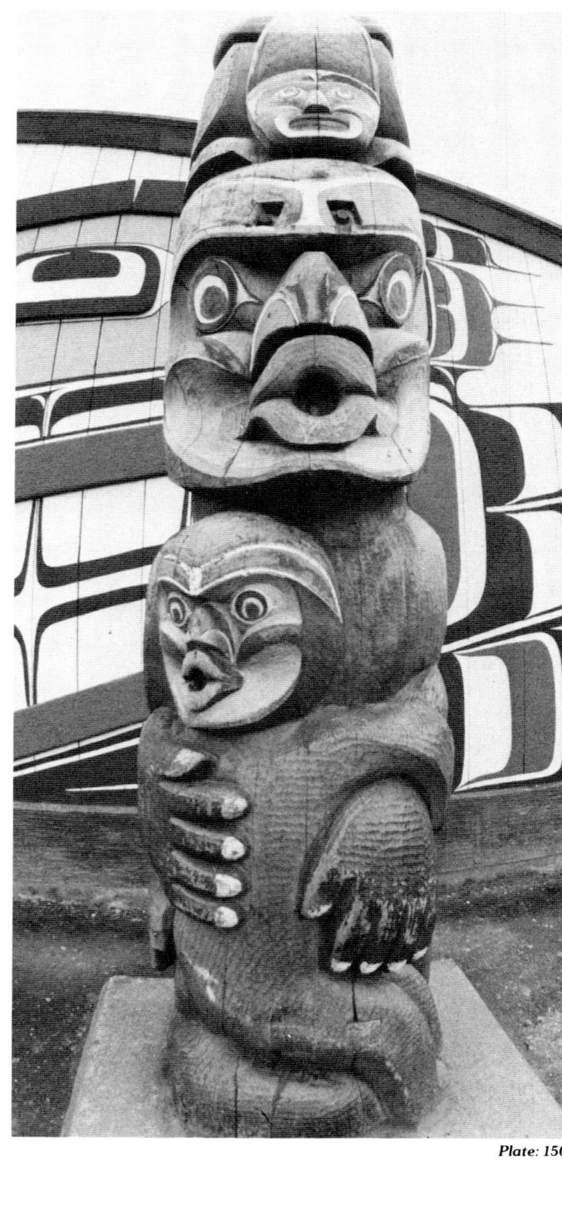

Plate: 150

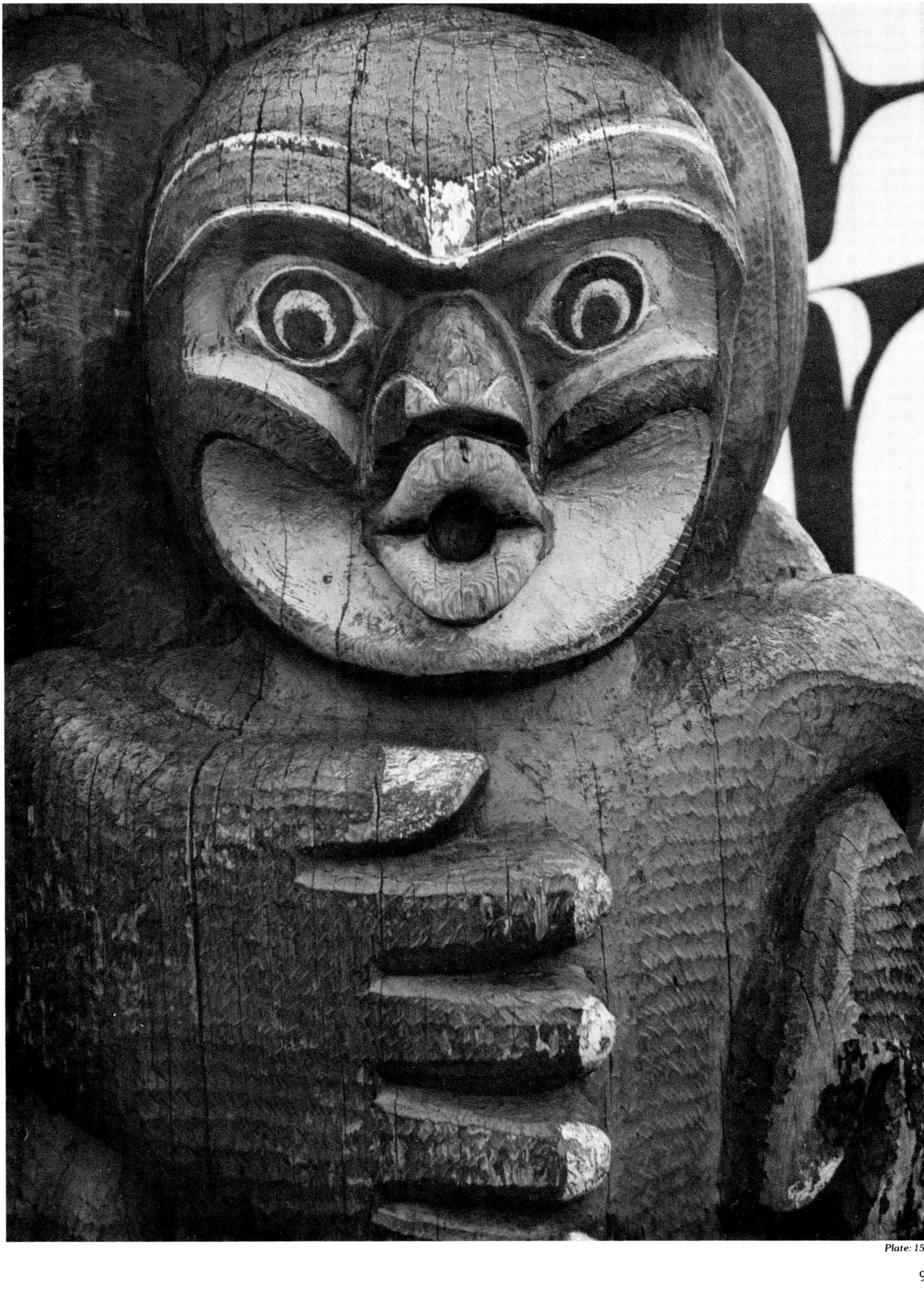

Plate: 151

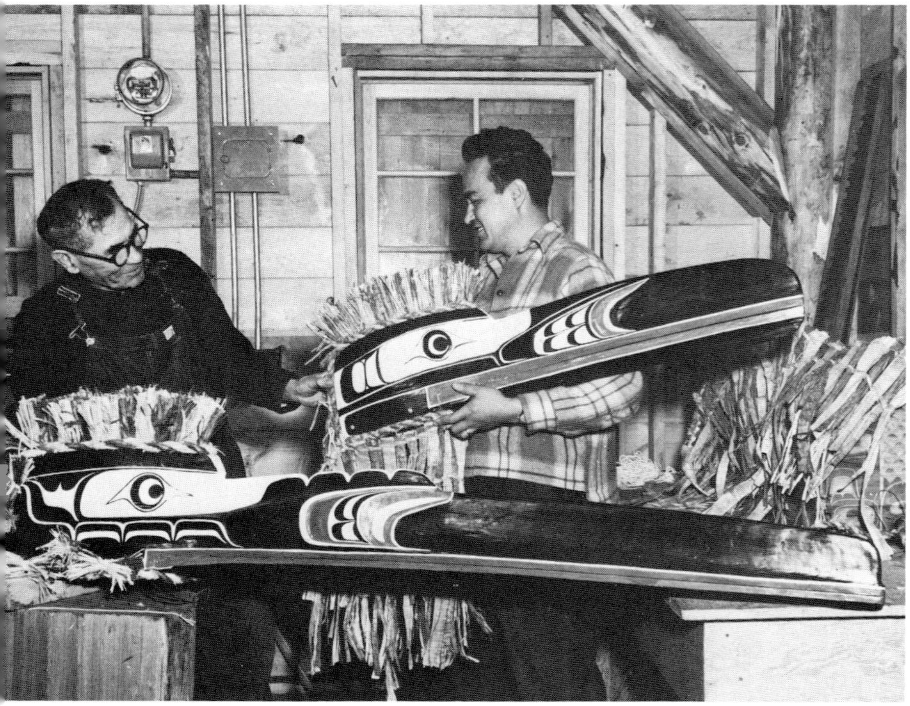

Plate: 152

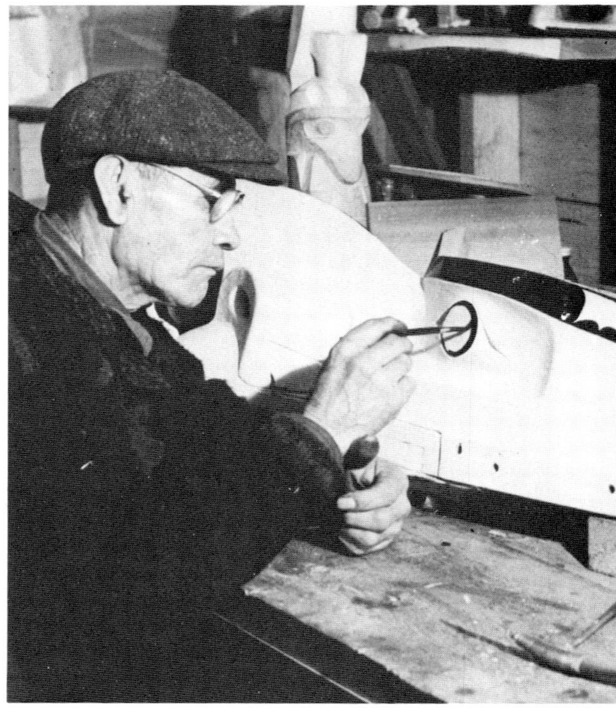

Plate: 153

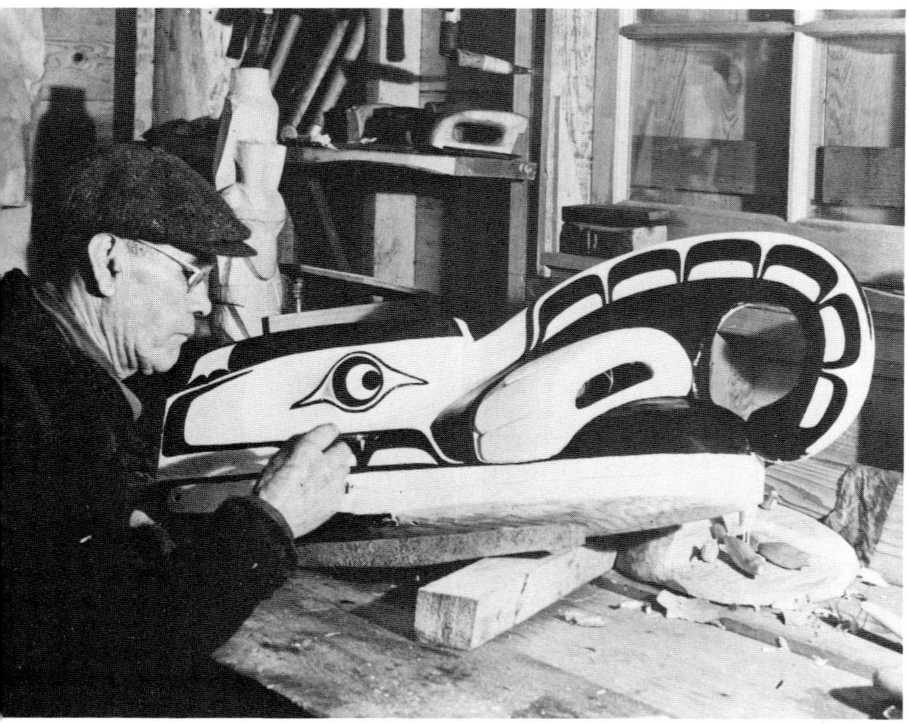

Plate: 156

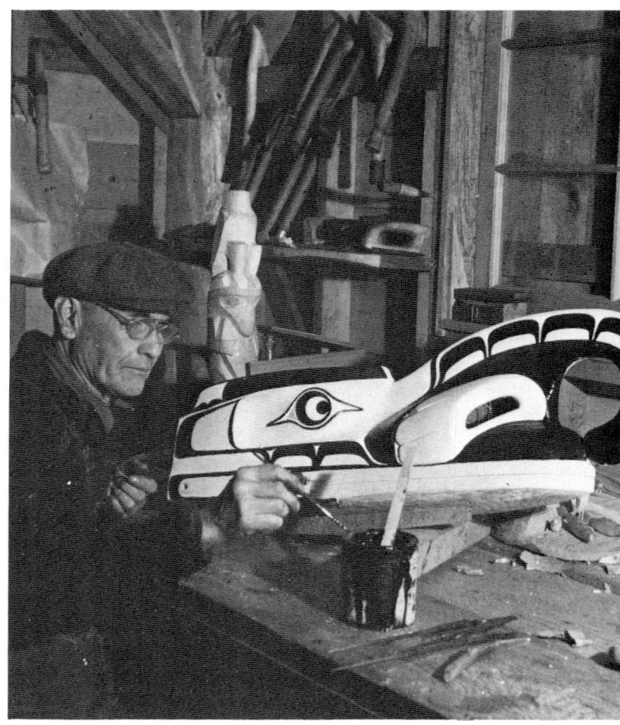

Plate: 157

Plate 152: Mungo Martin, left, stands behind a huge 'Huxwhukw' or Cannibal Bird mask, while David Martin holds a 'Hamat̓sa' or raven mask. The cedar bark hangings for the large 'Huxwhukw' are seen to the right. Both of these masks were used in the 1953 potlatch to dedicate Mungo's house at Thunderbird Park. (1953. Photo: Tourism, B.C. 7507.)

Plate 153: Mungo is shown painting the outer eye-ring on a representation of 'Galokwudzuwis' of the 'Crooked Beak of Heaven.' One of several masks that Mungo made for the opening potlatch of his house. Note how his left hand and thumb steady the right in a manner similar to a modern sign painter. (1953. Photo: B.C.P.M. PN-13328.)

Plate 154: One of the two miniature ravens that will appear on each side of the 'Crooked Beak' mask is held in place by Mungo. (1952. Photo: Tourism, B.C. 537.)

Plate 155: Note the small 'Hamat̓sa' raven rigidly mounted to the top of the 'Crooked Beak' mask. The lower portion of the Raven's beak is articulated and operated by a pull-cord. (1953. Photo: Tourism, B.C. 7502.)

Plate 156: Mungo continues to apply the glossy black enamel over the base coat of flat white. The finish detail begins to appear on the 'Crooked Beak' mask. (1953. Photo: B.C.P.M. PN-13327.)

Plate 157: Mungo continues work. The 'Galokwudzuwis' or 'Crooked Beak' is one of several emissaries of 'Baxwbakwalanuksiwe' or the 'Cannibal-that-lives-at-the-north-end-of-the-world.' The mask itself is called a 'Galokwumhl' or, simply 'Crooked Beak Mask.' This was taken in the carving shed at Thunderbird Park. The finished mask is shown in ***Plate: 158.*** (Thunderbird Park, Victoria, 1953. Photo: B.C.P.M. PN-13008.)

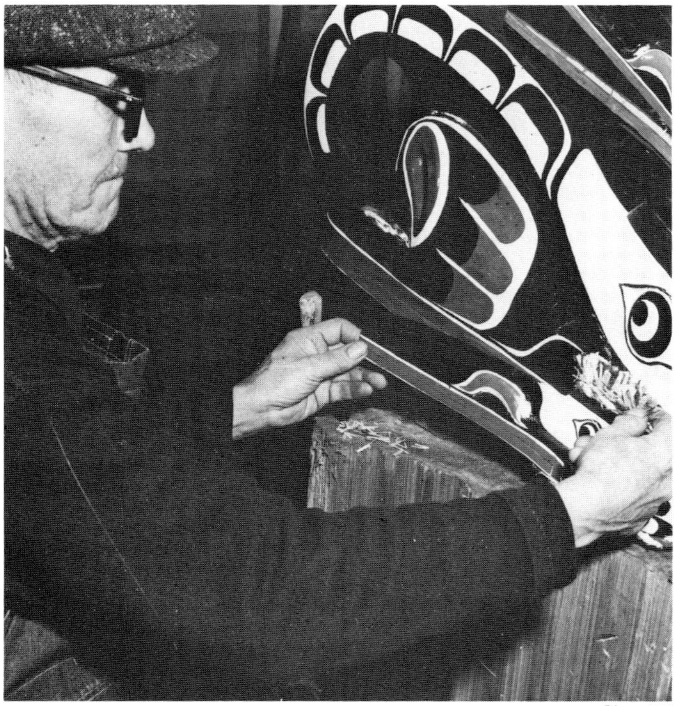

Plate: 154

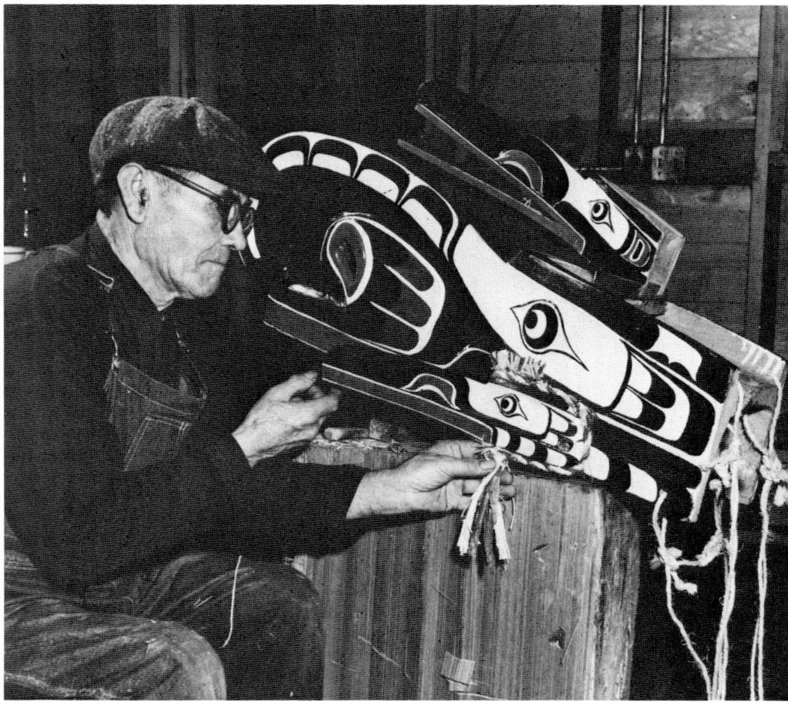

Plate: 155

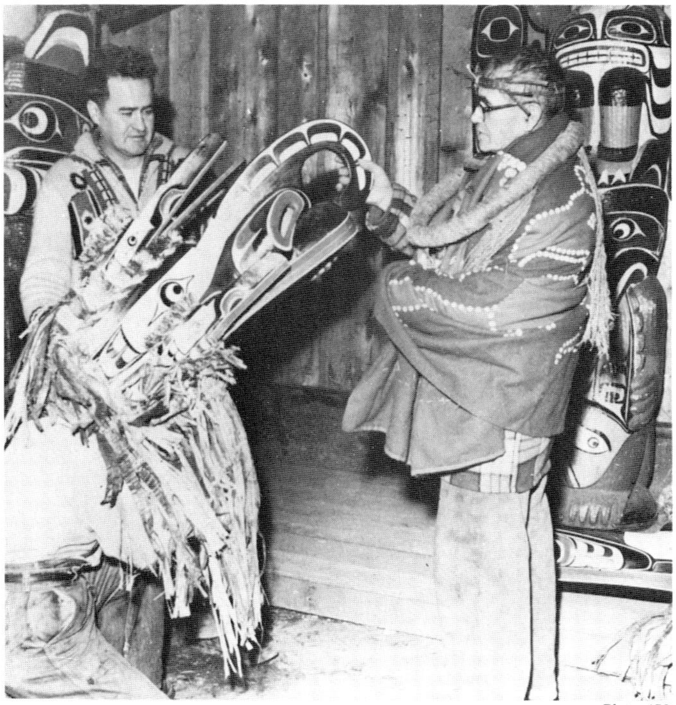

Plate: 158

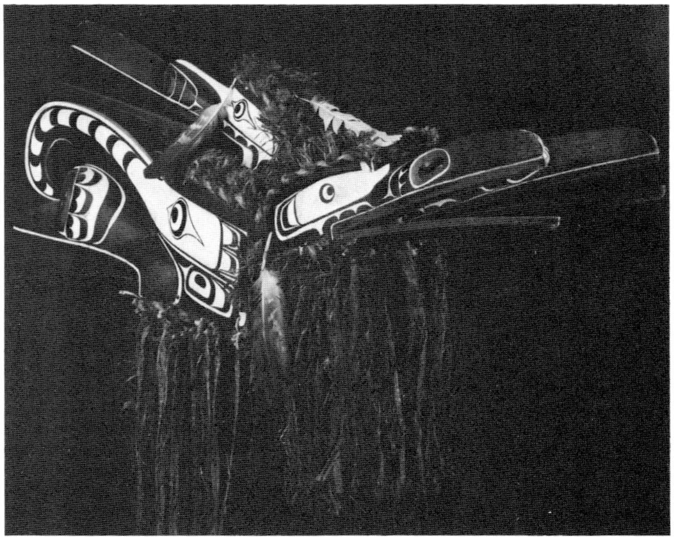

Plate: 159

Plate 158: Mungo Martin, on the right, and Dave Martin. A dancer (probably Henry Hunt) models the finished 'Crooked Beak of Heaven' mask. (Thunderbird Park, 1953. Photo: B.C.P.M. PN-14096.)

Plate 159: Another 'Crooked Beak of Heaven' mask made by Mungo Martin in 1953. This is a much larger mask than the mask shown in *Plates: 152-157*. The 'Hamaťsa' ravens are fully articulated and face rearwards, while the top figure is a 'Huxwhukw' or 'Cannibal Bird.' Mungo made this mask to replace one that he had previously owned (see *Plate 160*). This large complex mask was used at the 1953 potlatch to dedicate Mungo's house 'Wawaditla' and is now in the collection of the B.C. Provincial Museum at Victoria. (c. 1953. Photo: B.C.P.M. CPN-9201.)

Plate 160: The prototype of Mungo's 'Cannibal Bird' mask. This mask was made for Mungo in 1938, by Kwakiutl artist George Walkus. The mask was sold in 1948 and is now in the Denver Art Museum, Denver, Colorado. (Fort Rupert, c. 1947. Photo: C.M. Barbeau. Courtesy: National Museums Canada 103121.)

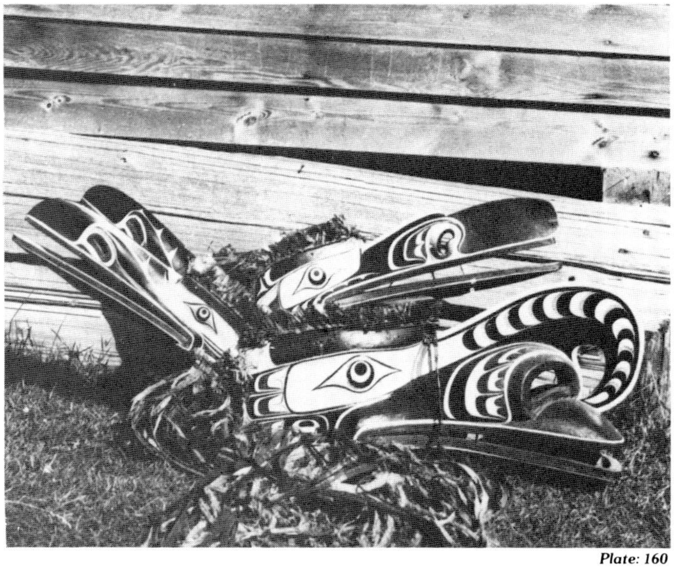

Plate: 160

come out and dance. Finally, the Ha'matsa dances again and the spirits disappear.

The Bee Dance .... Eugene (Tony) Hunt

The Women's Dance

..... Emma, Helen, Mildred, and Marion Hunt

Concluding Speech .... Mungo Martin

Wednesday, December 16th, 1953

A similar program will be given for the general public.

It is fortunate that a detailed record was taken on December 14th 'Indian Day' by the Provincial Museum. Through this transcript, one can get at least a feeling of just how important this potlatch was to Mungo and his family. It stands as a small piece of Kwakiutl pride—the first really public potlatch since the Indian Agent, W.M. Halliday's fervent attempts to abolish the potlatch over 30 years before. The transcript reads a little roughly—because it was not intended as a finished report. But here it is, exactly as it appears in the Museum files:

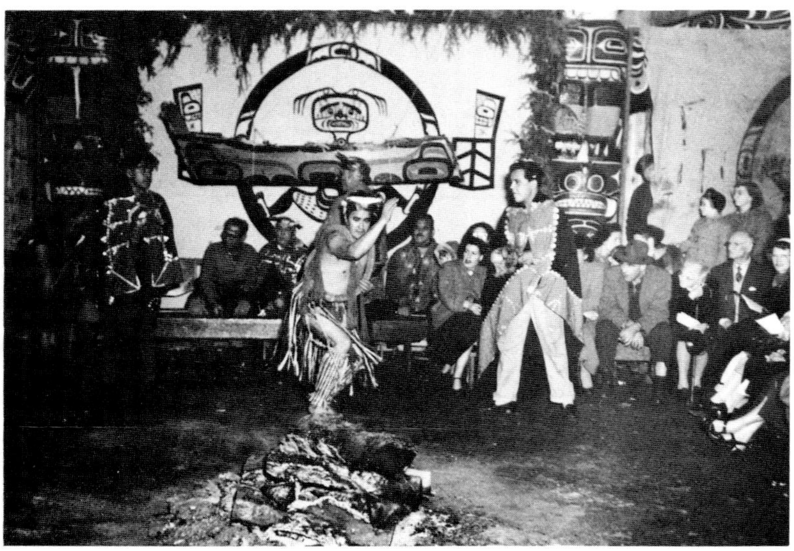

Plate 161: **David Martin comes out as the 'Hamatsa' or 'Wild Man.' His attendants flank him on either side. Note the cradle hanging above and behind him. This cradle was used earlier in a 'cradle song,' and served to introduce the first entrance of the 'Hamatsa.' (Thunderbird Park, Victoria, 1953. Photo: N.M.C. 71-6905.)**

Transcript of Potlatch

The ceremonies began at 1:00 p.m., December 14th, 1953.

Inside the house, the Indians were gathered around the three sides of the building, with a large fire burning in the centre floor. The end of the building was partitioned off by a series of three muslin quarters painted with some of Mungo's family crests, behind which the dancers were hidden, and into which they went, after dancing. In the centre front, were two parallel benches, on which were seated the chief guests of the potlatch, facing each other. These were the old men who retained the knowledge of procedure and protocol; they knew the songs and the order. Chief Tom Moody of Kingcome Inlet; Charlie Nowell of Alert Bay; Dan Cranmer of Alert Bay; Tom Ohmid; John Nolie and Mungo Martin. Mrs. Martin sat by his side, in a chair. All were in button blankets and ceremonial headpieces, except Mungo, who not only wore his old sweater, but had not shaved that day (when I questioned him later, he explained he had felt too busy to take time off to dress up). It was evident throughout the proceedings that he was tense and keyed to a high pitch. Dan Cranmer translated, infrequently.

Mungo spoke, standing, to the collected peoples; his spokesman also stood with him, taking the speaker's staff in his hand every time he was to take over the speech. This speaker was Mr. Nolie. Mungo welcomed the people to his gathering, but said that now, first, they must have a mourning ceremony for those who had died since the last ceremony (a potlatch three years ago). An old woman, from Comox, and Mrs. Paul from Blunden Harbour, borrowed three blankets, put them on, and were seated as the chief mourners on two straight chairs in front of the benches where the men were seated. The song leader started to sing a few phrases, the others on the benches joined in, beating the rhythm with sticks; from time to time another voice would call out a few phrases,w hich made an antiphony to the song. These songs continued for about 40 minutes; no recklessness on the part of the audience. The two women sat with head bowed, but now and then looked about with interest. New arrivals came in from time to time, and were escorted to their places by Wilson Duff. Very low-voiced greetings. Dress was of all degrees, from some well-dressed, prosperous-looking women, to the oldest shawls and calico long dresses of two long-haired old women. Children sat quite quietly, except some very young ones who ran back and forth happily, between relatives in different parts of the floor.

After about 40 minutes, the singing stopped, the women stood up and took off their blankets, and Mungo announced that they had finished the mourning period. The women returned to their seats among the spectators.

'Now,' said Mungo, 'the winter ceremonies can begin.'

Helpers in the front came out with the long garlands of cedar bark, dyed red. This was quickly split by women sitting in the audience by the door (relatives of Mr. M.) and strips were passed out by about six of the participants. They would hand it over to each person in the audience, who then wound it around his head, and tied it over the forehead. From time to time the distributors murmured, 'Here is red cedar bark. Put it on, so you'll feel happy,' or urged, 'When you wear this, you'll feel good.' (Dan Cranmer later said, even people in recent mourning, when they put this on, felt cheerful and forgot their grief.) After all the cedar bark was tied on, helpers went around with baskets of eagle down, and put a few wisps on each person's head. Mr. Nolie stood and addressed the people, which Dan C. later interpreted—'This eagle down means peace. Everybody wear it, and you will enjoy this time.'

Now Mungo arose, and announced (through Dan) that he was going to name some people. First, his newest grandchild (who was not really there in the cradle). In the front of the room, above the bench, was a great wooden cradle eight feet long, suspended by ropes from the central house beam. Now, two young men in button blankets stood on the platform behind the cradle (these were young David Martin and Dan

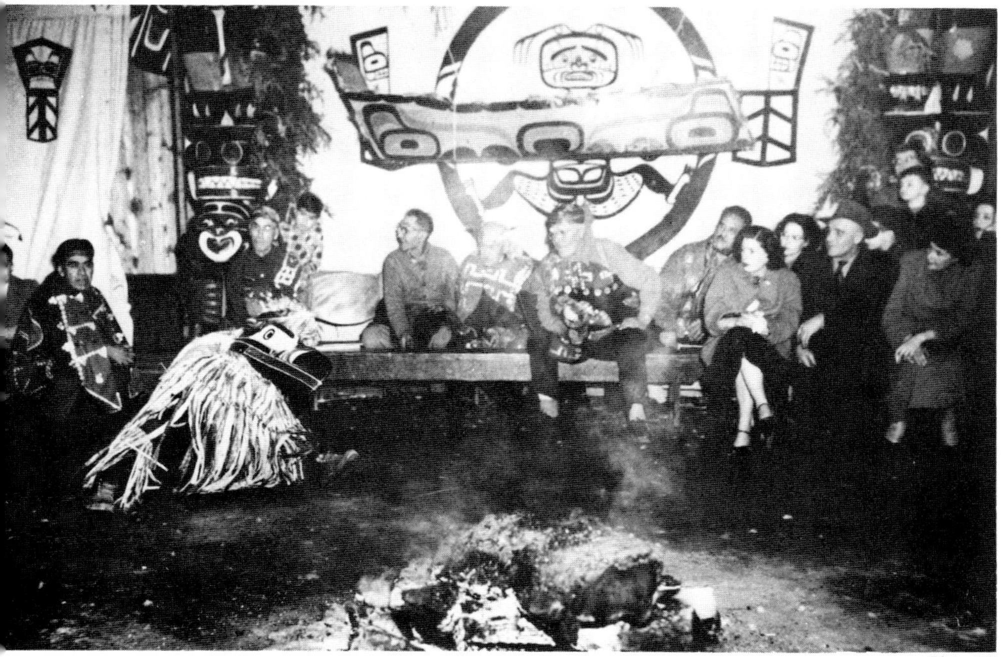

Plate: 162

Plate 162: The guest chiefs of the potlatch watch a 'Hamatsa' raven dancer. (Thunderbird Park, Victoria, 1953. Photo: N.M.C. 71-6900.)

Plate 163: A 'Hamatsa' raven dancer—Phillip Hall of Blunden Harbour, B.C. The 'Hamatsa' is another of the representatives of 'Baxwbakwalanuksiwe"—The Cannibal that lives at the north end of the world.' (Thunderbird Park, Victoria, 1953. Photo: N.M.C. 71-6925.)

Plate 164: The complex 'Crooked Beak' mask being danced inside Mungo's house 'Wawaditla'. The cedar bark hangings alternate sections dyed red and the natural light brown of the undyed bark. The hangings effectively conceal the dancer and his motions of pulling the strings to operate the articulated beaks. (Thunderbird Park, Victoria, 1953. Photo: Tourism B.C. 7054.)

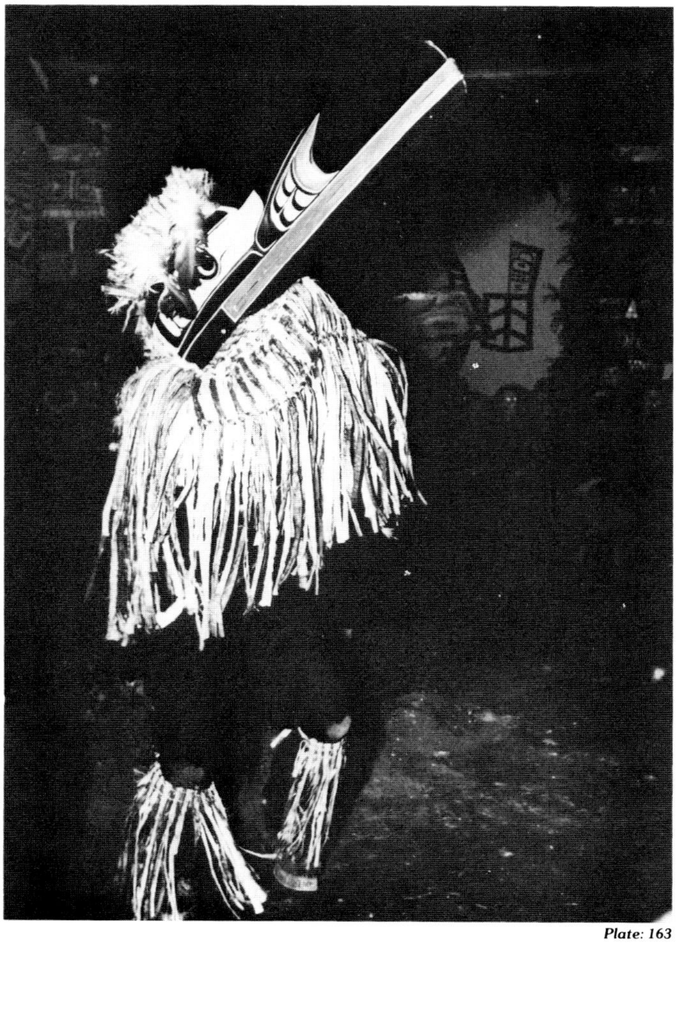

Plate: 163

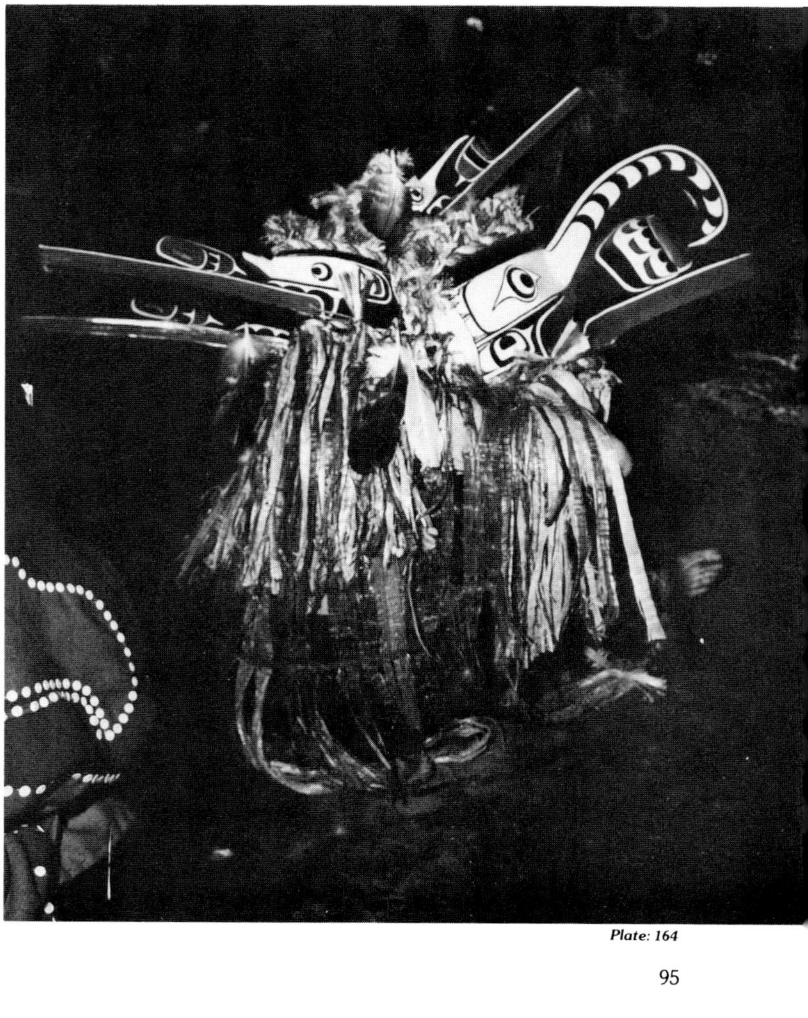

Plate: 164

Plate 165: Helen Hunt (left) escorts a 'deer' (Thomas Hunt Jr.) while a young 'deer' (Tony Hunt) brings up the rear. These figures are part of the Animal Kingdom presentation. (Thunderbird Park, Victoria, 1953. Photo: N.M.C. 71-6899.)

Plate 166: The 'Marten' dancer. Part of the 'animal kingdom' series. (Thunderbird Park, Victoria, 1953. Photo: N.M.C. 71-6912.)

Plate 167: The 'Field Mouse' dancer—part of the 'animal kingdom' series. (Thunderbird Park, Victoria, 1953. Photo: N.M.C. 71-6911.)

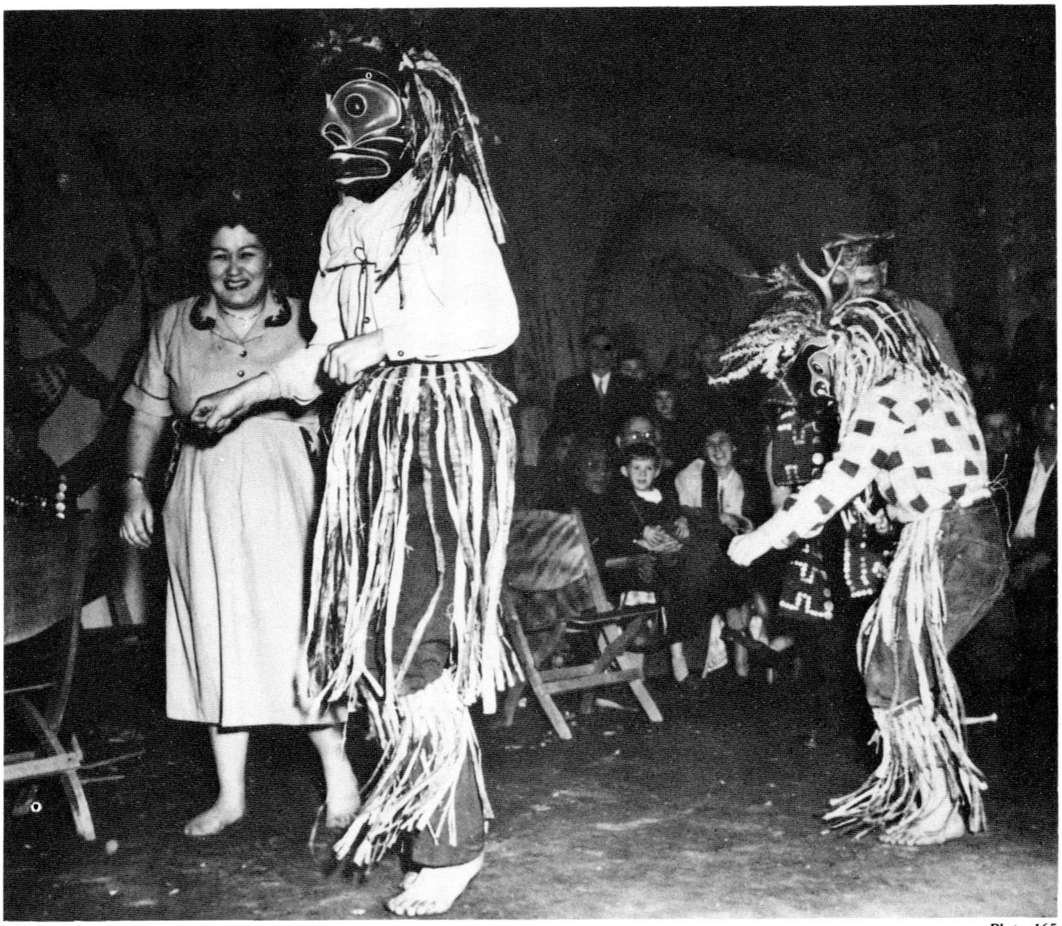

Plate: 165

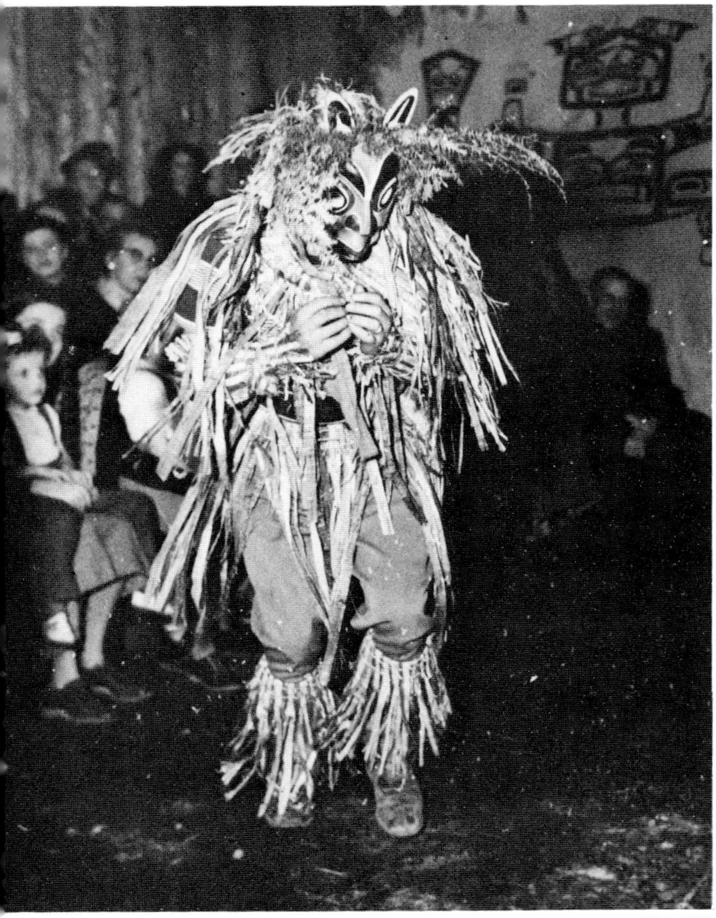

Plate: 166

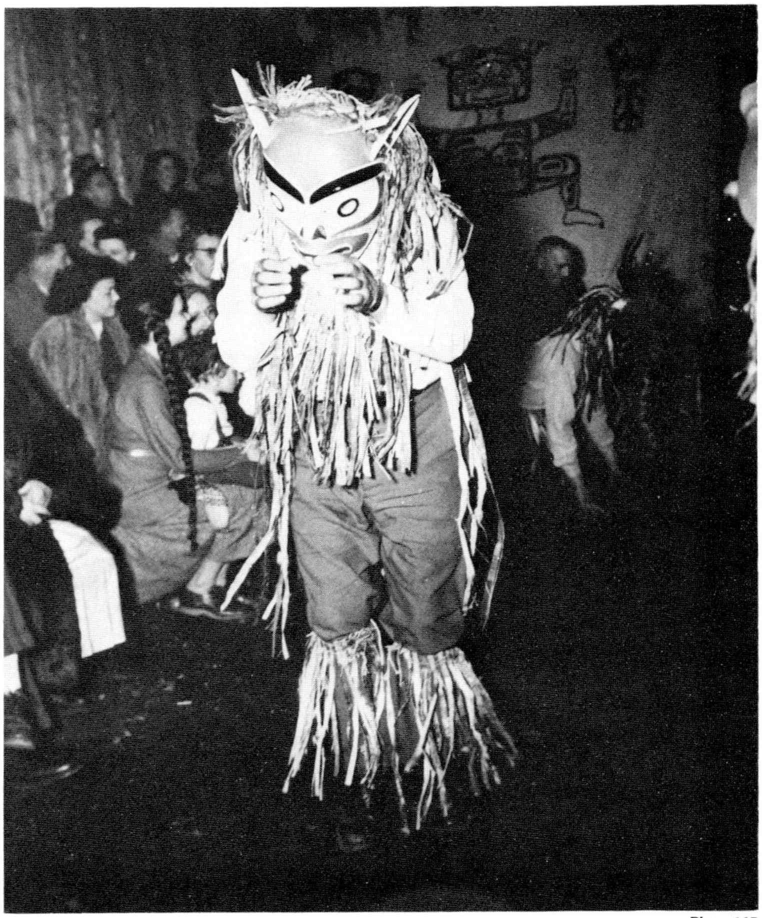

Plate: 167

Cranmer's son); for both it was the first time they had done this, and they had to be instructed by whispers from the old men at the beginning. Dan Cranmer, as a relative on his mother's side, stood in a corner of the centre floor, to the left rear of the fire. He said there should be a rope there, for him to swing the cradle with.

Now the song began. The men sang it, beating their sticks. It was punctuated periodically by a cry from the rear, pretending to be the baby's cry—'ooo-ooo-ooo'. Then the song would grow louder, and for emphasis the men would beat heavily with their sticks on the platform. The two men behind the cradle would keep time with their rattles to this emphatic portion, with a crescendo at the end of several bars, of waving a white wing of song feathers over the cradle, thus fanning a thick blanket of eagle down up into the air. Then the song would return to its usual tempo.

The song, as translated by Dan, was 'Hush, baby, don't you cry. Don't make any noise. Over in that corner is a wild man. He will hear you.' This was repeated four times, with the baby's cry four times, and the elaborate rhythm beating four times. Then all stopped. In the back, the cry of the wild Hamatsa was heard—a hoarse, throaty, chilling cry. In rushed the Hamatsa (Dave Martin) dressed in long shredded cedar bark over red bathing trunks. He circled in each of the four corners, in the centre square, while his attendants who were with him seemed at a loss as to what to do. They followed, some distance behind. They wore button blankets, toga fashion, turned inside out so the stitches showed. After he was returned, the interpreter said that the Hamatsa would dance tonight, so be ready for it.

Then, attendants took around bags of 50 cent pieces, newly minted Queen Elizabeth pieces, and passed one to each person in the audience. They were all thanked for coming to this potlatch, to dedicating this house. Then everyone was reminded that the evening would begin promptly at 7:15, and people should go to the Crystal Garden Restaurant across the street for dinner. (There were no cooking facilities available here.) Then, meal tickets were handed out to everyone. Without further dismissal it was evident that the afternoon session was over. People broke up and drifted out. I heard later from Dan Cranmer that a special sum of money was given to the Cape Mudge people.

Dinner was in a long room like a church meeting hall, with long tables set. Beef stew, apple pie and coffee, with white bakery rolls. There was no toasting or public speaking. Families and friends sat together in small groups.

We arrived back at the big house early enough to watch everyone saunter in. There were family groups from 30 different tribe branches, according to Wilson Duff who had helped with the mechanics of invitations.

The house was decorated with boughs of green hemlock over the door and framing the front stage. This was sprinkled with eagle down and looked festive. The fire roared and crackled, the flood lights in the ceiling were dimmed down, so the whole place had an intimate old-fashioned air. Everyone continued to wear the strips of red cedar bark.

Mungo rose and addressed the crowd. He said (through Dan C.) that everyone was welcome to the house of Chief Naka'penkim, nephew of Chief Naka'penkim of Fort Rupert. This house, Wa'waditla, was a model of the old house of the same name, built about 100 years ago. But, the old house was 90 × 90 ft., large enough to hold everyone of the Kwakiutl nation, gathered under its one roof. This house was going to be celebrated by this potlatch, and everyone here should watch the dances of Chief Naka'penkim's family history, as they had always been done.

Then there was a little statement made about the carved house posts, copied from the old house. The Hok Hok, at the top of the pole, moved their great beaks with a clapping sound.

Now Mungo is going to give some of his family their winter names. The person to be named was called up from the audience by either Mr. or Mrs. Martin, then went behind the front curtain and put on a button blanket and head-piece. (There were four button blankets and one Chilkat, woven by Mrs. M. which were circulated among the persons.) Named were: the

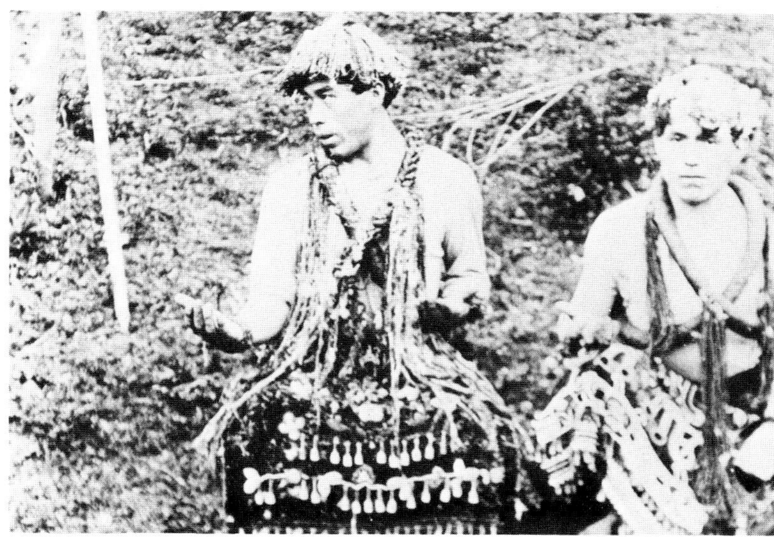

Plate 168: **One who would have appreciated Mungo's potlatch of 1953, his brother, Herbert Martin 'Meetsa' (at left). Herbert was a noted dancer and athlete in his time. Herbert is shown with Ed Whannock (right), both dressed in 'Hamatsa' or 'Wild Man' outfits. (Alert Bay, no date given, but probably around 1920. Photo: Rev. W. Corker. Courtesy: B.C.P.M. PN-2314.)**

great nieces and nephews, six of them, children of Ellen Neel of Alert Bay.

They stood still while the naming song of the singers bench was sung over them. They ranged from 7 to 16, and were very proud and thrilled. An old, old woman, looking a little long-headed, who had danced in the old house at Fort Rupert, was named. While the singers sang and drummed, she stood, gently dancing from side to side, feet in place, moving hands, palms outstretched and parallel, from side to side. After she was named, Mungo announced how proud he was to have this old woman in his house today.

Then, a tall, handsome woman, in very smart European clothes, who looked very non-Indian. She was a niece from Alert Bay.

Another young niece from Alert Bay—for each a song, using rattles, drums and music sticks, was sung. Mrs. Martin danced over to the audience, and selected a grey-haired man sitting there. She took him by the arm, and had him walk once around the room with her,

Plate 169: Tony Hunt dances at the potlatch, earlier dressed as a 'Bumble Bee', Tony 'stung' several guests and Mungo send over a dollar bill 'to put a bandage on it.' Tony now owns a gallery called 'Arts of the Raven' in Victoria; and his son Tony Jr., is a fine upcoming young artist in the tradition that his father and grandfather learned from Mungo Martin. (Thunderbird Park, Victoria, 1953. Photo: N.M.C. 71-6918.)

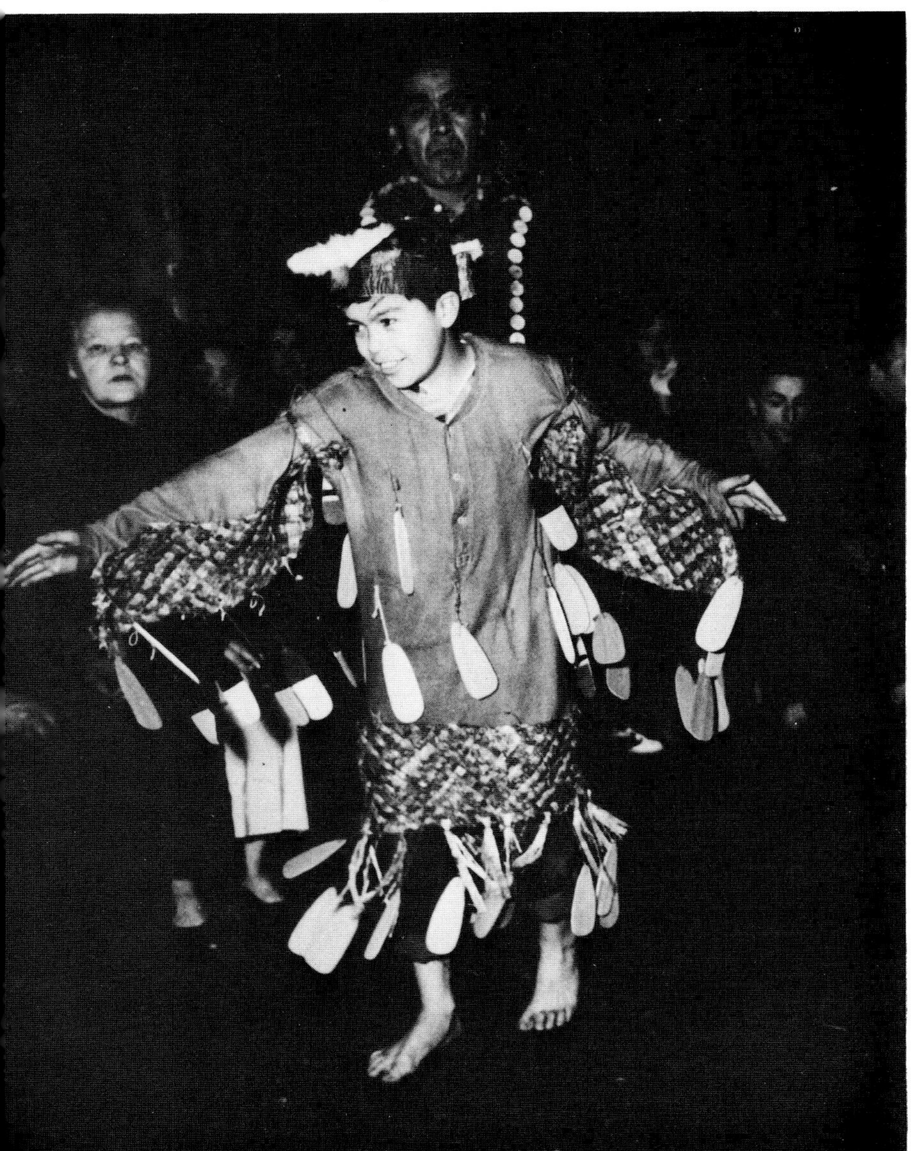

and when he sat down, she tweaked his nose, pulled it, and laughed. Many others laughed too. Interpreter said: 'You will be called nosy. If anything touches your nose you will feel crazy. We will make you a mask.'

(Bill Holm remembered this incident. He said, 'I believe the man's name was Hamilton... the name he was given was 'NOOHLEED'—it doesn't actually mean 'nosy'... it probably means something more like 'having recklessness or foolishness'—P.N.)

Then cartons of Mandarin oranges were brought out and opened up and distributed, everyone getting two, three or four. Dan saying, 'Chief Naka'penkim got you these oranges to enjoy yourselves. Eat them up now. Now you have seen all these new named people.'

Behind the curtains came the hoarse cry of the Hamatsa. It was followed by an interval of rattles vibrating, then silence, then the cry again. This sequence was repeated four times. Then David M., dressed in a shredded cedar bark shirt, fringe on legs, tied into hair two red cedar bark rings crossed into an 'X' at his back, came in head lowered, turning right and left, one arm outthrust, hand shivering and rotating left to right, on alternate arms. He was followed by the two attendants, who still followed rather laconically from a distance, not restraining or gentling him. he danced in a circular rotation in each corner, slowly, going with halts and starts up to the next corner, with some backward coverage. Now and then he would give the cry. The music sticks, rattles and voices, were very tense and emphatic. Now and then he would have to stop to rest and would simply kneel, head down. The singing would continue without him. His dance, four times around the square, must have been 20 minutes. At this point a woman in button blanket came in, arms forward, palms upright, carrying a copper. He followed with steps suited to hers, as though following the copper. After circling the fire and the squares once, she put the copper down, and then danced in the left corner by herself, as he finished another circle of the room. When he went out, the two Hamatsa bird monsters came in, covered in shredded cedar bark, beaks pointed upward, lurching from side to side, sometimes balanced by shoulders hunched, elbows akimbo. They squatted in each of the four corners, beaks turning in exact rhythm to the music.

After that, in came the Hamatsa men, without the masks. David Martin now in the Chilkat robe, his attendants following, two bird figures in shredded cedar bark. They all circled the floor four times, too. The music seemed the same as for the Hamatsa, but not sure.

After this, a small boy figure, (Tony Hunt) dressed as a bumble bee came darting out, followed by a woman attendant. He darted, and flew around the fire. He stopped, seeming to hover over an old woman in the audience, and 'stung' her. After circling the fire once, he left. Mungo sent an aide over to pay the old woman a one-dollar bill 'to put a bandage on it'.

The women had their dance after this. Six women, in button blankets, covered with eagle down came out. They had four different rhythms to the music, and circled the fire four times.

The dance, which came next, was a Tok-wit dance.

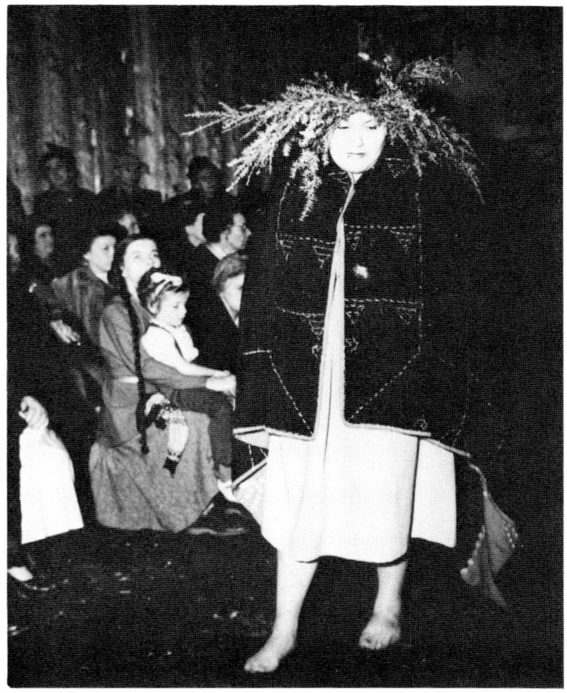

Plate 170: **Helen Hunt dances at Mungo's potlatch. Helen, Henry Hunt's wife, often acted as an interpreter for Mungo Martin. Here she played the part of a very pregnant lady, dancing in small mincing steps. (Thunderbird Park Victoria, 1953. Photo: N.M.C. 71-6909.)**

In the background came a woman's voice, floating out, very poignant, a little refrain of about six bars. This was repeated four times, then emerged a woman (Helen Hunt) with a hemlock branch crown, button blanket turned the wrong way, bare feet. She held her elbows akimbo, palms forward, so that blanket was belled out, and she looked very pregnant. She danced with small, gingerly steps, in a fashion to show this. Singing the plaintive little refrain, she danced once around the floor up to the bench where the Chiefs sat. She knelt before them, seeming to consult them. Everyone began to snicker and giggle, the Chief included. Then she stood up, and Mr. Nolie took his speaker's staff and poked her in the side with it. There was some sort of concealed bladder, which made a bleating sound. Everyone roared—this woman had something wrong with her. The staff prodded her, and she danced backward and sideways in a frenzied manner. Going up to the bench again, she knelt, consulted, stood up, was prodded (laughter now hilarious) and danced backwards four times.

The fifth time she approached the bench and knelt, a little carved figure was pushed forward from under the Chief's feet so when she arose it was seen she had given birth to a frog. The people all enjoyed this hugely. She now danced off in a bright and brisk manner, while the frog glided backwards, under the bench.

Now, a shrill whistle behind the curtain was followed by a variety of shrill blasts on a number of different sounding whistles, and a stampeding sound of feet. These were the forest animals (said Dan) who were coming to dance. There is a cave on Gilford Island, where in the beginning—all the animals used to gather to dance. Three more times, the whistles and the dancing of feet. Then wolf came out. He was in a woolly suit, with upturned snout. He gave a long wolf call, ran around the floor once, went back to call out the next animal. He came out, followed by the mouse. (As Dan C. said to the European audience the next night, 'the mouse was important and nice, not like the dirty rats you white people brought over to us!'), who mimicked wonderfully, the tiny, shy, mincing gestures of the field mouse. It stopped in the front right-hand corner, and danced in place, in time to the music. Wolf ran around and called in Raccoon, with his little hands held in front of him and diving, King fisher—swooping, Martin, Wren, Squirrel, Owl, two deer (one a child), each dancing in place, strung along the square, three times. Mouse ran outside, to see if the humans were coming. He called out the all clear, via an attendant, each time. Then the dancing continued. After about 20 minutes, the first one, Raccoon, left his place to file out, the others following, dancing all the while.

Then Mungo arose again, and thanked the audience for coming; for seeing all his relatives get names, and for watching the dances of his family. He said he had many more masks, but no one to wear them, so what we saw tonight was just some of his family history. Then he added he would like to give one more name, to Wilson Duff... a named to be used summer or winter.

Then eveyone left. It was after midnight and the fire had died down.

For the white invitation evening, the ceremony was even more careful, the 'stage managing' went along a little quicker, and no long pauses in it. The audience clapped at each item, which increased the feeling of a stage production. It was very much shorter.'

Although the museum notes seem to indicate that Mungo was 'tense' and 'keyed to a high pitch' during the course of the potlatch, that should not be taken to mean that he was a novice to such public affairs.

As a song-writer and singer at numerous potlatches, he was expected to be, and was, an accomplished performer. He was a powerful orator and it is said that he often made suggestions about the ceremonies, dances, and costumes—suggestions that were designed to wring the maximum dramatic impact from the specific moment. His insistence on calculated observation of the nuances of a particular segment showed a keen grasp of the psychology and a sense of timing of the type found in professional performers.

Mungo was even a movie star, of sorts! The colour film 'Making a Totem Pole,' shot a few years before, has already been mentioned, but nearly a quarter of a century before, Mungo had participated in a film made by one of the most venerated ethnographers ever to visit the B.C. Coast.

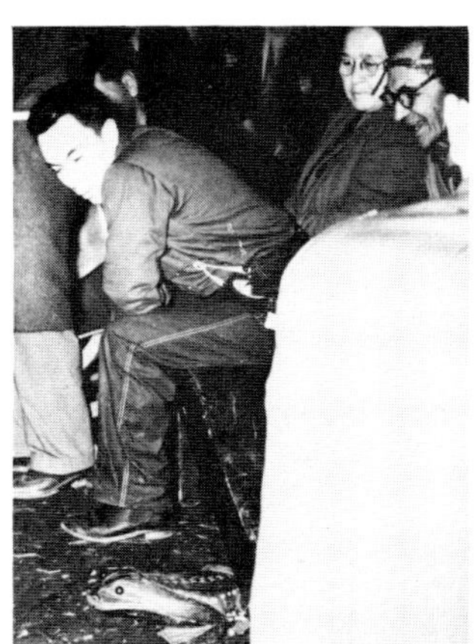

Plate 171: **Helen Hunt's 'Baby'—Henry Hunt looks askance at the frog while 'A̱baya̱'a' and Mungo (upper right) are obviously enjoying this bit of humour. (Thunderbird Park, Victoria, 1953. Photo: N.M.C. 71-6908.)**

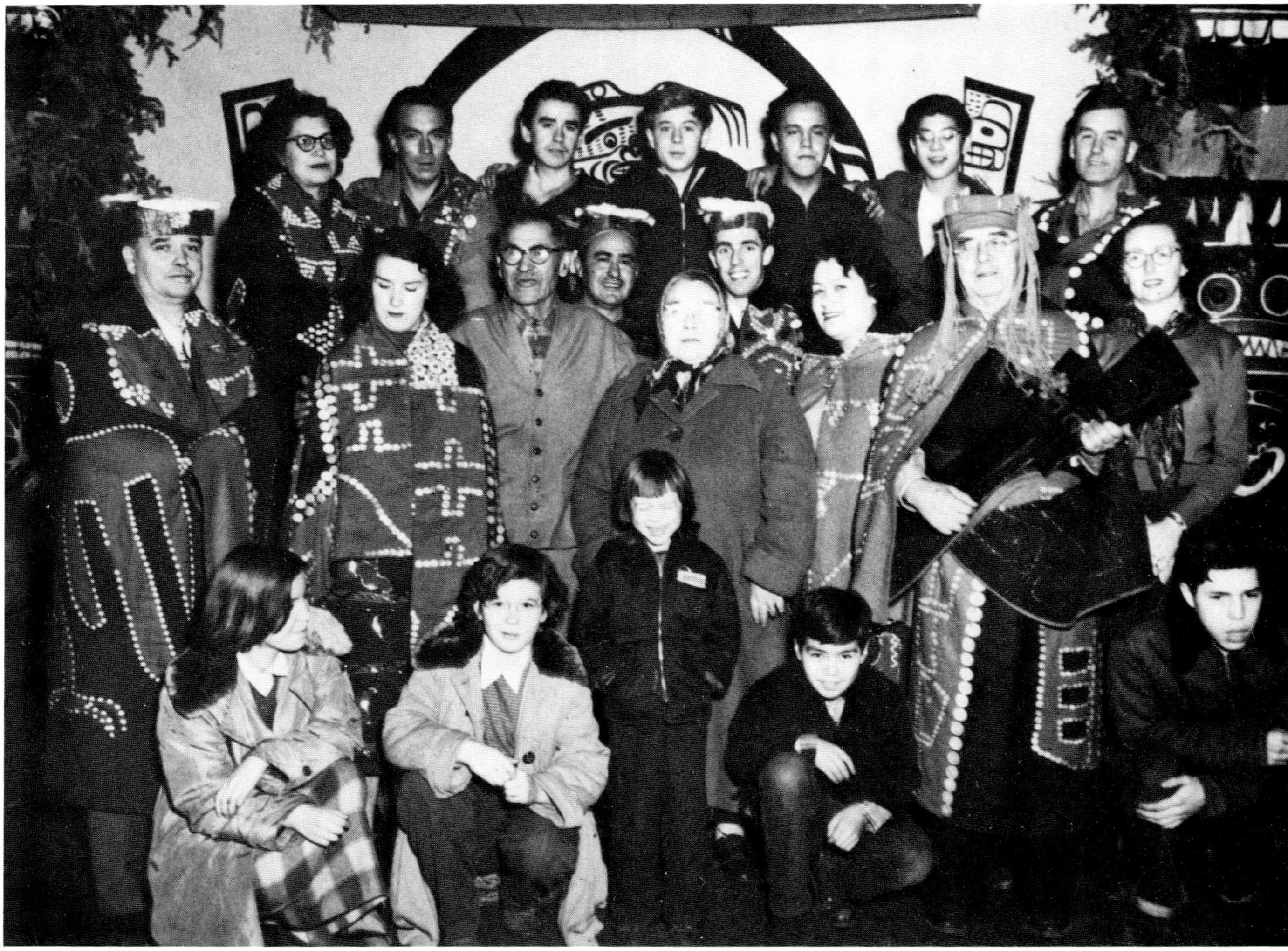

Plate 172: **After the potlatch, tired, happy, proud. (From left to right.) Front row: Theo Neel, Cora Neel, Bitty Neel, Tony Hunt, and Ted Neel. Centre Row: Ted Neel Sr., Mildred Hunt, Mungo Martin, David Martin, Sara Martin, Wilson Duff, Helen Hunt, Tom Hunt, and unidentified. Back Row: Ellen Neel, Henry Hunt, Danny Cranmer, Bob Neel, unidentified, Dave Neel, and unidentified.**

In 1930, Franz Boaz visited Fort Rupert, B.C. and filmed many of the dances that he had written extensively about, during the previous 40 years. The films were an attempt to use motion pictures as an ethnographical tool in the same manner that sketches and still photographs had been used in his many published texts.

Mungo was one of the participants in a 'West Coast' dance in Boaz' film. The dancers move in a line with singing, drumbeating and steps related to the words of the song. An impromptu piece of action (that never fails to draw a laugh from viewers) occurred when a village dog ran into the camera frame and began to nip at the heels of one of the line dancers—only to be dispatched by an accurate kick; accomplished without the dancer losing either time nor step. Bill Holm has edited and annoted this documentary film and it is available from the University of Washington, Seattle, Washington, U.S.A.

Mungo was no stranger to public performances! Veteran Victoria photographer, Jim Ryan, remarked several times on Mungo's ability to strike just the pose called for, without 'hamming it up', or causing the pose to appear contrived. If Mungo Martin was 'tense' at the potlatch for the opening of 'WA'WADITLA', it certainly was not stage fright. It could only then serve to underscore how important the event was to him.

It would seem that Mungo's 'opening night' was an unqualified success! In March of 1954, a good account of the potlatch appeared in the magazine 'Beaver'. The article was written by James K. Nesbitt and contained a careful description of the event and some interesting quotes:

'The public almost stampeded. One night nearly 2,000 people lined up for blocks, two and three deep, but couldn't get in. The new house only holds 300 people. Mayor Harrison immediately said Victoria should have a genuine Indian village, that the potlatch should become a part of Victoria's uniqueness and culture.

Provincial Government anthropologist, Wilson Duff, was more than delighted. For it uncovered, as he said, a wealth of native dances and a knowledge of traditions that we didn't know existed—and it showed just how colourful they can be and what amazing public interest this sort of thing arouses.'

Nesbitt wound up his article by saying:

'Sitting in that big house, warmed by the open fire, the smoke in our eyes, it seemed impossible to believe it was 1953 and we were in the heart of busy Victoria. It was easier to imagine that house on some lonely beach far up the coast—one of the long, curving beaches washed by the swells of the Pacific, a beach with Indian dug-outs drawn up. We could almost hear the waves washing the pebbles, the sigh of the fir trees over the house, the lashings of the rain...'

'There are many who would know how he felt, had they been there. The culture of the Kwakiutl casts this sort of spell... over some people.'

When everything had calmed down, Mungo went back to work. In the 1955 Museum Annual Report, his activities were described thus:

Totem Pole Restoration Program

'Carving operations were continued in Thunderbird Park. Mungo Martin and David Martin worked steadily from January 1st to December 15th, and Henry Hunt was employed from April 1st to December 15th. During the summer, thirteen poles and other exhibits were erected in the park. This was a major undertaking and more costly than had been foreseen, as excavation for the bases required the use of power machinery and, in some cases, blasting.

Painting and preparation of the exhibits took much of the carvers' time. In addition, four Haida poles and one Kwakiutl pole were carved. Two of the Haida poles were corner posts for the house front framework erected in the park. These were copies from a photograph of an old house in Skidegate. A third was a copy of the massive mortuary pole collected from Tanoo in 1911. The original was removed to storage after being copied. The separate bird figure on the top of this pole was copied from the original, which has been in storage since it was collected. The fourth Haida pole carved was a copy of the Tanoo beaver frontal pole, salvaged in 1954. Since the park is now full, this pole was stored awaiting assignment to a suitable place, elsewhere in the province.

Plate 173: **Mungo takes time out to talk to a group of 'Wild Indians.' Thunderbird Park had an almost irresistable fascination for children of all ages and Mungo always had time to explain what he was doing . . . and why. (Thunderbird Park, Victoria, date unknown. Photo: Jim Ryan.)**

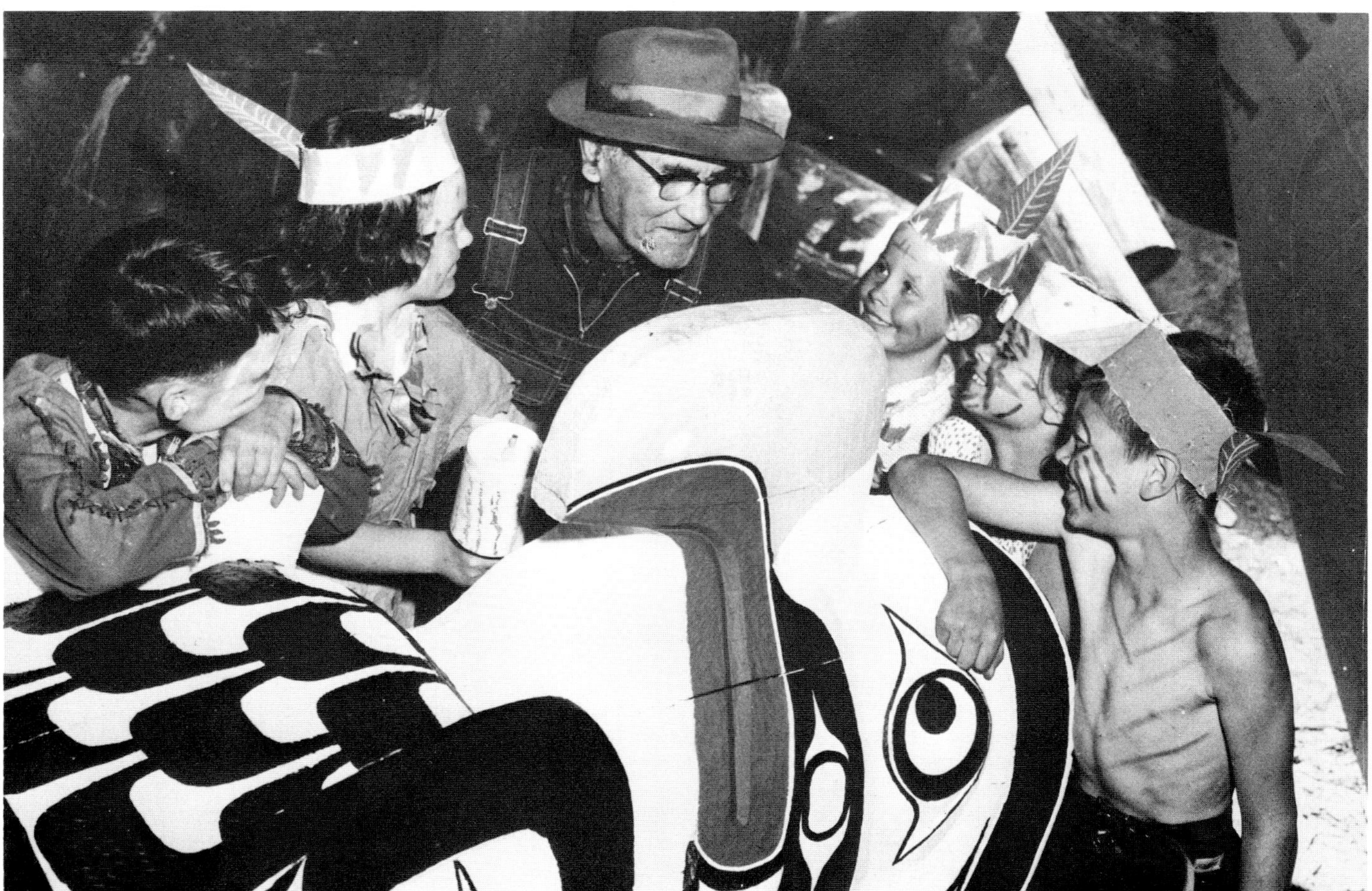

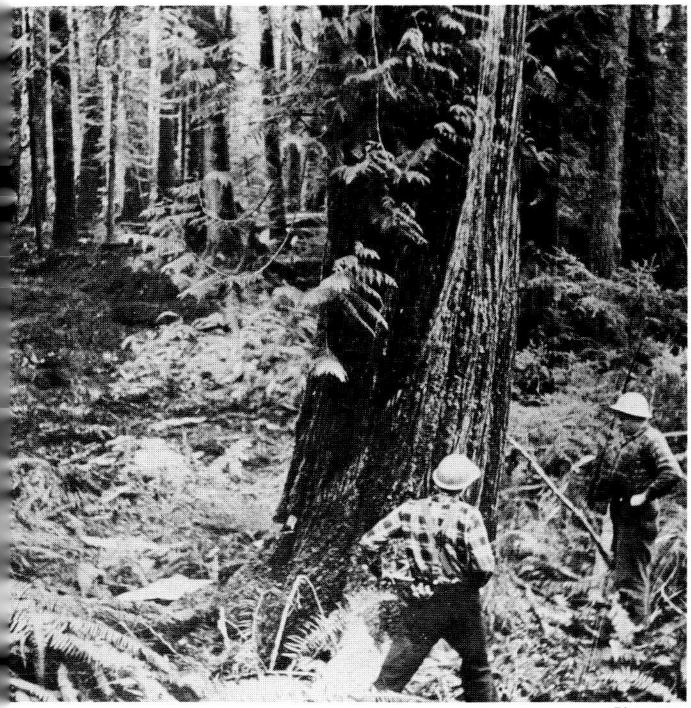

Plate: 174

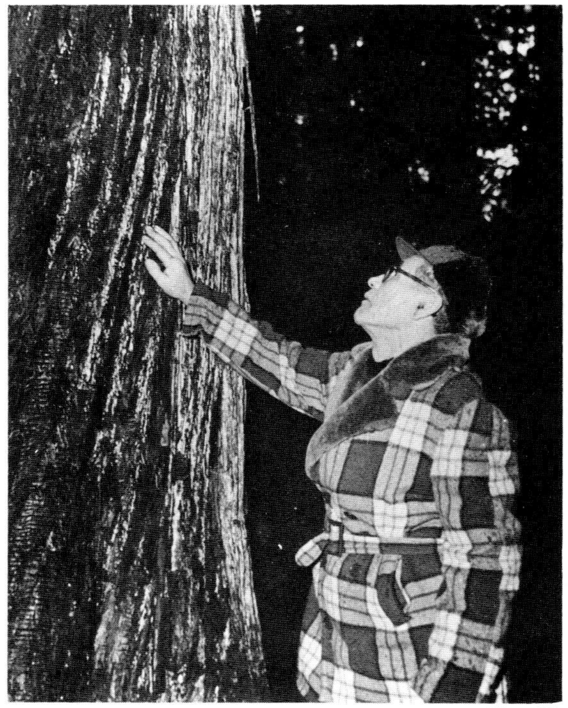

Plate: 175

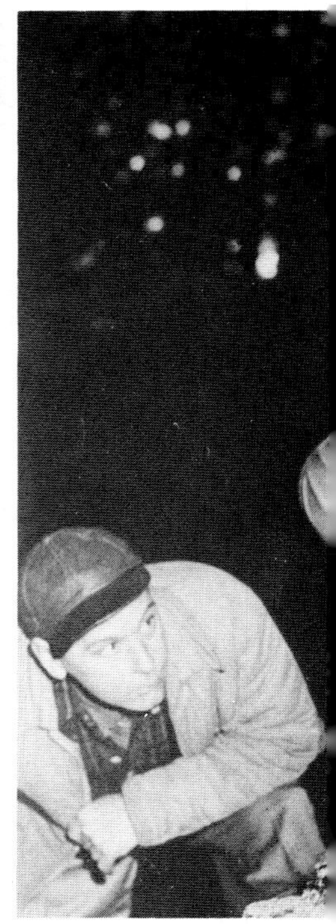

Plate 174: **The cedar tree that was destined to become the 'world's largest totem.' Loggers from the Elder Logging Company look it over at Muir's Creek, near Sooke, B.C. (Sooke, 1956. Photo: Victoria Daily Colonist.)**

Plate 175: **Mungo looked over the huge cedar at Muir's Creek... the 18th one examined... and said briefly, 'Will do.' (Sooke, 1956. Photo: Victoria Daily Colonist.)**

Plate 176: **The loggers look delighted. The deep 'Kerf' cut in the tree to become the 'world's largest totem' shows that it is sound internally. (Sooke, 1956. Photo: Victoria Daily Colonist.)**

The Kwakiutl pole carved was a copy of one of three houseposts collected at Knight Inlet in 1914. It was copied and stored at this time because the original was too badly decayed, even to move to storage.

New descriptive labels were printed and ensheathed in plastic, and attached to the exhibits in the park.

At the beginning of the year, the possibility seemed good that extra carving contracts could be obtained to pay the carvers' way for part of the year, and it was decided to employ three carvers, instead of just the two, so that Henry might obtain a year of training. Such outside work did not materialize, and, as mentioned above, other expenses were greater than had been foreseen, and it was necessary to lay the carvers off on December 15th until the beginning of the next fiscal year. It is heartening to note that a community project was organized by the Victoria Daily Times to employ the carvers, during that three months, in the carving of the world's tallest totem pole. The pole is to be given to the City of Victoria, when completed. Public support in the form of purchase of shares in the pole has been heavy, and much good publicity for the carving program has resulted.'

The world's tallest totem pole—the people of Victoria loved the idea! It would provide much needed income to Mungo and David Martin and Henry Hunt. Their pay scale, at that period in 1955 ran: Mungo Martin—$2.20 per hour, David Martin —$2.10 per hour, and Henry Hunt—$2.00 per hour.

In January 1956, the project began. Through the efforts of the *Victoria Daily Times,* the financing of this 'tallest totem' was accomplished by selling shares to the public at 50¢ each, and each share entitled the shareholder to view the progress of the carving and to have their name printed on a scroll that was to be buried at the base of the totem pole.

The people of Victoria were solidly in support, but they were not alone. By the time the shares had been 'on the market' a couple of weeks, there were shareholders in the form of individuals, communities, and organizations across Canada, in the United Kingdom, Australia, France, South Africa, Russia and Mexico. Clearly, this project had captured the public imagination.

The finished pole was to be 127 feet high and the red cedar tree from which it was carved weighed some nine tons and was about 250 years old. The tree came from the Muir's Creek area of Sooke, B.C., about 35 miles from Victoria.

The tree was, by actual count, the 18th tree examined by a search party comprised of officials from B.C. Forest Products Ltd., Elder Logging Ltd. and Mungo Martin. Mungo examined this 18th tree and said, briefly, 'Will do.'

The tree scaled 3,000 board feet of timber and the problem of falling it, undamaged, was formidable. When it was finally down, Mungo and David Martin examined it, foot by foot, and finally announced, 'O.K.' to a sigh of relief by the onlooking officials and forest workers.

The tree, with its massive five-foot butt end, was transported to Victoria, and the work began. The bark was stripped on January 16th, 1956. The finished totem was dedicated in a ceremony on July 2nd, 1956, at Victoria's Beacon Hill Park, where the pole was erected and where it still stands.

During that period, Wilson Duff noted in a letter to a colleague: 'The carving of the world's tallest totem poles goes on apace. The chips are flying as never before and public interest is at a new high. The idea may seem slightly corny to some, but it sure appeals to our Kwakiutl friends, and it bailed me out of an uncomfortable spot.' (Having to lay-off the carvers since the museum budget had been spent for that fiscal year... P.N.)

As Duff pointed out, the public interest in this project was tremendous. A good indication was the final tally of 'shares' sold, in excess of ten thousand. The best indicator, however, was the small, bronze plaque set into granite at the base of the pole. It reads:

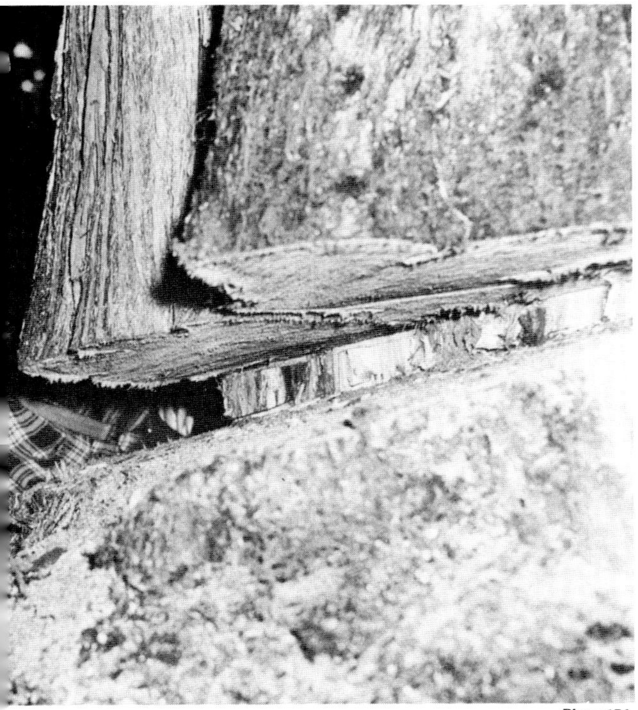

Plate: 176

'Symbolic of a proud race: Memento of the Nation's infancy: Monument to a rare native art: Proof of a united community interest: And the purest form of Canadiana.'

For the figures on the pole, Mungo decided to use the figures of the Gi'Ksem legend, previously described in connection with Mungo's house building project. Along with the figures of the Gi'Ksem legend, Mungo added two other figures to use up the length of the pole. They were two 'first men' who originated other clans of the Kwakiutl.

If finding employment as carvers was a problem before this project, it was certainly not immediately afterwards. In August, 1956, they were back at work for the Provincial Government at Thunderbird Park. If before there had been too little work to support the three of them, now there was too much. Probably due to the publicity generated by the 'tallest totem', the orders began to pour in. Orders from museums, governments, and private citizens, (mostly in the U.S. who wanted 12-foot or 15-foot totems for their private collections). The museum had ordered an additional eleven poles, and there were numerous commissions for masks, tourist poles, and the like. David Martin was moved to remark to a reporter that putting in a full day's work for wages 'makes our work just like an ordinary job, and the temptation is to be mechanical, and just when we think we'll get a few days off, boom comes another big job!' Just as Ellen Neel was saying, across the Strait of Georgia . . . it was either feast or famine or near mass-production.

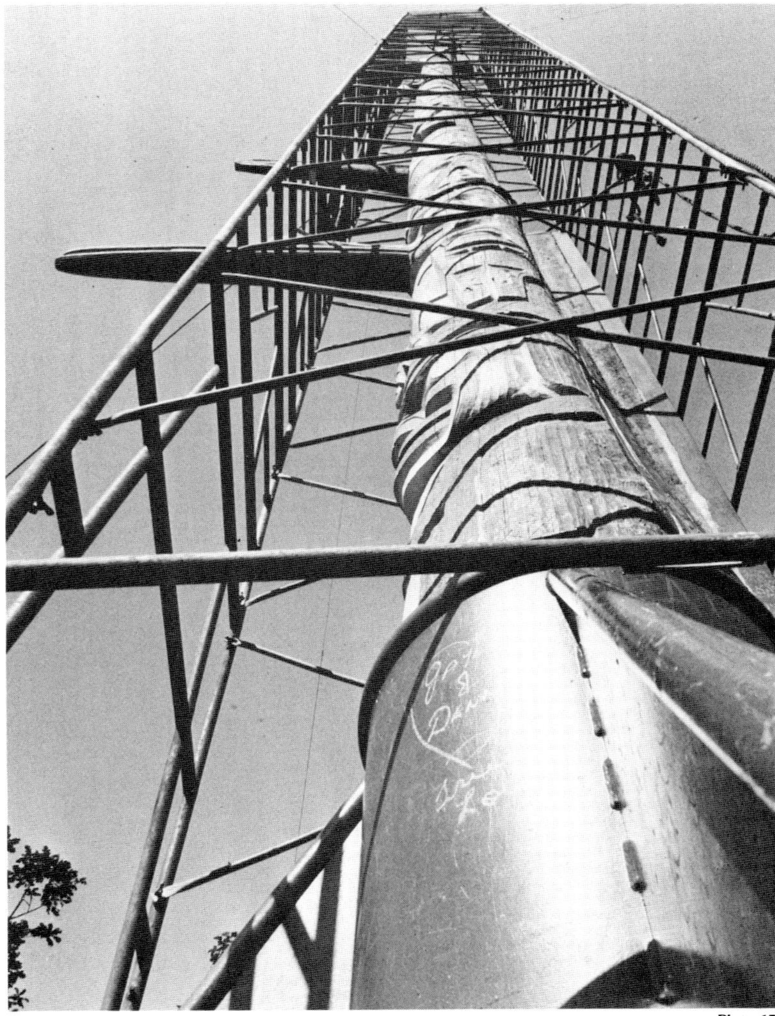

Plate: 177

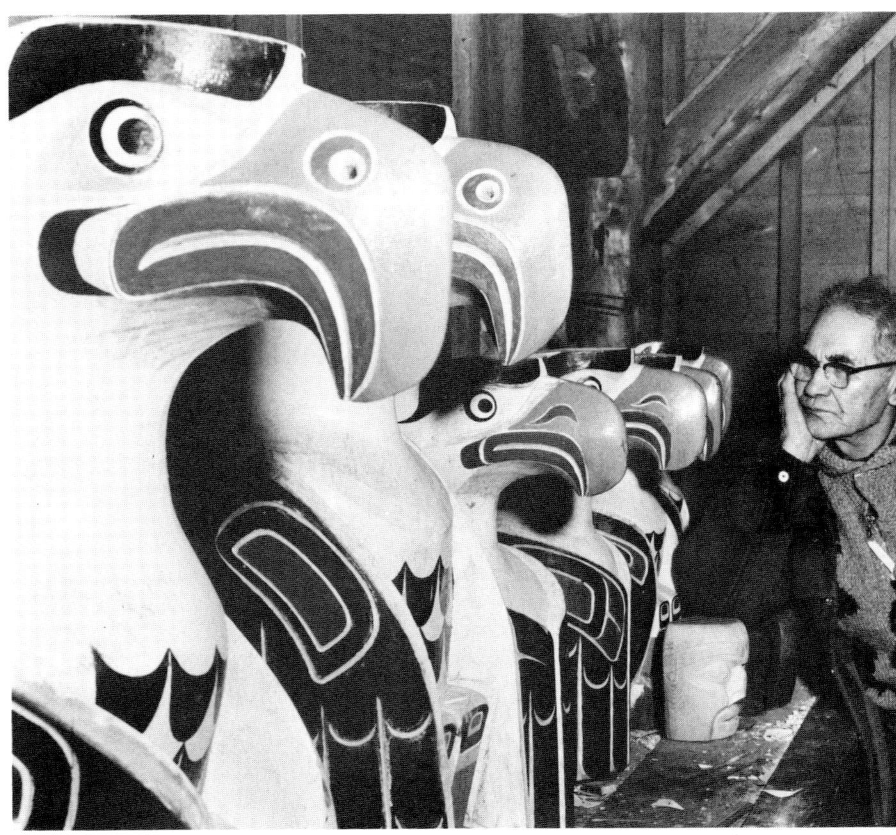

Plate: 178

Plate 177: The 'world's tallest totem' at Beacon Hill Park, Victoria, B.C. The elaborate scaffolding allows periodic repainting. The steel collar to reinforce the base was put on many years after it was erected in 1956. (Victoria, no date given. Photo: Jim Ryan.)

Plate 178: Mungo contemplates some of his carvings —a group of 'Kulus'—young Thunderbird figures. Photo taken in the carving shed at Thunderbird Park. (Thunderbird Park, Victoria, no date given. Photo: Jim Ryan.)

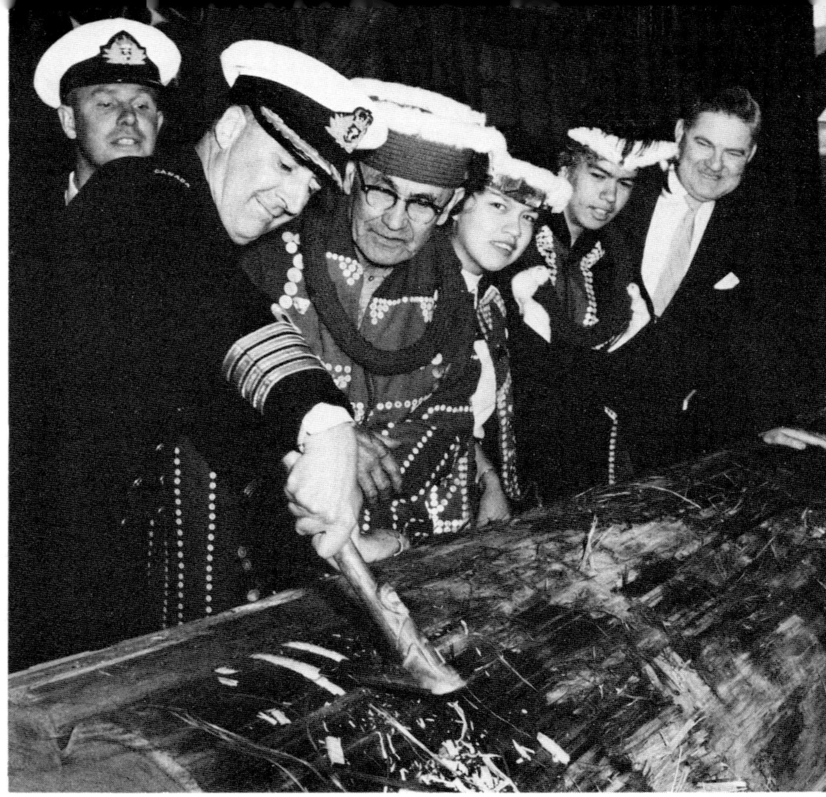

Plate 179: **A uniformed official takes one of the first swings at the log that will become a 100-foot birthday present—to the Queen of England! Several 'first cuts' were made... as many as there were officials. Mungo and young Tony Hunt, dressed in 'Hamatsa' neck-rings, button blankets and head-rings, look slightly apprehensive as the razor-sharp elbow adze is plied ... in the centre, one of Mungo's pretty 'nieces' looks directly at the photographer. (Thunderbird Park, Victoria, 1957. Photo: Jim Ryan.)**

It was just after this busy period that Mungo is supposed to have passed his carving skills to Bill Reid, a noted Haida craftsman and artist, during a brief 'apprenticeship'. Reid had been given the formidable task of creating the Haida Village portion of Totem Park at UBC and spent some time with Mungo before beginning the actual carving there. Reid is a famous man today, and all of the published texts on his training and early career mention this 'apprenticeship' with Mungo. When I asked Bill about it, he laughed and said:

'The story of my learning from Mungo is a myth. It's prevalent in the published stuff because it makes a nice story—you know, handing down the skills, etc., etc. Actually, my total exposure to carving poles with Mungo was limited to about 10 days—in 1957, I think it was. I was still working for C.B.C, and had a couple of weeks holiday coming. Wilson Duff arranged for me to go over to Victoria, and I spent the two weeks carving on a duplicate of an old Haida pole that Mungo was doing for the museum. As far apprenticing, Mungo just pointed at a blank space on the partly-carved pole and said 'You're an artist—go to it.' I wound up doing a small figure on that pole. That's the pole that's in Peace Arch Park, in Blaine, Washington.

Doug Cranmer was in Victoria then, staying at Mungo's house. I don't think he was actually working for the museum, but was doing some carving on his own. I met him while I was over there and subsequently hired him to work with me on the Haida village at U.B.C.

We started in 1958 and the village was opened in 1962. Mungo used to come over to visit while he was in Vancouver, and I finally got to know him pretty well.

Bill finished by saying: 'No, I didn't apprentice under Mungo,' he paused thoughtfully. 'Although that little figure on the Haida pole was the first large wood carving that I'd ever done.'

So the work went on... early in 1957, Mungo was commissioned to carve a 100-foot totem pole as British Columbia's centennial gift to the Queen of England!

Mungo started carving this unusual gift on March 23, 1957. One of the 'first cuts' on the giant log was made by the Lieutenant-Governor, Frank Ross, in an official ceremony at the Thunderbird Park carving sheds and more than 300 persons, including government and civic officials witnessed the event.

Provincial pride ran high that year, as hundreds of projects were planned to commemorate British Columbia's one hundredth anniversary the following year, 1958. B.C. had become a crown colony one hundred years before and, as gift to Britain from 'Totemland', a totem pole seemed particularly appropriate.

At the ceremony, Mungo Martin delivered a greeting to the Queen, through the Lieutenant-Governor. In sonorous Kwak̓wala translated by Henry Hunt's wife, Helen, Mungo gave this message:

'I want to say that I am happy to have this chance to speak to you, and through you—to send a message to Her Majesty, the Queen. I would ask you to convey my message to Her Majesty.

'I send my greetings. I send her greetings of my whole family, my whole tribe, the Kwakiutl, and all of the Indian people.

'We are honoured that she would accept this totem pole. Totem poles are things that we make—no one else in the world makes them. We are happy that Her Majesty will accept this pole and will put it up in one of her parts of England.

'Your Honour—I have made many totem poles. I have carved totem poles for over fifty years, but this will be a very special one. I have never made one for such a high personage before. I am honoured that I was chosen to carve this pole and that the work of my hands will stand in London for many years to come.

'This will be a real totem pole. I designed this to show the family stories of my tribe, the Kwakiutl. This is the way we show our history. This pole will show the crests of ten tribes.

'Thank you for the honour of speaking to you and sending this message to Her Majesty, The Queen.'

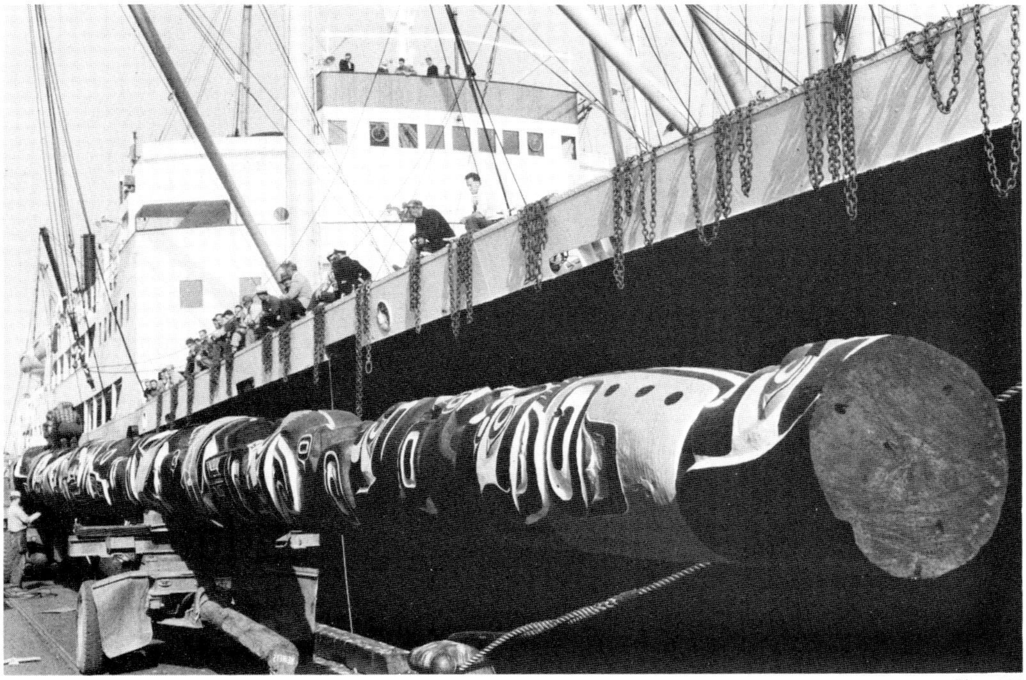

Plate: 180

Plate 180: B.C.'s present to the Queen of England. The totem is shown being loaded aboard ship for the long journey to the British Isles. The holes in the top figure accept a separately-carved 'potlatch hat.' (Victoria, 1958. Photo: Jim Ryan.)

Plate 181: The 'Queen's Pole' is secured to specially cut blocks on the deck of the vessel. Cardboard and cedar shingles were used to protect the figures at the tie-down points. The next time Mungo saw this pole—he and it were in the British Isles. (Victoria, 1958. Photo: Jim Ryan.)

Mungo concluded the ceremonies by giving the Lt. Governor a Kwakiutl name 'GIUTLAS'. It was a name held by Mungo's great-grandmother's father and it meant: 'Everyone is always going in the same direction'. That is, to the house of this man who always makes them welcome. Helen's best translation was 'Man of great hospitality'. It's interesting to note that this name is close, in both sound and meaning, to 'GAI-YUS-DIS' and 'HAYUSDIS', the name of Arthur Dick and a shortened version of Helen Hunt's name, respectively.

The carvers finished the Queen's totem pole in due course and arrangements were made (courtesy of a $1,000.00 donation from a private Victoria citizen, Mr. J.G. Nordal!) for Mungo to attend the dedication ceremonies in Windsor Great Park, London, along with Helen Hunt to act as his translator. The event was scheduled for July 19, 1958 and Mungo said little about his pending trip to England, until the eve of his departure July 16th. Then he said, simply, 'This is a great honour. The Queen is bestowing an honour on the Indians of British Columbia.'

When he returned to Canada, a week later, Mungo had much more to say. 'The English are a wonderful people. What impressed me was the hospitality of the English. They respected and honoured the traditions of my people.'

Mungo Martin was seventy-eight then, and the long trip had tired him, but he was genuinely moved by his experiences in England. He and Helen Hunt had been presented to the Queen Mother, when Queen Elizabeth was unable to attend the dedication because of a sinus infection.

Helen Hunt said, 'The Queen Mother was charming and kind. She took a real interest in the totem pole.'

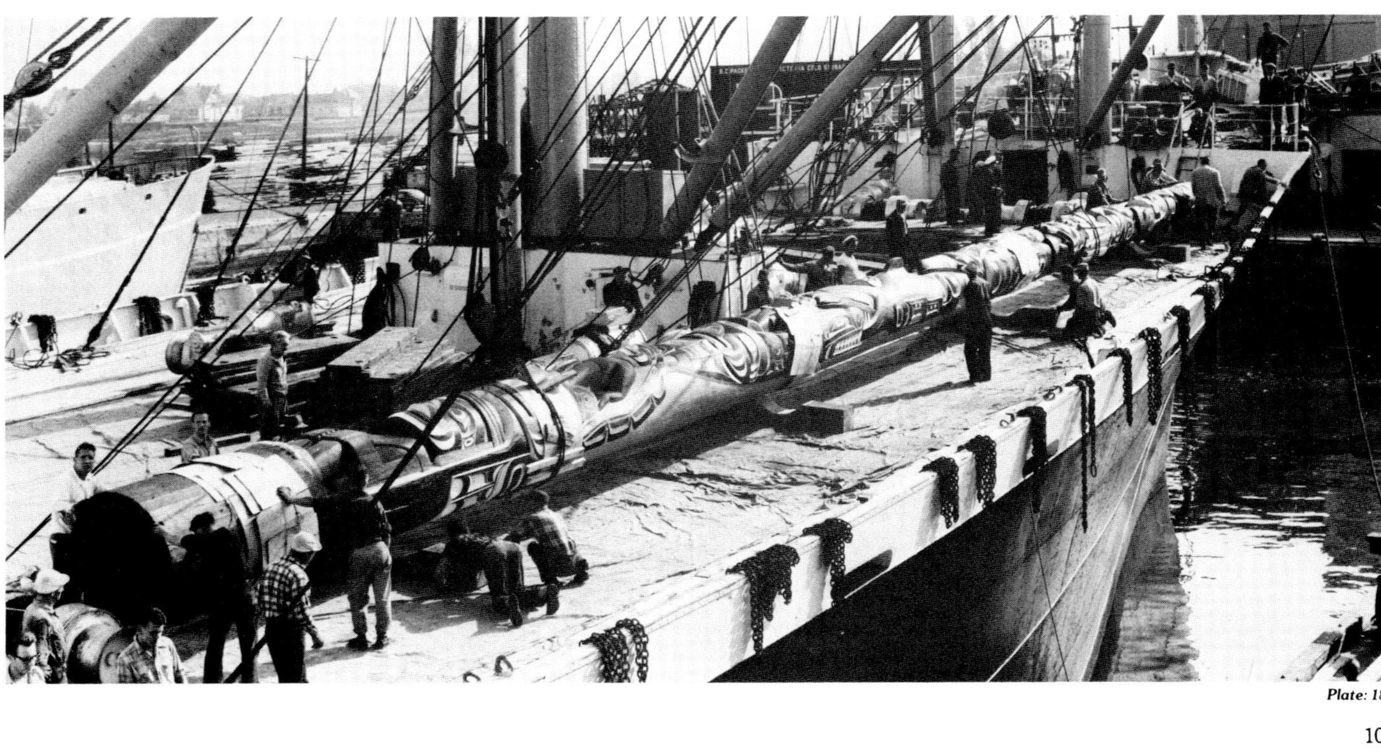

Plate: 181

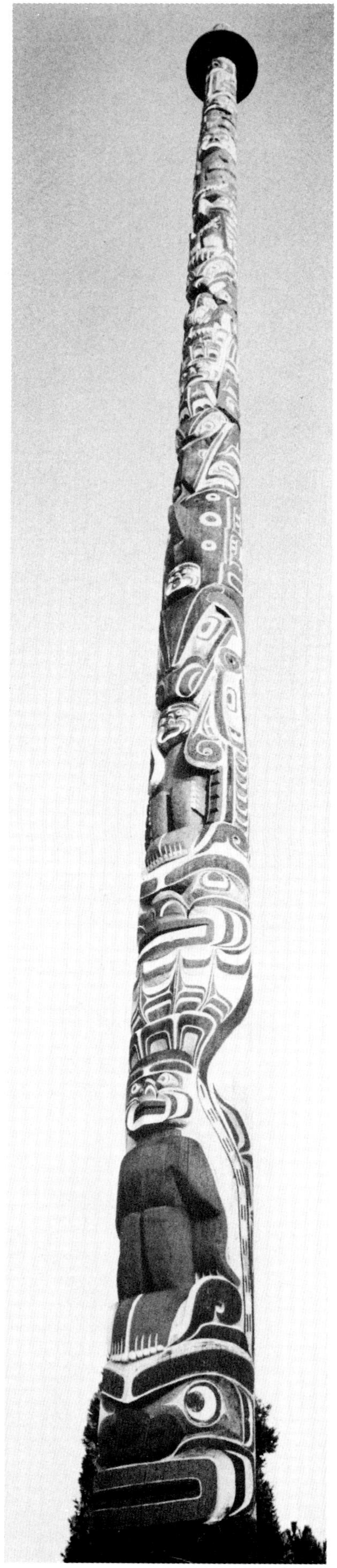

Plate 182: **Vancouver's 'Centennial' totem pole, outside the Maritime Museum at Hadden Park, near Kitsilano Beach. Mungo carved this pole in 1958 in Victoria. This pole has an exact twin in Great Windsor Park, England. (Vancouver, 1979. Photo: Author.)**

Helen Hunt went on to explain that from the first moment of their arrival, English officials had looked after them, had seen to their needs, taken them on whirlwind tours of the city and entertained them at their private, homes.

Mungo was surprised at the size of London, for this was his first trip out of the Northwest. 'For as far as my eyes could see—there were houses and more houses,' he said, 'I just couldn't believe it.'

The English people threw a lavish dinner and reception for their visitors and Mungo said, 'In return, we sang an old Indian song of thanks.'

While visiting the Tower of London, they met the Resident Governor, Brigadier Leslie Wieler, who later invited them to his home for tea.

Mungo also visited the Oxford University Museum and the British Museum, where he examined carvings collected from British Columbia—many collected before Mungo was born. Mungo was most impressed with his plane trip. It was the first time in his life he had travelled by air.

'The world looked to me from the air,' Mungo said, 'looked to me like a long sand bar, with lots of clams!'

Concurrent with the carving of the Queen's totem pole, a duplicate was made for the people of British Columbia to enjoy. Both poles bore these figures; from the top, Man, Beaver, Old Man, Thunderbird, Sea Otter, Raven, Whale 'SISIYUTŁ' (double-headed snake or sea serpent), Halibut Man, and Cedar Man.

The pole that remained behind was erected at Vancouver's Hadden Park, near Kitsilano Beach in October, 1958. This hundred-foot pole (one foot for each year of B.C.'s growth), saw much the same scene as its twin . . . the sun shone, Centennial flags fluttered, a band played, and dignitaries gave speeches.

The following year, Wilson Duff, writing in 'Museum News' of May, 1959, used the twin poles as the lead-in to a tribute to Mungo. It was titled:

Mungo Martin—Carver of the Century

'Towering above the grounds of the new Maritime Museum, is the magnificent Centennial Totem Pole, a massive 100-foot cedar column boldly carved and painted with symbols of British Columbia's Indian past. Dominating great Windsor Park, in England, is its exact duplicate. Erected there as a gift to Her Majesty, from the people of the Province. This most imposing pair of totem poles ever carved will stand through the next century as striking reminders of British Columbia's first centenary. They will also stand as memorials to the remarkable man who created and carved them, Mungo Martin.'

Duff continued . . .

'The idea of carving these two poles originated with the Vancouver Centennial Committee. It very soon became obvious that Mungo Martin was the only logical man to carve them, and he was eager to accept the challenge. Since 1952, he had worked in Victoria as chief carver for the Provincial Museum's Totem Pole Restoration Program, in Thunderbird Park, a position he still holds. The carving of the Centennial poles was readily made a part of this progam, and Mungo Martin was asked to create the design. He had a certain amount of assistance of a practical and adminisitrative nature, and he had strong young men to help him with the actual carving, notably the talented Henry Hunt, but the act of creation was his own.

The days ahead were to bring great events in his life: the dedication ceremonies, the visit to England and the presentation to the Queen Mother, the many occasions that brought public acclaim. He enjoys such events, they are now happy ceremonies for him. But, in addition to these memories he will always carry in his mind a deep satisfaction, the satisfaction of an artist who has crowned his career with a great masterpiece.'

Duff pointed out how he had hesitated to pay a personal tribute to Mungo—out of fear of doing so in an inadequate manner. Yet he had come to respect Mungo Martin and to know him as few white men could. Because of Duff's training as an anthropologist, he could bridge the gap between men of different cultures and his association with Mungo was virtually on a daily basis.

'I have been his (Mungo's) 'boss' since his arrival at Thunderbird Park in 1952. I have been his friend, advisor, intermediary, secretary, announcer and interpreter. (Not interpreting from English to Kwakiutl—but, from the incomprehesible English of officials, journalists and visiting anthropologists into Mungo's English—and vice-versa).'

Duff continued with a description of Mungo's early life, most of which has already been recorded on these pages. That Mungo had passed to Duff a comprehensive account of his own personal history was evident through the knowledge of specifics that Duff displayed and expressed—knowledge important to future scholars and researchers. Important, as well, to Mungo's progeny and their relatives—for when Mungo and his striking memory had passed, these people would still have a clear record of at least some of that what had gone before. Duff recorded these things with rare perception, and he continued:

'Every Kwakiutl of any importance assumed a whole series of hereditary names of higher and higher rank, as he went through life. So far, Mungo has had eight. His first name was 'KASALAS' ('proficient on the shore'), and his latest and highest is 'NAKA'PANKAM' ('ten times Chief'). His others—they all lose much in the translation—have been: 'YAYAKALAS' ('always has a house full of wealth'), 'GWOYIMSI' ('big whale'), 'TLATHBAI' ('leader of a school of whales'), 'SIEKWALAS' ('proficient on the sea'), 'KISUYAKULIS' ('great ceremony'), and 'HINAKYALASU' ('invulnerable to ridicule'). Spruce Martin outranked Mungo and held the name 'NAKA'PANKAM' until his death. Now Mungo holds the highest name and rank in his clan.'

Experts may disagree on the precision of translation. Mungo's peers may argue over Mungo's specific rights to privileges that he claimed. Duff, at least, recorded what Mungo told him, and possessed the inquisitiveness and over-view to search out the questions that could link isolated data.

Duff continued describing Mungo's early life and concluded:

'Today, Mungo reads a little, writes a little, and speaks a little English, and finds that quite enough. He doesn't want to be a white man. I don't mean that Mungo could not make the best use of white man's inventions when it served his purpose to do so. Once, using a handsaw, and sheer ingenuity, he converted a two-cylinder engine into a single cylinder engine—or so he told me. With equal ingenuity he could transform the noses of sea-lions into those of seals, and collect the bounty. I am quite sure that he was the first of his tribe to own and use a tape recorder. Learning the potential of this machine through his association with anthropologists, he purchased one in 1954, and he is still working systematically, at the task of transferring hundreds of songs from his mental storehouse to the more permanent memory of magnetic tape.

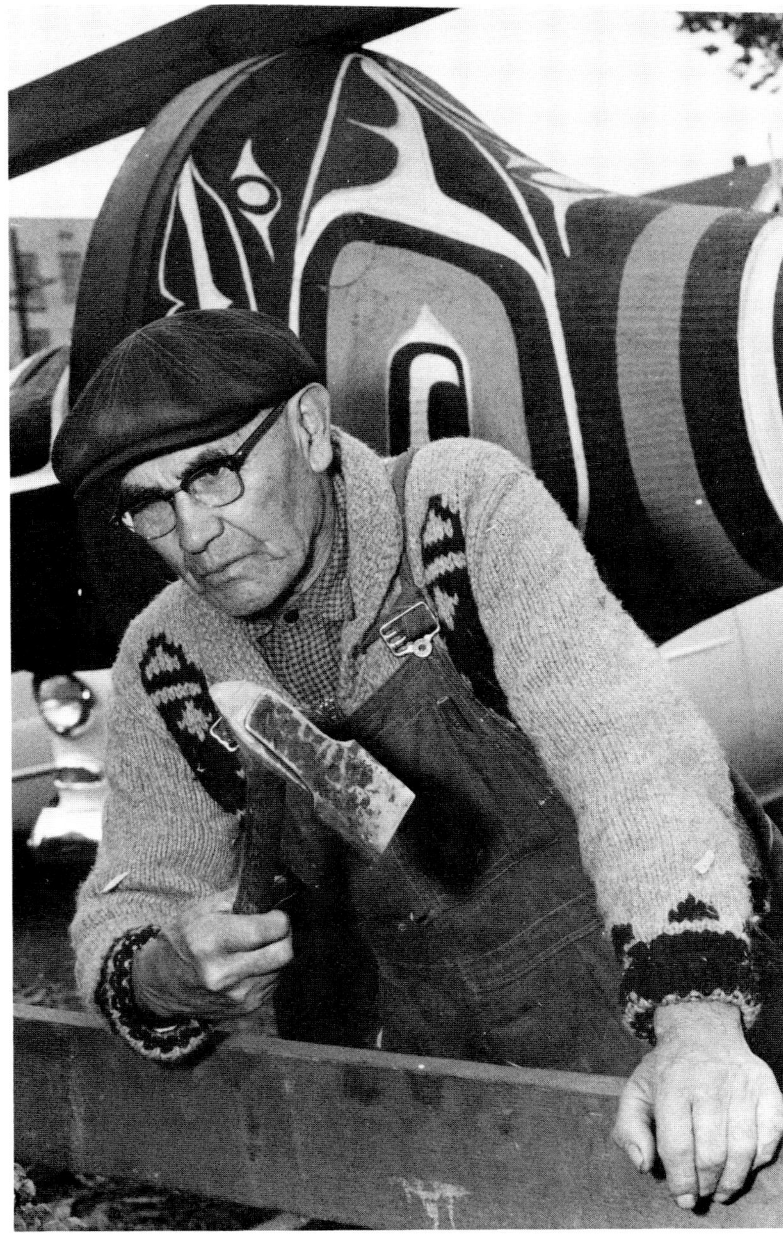

Plate 183: **Mungo looks thoughtful... this photo was taken after the completion of the 'Queen's Pole' (shown in the background). Mungo was aware at the time, of his impending trip to England. Well-known Victoria photographer Jim Ryan asked him to hold an adze in his hand for the photo. Mungo snorted and responded 'This pole already finished.' But he held the adze and struck a serious pose. (Thunderbird Park, Victoria, 1958. Photo: Jim Ryan.)**

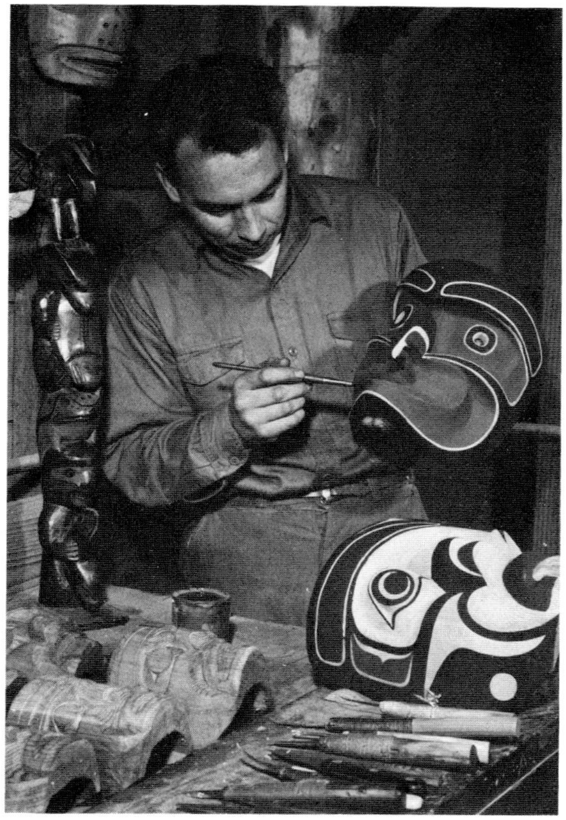

Plate 184: **Henry Hunt paints a 'Bookwus' or wild man mask, a 'Pugwis' or merman mask lies on the table in front of him, and a model totem carved and painted by Charlie James is immediately to his right. These 'tourist' and 'souvenir' masks helped carry Henry over the times when the Provincial Museum's budget ran out and he and David Martin—and sometimes even Mungo—were laid off. Photo taken in the carving shed, Thunderbird Park. (Victoria, no date given. Photo: Tourism, B.C.)**

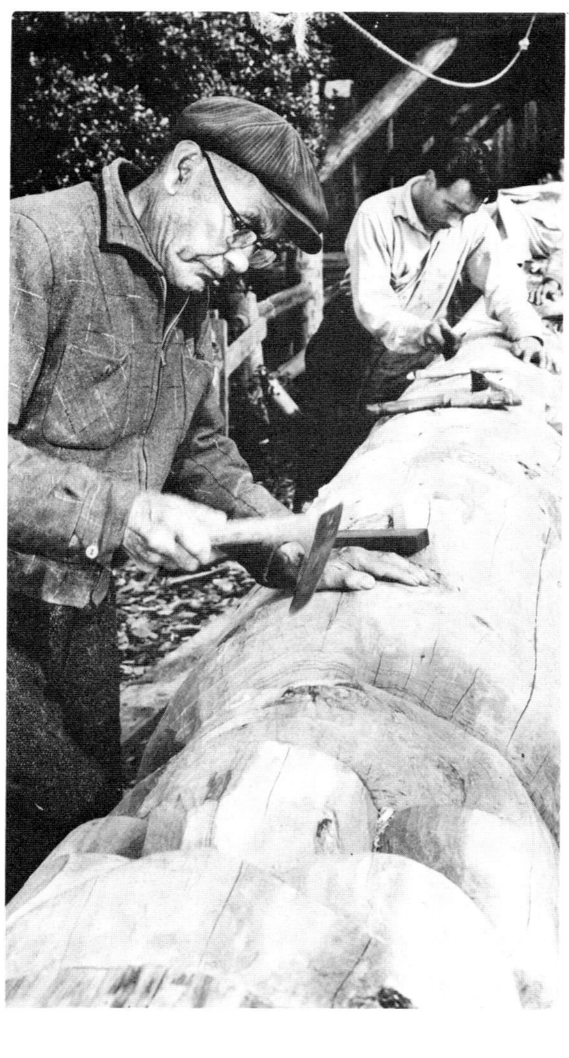

Plate 185: **The carving goes on. Mungo in the foreground and Henry Hunt working on another massive cedar monument. (Victoria, 1956. Photo: Jim Ryan.)**

'(Mungo) regrets that the arrival of the new civilization had such destructive effects on his people and their culture—but, he accepts the situation as it is. Furthermore, he has assigned himself the task of preserving all he knows about Kwakiutl culture. Whether it is by knife and adze, paintbrush, on the tape recorder, or in the note-books of his anthropologist friends, he is determined that this knowledge will be recorded for posterity.

'In my view, this objective appraisal of the situation and this conscious dedication to preserve the culture are Mungo Martin's clearest claims to true greatness.'

That was in May, 1959, and it must have given Mungo satisfaction to hear words of tribute and praise from one he had come to regard as a good friend. But, words of praise buy few groceries, and once all the heavy work-load was over, David Martin and Henry Hunt were laid off again. Mungo continued; Henry Hunt carved souvenir totems and masks; and David Martin said 'to hell with it', and went back to commercial fishing.

On Friday, September 3rd, 1959, David Martin drowned while crossing from Comox to Steveston on the salmon seiner *Annadale.* Dave had gone overboard in heavy seas and an intensive search by fishing vessels and search-and-rescue aircraft failed to find a trace of him.

With David Martin's death, Mungo lost not only his son, but his successor. Mungo Martin had preserved, intact, his family culture as few Kwakiutl had—and now there was no one left to carry it on.

It is said that Mungo remained stoic and said little during the time when his emotions must have nearly overwhelmed him. The depth of his grief was not shown until several months later.

In December of 1959, Mungo Martin turned over his family's collection of dance masks and potlatch regalia to the Provincial Museum. These items included the masks that Mungo had painstakingly made, and those he had commissioned others to make, to illustrate his family's privileges at the opening of his house . . . the 'HAMAT̓SA' pieces. All those things that would have passed to his son.

To a small group gathered in the house of 'NA<u>K</u>A'P<u>A</u>NK<u>A</u>M' at Thunderbird Park, Mungo spoke:

'Today, I am in darkness—I cannot carry on. All my life I have worked so that we would be known by the different nations. I carried on alone when the different tribes had stopped, because I wanted to prove my love for my son.'

Mungo stopped and gazed away for a long moment, then continued: 'When this is gone, I will have a new life.'

Mungo spoke slowly in Kwak̓wala and Helen Hunt, always by his side, translated for him, 'My wife and I thought night after night, if it was right or wrong to give these things away. But with them, we could not forget our son,' tears welled in his eyes and threatened to spill as he said with finality, 'Now he is gone. Now I am alone, I don't want to see these masks anymore.'

A sad picture from this time shows Mungo working on a memorial pole to stand in Courtenay, B.C. in memory of David Martin. The pole was erected on May 28th, 1960.

Almost a year after Mungo turned his face away, an article appeared in a Vancouver newspaper under the heading:

VICTORIA'S TOTEM CARVER LOSES JOB

December 1, 1960—Victoria

Mungo Martin, last of the great totem carvers in the Pacific Northwest, Wednesday was given notice that he cannot be kept on the government payroll.

For the past eight years, Mungo, now 82, has been carving poles in the Thunderbird Park courtesy of the B.C. government. He and his assistants have been responsible for the most famous poles in Canada and the United Kingdom.

Also given notice was Henry Hunt, Mungo's 37 year old grandson-in-law, who learned the carving art from Mungo and worked with him fashioning totems, masks and vessels.

Dr. G.C. Carl, director of the Provincial Museum said the project, which has attracted thousands of tourists, will be closed at least from December 31st to the end of April.

He said, 'It has been supported in the past two years mainly by contracts from agencies. However, there have been none this year and there are no funds available from the budget.'

A cold rain fell in Totemland that day, and the clerks and typists and other museum employees had their umbrellas up as they scurried to the parking lot.

That same month, December 1960, Mungo put into the Provincial Museum, his 'copper' called 'MA'HAYNOOTSI', (great killer whale). Wilson Duff arranged this acquisition for the museum.

It is significant to note that the previous year when Mungo turned over his masks to the museum, he offered to do so—free. But Wilson Duff applied for 'special funds' of $1,000.00 to make the purchase, and that money saw Mungo through the winter lay-off at almost precisely his usual salary. A year later, at lay-off time, Duff again had Mungo donate something of such value that 'special funds' would have undoubtedly been available. Did the museum purchase Mungo's copper in 1960? I don't know, but it would be no great surprise if Duff had so arranged it and made sure that the amount was roughly equal to what Mungo would have earned through the lay-off period, until the new fiscal year funds were available once again.

Duff could not spend more than his budget for the 'Totem Pole Restoration Program' in a given fiscal year, but years of experience in a

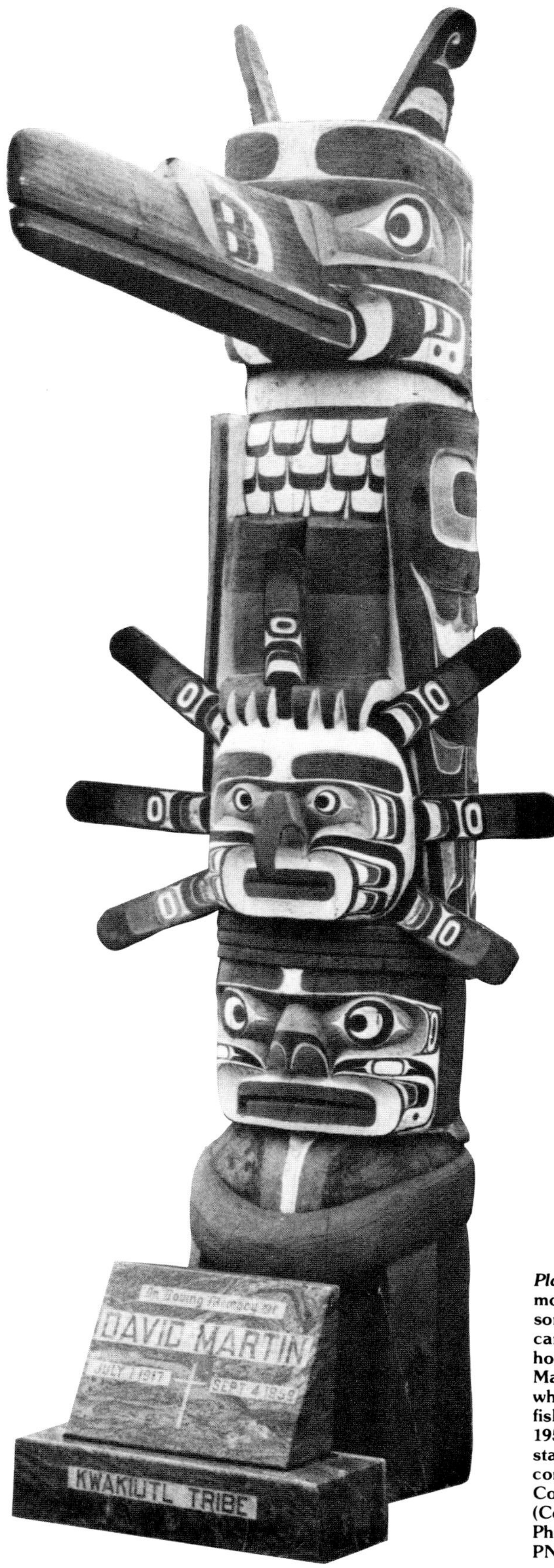

***Plate 186:* A chief's monument to his son. Mungo Martin carved this pole in honour of David Martin who was lost while commercial fishing in September, 1959. The pole stands outside a communal house in Courtenay, B.C. (Courtenay, c. 1969. Photo: B.C.P.M. PN-2856.)**

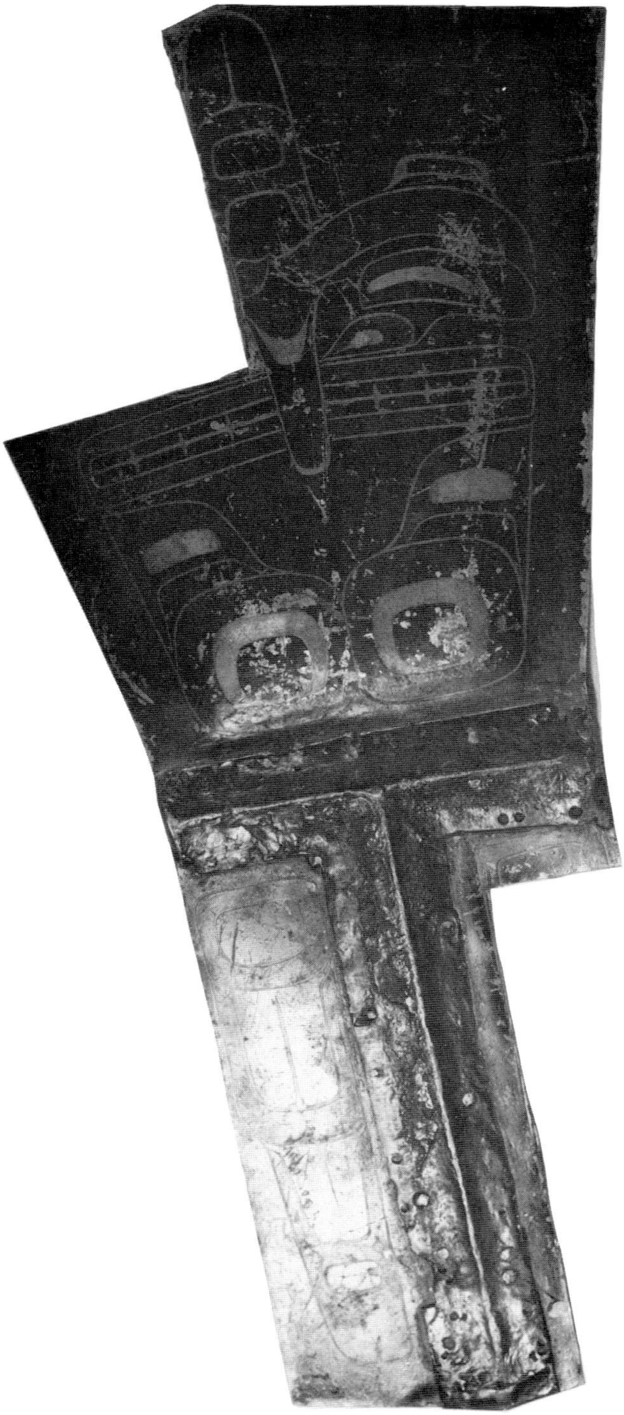

***Plate 187:* Mungo Martin's 'copper' 'Mahaynootsi'—big killer whale. (Victoria. Photo: B.C.P.M. PN-9251.)**

bureaucratic system makes one knowledgeable in its by-ways. There is no doubt that Duff counted Mungo as both a friend and a national resource of immeasurable value.

In 1961, Duff published the history of Mungo's 'Killer Whale' copper 'MA'HAYNOOTSI'. It was part of the 'Report of the Provincial Museum of Natural History and Anthropology—1960'. It was also one of Duff's finest pieces of detailed reporting on a single object that was, at once, both artifact and culmination point of a sophisticated cultural heritage.

Although repetitious of some descriptions already given, Duff's paper follows in its entirety as an example of the detail that he was able to extract in pieces and weave into usable fabric.

THE KILLER WHALE COPPER
A Chief's Memorial to His Son

By Wilson Duff, Provincial Museum, Victoria, B.C.

In December, 1960, Chief Mungo Martin put into the permanent care of the Provincial Museum his valued 'copper' Ma'haynootsi 'Great Killer Whale.' It had been his intention to fix it to a stone monument which he had erected in Centennial Park, Courtenay, in memory of his son David, who lost his life by drowning in September, 1959. However, the suggestion was made to him that it would be safer, and would make a more meaningful memorial, if it were placed on permanent exhibit in the Museum. To that he agreed.

The history of the copper was recorded on tape, with Mrs. Helen Hunt acting as interpreter. It is the purpose of this brief article to put the story into print, along with enough introductory information to give it a context. Certain sections are given verbatim from the tape, as they convey some of the eloquence of the original Kwakiutl phrasings.

Mungo Martin was risen to a high social position among his people. A member of the 'real' Kwakiutl tribe of Fort Rupert, he holds at present the name Naka'pankum. He is the leading chief of the second-ranking clan of the tribe, and ranks third in the entire tribe, after Tom Johnson (Tla-kwageela) and James Knox (Tla'kodlas). At the time he purchased his copper, however, he had not yet attained such a high position of rank. His older brother, Spruce Martin, preceded him as leader of the clan and holder of the name Naka'penkum. It wasn't just the highest chiefs who could own coppers.

Coppers

Coppers were owned by the Indian tribes of the Coast from the Tlingit of Alaska to the Kwakiutl of Vancouver Island. Their only use, aside from the tiny ones sometimes used as ornaments on costumes, was as objects of wealth and prestige. They served, in general, as the currency of the highest denomination in the complicated native systems of high finance. They were bought and sold (for ever-larger prices), given away, 'broken', and even thrown into the sea as the chiefs who owned them strove for superiority by 'fighting each other with property'. The most important coppers had their own names—Mungo remembers the names of thirty-two others which belonged to various tribes of the southern Kwakiutl—and their histories and values were widely known.

The origin of the custom of using coppers had not been satisfactorily explained, nor has their distinctive shape. It is generally believed that coppers were used in pre-contact times, being made of native copper from sources far to the north, in Alaska. Native traditions reveal that the metal was held in very high esteem, and the first explorers to the Coast did find a small amount of it already in use in the form of weapons and ornaments. However, native copper went out of use very quickly as the traders flooded the market with sheet copper. We do not know directly of any existing 'copper' which is made of the native metal.

The Copper 'Ma'haynootsi'

This copper is 26 inches high and was about 13 inches across at its widest point; its size is not unusual, but its proportions are somewhat more long and narrow than most. It has been 'broken' in two places. It was not uncommon for pieces to be removed from a copper in this way until only the raised T-shaped central ridge remained, and in fact this copper actually consists of an old central T riveted to a new copper-shaped sheet. The arms of the T, as was customary, form a shallow inverted V in cross-section, although they have been somewhat flattened out when riveted to the flat sheet below. The upper (larger) part of the copper is shallowly dished out from behind. The entire surface has been blackened with some type of lacquer, and a design of a killer whale has been engraved on the front.

History of the Copper

Mungo bought Ma'haynootsi from Peter Scow about 1942 for $2,010. He does not know its earlier history, except that it is an old T on a new copper, and Peter Scow had it remade in a machine shop at Alert Bay. Willie Siwid engraved the design on it.

Most of the money which Mungo used to buy this copper was obtained in earlier transactions involving another copper. In the late 1930's, when he married Abaya (the present Mrs. Martin), her 'cousin' Willie Siwid gave him many things as part of her dowry—money, blankets, pots and pans, a Hamatsa mask and Hamatsa name, and other privileges (ki-su). In addition, he bought a copper named Tlaksoo'yala and gave that to Mungo as well. Some years later Mungo sold Tlaksoo'yala to his brother Spruce for $1,600.00. He kept the money and later used it to buy Ma'haynootsi.

Mungo bought Ma'haynootsi with the thought in mind that he didn't want to put up a potlatch or winter dance without a copper for his children to dance on. Another reason was that if he died, his son would never be ashamed, but could say, 'I have a copper to dance on, and for my children to dance on, through my father.' And nobody could say otherwise.

The first time Mungo showed the copper in public was at the initiation of his son David into the Hamatsa 'secret society'...

After Mungo had the copper to use as a shield against anyone who would say anything wrong against his family, after he had his security, then he put on a big winter dance and brought out Dave as a Hamatsa on that copper. Mungo selected one of the big chiefs, Harry Mountain, to place the copper in Dave's arms the moment he came back from being initiated back to the tribe. Mountain made the motion of having Dave swallow the copper, tail end (small end) first. Then it was placed on the floor. Now it was said that Dave had had a feast of copper.

The copper was then 'broken for the first time...

The Chiefs of the tribes were then invited to break the copper. Not all Chiefs can break copper—only the Chiefs that had the right to break copper were invited. They got eagle down and put it over the copper, so that it would be perfect, and te'lkw (tender, soft). The Chiefs all put their hands on it as Harry Mountain broke it. All the Chiefs are said to have broken it because they had their hands on it.

Then they got the piece off (it is the piece off the top of the copper). They gave Mungo the piece, and he gave it to Frank Walker. In that way he only returned what Frank Walker had given to his brother Spruce. Frank Walker was a Kwakiutl who had broken a copper for Spruce. They didn't want to have the name of not returning against them. This cleared that.

The next occasion on which the copper was shown in public was during the performance at Gwayastums, Gilford Island, at one of Mungo's own ceremonies (ki'su), which he used to celebrate the coming of age and naming of a young girl in the family. The ceremony makes use of a very large decorated wooden cradle, which is hung at the back of the house. The copper was placed in the cradle as a 'comforter' (blanket) for the 'baby' concerned. This ceremony was repeated in Thunderbird Park in 1953, and will be described in more detail below.

The story behind the other piece 'broken' from the copper is as follows:

Mungo got quite angry at Chief Tom Omhid one time about 1944, and made all the arrangements to break his copper to give to Omhid. But after he had the piece broken off he changed his mind, because Omhid didn't have any power to do anything about it if he did give him the piece.

Omhid had spoken out of hand and said that Dave was a Hamatsa without a copper. He was a Hamatsa with an empty stomach. That is what angered Mungo.

Mungo disposed of the piece of copper when his brother died:

So instead of giving it to Omhid (when he changed his mind and didn't want to hurt anybody with that piece of copper), when Spruce died, to comfort his own sorrow, he threw it in the water. He didn't want to bring up hard feelings about things that had happened years before, so he just vanished that piece with his brother. That was at Fort Rupert, when he invited the tribes to have the sa'la (mourning) for his brother.

The copper was shown again in December, 1953, when it played a very prominent role in the opening ceremonies of Mungo's Kwakiutl house in Thunderbird Park. First, Mungo went through the motions of financing the event by 'selling' the copper to his wife Abaya for $1,500.00. The cradle ceremony was performed in honour of David's daughter Dorothy, with the copper serving as her 'comforter' in the large wooden cradle. The copper also appeared at times during the Hamatsa dance, carried on the arms of the Hamatsa, David Martin. The following summaries of these events are taken from the complete transcript made at the time, and now in the Museum files.

The 'sale' of the copper took place, with proper speeches and ceremony, during a rehearsal on the evening before the main performance. The procedure was that Mungo 'took up' (brought out) his valued copper and 'sold' it to Abaya for $1,500.00, so that he would have money to give away and thus show the extent of his pride in his new house. In actual fact it was Mungo's own money, and the figure included expenditures which had already been made in the preparations for the event.

Tom Omhid, who was Mungo's speaker, took up the copper and said (in part)...

This is what the Chief has taken up, this that has a name, the name Ma'haynootsi. He doesn't want to take up just anything. He comes from a proud tribe. He is proud of the new house. You will recognize this house, Chiefs... It is a copy of the first house that all you tribes used to gather in, the house that belonged to my Chief, the house of Naka'penkum... and now I am selling this... There it is.'

Omhid placed the copper on the floor. George Scow, who spoke for Abaya, picked it up and made a speech. '... She will take it, you Chiefs. She will buy it...' He placed the copper down in front of Abaya and took from her a bag of money.

'...Now we will need your help,' he said, addressing Omhid and Daniel Cranmer. Mr. Cranmer took the money and he too made a speech, praising Abaya and Mungo for what they were doing. He passed the money to Omhid, who spoke again, then handed it to Mungo.

Helen Hunt later explained the speeches:

'They were talking about the copper being brought out. It was given to Mungo by Abaya in the first place, and now Abaya has bought it back so that Mungo will have money to distribute to the people... so that all the performers will not be ashamed of themselves. They will have the copper to dance on. That is the value of the dance that is going to be performed.'

The cradle ceremony was performed early on the first day of the opening ceremonies, at a performance to which only Indian guest and anthropologists had been invited. It followed the set of mourning songs which had opened the performance, and preceded the dances, which were of the winter ceremonial type. The large cradle had been suspended prominently in front of the painted screen that closed off the rear of the house. The main performers grouped themselves in front of the cradle. There were strange sounds as the voices of spirits were heard from the back corners of the house. Mungo called out, as though to a baby in a cradle, not to be afraid. Then the song was sung, there were speeches, and the ceremony ended with 50-cent pieces being distributed to everyone in the house.

Omhid's speech was in the typical figurative language of Kwakiutl speeches, referring to the copper as a blanket, and to Dorothy as the new-born baby:

'The blanket to keep this child from getting cold has already been prepared. This man with the great name has already bought it. The softest of all blankets. Its price is enough to distribute to all your tribes. That is why it can never be cold, the new-born baby, it starts its life by keeping warm.'

At other points during the 1953 ceremonies references were made to the copper. In one speech Omhid pointed to where it rested on the floor:

'This is the work of Naka'pankam. This is proof of his courage, lying right there. This belongs to the Chief, and he can never fail the name of it.'

But at some point Omhid must have said something that made Mungo angry, because Mungo renewed his threat to break the copper for Omhid. However, that was not done.

Mungo brought the copper out once more before David's death.

When Dave decided to marry Robina Ferrie, of Campbell River, Mungo gave her father Johnny Ferrie $2,000.00 and the copper to make the ceremony big enough and known. Johnny Ferrie couldn't keep the money or the copper; he had to give it to Dave. That's what Robina carried to her husband, the copper and that money.

So then the copper belonged to Dave.

Mungo didn't want it to go and stay with Dave—he bought it back from him, so that Dave would have the money to throw a big potlatch. That was the last one that was at Gilford, that last winter before Dave died. That is how the copper came back to Mungo.

On the death of his son, the grieving Chief determined at first to comfort himself and erase the memory of the old insult by breaking the copper for Omhid. From this he was soon dissuaded, and decided to use the copper as David's 'coffin'.

For a while, Mungo wanted to cut off the T and give it to Omhid. It was just to erase the memory of the name he gave Dave when he said he was an empty stomach Hamatsa, and he wanted to get that off his mind. But the family said no, because they didn't want to shame the copper.

The copper was never brought out in public again, but Mungo told different tribes that it was Dave's coffin. In the old days, he would most likely have used it as a tombstone—as you have seen in some of the old graveyards. In the olden days they placed them over the graves. It is said to be the coffin. Because it is valuable, not only for the price that was paid for it, but for the name and all the things the copper has come through and covered for the family, and it comes to an awful lot of money. That if why he used that copper as Dave's coffin.

Earlier in the interview Mungo said that he had always tried his best to use his copper as he had been taught it should be used.

He said that he had tried to bring it out in any kind of circumstances the way it was supposed to be brought out, right up to now. And it stopped because he lost his son. It was as far as the copper can go.

Reprinted from the Report of the Provincial Museum of Natural History and Anthropology, 1960.

I was surprised when I read of Mungo threatening to break his copper 'for' UMX'ID. I always heard they were firm friends. I asked an old man who had known them both and he laughed and said, 'The old chiefs always used to shout and argue with each other at potlatches. They even used to rehearse it—first one way—then the other—to get the most out of the insults.'

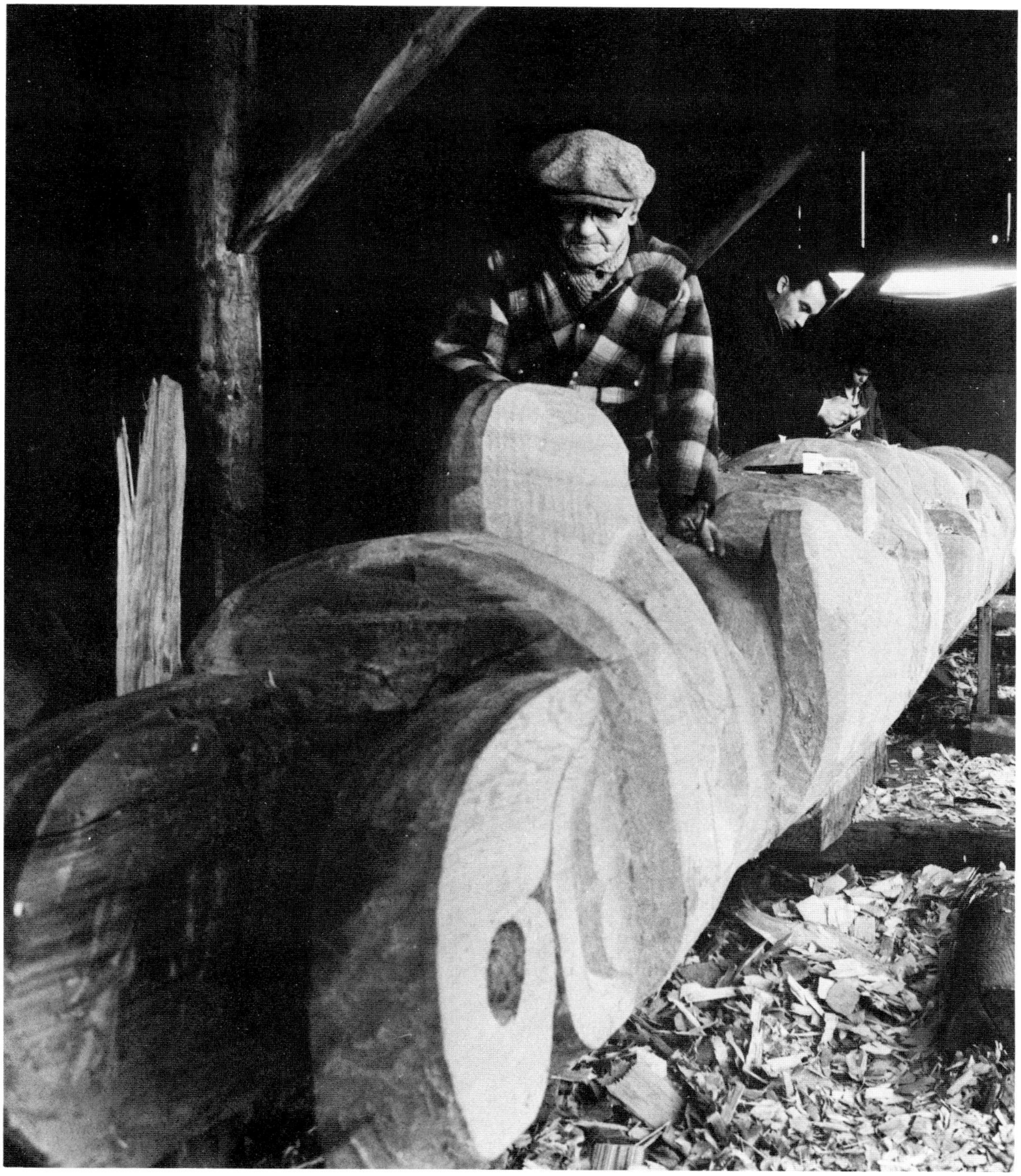

I told him of the circumstances of Mungo's copper and he thought for a while, then said—seriously, 'I don't know—but when you really like someone and he's a good friend, then you might say something insulting that you know isn't true—so's the other guy can prove you wrong. And that last time, DATSA would be making Dave's memory bigger by defending him with a copper—I don't know, but DATSA didn't go through with it. It's pretty hard to figure out when it's for real and when it's not.'

In the summer of 1962, Mungo went into the Royal Jubilee Hospital, in Victoria, with a heart ailment.

The tourists looked for Mungo at the carving shed in Thunderbird Park and for the first time in many summers, he wasn't there.

On August 16th, 1962, at seven o'clock in the morning, Mungo passed peacefully away in his sleep and went home.

Plate 188: **Mungo Martin kept working until shortly before his death. He is shown here in the carving shed at Thunderbird Park. This is the shed where he did some of his finest work. Almost symbolically, behind Mungo is Henry Hunt, and behind him, Tony Hunt. (Thunderbird Park, Victoria, no date given. Photo: Jim Ryan.)**

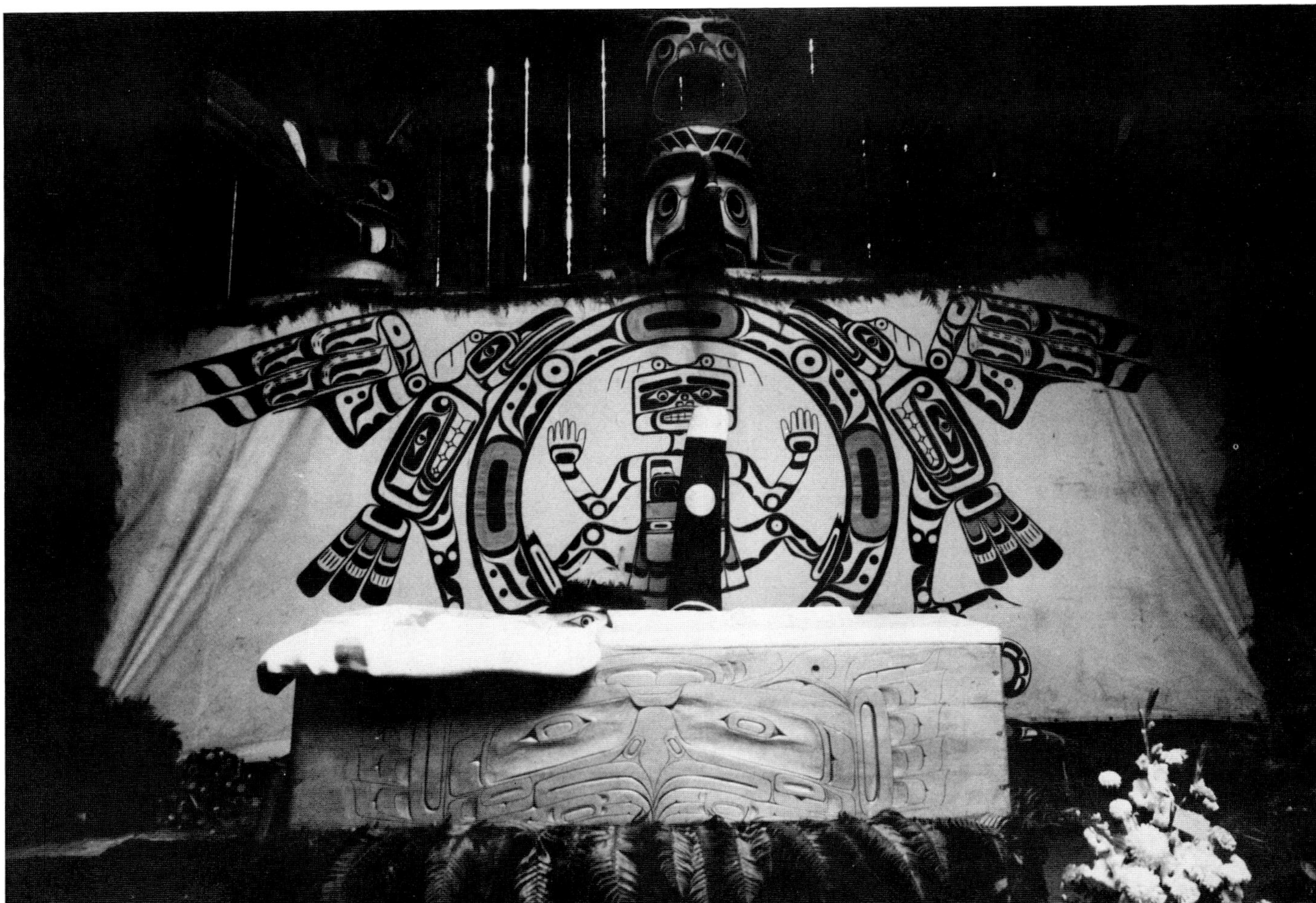

Plate: 189

Services were held on the morning of August 20th at the Anglican Church near the Esquimalt Naval Base. The ceremony was somewhat different than usual in that the Minister Reverend J.A. Roberts said two of the prayers in Kwak̓wala. Mungo's body was taken to the house of NAKA'PANKAM, in Thunderbird Park, where it lay in state from 10:00 to 4:00 p.m.

Mungo lay in a yellow cedar coffin, carved the previous day by Henry Hunt, his son Tony, Ellen Neel, and others who had worked with Mungo. The coffin was carved on the sides and ends with emblems of the Thunderbird and Grizzly Bear, and had on top a wooden replica of a copper. Mungo was dressed in a plain grey suit and lay atop a Hudson's Bay blanket. Near the coffin were arranged carvings that Mungo had owned, masks and headdresses, and around the end of the coffin were the flowers sent by friends and admirers.

WA'WADITLA—the house of NAKA'PANKAM—of Mungo Martin, was specially decorated. The benches covered in sword ferns and rag rugs; the doorway heavily hung with sword ferns, to indicate that in this house, the body of a great man lay.

Anthropologist, Frederica de Laguna of Bryn Mawr College and representative of the American Anthropological Association was present and later wrote:

'After the doors of the house were closed at 4:00 p.m. there was a brief prayer by Chief Jim King, who acted as Master of Ceremonies. The family said a last goodbye to the deceased, the coffin was closed and carried out to be taken to the HMC Dockyard at

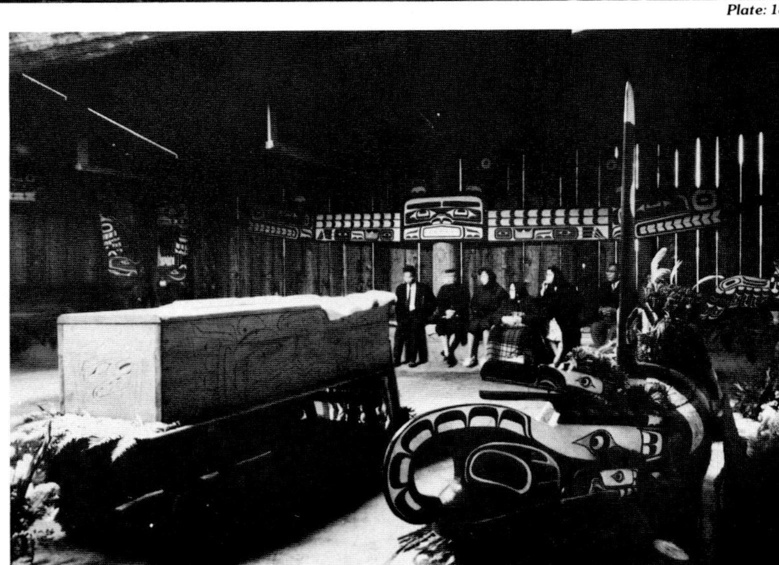

Plate: 190

Esquimalt. Here, at 6:00 p.m., with Navy Pallbearers and a guard of honour, the body was piped aboard the HMCS Ottawa, where the coffin was placed on the after deck, covered by flowers and guarded by four sentries with fixed bayonets. As the destroyer escort sailed out of Esquimalt Harbour, every flag in port dropped to half-mast. This is the first time the Canadian Navy has paid such an honour to an Indian.

Meanwhile, in the Kwakiutl house, a mourning song was played on a tape recorder (this was Mungo's voice playing on Bill Holm's tape recorder... someone

***Plate 189*: Mungo Martin, Chief 'Nakapan'kam', lies in state in the house 'Wawaditla.' The sword ferns under the coffin and hanging elsewhere in the house indicate that in this place, a great man lies. (Victoria, August, 1962. Photo: Jim Ryan.)**

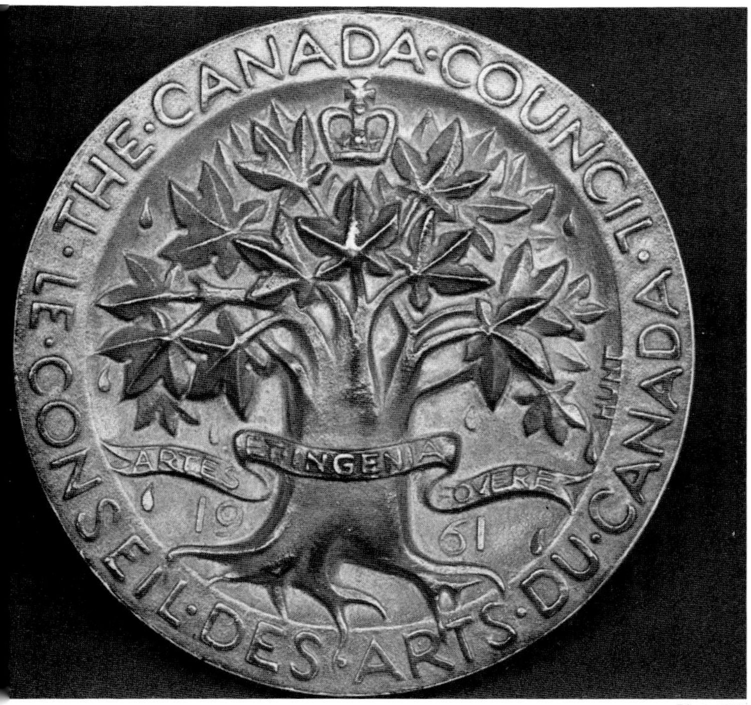

Plate: 191

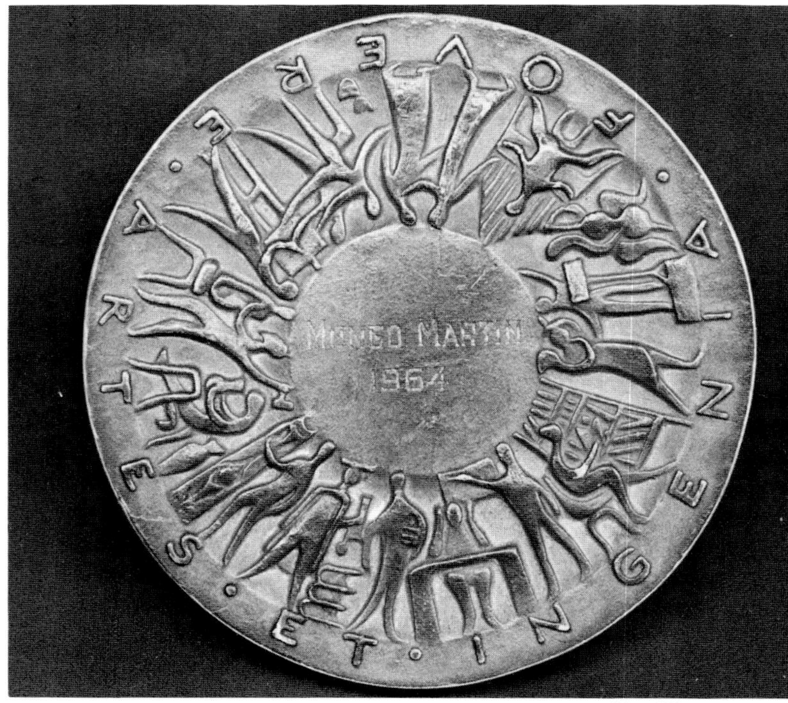

Plate: 192

Plate 191: **Face of the Canada Council medal presented, posthumously, to Mungo Martin. (Victoria, 1964. Photo: B.C.P.M. PN-13798 F.)**

Plate 192: **Back of Canada Council medal. (Victoria, 1964. Photo: B.C.P.M. PN-13798 B.)**

Plate 193: **Mungo Martin's wife A̱bayu̱'a, works on a Chilkat style blanket. Photo taken while Mungo worked at the University of British Columbia, on the totem pole restoration programme, in the early 1950s. (Vancouver, exact date unkown. Photo: B.C.P.M. PN-13167.)**

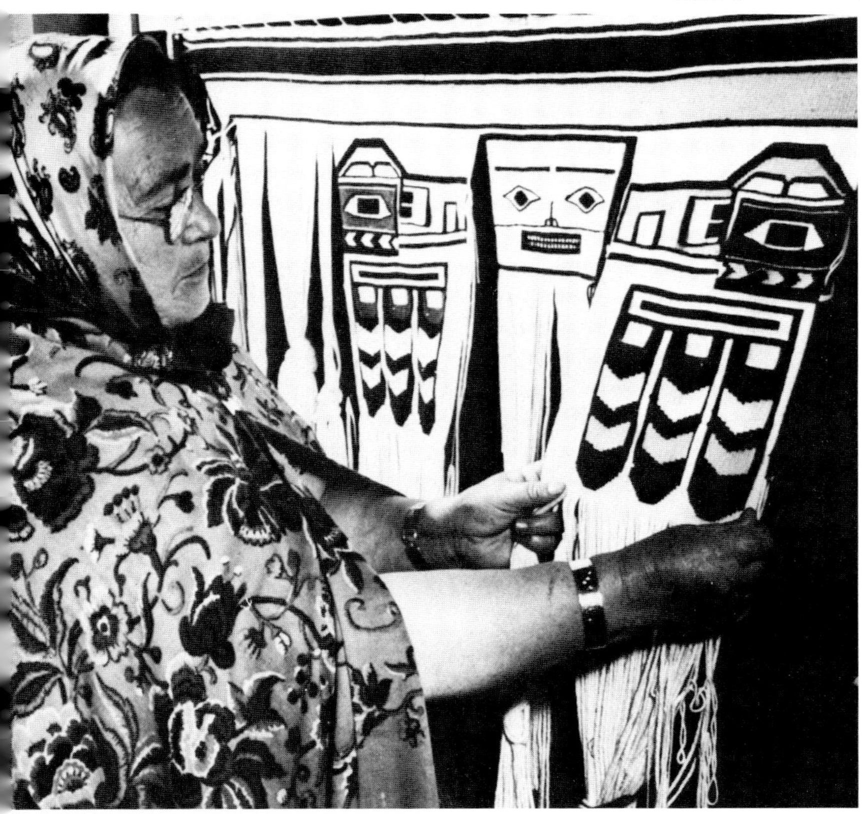

Plate: 193

Plate 190: **The 'Crooked Beak' mask—in previous illustrations shown during its creation—stares out with sightless eyes at Mungo Martin's coffin. (Thunderbird Park, Victoria, 1962. Photo: Jim Ryan.)**

asked Bill, at the last moment, if he had his recorder and tapes... and he ran out to his car and got them. P.N.), Chief Martin's handsome granddaughters sat in button blankets at the back of the house. Then Chief King sprinkled bird down around the house, explaining that the mourning was over, and all must be happy again. No one should feel any more sorrow, for Mungo Martin had lived a good and full life and had died without debts or anything to regret—honoured by all.'

Frederica de Laguna was asked to give the farewell speech and prayer:

'Perhaps no Canadian Indian did more than Chief Martin to secure recognition and honour for the culture of his people—and so helped to win for the Indian, equal rights under Canadian laws.'

A̱bayu̱'a, Mungo's widow, later made Mungo's wishes known. She said that he originally wanted to be buried at Fort Rupert, where he was born, but had changed his mind. Mungo felt it would be easier for his friends and relatives to visit his grave at Alert Bay, B.C. His last wish was a plea to the Provincial Government that his proteges—Henry Hunt and his son Tony Hunt—be allowed to continue his carving work at Thunderbird Park.

A̱bayu̱'a—Sara Constance—followed her husband barely a year later and she was buried next to Mungo at Alert Bay.

But Mungo's story was not quite finished.

In late 1963, Mungo was posthumously awarded the *Canada Council Medal*. This honour is reserved for those persons in Canada who demonstrate outstanding accomplishments in the arts, humanities, or social sciences. Mungo Martin was the first Indian to be accorded this honour and the second Canadian to receive it posthumously.

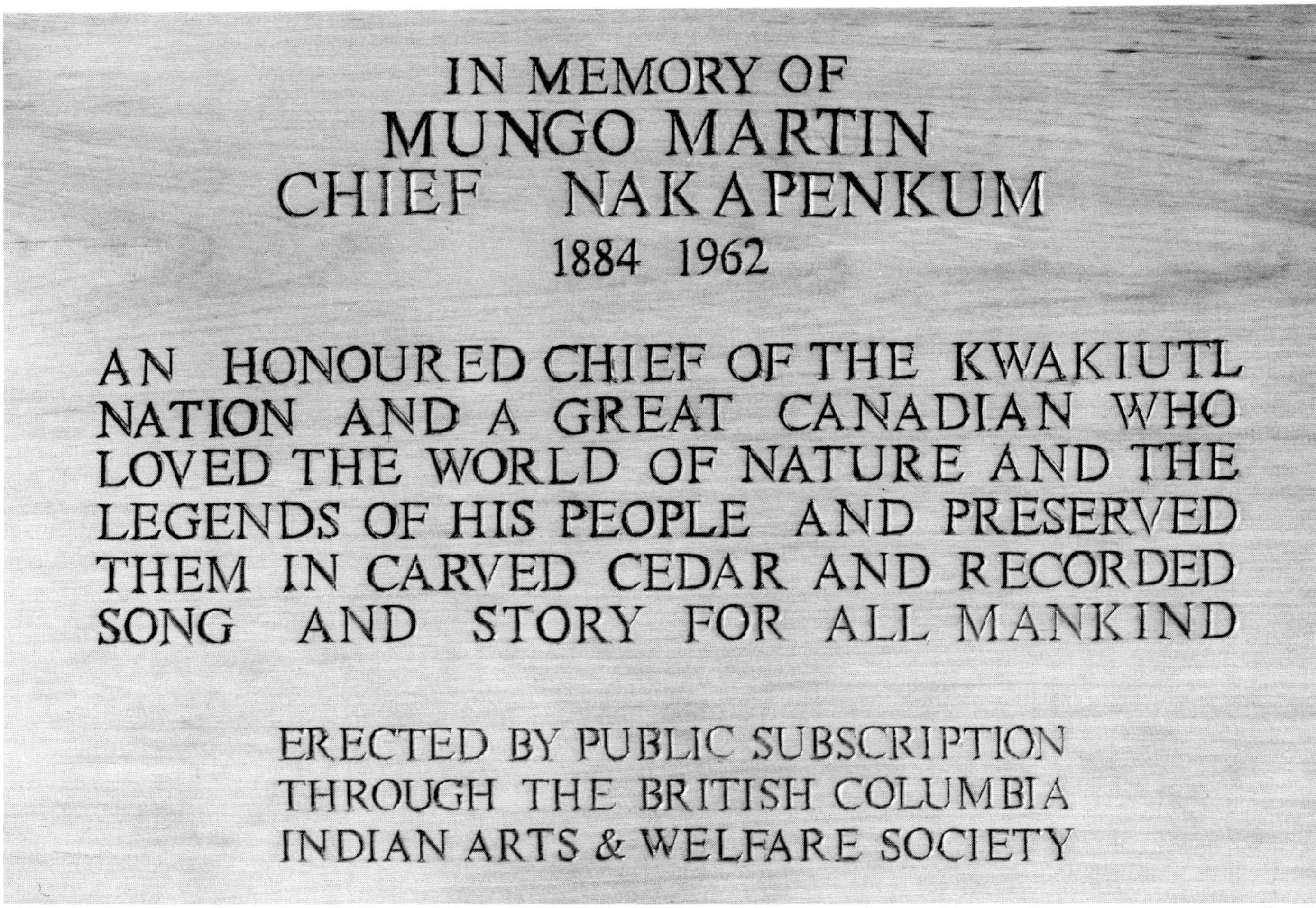

Plate: 194

Plate 194: **Inscription for a memorial plaque in B.C. Provincial Museum. Carved by Peter Macnair. (Victoria. Photo: B.C.P.M. PN-15151.)**

Plate 195: **John Livingston. Trained in the Mungo Martin/Hunt style of Kwakiutl art, Livingston is considered one of the best non-Indian artists to be working in the North-west style today. (Victoria, 1978. Photo: John McKillop. Courtesy: Arts of the Raven Gallery.)**

In making the award for 1963, the Council cited his 'contribution to Canada's artistic, cultural and intellectual life', and made note of his work in 'recordings of songs, ceremonies and other Kwakiutl culture'.

Later, plans were made to install an elaborate plaque in Thunderbird Park, in Mungo's memory, but it never came to pass. Mungo's house and his poles stand there today. Those poles in the Park are not alone, for Mungo's poles stand in England, in Ottawa, in Blaine (Washington), in Vancouver, in Argentina and in Mexico City. Yet in 1963, Mungo's story was not over. There was one more totem pole to come.

In April 1970, nearly eight years after Mungo's death, the Provincial Government authorized the carving of a memorial totem pole in his honour.

The 32-foot pole was to be carved and painted by Mungo's proteges Henry Hunt and his son Tony, and they would be assisted by John Livingston.

The work was carried out in the carving shed at Thunderbird Park, the same shed in which Mungo had spent so many hours. Watching this pole emerge from the cedar log was, in many ways, like hearing the tape recording of Mungo's voice singing a mourning song as his body lay in state. Through the skills that Mungo imbued in these artists' hands, he might well have been carving his own memorial pole. By August 1970, the pole was nearly complete and Peter Macnair, the Provincial Museum's enthnologist, reported that the carvers were well pleased with their work.

The pole was shipped to Alert Bay and on the Friday morning of September 18, 1970, the pole was raised in

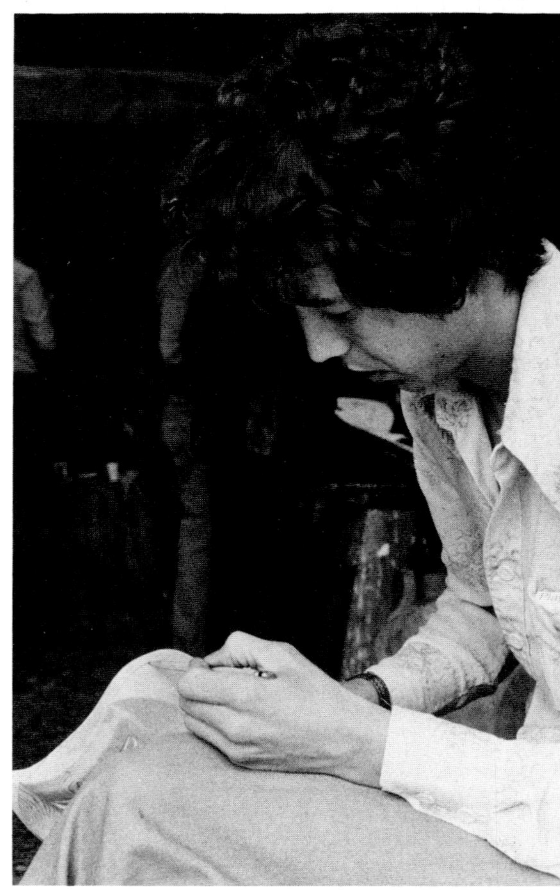

Plate: 195

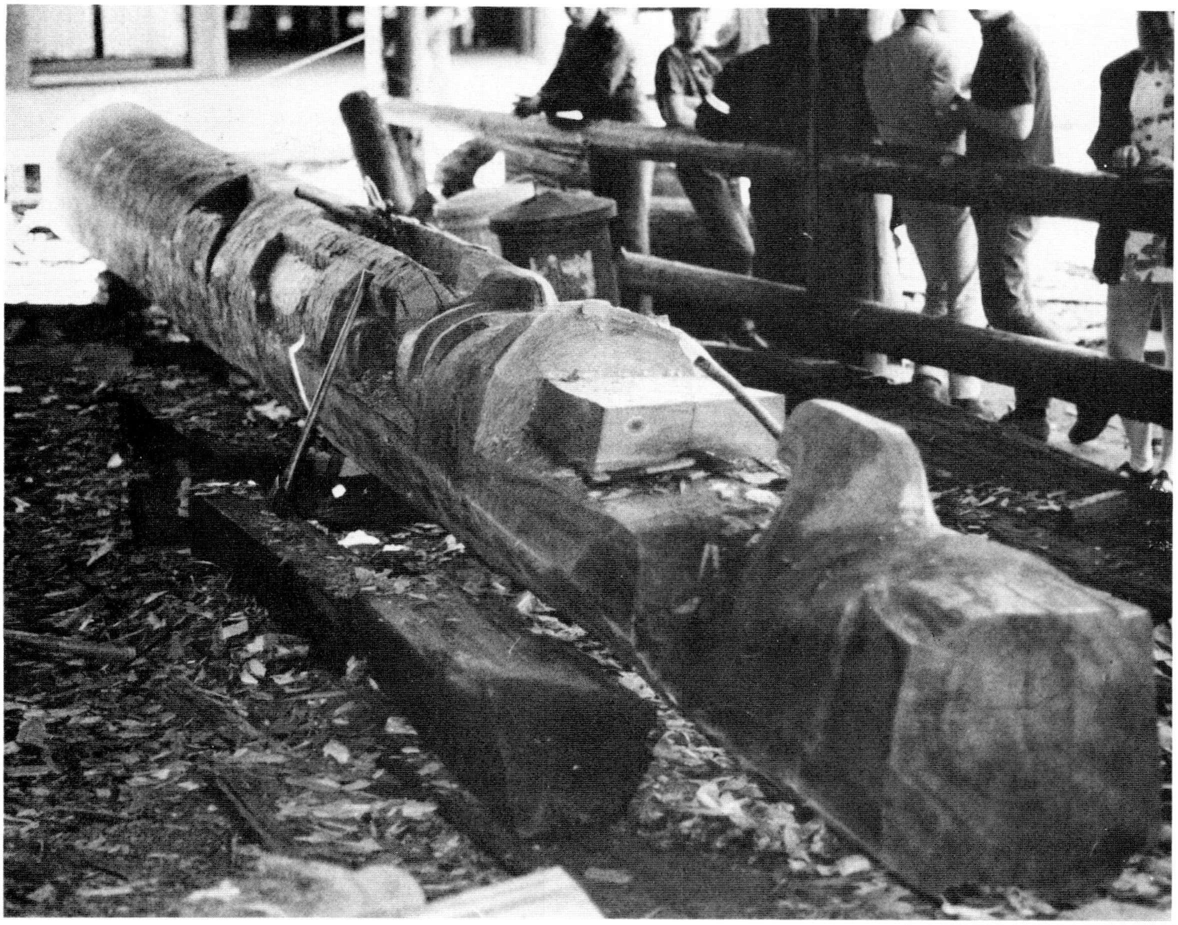

Plate 196: Starting the Mungo Martin memorial totem. This rather blurred shot shows the rough blocking-out of two figures: the Thunderbird and 'Cedar Man' (shown as a 'Chief-with-talking stick). In the lower right of the photo, the Thunderbird's beak is evident. The square block below the curved beak will be the Thunderbird's 'knees' and legs. The next protrusions are the eyes and nose of the Chief—below that and to the left, the Chief's hand holds the talking stick... yet to be released from the log. (Thunderbird Park, Victoria, 1970. Photo: B.C.P.M. PN-7750-3A.)

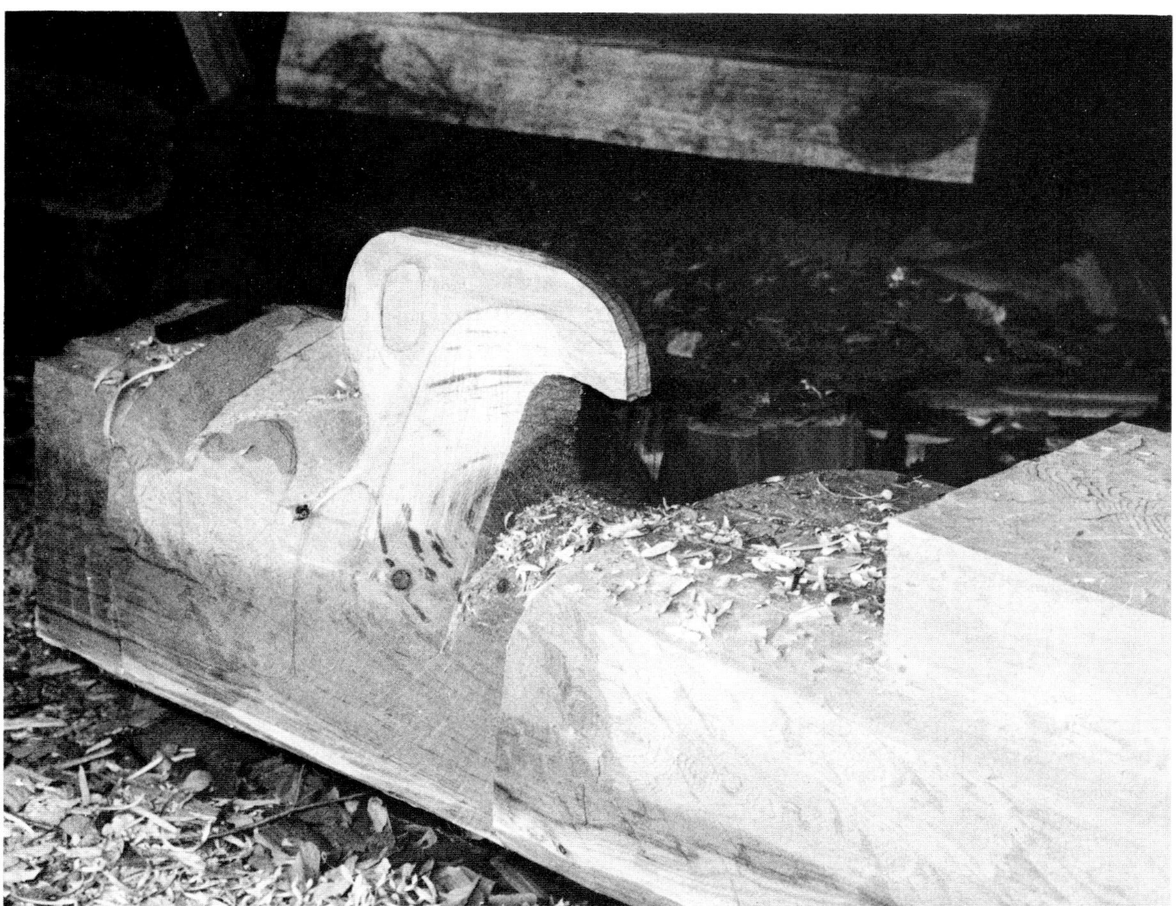

Plate 197: Mungo Martin's Memorial Pole. A more detailed look at the Thunderbird from the other side. Note the black crayon marks outlining the lines of the eyes, mouth, cheek, naries (nostril), etc. (Thunderbird Park, Victoria, 1970. Photo: B.C.P.M. PN-7750-6A.)

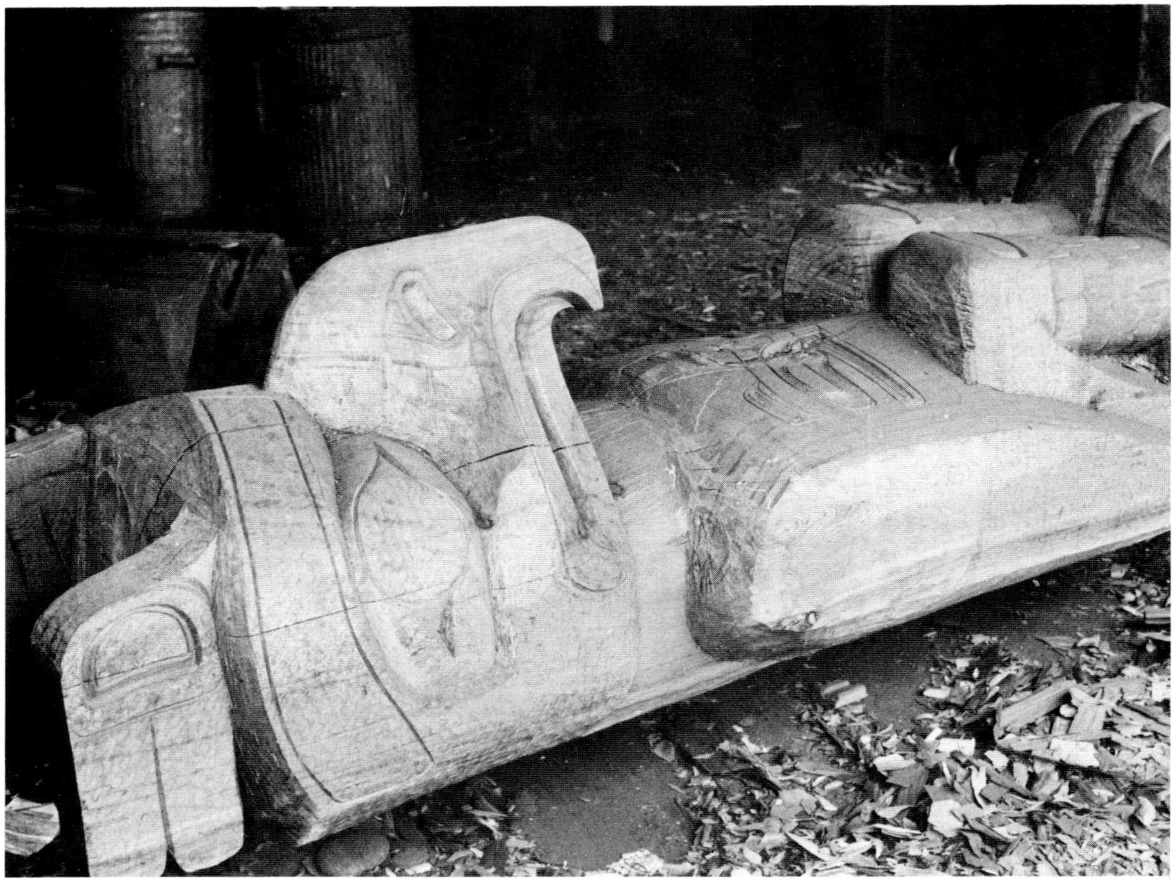

Plate 198: Mungo Martin Memorial Pole. The carving of the Thunderbird almost complete. The square block on the chest of the Thunderbird in the previous picture has become its legs. (Thunderbird Park, Victoria, 1970. Photo: B.C.P.M. PN-7753-3.)

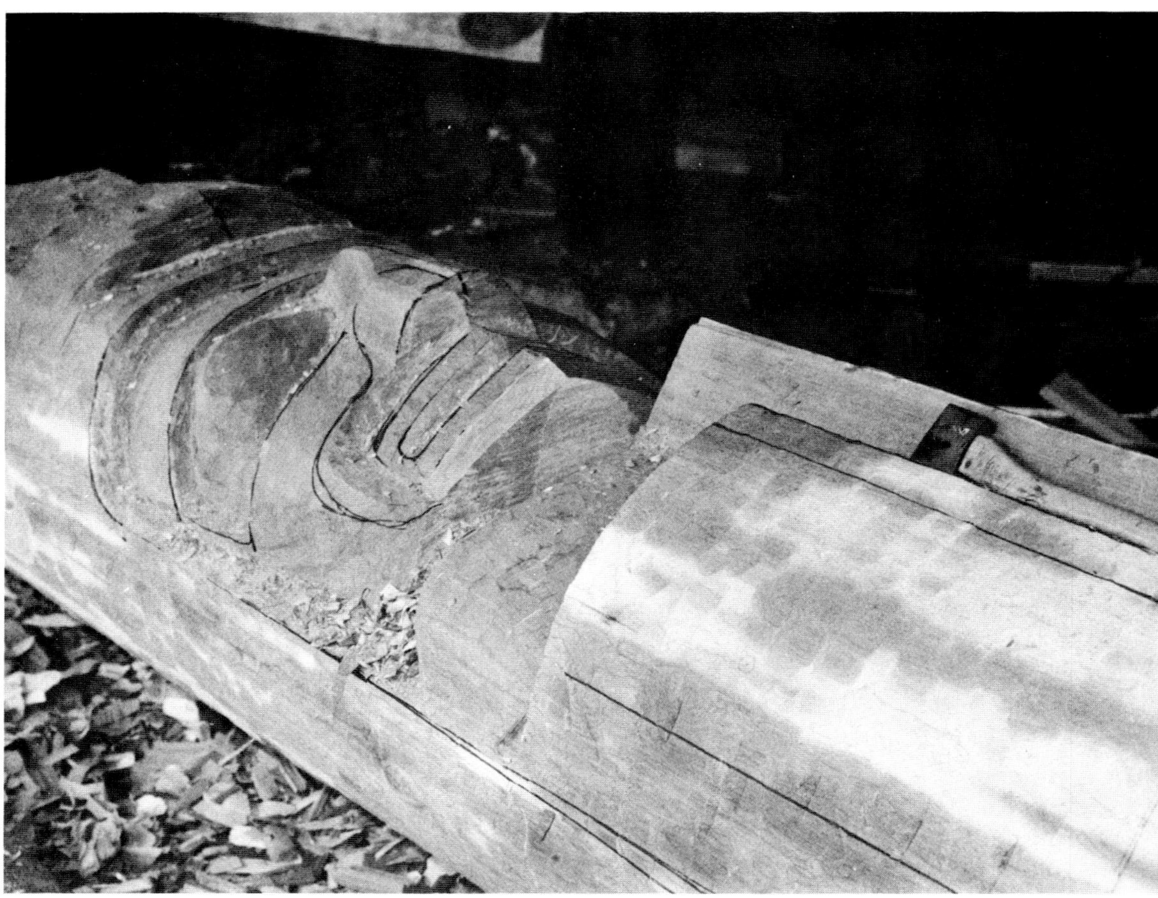

Plate 199: Mungo Martin Memorial Pole. The 'Chief-with-talking stick' is blocked out. The face is evident. The section in the upper right, with the hatchet lying against it, will become the talking stick and the Chief's hand. The mass in the lower right will become a 'copper.' (Thunderbird Park, Victoria, 1970. Photo: B.C.P.M. PN-7750-7A.)

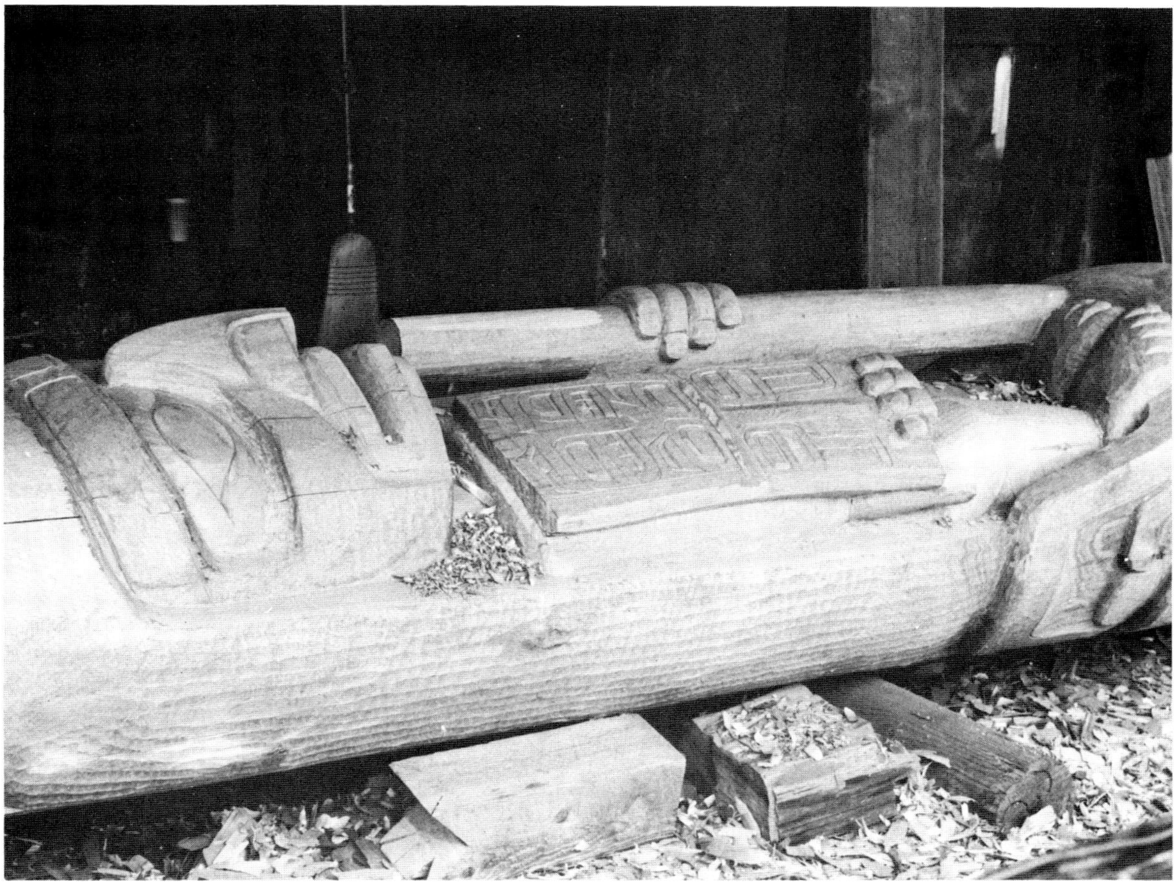

Plate 200: Mungo Martin Memorial Pole. The 'Cedar-Man' or Chief is nearly finished. The head details and the 'copper' have been carved. The talking stick is free-standing from the log, but has yet to have the miniature totem details carved. (Thunderbird Park, Victoria, 1970. Photo: B.C.P.M. PN-7753-4.)

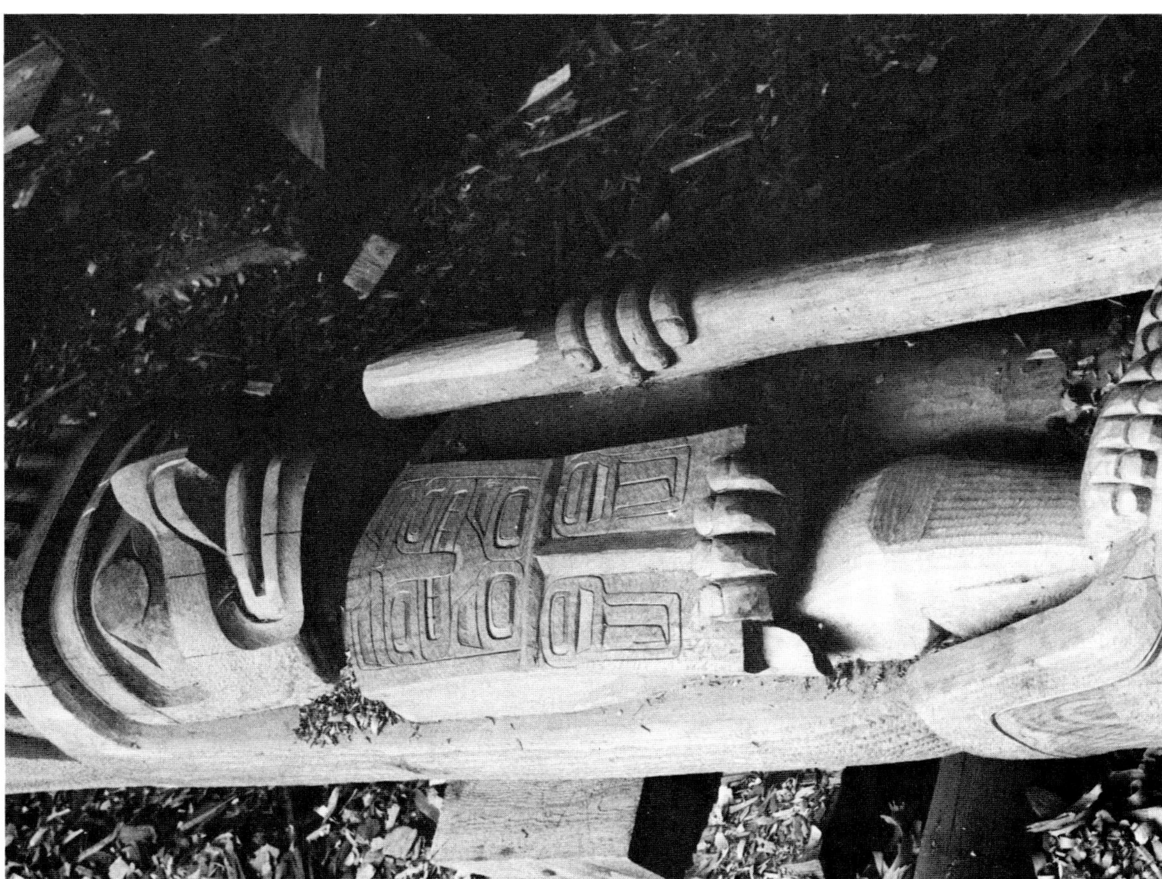

Plate 201: Mungo Martin Memorial Pole. A more detailed photo of the 'Chief-with-talking stick,' showing the crest on the copper. The crest is of the killer whale, the 'copper' probably represents 'Ma'haynootsi', 'Big Killer Whale,'— Mungo's 'copper' acquired by the B.C. Provincial Museum in 1960. A fine piece of carving. (Thunderbird Park, Victoria, 1970. Photo: B.C.P.M. PN-7753-7.)

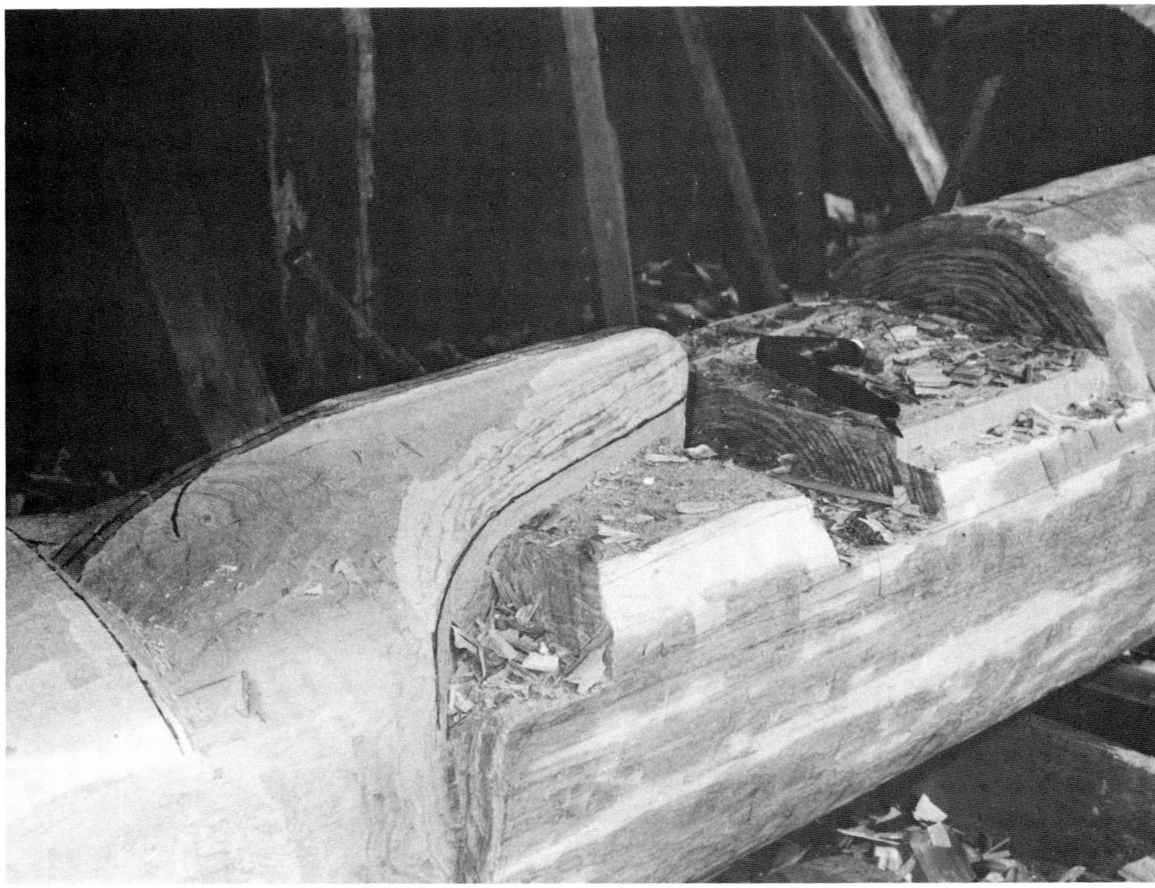

Plate 202: Mungo Martin Memorial Pole. The beak of the raven is roughed out. Because of the length of the beak, the raven is often shown in this position; head down with the long beak tucked into its chest. To extend the beak would require a separate piece, mortised on. The block under the beak will become another copper, while the block to the right will be the raven's knees and legs. (Thunderbird Park, Victoria, 1970. Photo: B.C.P.M. PN-7750-8A.)

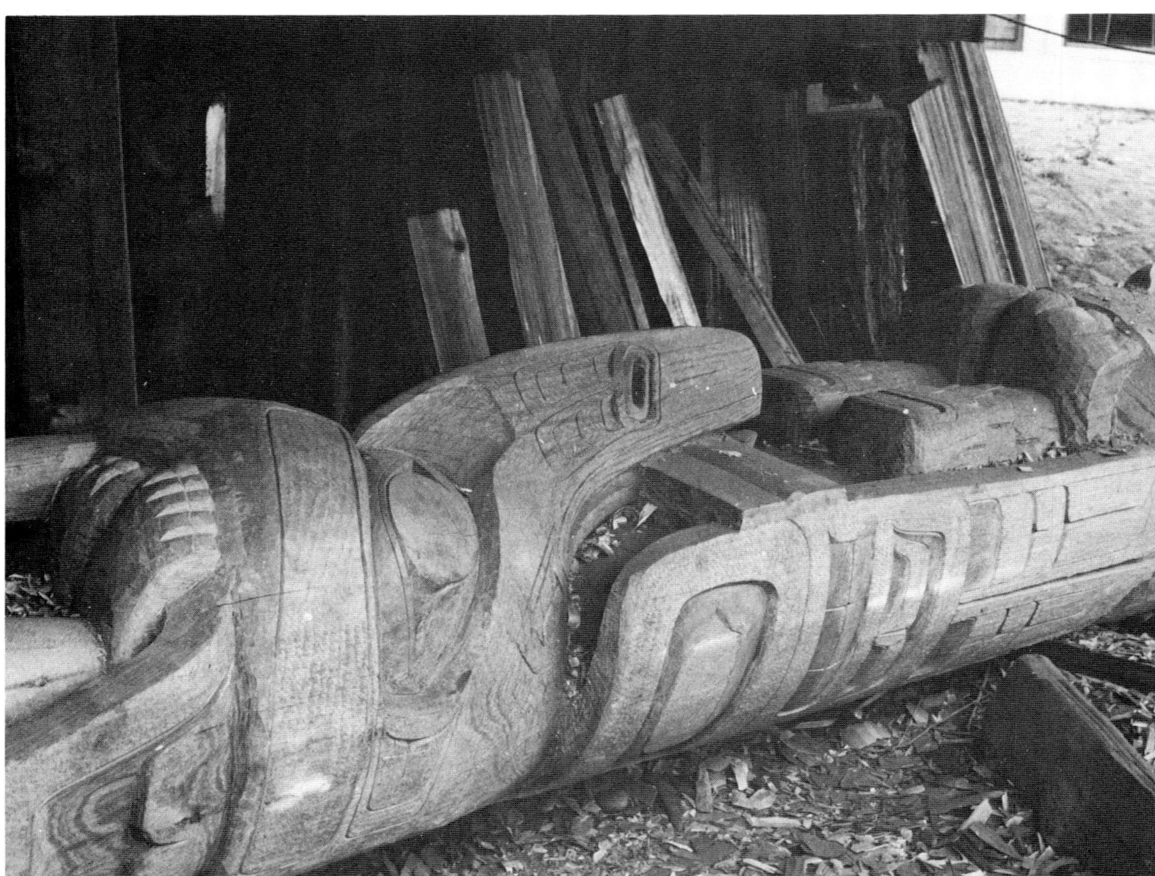

Plate 203: Mungo Martin Memorial Pole. The raven finished. Note how the 'ears' of the raven provide a natural place for the 'Cedar Man's' feet and the base of his talking stick. (Thunderbird Park, Victoria, 1970. Photo: B.C.P.M. PN-7753-5.)

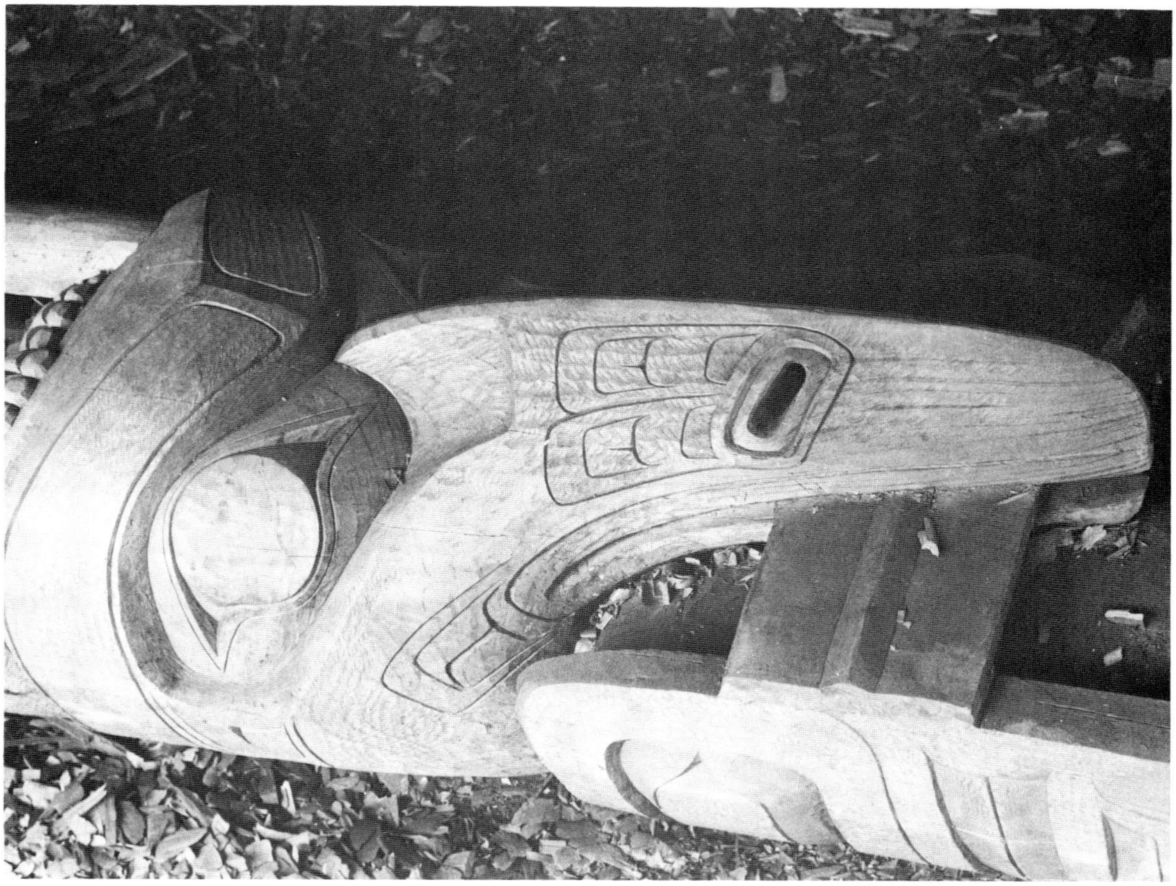

Plate 204: Mungo Martin Memorial Pole. A close-up photo of the detail on the raven with a 'copper' in his beak. Again, a fine piece of carving in design, proportion, and finish. (Thunderbird Park, Victoria, 1970. Photo: B.C.P.M. PN-7753-8.)

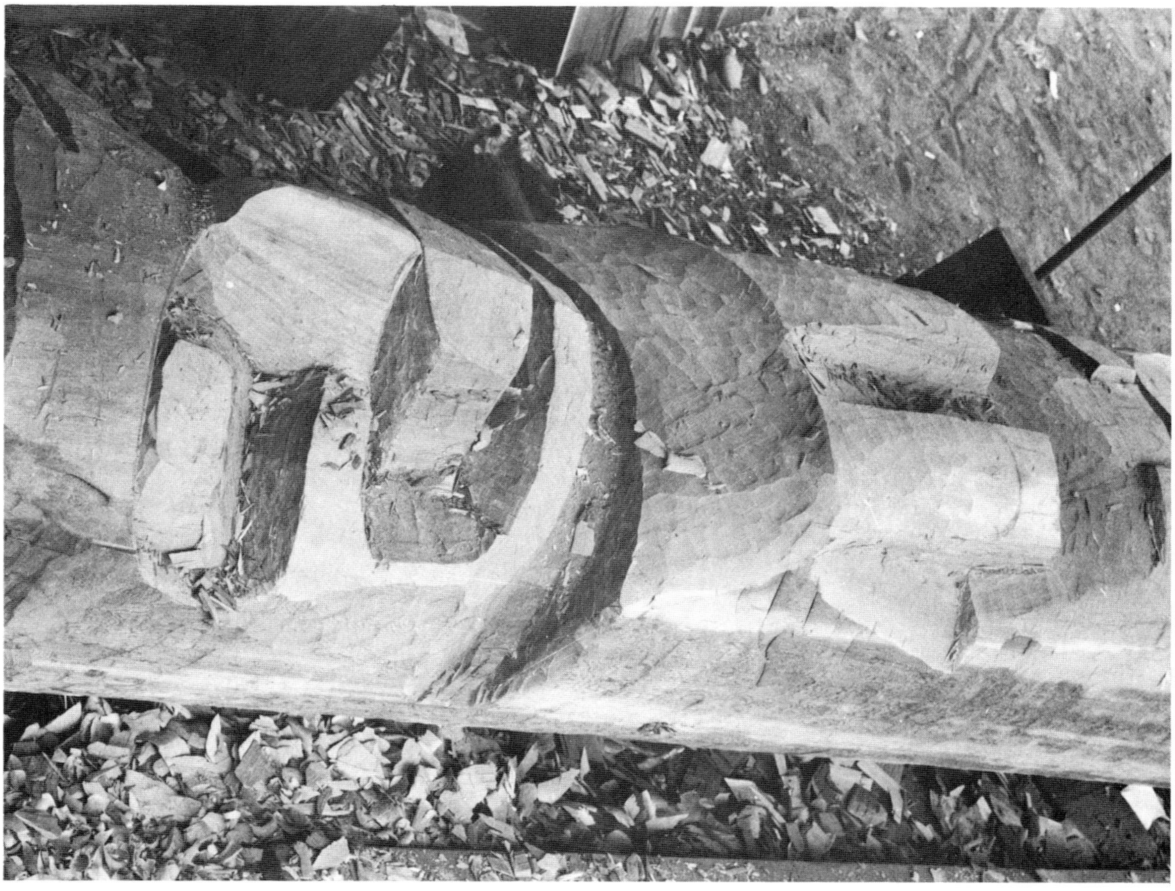

Plate 205: Mungo Martin Memorial Pole. This photo shows the very rough blocking-out of the 'Dzunuƙwa,' or 'Wild-woman-of-the-woods,' the bottom figure of the pole. Although it may be difficult to see, at this point in the carving, the blocking in the upper half of the photo will be the 'Dzunuƙwa's' head. The brow, nose, and start of the protruding mouth and the prominent cheekbones are shown. In the lower half of the photo, the two rectangular masses with the channel between them, will become the pendulous breasts of the wild woman. (Thunderbird Park, Victoria, 1970. Photo: B.C.P.M. PN-7753-6.)

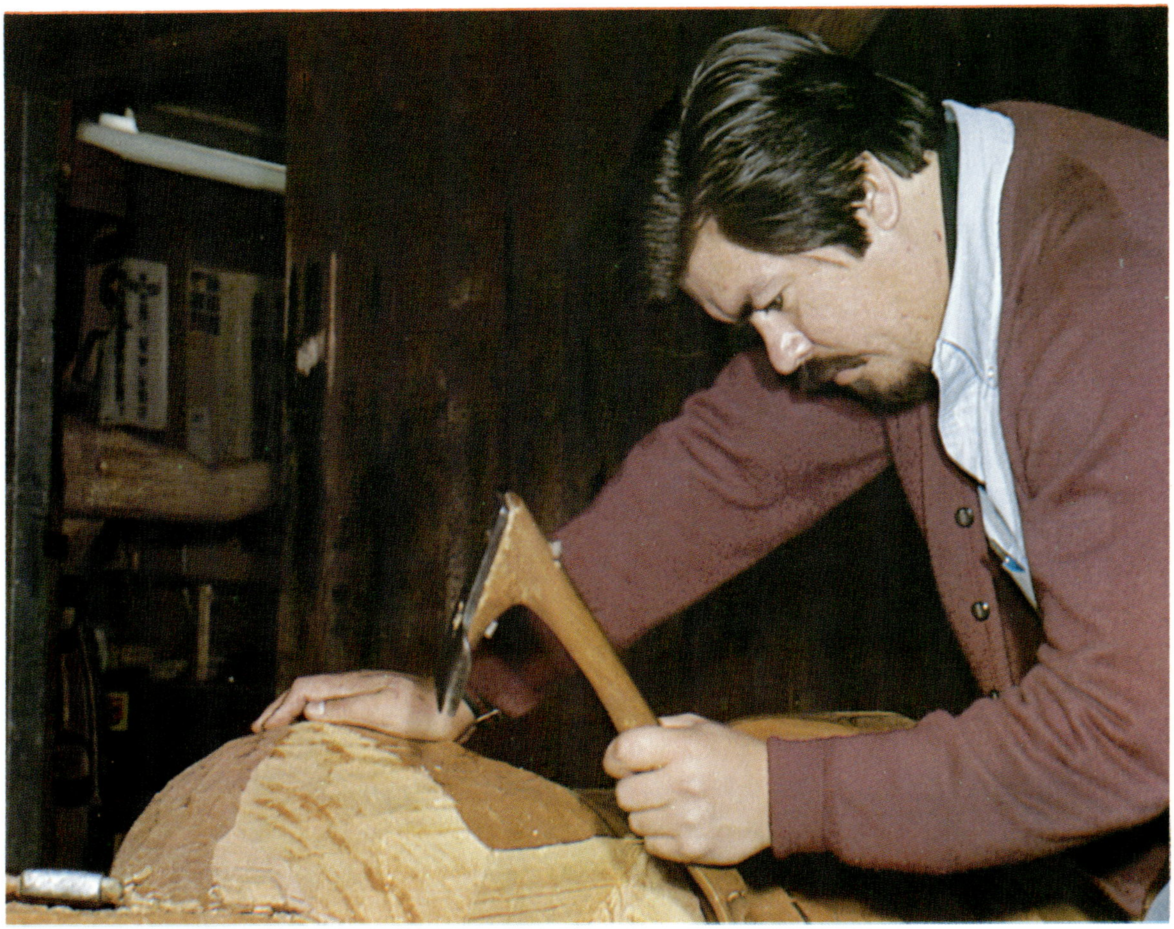

Plate 206: Tony Hunt uses an elbow adze during the roughing-out of Mungo Martin's Memorial Pole. Although it is difficult to tell, at this stage, Tony is working on a block that will probably become the claws of the Thunderbird. The open doorway in the background leads to a small room separate from the rest of the open carving shed. Here the tools are locked away at night; drawers hold personal correspondence to the carvers, notices from the museum, and 'private' projects, commissions obtained outside the aegis of the Provincial Museum. (Thunderbird Park, Victoria, 1970. Photo: Tourism, B.C.)

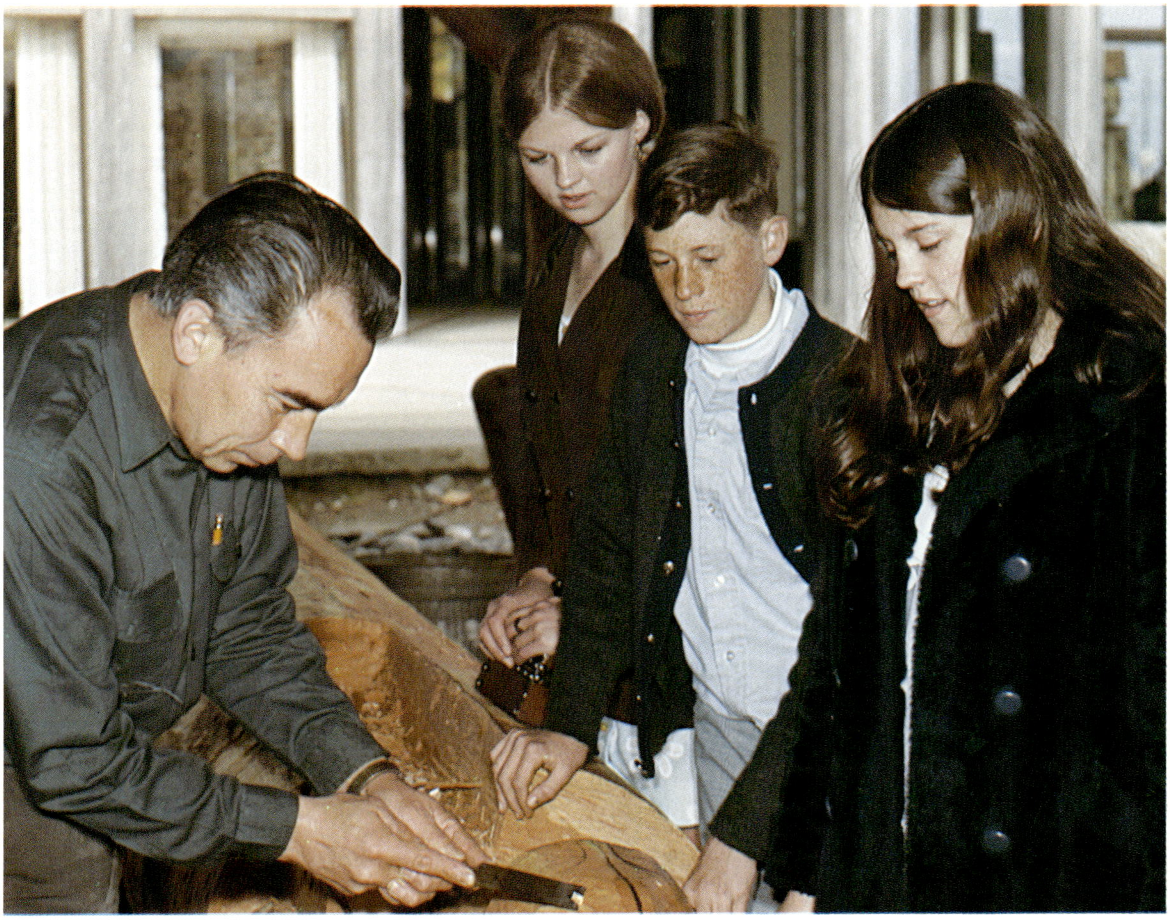

Plate 207: Henry Hunt works on the 'Chief-with-a-talking stick' figure of Mungo Martin's Memorial Pole. A group of interested young spectators watch attentively. (Thunderbird Park, Victoria, 1970. Photo: Tourism, B.C.)

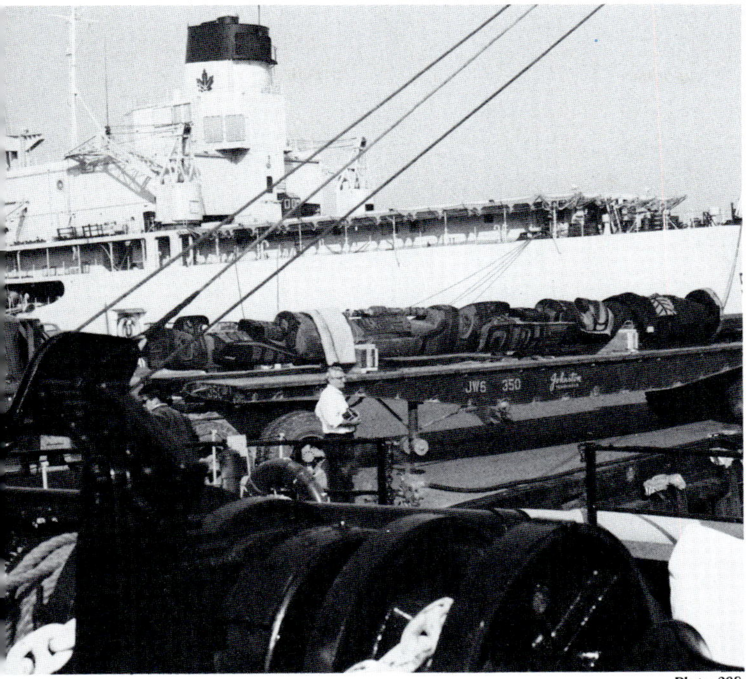

Plate: 208

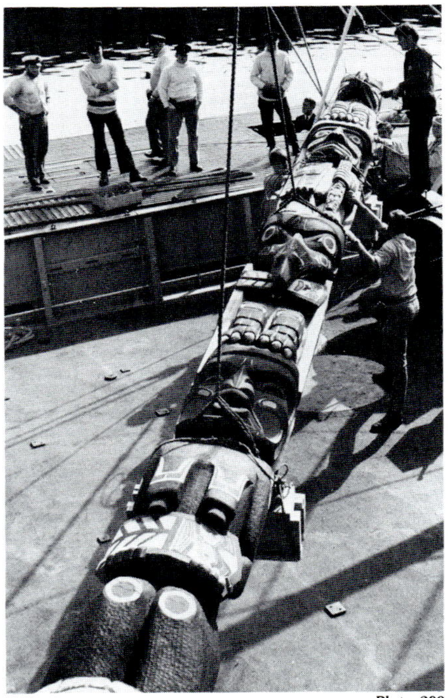

Plate: 209

Plate 208: Mungo's Memorial Pole just prior to being loaded aboard the vessel that will take it to Alert Bay. (Victoria, 1970. Photo: Tourism, B.C.)

Plate 209: Mungo's Memorial Pole is carefully slung aboard the government vessel as members of the armed forces look on. (Victoria, 1970. Photo: William Boucher. Courtesy: Victoria Press.)

Plate 210: A small child points at the Memorial Pole as it lies in a trench prior to being raised . . . or perhaps she's waving goodbye. (Alert Bay, B.C., September, 1970. Photo: Tourism, B.C.)

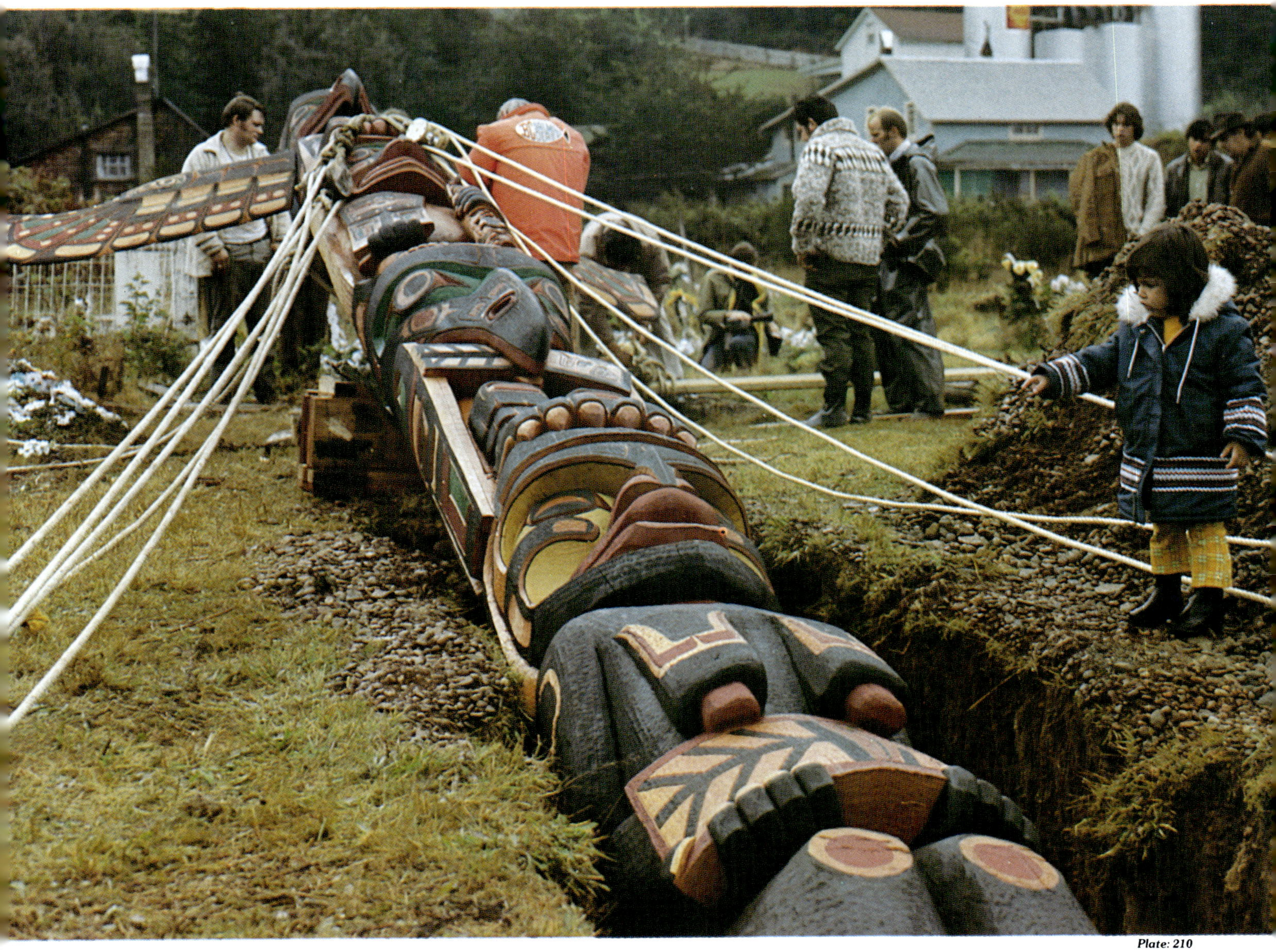

Plate: 210

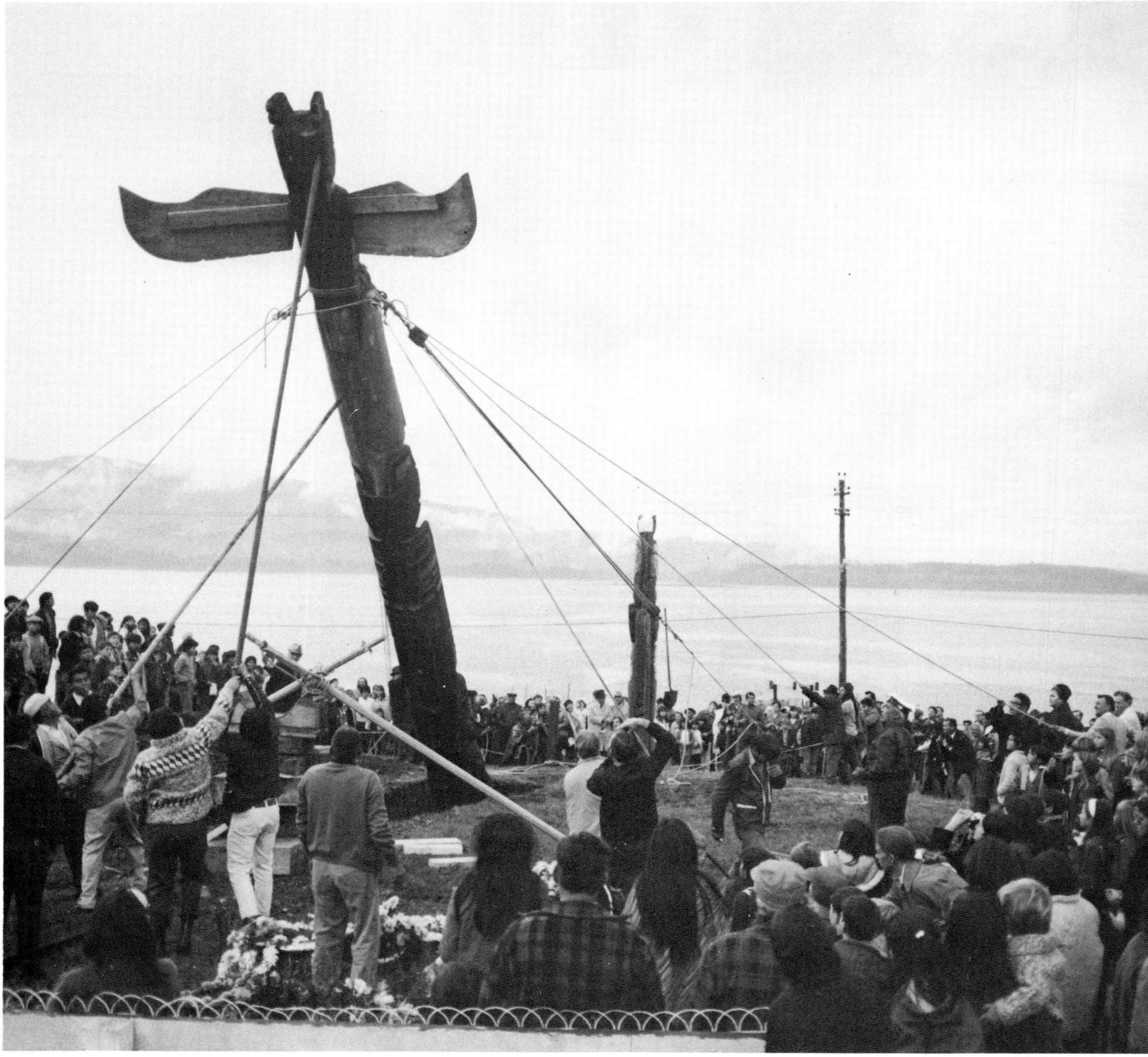

Plate: 211

Plate 211: **With many helpful hands, Mungo's pole starts up. This totem will look out from the shore of Cormorant Island, across the inside passage to the Nimpkish Valley and the Cluxewe River on Vancouver Island. (Alert Bay, B.C., 1970. Photo: Tourism, B.C.)**

Plate 212: **Almost up. The photographers move back and the crowd falls silent. Under their feet, the spirts of many proud Kwakiutl people slumber quietly . . . or perhaps they watch, with interest. (Alert Bay, B.C., 1970. Photo: Vancouver Sun.)**

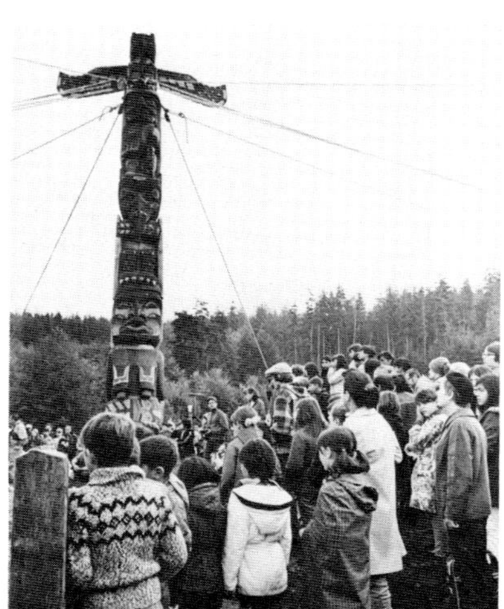

Plate: 212

the Alert Bay cemetery. The first pole to be raised there in nearly forty years.

The pole raising was climaxed by a memorial potlatch that was attended by hundreds of people.

Peter McNelly wrote of the raising:

'Henry Hunt's brothers, sons, and cousins pulled the ropes which raised the totem—50 feet from Mungo and Sara Martin's graves.

'A quiet sense of drama filled the crowd as the pole rose. Photographers jostled for angles in the mud, half-driven to get their shots, half concerned that they might offend.

'Babies, children, young and old men and women watched. Many white people were present.

The technology of microphones, cameras and tape recorders, and the presence of crosses and Christian ephitaphs (in the cemetery), created for me a melancholy mixture of two life-styles.

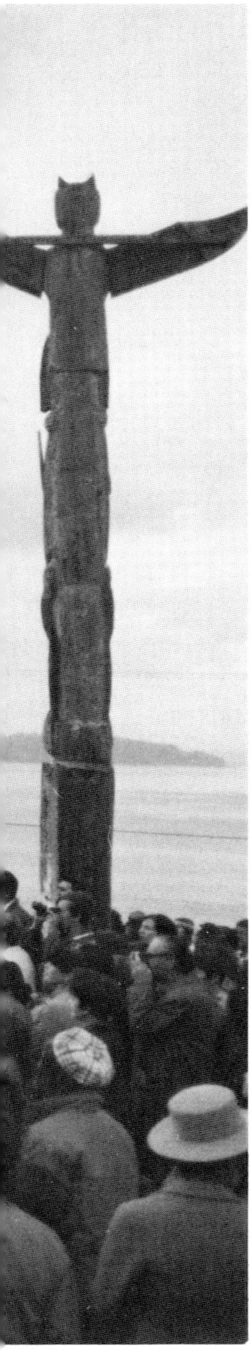

'Chief James Sewid said that the interest in the Potlatch and pole raising proved Mungo's greatness. The obvious impression was that he was pleased to see the culture getting the recognition he knew it deserved.

Between the pole raising and the potlatch came a buffet luncheon and more speeches—all in Kwakiutl—at the Nimpkish band council hall. Just before lunch began, Chief Tommy Hunt of the Kwakiutl Tribe in Fort Rupert, suddenly stood out of the crowd and began speaking agitatedly in Kwakiutl.

'Then, speaking in English, he said, 'Ladies and Gentlemen, you are to go like this when I start . . . he clapped his hands rapidly.

He began to sing a song in praise of Mungo Martin. We clapped rapidly and three Indian women from Neah Bay, Washington, stood up dancing.

Chief Hunt was singing loudly and the three women were flowing in short steps and glowing with large smiles. Suddenly, the song was over and a more formal mood returned.

This kind of spontaneous gaiety was repeated only once or twice more that day. After lunch the gathering adjourned a mile up the road to the Kwakiutl long-house, a massive cedar structure, for mourning songs to Mungo Martin. Tradition requires that the songs be sung before sunset.'

During the raising of the pole that morning, the figures on the pole were described by several of the chiefs, each one describing a figure and its significance to Mungo Martin. The chiefs spoke in Kwak̓wala and their words were interpreted to the crowd by William Scow, a provincial court judge, and a Kwakiutl from a prominent family.

Chief Jimmy Sewid told first of the top figure, the mythical bird, 'K̲ULUS', close kin to the thunderbird. K̲ulus is said to have arrived at Viner Sound and built a great house from whose inhabitants Mungo Martin's family descended.

Chief Jim King of Kingcome Inlet told of the second figure, 'TSEK̲A̲ME', the cedar man—once a large cedar tree, transformed into a man. 'TSEK̲A̲ME' holds a talking stick and clutches a copper, indicative of his position as a chief and his wealth. Mungo's right to this crest came from his father's people at Gilford Island.

Chief Tommy Hunt of Fort Rupert took up the tale as Jim King finished. He went on to describe 'G̲WA'WI-NA', the raven. This crest originated in Tongass, Alaska, and was a crest of Mungo's son, David, transferred from David's wife by marriage into the Martin family.

Finally, Chief Peter Smith described the bottom figure of the pole—the 'DZUNUK̓WA', or wild woman of the woods. This crest Mungo obtained by marriage. The wild woman held in her arms a huge copper, symbolic of Mungo's position as Potlatch Chief—'ten times over'.

Important people, white and Indian, had paid their respects to an important man. When the occasion was over and everyone had gone home, Cormorant Island was as before. Just a little point on the map, a point that indicated both the beginning and the end of many interwoven circles. And now Mungo's pole stands in the sloping graveyard at Alert Bay. Across the street is the stretch of beach where Mungo's stepfather, Charlie James, once carved. The same beach that Ellen Neel played on as a child.

Sparks fly up through the smoke-hole of the potlatch house and disappear in the darkness beyond—but for a brief instant the sparks live and burn brightly.

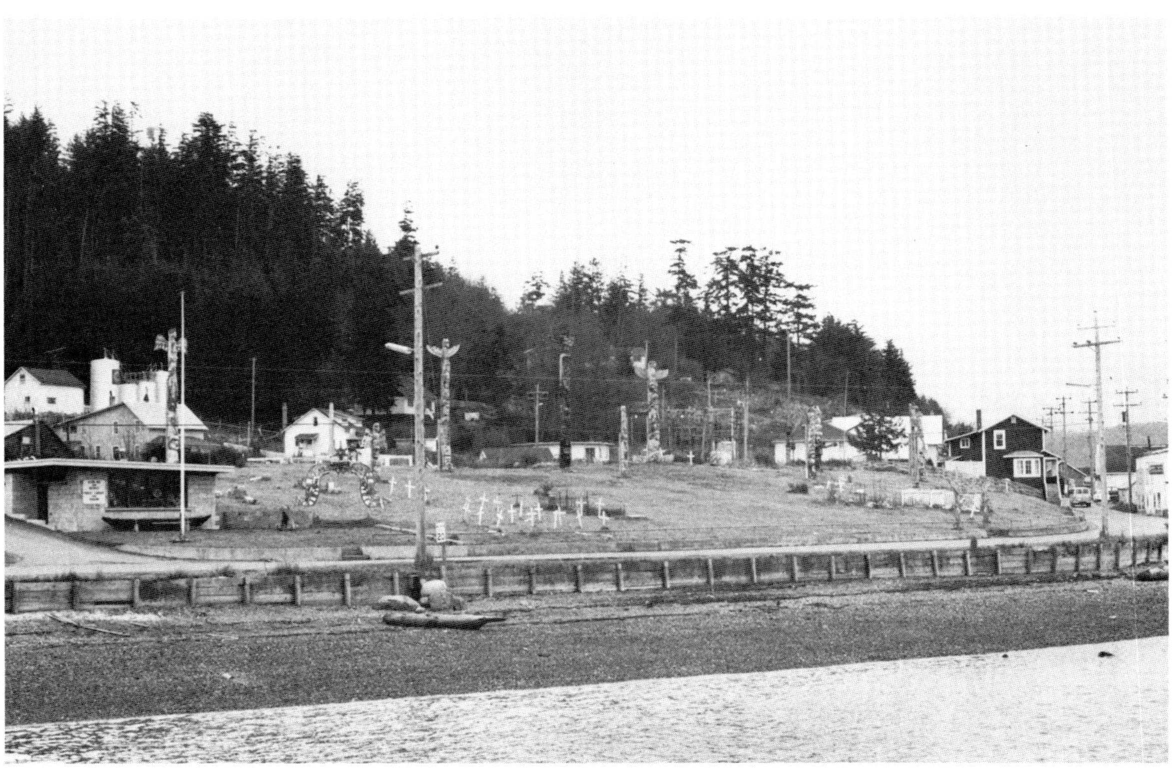

Plate 213: **The cemetery and beach at Alert Bay. (Alert Bay, B.C., 1970. Photo: B.C.P.M. PN-7808-10.)**

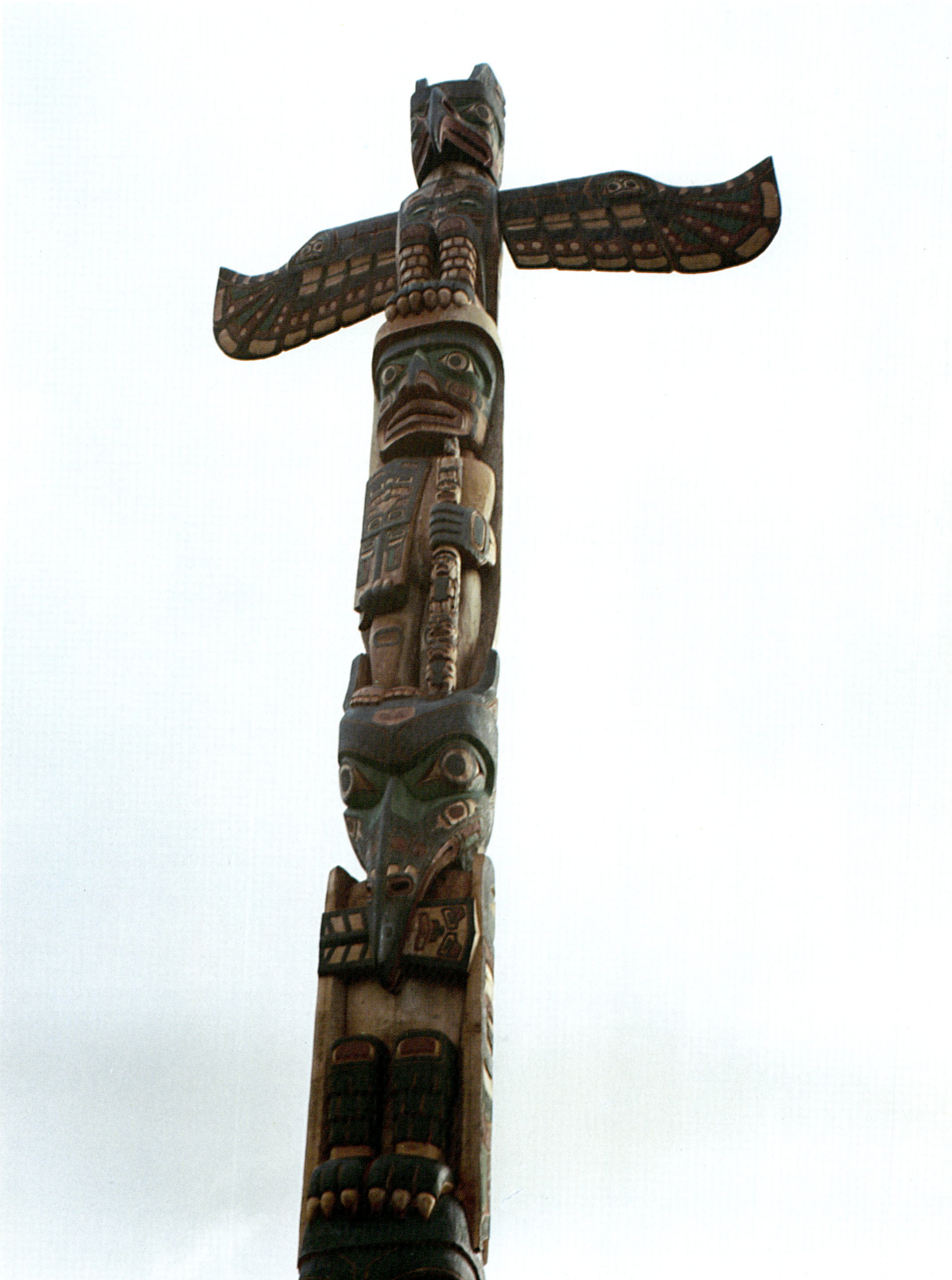

EPILOGUE

Mungo and Dave Neel sat at the dining room table, and I sat off to one side. Ellen was ironing clothes, the legs of the ironing board half into the living room.

Dave had brought out some sheets of artists' sketch paper and Mungo was hunched over one, drawing with a flat carpenter's pencil. He didn't sketch, but drew heavy lines from point 'A' to point 'B', with no preliminary light lines or reference points.

He straightened up and I could see that he'd drawn an ovoid with a second ovoid in the centre of it—an 'eye', or the start of one.

Mungo said 'O.K.'—a statement , not a question—and pointed to Dave's paper. Dave sketched on his paper for a few seconds and then said 'O.K.—now what?' Mungo shook his head, 'No.'

Mungo turned to Ellen and said a few words in Kwak̓wala, and Ellen came and stood behind Mungo's chair, her hand on his shoulder. Mungo pointed again at Dave's sketch and, half-turned, spoke to Ellen. She repeated his words in English.

'See this line?'

She pointed to the bottom of the ovoid. 'The line rises a bit at the bottom—not straight like you have it.'

Dave shrugged, 'Well—I've seen you do it this way.' Mungo stirred his tea and reflected a bit then spoke again to Ellen.

Ellen said, 'He says, you can paint it any way you want, but if you're going to carve it, you can't make straight anywhere.' She traced the ovoid with her finger. 'It's always best to cut across the grain, even at a very shallow angle, but always across.' She tapped the bottom line, 'See, you can cut down the side, around the corner and along the flat part, but when you got to turn up the blade will follow the grain and ruin it.'

Mungo nodded affirmatively. Dave thought about it for a few seconds and said, 'O.K.—I see what you mean, but boy, the old guy's sure made it hard to do!' Mungo laughed and spoke to Ellen and she said 'No, no. The whole thing is that they made it easy—all the little things are to make it easier, not harder.'

Mungo hunched over the paper again, obviously warming to the subject. I leaned closer, Dave leaned closer, and even Ellen bent over to get a clearer view. Mungo spoke and Ellen translated:

'Two things you gotta know,' Mungo drew a number of fine parallel lines representing the grain of the wood. 'The shape,' he repeated a quick rendition of the ovoid, 'and the position. See how you put this so you don't go along the lines?' He indicated the parallel lines, 'except for just a little bit?' Mungo leaned back and looked at Dave. 'Lots of guys do it O.K. because they've seen it done many times, but they don't know how come it's O.K. so they can't do changes very good.'

Ellen said, 'That's why some people can copy pictures, or even things that others have made, but when they come to do their own stuff it doesn't look right because they don't know the principles. Once you know the principles, then it comes easy.'

Dave said, 'O.K., I've got an eye—now what?' Ellen said, 'You've got the right shape in the right place. Now you can build the rest. But, remember all the straight lines go across the grain. Curved lines can go anywhere, cause they're not straight.'

Mungo drew a smaller ovoid off to one side of the large one. He drew a few heavy lines to join the two and the bold shape of a raven's head began to appear; a few more strokes and ears grew out of the raven's head. I looked closely. No heavy lines ran along the fine parallel lines that Mungo had marked in to indicate the grain. Each heavy line ran across the grain or at right angles to it. When it seemed it must run along the grain, it broke sharply into a curved line.

Mungo drew several different designs on additional sheets of papers as Dave laboured to keep up. One was a sea eagle and it looked great!

Dave continued drawing, Ellen and Mungo went out to the kitchen and I went downstairs to work on the tourist poles. Bob and Ted showed up a short while later and clumped down the stairs.

Ted said, 'Jeez—Dave's scratchin' away to beat hell up there. What have you guys been up to?'

***Plate 214:* Mungo Martin's Memorial Pole framed against the sky in 1970. By the early spring of 1981, the paint had faded and the right wing had fallen to the ground . . . my young daughter pointed out a raven perched on the left wing as we drove by the cemetery. (Alert Bay, B.C., 1970. Photo: Tourism, B.C.)**

I explained, and Bob said, 'Well, he ain't gonna make any money drawing!'

When the afternoon was over, I went upstairs and got my jacket on, ready to go home. Dave saw me wistfully eyeing the sea eagle sketch that Mungo had done.

'Hey kid, I need that to check my stuff with. Here, you can have one of mine.' He pushed one of his hastily done sketches in front of him and wrote on it with his soft artist's pencil. He handed it to me and I read

Drawn for Phil Nuytton, by Dave Neel.

I pointed out that he had spelled my last name wrong. He laughed and said, 'Big deal! See kid, personally autographed, and it didn't cost you a cent.'

I still have that sketch. Mungo, Ellen and even young Dave and Ted Jr., have all gone to be with the old people, but that simple sketch and the bright sun that shines across my desk still reminds me of the laughter and the good times, and the lessons learned so many long summers ago.

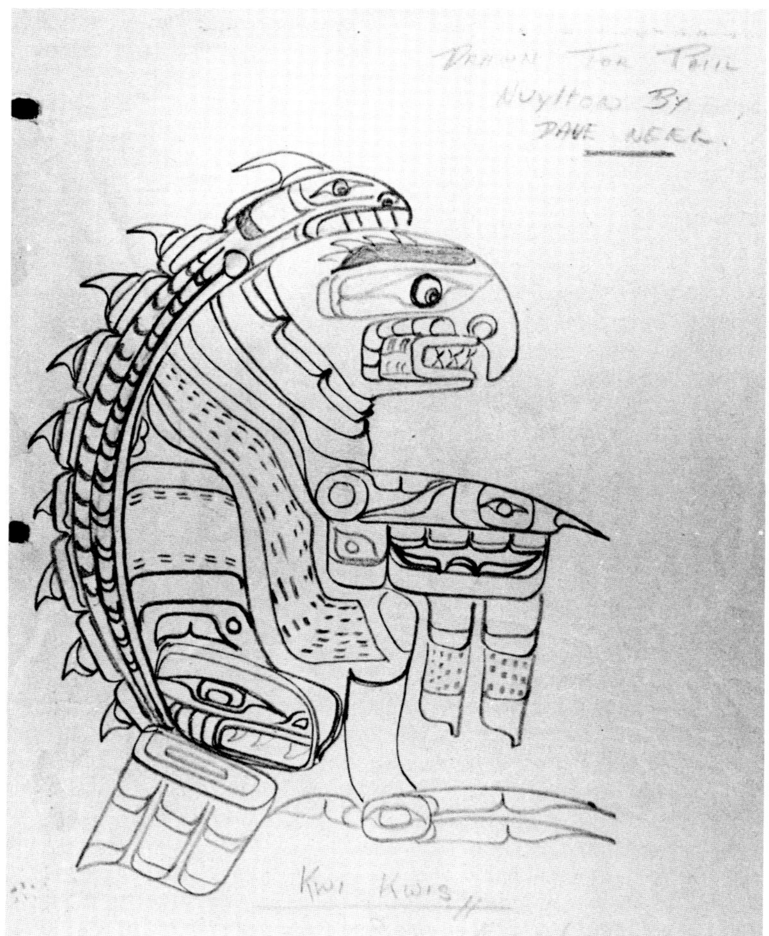

APPENDIX I
A Note on Indian Names

Among the Kwakiutl people, it is common to have more than one 'Indian' name. In the old days, as a person rose through the potlatch system, he or she acquired many names, usually of increasing importance. These were 'formal' or 'potlatch' names.

In addition to the formal names, almost every Kwakiutl has a 'pet' name or 'everyday' name—probably the English term 'nickname' comes closest to defining this pet name. Often the pet name is an endearing term. Frequently it is a humourous name—sometimes erotic in reference. Other pet names are shortened versions of the formal names, and once in a while, a word that has no meaning or whose meaning or reference was lost generations ago.

When a person has a number of names, it is usual to refer to only two; their highest or most recent potlatch name and their nickname. A common way to say this is, 'His name is (formal), but he is called (nickname).'

In Mungo Martin's case, his name was NA̱KA̱'PA̱NKA̱M, but he was called 'Datsa'. Charlie James was named YAK̲UDŁAS, but he was called 'Dak̲uma'. Ellen Neel was K̲AK̲A̱SO'LAS, but people called her 'Ellen-ah'.

Although the Kwakiutl people have been very keenly studied since the last half of the 19th century, it is often difficult to determine specifically and chronologically to whom the scholar, or his informant, is referring. Much of the confusion is brought about by a fondness for naming male offspring after their fathers or grandfathers.

For example, Amos Dawson is a chief among the Kwakiutl (Fort Rupert) and among the Mamalilik̲ala (Village Island). He holds the name NA̱K̲A'PA̱NKA̱M on the Kwakiutl side and KWAX̱SILA̱NAGA̱ME' on the Mamalilikala side. His father's name was Amos Dawson and so was his grandfather's; Amos' son is named Amos Dawson also. Likewise, Amos' 'Indian' names belonged to his father and grandfathers. Since his son is being trained in the potlatch system, Amos' 'Indian' names may pass to him.

When George Hunt (writing to Franz Boas) in 1925, refers to NA̱K̲A'PA̱NKA̱M, it is impossible to know whether he refers to the present Amos Dawson's grandfather or even his great-grandfather, because the stories that Hunt relates, in 1925, may have been set many years earlier.

To give a further example of the complexity, George Hunt writes, in 1925, about his daughter-in-law:

'And now Lalayagilis (Hunt's daughter-in-law) that is the Princess (daughter) of the late Hawilkulal, although she is a woman, took the seat of her uncle, Hamasaga and the office of giving away property, and all of his privileges. And when Hamasaga died, Lalayagilis had the name Wakadze in the secular season and she had the name Lemkala in the winter ceremonial; and she had the name Maxenox for the giving-away ceremonial of the young man. She had the name Kwaxsestaladze when she went to a feast. She, Lalayagilis, who had the name Wakadze had as a wife of the other side (a different tribe or band) the name of her late aunt Tsetsalal in the secular season, and she had the name Qegemala in the winter ceremonial, and she had the name Kuskus in the giving away ceremonial of the young men... and she had the name Tsexula, when the women gave away property to one another.

She had all eight names in addition to her woman's name (Lalayagilis). She is married to my son, Kwakwabalaseme and I am George Hunt, and that is how I really know all about the nine different names of Lalayagilis.'

Hunt preceded this summation by explaining, in minute detail, how each of these names had been acquired, how long his daughter-in-law held them and to whom she gave them. The problems of identification, are further compounded by names that are spelled differently, using various orthographic systems, or phonetically as they were heard by different ears. This happens with a number of common words, not just names. For example, 't'ł'na' (oolichan oil) is variously spelled 'gleana' or 'kleena', depending on how it was heard by English ears.

Charlie James spelled his name 'Yakuglas' in a system taught to him by the Reverend Alfred Hall. If you add the potlatch appendage 'ame" phonetically, you wind up with 'Yakuglasamai'—very close to 'Yagotglasamai'—Mungo Martin's eyelash plucker!

The difference in spelling is not particularly alarming. I have heard people who knew Charlie James pronounce his name (Yak̲udłas) as 'Yagotlas', 'Yakuglis', 'Yakoglis', etc. I submitted a number of the 'Indian' names used in this book to the U'mista Cultural Society in Alert Bay, B.C. to have those that were recognizable put into the U'mista written Kwakwala system. Among the names were 'Yak̲ugłas' (Charlie James) and 'Yagotglasimai' (the eyelash plucker!)—they came back as 'Yak̲udłas' and 'Yak̲udłasa̱me". Boas (Secret Societies, 1897) records a number of potlatch names—among them, 'Yagolas'—(which he translates as 'giving wealth') and 'Yagolaseme' ('from whom property comes').

Boas, writing in a later volume 'Contributions to the Ethnology of the Kwakiutl—1925' or, rather, translating George Hunt's words literally—makes it quite clear that Yagolas and Yagolalaseme (note slight change in spelling) are the same person. Boas also gives the form of a potlatch appendage to other formal names:

'This is my name, my own name, Maxmewis, the great Maxmewisageme.'

And: 'Go on great chief, call your great name, your own name, Naxnagem, Naxnagemgame.'

And: 'The true name of my great-grandfather, whose own name is Yagolas, Yagolalaseme.'

Halliday, (Potlatch and Totem, 1935) mentions 'Yakoglasemai'—probably referring to Charlie James—since the book was written using real names at Alert Bay, during a time when James was a prominent carver there.

It is reasonable to conclude that all sources on the 'eyelash' matter agree—to a large extent. Charlie James might well have been considered an 'uncle' and he very probably was called 'Yak̲udłasa̱me" as an extension to his formal name, Yak̲udłas.

This helps to illustrate the incredible complexity one encounters when trying to understand and explain even the smallest of Kwakiutl mysteries. Even then, the conclusion can only be an opinion, at best.

Finally, it should be noted that 'potlatch' or formal names are often a type of shorthand, and do not translate in the literal sense. You are expected to know the complete name and the nuances of its meaning. If you do not, no amount of dissection with a Kwak̓wala /English dictionary will help. The shortened versions of the names simply do not contain enough information to decipher.

The analogy would be trying to explain to a non-English speaker that 'everyone knows' that Bob is short for Robert, or Bill for William.

For example: Arthur 'Dai-yu' Dick's formal name is (phonetically) 'Gai-yus-das' which means, literally, 'coming up from the beach'—but what it actually means is 'coming up from the beach where the canoes arriving for a potlatch have landed', (personal communication—A. Dick, 1981).

'So,' you might ask, 'if his name is Gai-yus-das, why is he called Dai-yu?' Simplest thing in the world! Gai-yus-das is long, so they called him 'Gai-yu'. His young child could not pronounce 'Gai-yu' properly and called him 'Dai-yu'. The name stuck, and now everyone knows him as 'Dai-yu'.

Great, if you happen to live in Alert Bay, but difficult to understand if you live in Kansas and are trying to fathom the complexities of Kwakiutl names from reference books!

For further interest, 'Dai'yu' is pronounced 'Dai' as in 'dyeing clothes', and 'you'—'Dai'yu', or so it seems. If you listen very carefully and hear the name said very slowly, it is pronounced 'dah . . . ee . . . yoo'—hence, the U'mista orthography's 'Dai-yu'.

As mentioned, virtually all of the people recorded in these pages have at least one formal name and a nickname.

Tony Hunt's formal name is "MAXWALAGALIS' which translates as 'giving potlatches all over the world', (Tony says it means 'the movement of a great whale on the beach'!) but Mungo always called him 'Wis' (nephew). Henry Hunt's formal name is 'MU'PA̱NKA̱M', meaning 'four times over', but he is called 'Kulut'a' (porpoise) because he was a noted swimmer in his younger days. Helen Hunt's highest potlatch name was 'HA̱YUSDISA̱'LAS' meaning 'place you go straight to' (to be made welcome)—but she was called 'Teen', (no meaning).

Knowledge of these nicknames or familiar names was important to me in attempting to find out about people who have been gone for many years—such as Charlie James. James had the name 'Ya̱kudła̱s' but the old people that I talked to knew him by his everyday name 'Da̱k̓uma'. When I first heard this name, many years ago, I wrote it as 'Dah-qwo-mah'. I talked to different people, listened attentively and realized it was pronounced 'Dak-U (as in 'rude')-Ma'. Then you drag the last 'a' out a bit, and you've got it—'Dak-U-Mahh'—Da̱k̓uma'.

I was talking to chief Bob Wilson, in Fort Rupert, and he was telling me how he'd worked for Edward Curtis, acting in a movie, almost half a centry before. Wilson was old, about 85, but mentally, sharp as a razor. He'd known Franz Boaş in the first part of this century and I sat spellbound while he told all sorts of anecdotes. Anecdotes about Curtis, Boas, the other people in the village, George Hunt, coppers, grease, potlatches and on and on. He spoke English well, but often lapsed into Kwak̓wala and I had to have Amos Dawson translate for me. On a high point of his reminiscences, I asked him if he knew 'Da̱k̓uma'. He turned to look at me, surprised, and said, 'Ah, Da̱k̓uma,' then proceeded to tell me many things about Charlie James. My tape recorder was running as he frequently paused to see if I understood his English, I would say in Kwak'wala 'I see' or I understand'.

Wilson grinned at me, 'You understand' our language . . . little bit?'

I replied to the effect that I tried hard.

He laughed and said, 'You work at it, every day and every night. Don't bother sleepin' for mebbe . . . six months . . . then you understand, O.K!'

I said that six years would be more like it. I finished by saying, 'You know, I can remember the words pretty good, but when I go to pronounce them, the way you do, it feels like a piece of my mouth is missing!'

The whole room-full of relatives laughed. Bob Wilson wiped his eyes and said, 'You know, you was asking about the big potlatch. I'm gonna tell you about it.' He told me about Dan Cramner's 'Christmas Tree' potlatch in 1921—'the one that caused all the trouble.'

When he finished, I asked if he had gone to jail as had so many of the participants of that particular potlatch. The 'Christmas Tree' potlatch was as much a final test of the law as anything else, and an outraged Indian agent enforced a rigorous 'get tough' policy.

'Naw,' Bob Wilson said, 'I got sick in my belly after that potlatch . . . get trouble with my appendix.' He pointed to his side, 'And I had to go to the hospital. I was in the bed layin' there, when the policeman came to arrest me. He says 'You pretty sick, huh, Bob?' I says, 'Yeah, pretty sick, maybe gonna die.' So he says, 'No good to arrest you, cause you're too sick to go to jail.' I says, 'O.K. thank you."

The room broke into laughter again. While Bob Wilson was talking, his wife had put some food on the table for myself, Amos and Amos's sister, Alice. The meal was composed of a salmon soup with a dish of oolichan oil and another of dried seaweed, on the side. Wilson pointed to the meal and said something in Kwak'wala to his wife and everyone laughed again. To my questioning, raised eyebrows, Amos said, 'He says he hopes that you don't get sick and die on this Indian food, 'cause he'll have to go and hide in the hospital again, so that they don't arrest him.'

When I left his house, to catch the plane in Port Hardy, old Bob Wilson came in the door with me, 'You come here again . . . an' I teach you Indian good . . . then I can tell you some good stories.'

I waved goodbye with a warm feeling inside.

APPENDIX 2
Genealogy

When asked what tribes she was from, Ellen Neel often said she was from the Nimpkish ('NAMGIS—'alone, by themselves').

This simply meant that she was from Alert Bay. Since Alert Bay was officially designated as the 'Namgis Reserve by the Department of Indian Affairs—anyone who moved there became listed as a 'Namgis regardless of their actual lineage.

Any given member of the Kwakiutl people could conceivably be from four different bands, on their mother and father's sides. Even more, if their grandparents were considered. It is the common practise to speak of coming from the prominent bands (i.e. highest ranking in the potlatch sense) on the mother and father's side.

In this case Ellen was a Gwatsinuxw and a Kwakiutl—(Kwagu'l)—through her parents and grandparents.

It may show Charlie James, Ellen Neel and Mungo Martin in clearer perspective to illustrate a brief, though relevant genealogy chart. For portions of this, I am indebted to Kathy Cook of Alert Bay, who painstakingly waded through old church records to establish information on her aunt, Ellen Neel.

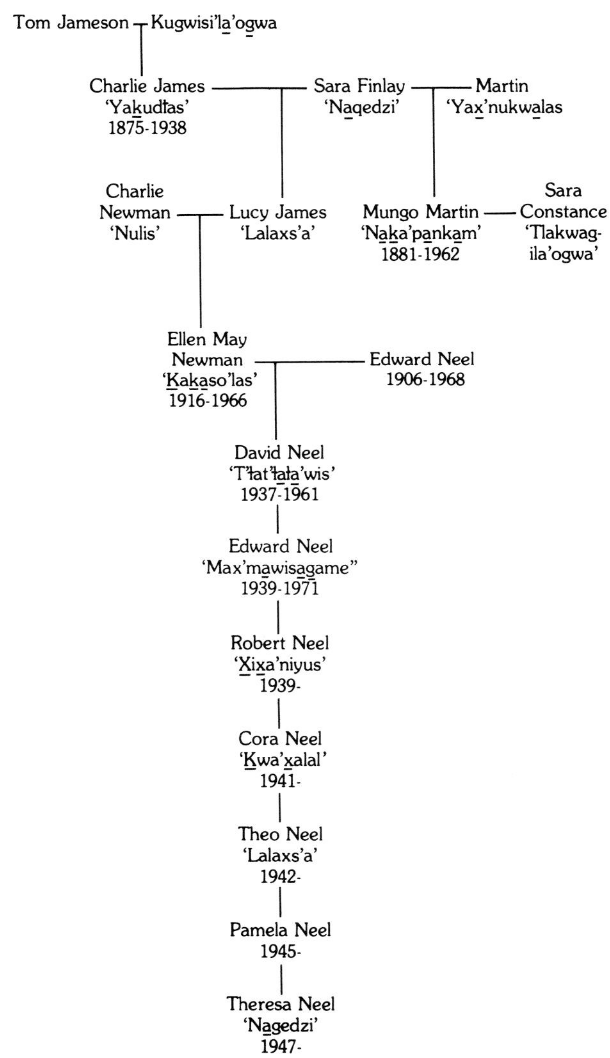

Genealogy is of great importance to determine the bands that one is from and, more specifically, what crests and privileges one is entitled to use.

For example, with Mungo Martin and his son gone, to whom would Mungo's names and privileges pass?

Henry Hunt and his son, Tony, were Mungo's proteges and his successors as carvers for the Provincial Museum in Victoria, but they were not closely related to Mungo. Helen Hunt, Henry's wife and Tony's mother, was often called Mungo's 'adopted daughter'. She grew up in his house and in Mungo's later years she acted as a daughter to him. But Helen was not formally adopted and had no blood ties to Mungo, although she was one of Mrs. Mungo Martin's (Abay'a's), granddaughters.

Wilson Duff, when asked this question in 1963,

stated: 'Mungo regarded Peter Knox, his son's (David Martins) first boy, as the logical successor for many of his Indian names and privileges.'

Peter Knox is a cheerful, personable man. He is about my age and we got on well. We laughed and joked about the usual antics around Alert Bay, but when I turned the subject to Mungo Martin, he grew quiet and reflective. 'You know,' he said, 'everybody called the old man 'Datsa'—'grandfather. Yeah, everybody called him that,' he paused, 'but he really was my grandfather.'

Trying to figure out the genealogy and band affiliations of various people can be almost as difficult as pinning down the meanings of Kwakiutl potlatch names.

For example:

While going through the extensive files in the Provincial Museum in Victoria, I came across a handwritten note of the type calculated to drive researchers crazy. The single page is titled 'Charlie James'—it has no date and no signature—although it appears to be in Wilson Duff's handwriting.

The note boldly says 'Through his (Charlie James) mother, he was related to four tribes: 'KWIKSUTENUK', 'TLITLEKIT', 'MAMALILIKULA' and 'NIMKISH.

Fine, except who on earth are the 'TLITLEKIT'?

It is absolutely unlike Wilson Duff to make a major error, particularly since he was quite familiar with the various bands and sub-bands of the Kwakiutl. Every other source says that Charlie James' mother was 'Fort Rupert' usually taken to mean 'KWAKIUTL' OR 'WALAS KWAKIUTL'—although there were several other tribes there.

Where did this information come from? Did Duff write it?

I don't know and no one else at the museum could help.

It bothered me enough to cause me to read and re-read the old listings and finally in E.S. Curtis' work 'The American Indian—Volume 10', I found it!

Under an appendix titled 'Tribal Summary', Curtis lists the 'CLE-LI-KIT-TI', and an alternate spelling 'TLITLUKET', a branch of the 'KOMKYUTIS' Sept of the Qaqyuhl (Kwakiutl)'.

It certainly would have made things easier if the writer of the museum note had simply written 'Kwakiutl' or 'Fort Rupert'. But the problem of who wrote the note or where the information came from, remains unsolved.

Enough to drive you nuts! Of course, on the other hand, most of the statements made in these pages contain no source footnotes. But, at least, any serious researchers can call me and I will dig up the source data for them! I can just see Bill Holm's face darken with indignation.

'Yes, but what happens if you are run over by a bus, or your office burns down and your notes are lost—what then?'

Indeed, what then? Oh well, driving serious researchers to the edge of sanity has been a popular Kwakiutl sport for at least a century—as an adopted member of the tribe, who am I to break the tradition?

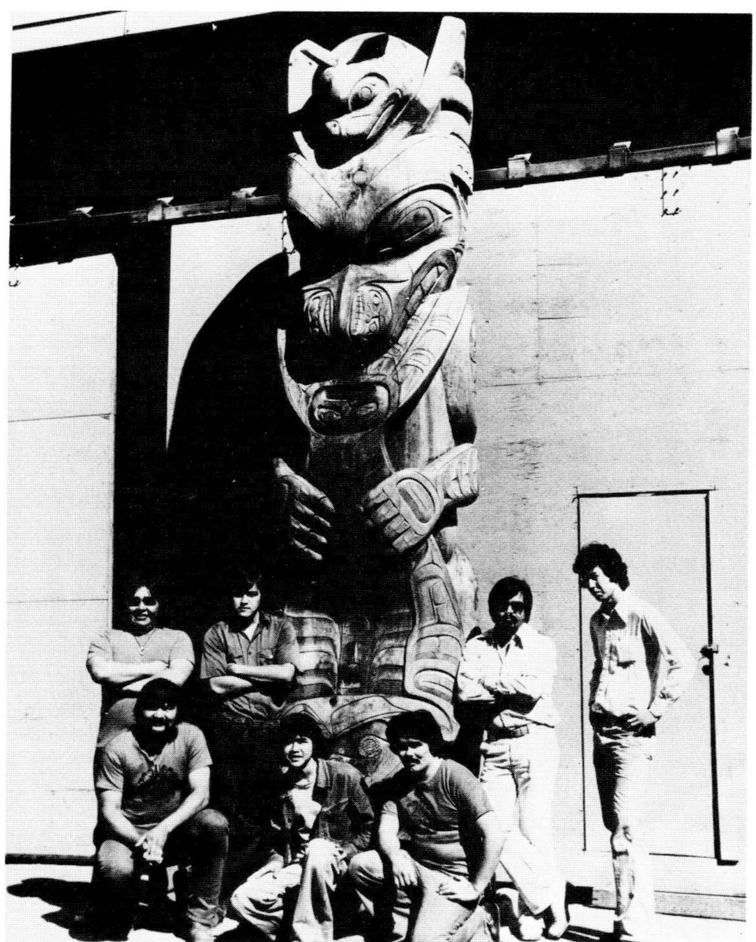

***Plate 216:* The legacy of Charlie James, Ellen Neel, and Mungo Martin continues. This truly spectacular pole was one of two commissioned by the National Museum of Japan and carved by Arts of the Raven Gallery. From left to right, back row (standing): Frank Nelson, Stan Hunt, Tony Hunt, and John Livingston. Front row, (kneeling): Nelson Leeson, Dwayne Simeon, and Ross Hunt. (Victoria, 1977. Photo: Courtesy of Arts of the Raven Gallery.)**

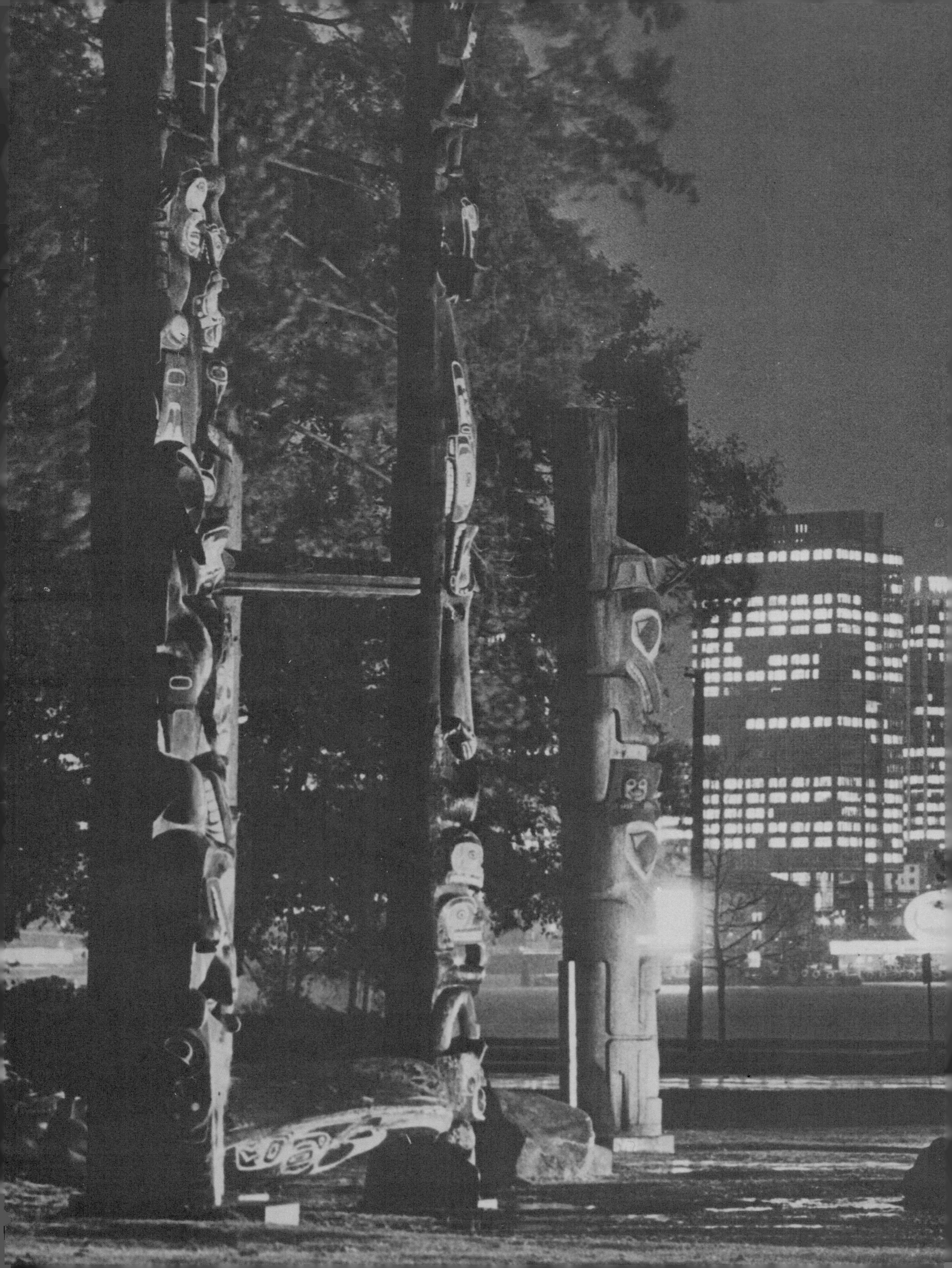